Bringing Theology Home

Bringing Theology Home

N. Keith Smith

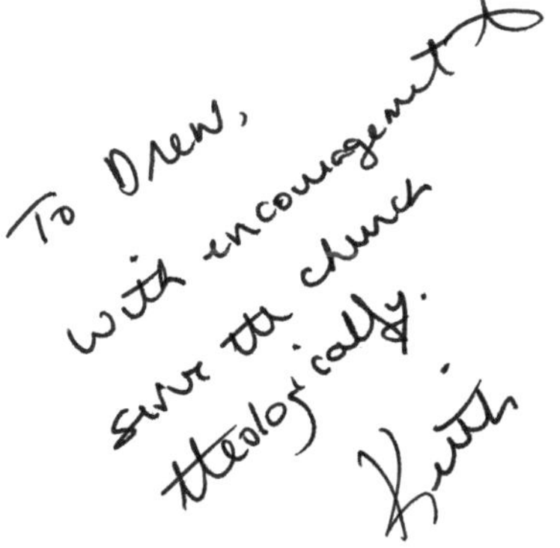

Hermeneutic House Books
Richmond, Virginia

BRINGING THEOLOGY HOME

Printed in the United States of America

Hermeneutic House Books is the publishing division of Hermeneutic House, which is a ministry of theological interpretation and education for Christian individuals, small groups, and congregations. Visit us at hermeneutichouse.com.

Book cover designed by Daniel Smith

ISBN 978-0-9993603-0-9

For Beth—
my wife, best friend,
and companion in the theological life

Contents

Introduction

Christian theology was birthed in and by the church.[1] Many local congregations formed and developed in cities, such as Jerusalem, Antioch, Ephesus, Corinth, and Rome. These assemblies were theological communities. They were places where theology emerged and was proclaimed, taught, practiced, cultivated, preserved, and transmitted. Believers learned and lived according to the teaching of the apostles, who had been taught by Jesus. They acted as stewards of the mysteries of God made known supremely in Christ.[2]

At the same time, the church was birthed by Christian theology. Since this theology was itself new, it required a new community. It attracted its own audience and formed its own body. Communities of faith sprang up locally as products of the truth Jesus taught, his apostles preached and taught, and Paul and others reflected on and put in writing. The church was the house theology built.

"Theology" comes from the Greek words *theos* (God) and *logos* (word, teaching, study, wisdom, or reason). Christian theology is the church talking, thinking, and teaching about God and about all things in relation to God, in the light of God's self-revelation in Jesus Christ. Theology is the wisdom by which human beings live in this

---

1. When I use the word "church," I am referring to the "communion of saints," or fellowship of persons—living and dead; past, present, and future—who share in common the life of theological faith patterned after Christ. The church is greater than any single congregation, or even all congregations together. A "congregation" is a local assembly of Christians. It is an empirical, social entity in and through which the church is becoming present and active, at least dimly and in part. I distinguish "church" and "congregation," while maintaining their proper, essential relationship. I do not refer to the "congregation" as "church," holding to the truth that there is only one church, while there are many congregations.

2. See 1 Corinthians 4:1–2.

world by faith, and thus as the church and as Christians. Theology and the church have always emerged and grown up together.

Today this union is diminished and estranged, if not on the brink of extinction. On the one hand, local congregations are no longer birthplaces and houses of theology. Ordinary Christians are not brought into existence and sustained by theology and for theology. They do not know and understand their own theological faith-tradition.[3] They have little to no interest in studying and learning this tradition, much less any sense of real responsibility for it. Not even clergypersons are serious students of theology. Although they are "all things to all people," they are rarely theologians and teachers.

On the other hand, theology remains at a great distance from local congregations, being the intellectual property of professional theologians in divinity schools and seminaries. While these schools are often affiliated with denominations, and are considered the teaching arm of the church, they are under the heavy pressure of the objectives, methods, and measures of secular higher education in the modern university.

Also, these schools are designed for the training of clergy who can perform professional tasks and meet the leadership needs of denominations, congregations, and agencies that are largely non-theological. Therefore, the typical minister produced by these schools is not a comprehensive student, teacher, interpreter, and shepherd of theological faith.

Consequently, neither theology nor the church is home to the other, despite any DNA evidence of the other that remains. Their

---

3. "Faith-tradition" is my term for the deposit of truth and meaning that has been and continues to be left behind by persons and communities who are living by and for faith. "Faith" is a particular mode of being, or manner of existence ("faith-existence"). Faith is primal. It is prior to believing, thinking, speaking, or acting. Yet, it does not remain hidden and silent. It comes to expression in words and actions. It seeks to be known. The resulting knowledge or wisdom is what I call "faith-tradition." It is what people of faith have come to know and understand, and thus is considered to be orthodox, authoritative, and normative for faith. Faith-tradition is not tradition in general (past customs, beliefs, or "the way we've always done it"). Nor is it any particular denominational tradition (Orthodox, Roman Catholic, Protestant, Baptist). It is the Great (Grand) Tradition behind, beneath, beyond, and before all Christian traditions. It is the church's theology. See my discussion in chapter 2 on pages 92-97.

estrangement occurred early, and has been the status quo so long that no one can remember when it was otherwise, or can imagine it being otherwise. The absence of theology locally is now taken for granted and assumed to be the way things are, as well as the way things are supposed to be.

Seminaries and divinity schools operate by the paradigm of the separation of clergy and laity. Their education is designed for the former. They would not know what to do if the whole church, the *laos tou Theou*,[4] suddenly demanded theological education and active involvement in the reflection, discussion, interpretation, articulation, and embodiment of their own theological faith-tradition. Neither would congregations know what to do if theology were to be brought back, demanding to be taught, learned, and lived.

Sadly, the chances of this ever happening are next to nothing. Congregations and Christians are not showing any signs of awakening and returning to their theological home. Our schools are not returning, or showing any interest in moving closer, to their local roots and to their responsible role in the ecclesial (church) home. If anything, both parties are moving further apart, leaving the future of both theology and the church in jeopardy.

Of course, congregations will continue. But their future as the church, which is a theological house, is imperiled. Without theology, the church cannot be the church. It is emptied of its distinctive matter that truly matters. It is cut off from its own history and tradition, leaving its congregational form to be nothing more than another social group, religious organization, social services agency, and a business for attracting and keeping consumers.

---

4. The Greek phrase *laos tou Theou* means "people of God." Strictly speaking, all Christians are the *laos*, or people. Clergy, or professional ministers, belong to the *laos,* along with the non-clergy. However, we commonly use words deriving from *laos* ("lay," "laity," "laypersons") as shorthand for the latter. "Ordinary Christians" are called "laypersons" in order to distinguish them from the few who quit being "as ordinary as everybody else" when they receive scholarly theological education and clergy ordination. This term has become the equivalent of "amateur" or "non-" (as in "non-clergy" and "non-theological"). While I retain limited use of "lay" words, I reject any connotation of amateurism. I always have in mind the whole church and the entire congregation, including clergy. Therefore, a "lay seminary" provides theological education for the *laos tou Theou.* See footnotes #11 on page 193 and #19 on page 199.

Without the church, theology cannot be theology. Theology may be allowed to continue hanging around congregations, since it has always been present in some form. But now it is little more than a "ghost of its former self." Some of it may be kept around because many older people are nostalgic. The sound of theology reminds them of their upbringing and what used to be. Theology can serve as a garnish for worship, giving just the right hint of mystery, nice poetic sound, and deep spiritual feeling. A few curious graduate students and serious scholars may still get something out of studying it and writing papers about it. But theology, apart from the church, is no longer living and is unable to bring about, sustain, and direct either faith or the community of faith. It is simply another dead science, philosophy, set of doctrines, or ancient tradition that has little or no relevance to the way Christians today typically think, talk, interpret, act, and relate to one another and to the world.

What is most needed for the survival of both theology as theology and the church as church is a homecoming. Theology must be brought home, back to the church, and specifically to its congregations. The whole church must be brought back to its home, which is theology. Both must learn to be at home with each other again.

Over four and a half decades ago, I was summoned to this ministry of reconciliation, and have been actively involved ever since in bringing theology and the church back together. My guiding vision has been a community of faith in which the theological tradition is sustained, and this community is itself sustained by its own theological tradition. The survival of both is at stake in the present dark ages of the post-Christian, postmodern Western world. I contend that this is a matter of salvation. Each can and will be saved only by relationship with the other, under the reconciling power of God in Christ. The church must become theological again, and theology must become ecclesial again. This is the only way you and I, as well as all humankind, will be saved.

Such a radical reconciliation, I have discovered, is difficult. First, theology remains firmly entrenched in schools far removed from where most Christians live. This is where theology has grown up and developed. It has known no other home. Therefore, the chances of its academic overseers bringing theology back to where it was born, sharing it with lay Christians, and staying to teach them are zero.

Second, students who attend these schools receive only a basic introduction to theology. The purpose of their education is not to make them theologians, but to train them vocationally to be clergy, who return home as preachers, leaders, entrepreneurs, community organizers, service providers (worship, weddings, funerals), shopkeepers, or just about anything and everything people may expect and demand of them. Consequently, the thought of bringing theology home with them when they return from seminary rarely, if ever, crosses their minds.

Third, in the rare instance when theology is brought back (as I have done), congregations and Christians do not recognize it. They do not know what it is or what to do with it. And, frankly, they are uninterested in meeting it and finding out. They certainly have no intention of welcoming theology in, and allowing it to have even a minor role or influence in their house, much less take over and have its full way with them. They refuse to be its students or stewards. Why would they? Theology has had no say in who they are, why their house is here, and what business they are in. And they are doing just fine, aren't they?

In view of these realities, I conclude that reconciliation is more than difficult. It is impossible. The gulf is too wide. The patterns are too set, and have been this way too long. Local congregations and ordinary Christians have moved on with their lives, without theology. Theology has adapted and grown comfortable in another place, and is subservient and secondary to other tasks, without ordinary Christians. There are too many people with too many other interests, too many more pressing needs, and too much at stake for either party (theology or the church) to pull up, leave, and come home.

Still, what is impossible for us, and can never be produced even by our clearest visions, noblest intentions, strongest determinations, cleverest strategies, most powerful energies, and fully charged efforts, is possible for God. Both theology and the church are the creations of God. Both have been entrusted with the same ministry of reconciliation of all things in the new creation that is centered in Christ, which is wholly from God. Therefore, both are called and commanded to participate in this ministry, which necessarily involves them being reconciled to one another.

How, then, can they possibly serve the reconciling God, or proclaim the reconciliation of God and humankind in Jesus Christ, without themselves participating and being reconciled? Although this is impossible, and will never happen if left to either party, it is being made possible and already coming about by the reconciling work of the Spirit.

Such reconciliation of the church and theology will bring about a new creation (as all reconciliation does). Everyone and everything that has been estranged from God, from each other, and from itself will be reunited and remade into the world God intends, which can exist only by the will and work of God. This is the Kingdom of God, appearing in its foreshadowing form as the church.

The Apostle Paul put it well: "So if anyone is in Christ, there is a new creation: everything old has passed away; see, everything has become new! All this is from God, who reconciled us to himself through Christ, and has given us the ministry of reconciliation; that is, in Christ God was reconciling the world to himself, not counting their trespasses against them, and entrusting the message of reconciliation to us." (2 Corinthians 5:17-19)

I believe that if you and I are reconciled to God through Christ, we will also be reconciled to the wisdom, thought, and discourse of the church and its faith regarding what God has revealed through Christ. This wisdom is Christian theology.

Both theology and the church will become new only within a new relationship, as part of the greater new creation now taking place. Theology will become ecclesial, although in a new way. The church will become theological, although in a new way. Together they will appear as a new community, radically transformed and different from what we now see as the non-theological church and as non-ecclesial theology. The church will exist to sustain theology, while itself being sustained by theology. Theology will sustain the church, while itself being sustained by the church.

Still, I have haunting doubts and questions: "Where is this new community? Is it anywhere? Even in seed-like form in the soil of our sacred institutions? If not, will it ever come about? If so, how? Who will be in it? How will these persons be called out of the crowd and its status quo, gathered, and made a new community? How will they know who they are, and who the other is? Are any of these people anywhere in our congregations, or in the larger world right now? Will they ever undertake the theological life and its education? Will they ever become a visible, audible, and influential body?"

I sometimes imagine that I have the eye of Jesus. I peer into the crowd and think I spot one, two, or three who are being called, or are about to be called, to be members of this new form of theological community. I trust that they are there, scattered among the 2.18 billion Christians across the earth and throughout the nations. But they are few in number. They are hidden. Nobody notices them or knows they are there. They do not even know who they are.

Unfortunately, I do not have Jesus' ability to perceive them, point to them, and call them out. All I can see is the anonymous, theology-less crowd. Therefore, I have to resort to a different technique. I call it "fishing for people" (reminiscent of Jesus' calling of his first disciples, who were fishermen).[5] I simply drag theology, like bait on a line, through the crowd. Those who are catchable, reachable, and teachable will do the rest.

This is the same idea behind Jesus' teaching that those who are his sheep will recognize his voice, come out, and follow him.[6] I believe that theology is the sound of the Good Shepherd's voice in all generations throughout the world. Therefore, if I "talk theology," or speak theologically, it stands to reason that Jesus' own sheep will detect the Shepherd's voice in mine, recognize it, and respond.

Borrowing a third image from Jesus, my task is to display pearls on the table. Then it will be made known who are the pearl merchants in this crowd. These are the persons who are drawn by the pearls, and to the pearls. Others are not. They do not value pearls, will only trample them underfoot, like swine, and then turn on me.[7]

This is how you, as a reader, should view and approach this book: (1) it is a display of the pearl of great price; (2) it is a calling out to scattered sheep; and (3) it is the dropping of a baited hook in the water. My objective is to discover those who will be responsive and receptive in the presence of theology. I want to find and teach those who will be students. I want to give them the knowledge and wisdom of faith they need. I want to make theologians.

5. Matthew 4:18–22; Mark 1:16–20; Luke 5:1–11.
6. John 10:1–16.
7. Matthew 7:6; 13:45–46.

My method is simple. I begin by inviting my audience to follow me into the wide, vacuous gulf between theology and the church, where I have devoted my life and work as a pastor-teacher-theologian.[8] I want my readers to enter into theology and get the lay of the land in much the same way as I did. I want each of you to learn through my experience both the problem of estrangement and the prospect of reconciliation. I want you to understand how we have ended up in this situation, and why we stubbornly keep ourselves in it, resisting the return of theology to the whole church as its home, as well as the return of ourselves to theology.

Finally, I want you to join others and me in the wide, vacuous gulf where the homecoming is taking place. Here a new community is being formed—a new creation—that can truly be the "meeting place" of church and theology, as well as the larger reconciling of God and God's people in Christ. Here the church will be sustained by its theology. Theology will be sustained by its church. They will sustain each other.

Do not expect from this book anything like a special church study course, midweek Bible study, Sunday School lesson, or even a seminary-type course. I am uninterested in offering a little more information or inspiration. Also, I have no interest in helping you "know what you believe," "develop your own theology," or "strengthen your daily walk," as a means of you creating your own Christian life.

My aim is more deeply existential: to make you the kind of person who is capable of being in the community that lives in this world theologically, or by theological faith. While I may bring theology *to* you, I succeed only if I bring you *to* theology, *into* theology, and you become *of* and *for* theology. I seek to bring you inside the theological life, and then, only from inside, explain to you the order, workings, and content of theology.

Consider this book to be your invitation and your entranceway. Once inside, I encourage you to take up residence and become fully engaged as a student and steward. Only by living here in this house among a theological community will you be able to learn theology. And only by learning theology will you be able to be part of this

8. See my discussion of this term on pages 246–247.

community, the church, and live the theological life. My hope is that you will be more than merely informed, but also will be transformed.

I have attempted to write in the full, multi-dimensional style of my vocation: pastor, teacher, and theologian. At times, I am colloquial and casual. At other times, I am scholarly and formal. I am trying to be a good theologian, who is writing and teaching as a pastor. Think of this book as an extended pastoral conversation. Here I attempt to baptize you in a prolonged immersion in theological waters. (Don't worry. I am a Baptist pastor. I know what I'm doing!)

I am writing with ordinary lay readers and clergypersons in mind. At the same time, I trust that academic theologians might overhear, benefit from, and join our conversation, since they, too, are members of the same theological body.

I do not take the usual path of instruction, however, approaching theology head-on as simply a science or another academic discipline: defining it, and then briefly running down the list of what Christians believe (or ought to believe), step-by-step, belief-by-belief. While this type of education is important and can be helpful, it fails to instill and cultivate theology as a mode of being, manner of existence, or way of life by faith. In other words, while theology has to be learned, it is learned for the greater purpose of being lived.

Therefore, I am taking a more autobiographical approach, telling my story of how I have lived in relation to theology, and thereby showing one example of how the theological life appears and what it looks and sounds like. Unless theology transforms, defines, frames, determines, and guides the person, and who he is and how he lives in this world, it fails to do its full, intended work. I want my own experience to be a case study for others who are trying to discern what it means to be Christian, to belong to the church, and to live in this world as persons of faith in the light of what God has made known through Christ and the host of saints following him.

I realize I am communicating with readers—you and others like you—who have had little or no exposure to Christian theology. This is another reason I do not come at theology head-on, as a purely academic exercise. There is enough "head-on theology" here to introduce you to the subject. But my first objective is to bring you in and get you involved in the theological way of thinking and talking, teaching and learning, embodying and living.

Just because you may be new to all of this, however, I refuse to talk down to you, or to water down this material. I try to write just "over your head" in order to expose you to theology, involve you from the start in higher education, and thereby entice you into greater knowledge, understanding, and embodiment. I trust that in the process of reading this book you will gradually acquire a familiarity with and aptitude for theological thinking and talking.

We must not forget that we are dealing with a subject matter that has its own integrity, makes its own demands, and forms its own community of faithful teaching and learning. Theology cannot be served with lip service, ignorance, attendance in a study course or two, a little reading, piety, or goodness. Only a life of serious, sustained intellectual discipleship and stewardship will serve theology. Hopefully, by reading this book, you will be brought in and will take up this faithful theological life.

In other words, I am confident that, among all the readers, a few will be revealed to be fish, sheep, and pearl merchants. To them I give the initial guidance and resources they will need. Since no beginner has a clue where to begin, I offer this book as a starting-point. I also provide a road map for making your way into a tradition that is too immense (and often too dense) to be fully covered and comprehended. Think of me as your docent and interpreter. Use the way I frame things to help you do the same. Consider my footnotes to be recommendations for additional reading. Have a New Revised Standard Version of the Bible close by, so that you can read the scriptural texts as you read my text. Consult chapters 5–7 for practical guidance concerning teaching, studying and learning, affiliating with a local teaching-learning community, or continuing education on your own.

My prayerful hope is that all of us, both readers and author, will be found faithful in the ministry of the reconciliation of theology and church that has been entrusted to us.

1
Leaving

The prodigal son in Jesus' parable left home, went to a far country, and returned.[1] I have left three times, and returned twice. I will not go back a third time.

To understand what I mean by this statement, you have to know the story of my life as a Christian believer, theologian, teacher, pastor, and professor. You also have to know where home is for me. Home is the local Christian congregation, i.e., the dwelling-place of the Christian community. For many, this place is Methodist (my mother was raised as a Methodist), Presbyterian, Roman Catholic, Orthodox, Evangelical, Fundamentalist, or non-denominational. But for me, throughout my life, home has been the Baptist congregation in Southern Christendom.

You also need to know what I mean by "leaving." Although I have left home three times, I have managed to find three different ways to leave. Each leaving was unique, having its own motivations and intentions. The third one—the leaving in which I am now living—has a finality that the first two did not.

I cannot speak of leaving without also speaking of "returning," or "homecoming." My first leaving lasted three years. It was ended by conversion and a homecoming. I returned to the home where I had been born and raised. My second departure stretched out seven years. Both times I came back to the local congregation, recharged with personal joy and promise.

---

1. Luke 15:11–32.

On my second homecoming, I brought Christian theology back with me. That set the course of my life's work as a pastor-teacher-theologian. The persistent refusal of the home folks to receive, learn, and embody theology, however, eventually brought about my third and final leaving, involving a second radical conversion. Conversion has catalyzed my entire life of returning and leaving, my coming and going.

But this time, there will not be another homecoming. Over a lifetime of theological study and theological ministry, I have gradually come to realize that the local congregation is not and will not be theology's home. It is impossible. Therefore, I can no longer be at home here either. Theology and the community it forms and houses are now my home. Explaining this is what this book is about, and why I tell my story here.

Home

I am one of Hannah's children.[2] I was conceived and born out of a desperate woman's prayer to have a child. After suffering a heart-breaking miscarriage, my mother, Virginia, remembered the Old Testament story of Hannah,[3] and retraced that ancient woman's religious moves. Virginia promised God that if He gave her a son, she would dedicate and give him to God's service.

I was that son. The bonus in the deal was my twin sister, Kaye. Later, my mother, along with the help of my father, Norman, had three more children: a son, Jerry, and another set of twins, Dennis and Donna. All five of us were born within four years, which automatically made my parents saints!

It was not until I was almost twenty-one years old that I learned what my mother had done. She was loading clothes into the washing machine in our basement garage when I told her that her prodigal

2. Hannah has a very large family. Among her brood is the theological ethicist Stanley Hauerwas (1940–), who is professor emeritus at Duke University Divinity School and Law School. Read his book *Hannah's Child: A Theologian's Memoir* (Grand Rapids: William B. Eerdman's Publishing Company, 2010). He is a prolific writer, popular professor, and widely respected theologian and ethicist.

3. 1 Samuel 1-2.

son had returned (my first return). She was delighted with tears beyond words, of course, but not terribly surprised. That's when she told me who I was and what I was destined to do.

I had no clue how much the vocational deck was stacked against me. The two most powerful forces in the universe, God and Mother, had colluded, and that was that! I was the product of prayer and providence (which explained a lot).

For one thing, I had always strangely felt a close connection to Hannah's first son, Samuel. I thought it was simply because, like him, I spent a lot of time during my growing-up years in the temple of the Lord (he at Shiloh, and I at First Baptist Church, Belton, South Carolina). I was born and raised in it. It was more than a "second home" or "home away from home" for me. It was home.

I was there all the time: Sunday School and "preaching" every Sunday morning (we never skipped, and rarely missed). Then we were back for youth choir rehearsal, Training Union, evening service, and youth fellowship group on Sunday nights. Wednesday night was spent at prayer meeting. The weekdays involved sword drills, junior choir, RAs, church baseball, and organ lessons after school. Annually, I was involved in January Bible Study, Vacation Bible School, spring revival, and summer retreats at Camp Buckhorn near Greenville, South Carolina, or Chapel by the Sea in Garden City, South Carolina. I was a born-and-bred, baptized-by-immersion, dyed-in-the-wool, steeped-like-sweet-tea, Southern Baptist Christian. The congregation at 105 Brown Avenue was home.

I found another fellow temple-dweller in Porter Osborne, Jr., the main character in three of eight novels by Ferrol Sams, a doctor-turned-Southern-writer in Fayette County, Georgia. In *The Whisper of the River,* Sams tells how important it was for a young man in the South during the mid-twentieth century, like Porter Osborne, Jr., to be religiously "raised right." This meant not only being "saved," but also spending his growing-up years in the Lord's house, attending Sunbeams, Sunday School, preaching, and prayer meeting.[4]

4. Ferrol Sams, *The Whisper of the River* (New York: Penguin Books, 1986), 3. Sams (1922–2013) was a family medicine doctor in Fayette County, Georgia, until his retirement in 2006. He wrote novels on the side, drawing heavily from the Southern storytelling tradition. His stories were based largely in his own life, growing up in a rural area during the Great Depression.

That was me. I was that saved, raised right boy: Porter and Samuel, all rolled into one.

First Leaving

By the time I graduated from high school and moved into the freshman military barracks at Clemson University, I had assumed the identity and role of another character: the prodigal son in Jesus' parable. I not only left home—congregation, town, and family—but I also left everything my home represented—the world of Christianity and its faith.

But please, do not assume any of this was intentional. I was not the least bit aware a prodigal-type departure was occurring. There was no crisis of faith, or "dark night of the soul." I had not been thinking about my religious options. There was no thinking. I was not setting out on some journey to find myself, or look for a purpose-driven life. Mostly, I was only being young and immature.

What I did want to do, pure and simple, was to "see the world." I knew there had to be a lot more out there, and I wanted to find out what it was and what it was like. I knew what was back here at home. I had been in it every moment of every day of my entire life. I wanted to expand my horizons.

In those days, leaving was not as easy to do as it is today. The world where I was born and raised was a world where the Christian church and American culture had not yet separated. Stepping out of the faith-community into the larger community was uneventful, since it all was basically the same. Protestant Christianity provided the dominant, default culture, which was pretty much the only world there was. Parents never worried about their children growing up Christian, because everybody did, simply by being born and raised in places like Belton, and breathing the air and drinking the water of Christendom, southern style.

The church was not only at the center of everything—family and community life—it *was* the center. Church buildings were prominent on the town square or the main streets. Businesses were closed on Sundays. So were the cotton fields and ball fields. If anything happened, it either happened at one of the congregations or within shouting distance. So, like the Psalmist, I knew the inescapability of God and the church: "Where can I go from your spirit? Or, where can I flee from your presence? Wherever I go—whether to the heights of the heavens or the depths of Sheol; into the light of the morning or the darkness of the night—you are there!"[5]

Where could a South Carolina boy in the 1950s and '60s go that was *not* God and church, or *not* Christian? The thing was, when I was growing up, I did not want to flee or escape. I did not know there was anywhere else to go—until the world changed.

William Willimon, who was born and raised four years ahead of me, about thirty miles up the road in Greenville, South Carolina, believes that the major shift occurred on a Sunday evening in 1963, when the Fox Theater in Greenville decided to open and show a movie, in defiance of the state's blue laws (the restriction or ban of non-religious activities on Sunday).[6] I believe it happened on another Sunday evening, one year later, on February 9, 1964, when 73 million people assembled at 8 o'clock in front of their TV sets to watch the Beatles in their first live performance on American soil on the Ed Sullivan Show. I did not see them, however, for I was at "Sunday night church."

Nevertheless, the world changed. And it would change far more by 1968 when I left for college. In those days, a Baptist boy wanting to experience what was beyond the Christian world had no choice but to play the prodigal. He had to pack up, leave, and go looking for "the far country." The "world" in all its worldliness was somewhere else, at a distance. As folks used to say about the small Reformed Presbyterian school, Erskine College, in Due West, South Carolina, where my twin sister Kaye attended: "It's located about twenty miles from the nearest known sin."

---

5. Here I am paraphrasing Psalm 139:7–12.

6. Stanley Hauerwas and William H. Willimon, *Resident Aliens: Life in the Christian Colony* (Nashville: Abingdon Press, 1989), 15–16. The sequel is *Where Resident Aliens Live: Exercises For Christian Practices* (Nashville: Abingdon Press, 1996). Willimon (1946–) is a pastoral theologian, who has returned to Duke Divinity School as Professor of the Practice of Christian Ministry. He formerly was Dean of the Chapel at Duke Chapel and Professor of Christian Ministry, before serving the United Methodist Church as Bishop of the North Alabama Conference. He is the author of more than sixty books, and is considered by many (myself included) to be one of America's best preachers.

Today people simply attend class in almost any public school or university. They go to work. They turn on TV or surf the internet. And they are there. The world is no longer "out there," somewhere else. It is here, where we are. It is everywhere. It is now the air we breathe and the water we drink. But fifty years ago, in the South, a Porter Osborne, Jr., or a Samuel, or Keith Smith had to go looking for it.

What I did not know at the time was that, just as I was leaving, the Western world was also going through a leaving of its own. After centuries of adapting to post-Enlightenment modernity, it was finally cutting loose and fleeing from traditional faith, thought, and practice. American society on the whole was becoming—far more quickly and radically than any of us realized at the time—"the far country."

The growing mood among young people my age in the mid-to-late '60s was not alarm or fear, but rather, ecstatic celebration that everything seemed to be both coming apart and coming together at the same time. Modern humans were finally "coming of age," just as we baby boomers were. At least that is what we thought. It was the dawning of the "Age of Aquarius," which was advanced as a new way of thinking, feeling, and living, supposedly filled with visions, euphoria, understanding, love, freedom, and harmony.

I was totally up for it. If the world's long, dark night was over, and the new, bright day was dawning, the advent of a new consciousness,[7] I did not want to miss a minute of it. I wanted to be up bright and early, awake, and out in it, soaking it all in. So, like the prodigal, I left home and headed for the sunshine. Surely I, along with like-minded, free-spirited youth, could make a difference, and even help to usher in a brand new era and construct a brand new world.

Unlike the prodigal, however, I did not take any of my inheritance with me. Not that I necessarily rejected or disowned it, but I simply did not need it where I was going. Besides, I had already learned that residents of the far country, especially in the dawning new age of enlightenment, looked on the Christian faith as part of the dark ages

---

7. In his manifesto for this New Age, *The Greening of America* (New York: Random House, 1970), Charles A. Reich promoted Consciousness III. Whereas Consciousness II accepted society, the public interest, and institutions as the primary reality, Consciousness III started with the individual self as the only true reality.

being left behind. So I left it back home in my room at my parents' house, along with my Bible, baseball cards, Cub Scout badges, and high school letter sweater.

I got swept up right into the middle of it all, providing the music. Literally. At age fourteen, inspired by the Beatles and the whole British Invasion, I taught myself to play guitar and organized a band called "The Avengers." We were one of hundreds of rock groups springing up across the nation to provide the soundtrack for the countercultural generation.[8] These were "garage bands," because they organized and practiced in the garages and carports of 1960s houses. Home base for The Avengers was my parents' basement garage, where my mother would later reveal to me my true identity and vocation. We played at school sock hops, teen clubs, Battle of the Bands contests, a nearby roller-skating rink every Saturday night, and a few times at the famous Myrtle Beach Pavilion.

During my freshman year at Clemson, I reorganized this group into a ten-member band named "Quicksand," and I switched from guitar to Hammond B3 organ. (I am sure my parents were thrilled that their significant investment in seven years of piano and pipe organ lessons was finally paying off.) We played at college dances, fraternity and sorority parties, Woodstock-inspired outdoor concerts, and nightclubs up and down the southeastern seaboard. We shared the stage with and backed-up many well-known singers and groups of the early '70s, including Jerry Butler, Percy Sledge, Arthur Conley, the Showmen, and Chairmen of the Board.

I tell you this to illustrate how "in the world" I was. Not only that, but I was also, as Christians say, "of the world." Truth is, I was no longer "in and of" the Christian community and its faith. I was "in and of" the secular community and its unfaith. This shift took place not only culturally, but also spiritually and morally, and even more so, hermeneutically.[9]

---

8. Ken Myers contends that rock 'n' roll became the dominant idiom of popular culture. See Kenneth A. Myers, *All God's Children and Blue Suede Shoes: Christians and Popular Culture* (Wheaton, Illinois: Crossway Books, 1989), 137.

9. Hermeneutics is the theory and practice of interpretation. Here I am simply making the point that living in any life-world is much more than mere presence, or residence. It involves a specific way of interpreting all things, including one's self, which is different from the interpretive ways of residents of other life-worlds.

Growing up at home in Southern Christendom, I had no idea that there was any other world. I thought everybody was more or less Christian, and the local congregation was their home, too—although they probably had not spent nearly as much time there as I had. I assumed everybody lived in the same world, although some people were open to playing cards, going to movies, dancing, smoking, drinking, and messing around.

This meant I was naive and didn't have a clue. Therefore, I had to learn to interpret, understand, and live the way people outside the Christian world, living in another world, do. To borrow and modify the words of Paul the Apostle: "When I was a child growing up Christian, I spoke, thought, and reasoned like a Christian. But when I became a countercultural, neo-pagan secularist, I put an end to Christian ways, which were believed to be childish ways."[10]

In other words, Christians and non-Christians are in different worlds, and are worlds apart. When I left the Christian world, I changed my citizenship. I became a brand new card-carrying member of another, very different realm, under the dominion of different authorities and powers, playing by different rules, cultivating different interests and aims, speaking a different language, and having a different way of existing.

For the most part, I was at home there. I do not remember being homesick for the world back home. I was off on an adventure of a lifetime, traveling and performing. I tie-dyed my T-shirts, put on bell bottom jeans, wore sandals, and let my beard and hair grow long. How could anyone shave or get a haircut, when the awakening of a New Age was going on, and we were surfing the huge waves of change into the future?!

There was one unexpected problem, however. It was not major, but it did prevent me from fully belonging and being totally acclimated and accepted by my fellow-citizens. I do not know how they picked up on it, since I never mentioned it; but somehow some people around me knew I was not really one of them. I was different.

How did the servant-girl of the high priest identify Peter as "one of them," who had been with Jesus, the man from Nazareth?[11] Had she

---

10. This is my adaptation of a statement by the Apostle Paul. See 1 Corinthians 13:11 for the original words and meaning.

11. Mark 14:66–72.

actually seen him with Jesus, or with Jesus' disciples? Or, did his thick Galilean accent give him away? Was it something about the way he acted? Or didn't act? Had Peter been asking too many questions?

Whatever it was, I realized I never was quite as free to be as uninhibitedly heathen as the people around me. I drew the line closer and tighter than they did. I hesitated sooner at certain language, thoughts, and behaviors. I questioned accepted norms. Because I had previously lived in another world, I was not as native and natural at this way of life as other people, who had lived only in this non-Christian world their entire lives. I had another perspective from another world, and thus was not as singularly experienced, captured, and obligated as everyone around me. Unlike them, I could see and come at things another way.

Therefore, in spite of all the energy and promise of the secular world, I began to perceive that it was not all it had been cracked up to be. I witnessed its harsh deception, violence, futility, and despair. Promising to rescue and fulfill, it most often numbed and cheapened, caused turmoil and pain, and disoriented and got people lost. There was much about that world that troubled me, and I could not accept or belong to it fully.

So, quietly inside myself, I began to rebel against "the rebellion." And that got me identified and called out at times, despite how much I tried, like Peter, to hide and deny it.

Still, my unrest was never strong enough to make me do what the prodigal son did:

> But when he came to himself he said, '…I will get up and go to my father, and I will say to him, "Father, I have sinned against heaven and before you; I am no longer worthy to be called your son; treat me like one of your hired hands." ' (Luke 15:17-19)

That primary home, or first world, remained distant and closed to me. The thought of going back never crossed my mind. I was never homesick. I was too entrenched and busy in the world where I was. Therefore, I did not "come to myself" (or, come to my senses) and decide I needed to go back and rejoin my Father and faith family.

It was never in my plan.

First Returning

One hot, humid summer night in 1971, between road trips with the band, the unexpected happened. I was hit as suddenly, hard, and out of nowhere as was Saul of Tarsus (whom we know as Paul the Apostle) by the approach of the Risen Christ.[12] The only two differences were: (1) Paul was a zealous Jew, while I was a lapsed Baptist; and (2) he was on the road to Damascus in the Middle East, while I was on Concord Road in Anderson, South Carolina. That particular night I was mysteriously confronted and claimed, resulting in a radical conversion. I was turned around and returned to the church and its life-world. The prodigal son was home.

However, I was not the same son who left. For one thing, I had lost my first naiveté, or "the first faith of the simple soul."[13] My initial, pre-critical, child-like, trusting, accepting-everything-at-face-value, doing-as-I-was-told faith was gone, and could never be recovered. I had been in a post-faith place, glancing back at Christian religion and its assemblies, Scriptures, beliefs, and practices from the outside rather than the inside.

Second, I had taken on a secular mindset and neo-pagan lifestyle to a large extent, which left an indelible mark on my being, and a permanent dent in my seeing and coming at things. I would never remove all of it, and would never be the same again. From then on, I would be aware that when I was among Christians, I was different. None of them had been where I had been, and could not imagine that such a world actually existed. They would not have believed me had I told them.

Third, and most importantly, no one can ever be the same again, post-conversion. I was a new, very different person—again. I was not the same person I had been growing up Baptist and Christian. But

12. The story of the conversion of Saul is told in Acts 9:1–22; 22:6–16; and Galatians 1:11–17.

13. Paul Ricoeur, *The Symbolism of Evil*, trans. Emerson Buchanan (New York: Harper & Row Publishers, 1967), 350–352. Ricoeur (1913–2005) was a French philosopher, who is widely considered one of the most significant philosophers of the twentieth century. He taught at the Divinity School of the University of Chicago from 1970 to 1985. His most important contributions were made in the areas of language, phenomenology, and hermeneutics.

neither was I the person I had been growing up secular and neo-pagan. I was a third person I had never been before. I returned to the church completely turned-around and radically transformed (having been changed from two forms of being human to yet another). Strangely, I retained residue or traces of both worlds, and carried the identifiable impressions of both. I suppose I always will.

Back in my home congregation in Belton, I jumped in with the full joy and enthusiasm of being home. My days as a rocker were over. I quit the band, and returned to my old Samuel-like pattern of living at the temple much of the time. I finished my final year at Clemson; and worked the graveyard shift as a drawing hand and oiler at Abney Mills in Belton on weekends to make some money. I went back to Concord Road almost every night during the summers of '71 and '72. I talked with and got to know the young people who flocked to that area. Often our conversations turned into impromptu counseling sessions about problems they were having with parents, boyfriends and girlfriends, or alcohol and drugs. I frequently told them what had happened to me by the power of God in Christ in that very place where we were standing or sitting. We discussed matters of faith. I began my ministerial career as an itinerant street minister.

At that time, the Jesus movement was in full swing, finally reaching the East Coast after its start on the West Coast in the late '60s. It swept like a great wind across the upper part of South Carolina, spawning youth groups in and around many congregations. These small groups were "getting high on Jesus" (a phrase I never liked or used) and taking the "one way" to heaven, which was not the way their parents were taking.

I went from congregation to congregation, attending two or three youth groups every week for singing, praying, and what was called "sharing." I was invited to "give my testimony" at all of them, and also at adult gatherings on Wednesday and Sunday nights. Soon I was bringing in over one hundred young persons every Saturday night in the basement of my home congregation in Belton.

My pastor, D. H. Daniel, asked me to take on more responsibility and become our congregation's first youth minister. That was my first real, official congregational position. My mother had taught classes and directed activities for junior and senior high kids all the years my brothers and sisters and I were coming along. Now I was building on the foundation she had laid. That was very meaningful to me.

Another important part of my life that came out of that early ministry was that one of the dedicated youth, a senior cheerleader in high school named Beth Burgess, later became my wife. So much happened quickly and forcefully in the wake of my major conversion. But meeting and marrying Beth, who would go with me through the leavings and homecomings of the Christian theological life, was one of the best gifts.

Finding myself back home and being Christian again, I had a strong, relentless appetite for Christian knowledge and understanding—a hunger that has never lessened or been satisfied. This is key to comprehending both me and my lifelong zeal for theology and its education in the local congregation.

I remember asking my two new friends, Ronny Whitfield and Danny Vehorn, who had served as midwives for my new birth in Christ, what I needed to give up and what I needed to take on. "Now that I am back as a follower of Jesus," I said, "Please tell me what to do." They responded, "Go to church, read your Bible, and pray. The rest will follow and fall into place. The Lord will tell you. You'll know what to do."

That was helpful in getting me started. I went to Sunday School and worship services. I randomly read from my Bible every day. I prayed. However, these were the same things I had done all my growing-up years, and I was still doing them the same way. Had I been confronted and claimed by the Lord, simply to go back to the same old culture to resume my former religious childhood and mostly childish ways? Surely there had to be more.

I went back to my new Christian friends. "Shouldn't I be learning something? Don't I need to know what it means to be a Christian, and come to understand the Christian faith?" They looked at me with the blank stare of incomprehension. "Keith, it's about inviting Jesus into your heart, making him Lord of your life, telling others about him, and following him, as the Spirit leads. That's all."

Still, I was suspicious there was more. There had to be more (a lot more) than my buddies knew or were telling me. If this tiny amount I now knew, that I had not known before, could make such a major difference in my life, just think what it would mean and what might happen if there was more, and I discovered it! I was starved for what I did not know.

Back at Clemson for my senior year, I slipped into the meetings of a couple of campus ministry groups, hoping for some further insight and instruction. However, those groups had nothing to offer either. Truth is, their exaggerated, emotional, uncritical, non-reflective piety repelled me. They seemed to be wide-eyed, religiously-robotic clones of one another and some absent leader. Obviously none of them had ever left home, nor seriously examined the faith with which, like children, they were so lightly and loosely playing.[14]

Sitting in one of those meetings, anonymously at the back, near the door for quick exit, I did hear the names of C.S. Lewis[15] and Francis Schaeffer,[16] who at that time were the leading gurus of college-age evangelicals. A few days later, I saw a couple of Schaeffer's books on a dorm friend's shelf, and asked him if I might borrow them. I excitedly went back to my room, propped myself up in bed, under the light of a desk lamp, and started reading Schaeffer's *The God Who Is There.*[17]

I was like the Ethiopian eunuch reading from the Book of Isaiah.[18] I did not understand what I was reading. I couldn't. My problem was exacerbated by the fact that, unlike the eunuch, I did not have a Philip to interpret and guide me. So, unable to make sense of what I

---

14. Read Annie Dillard's description of Christians today in *Teaching a Stone to Talk: Expeditions and Encounters* (New York: Harper & Row Publishers, 1982), 40–41.

15. Clive Staples Lewis (1898–1963) was a novelist, poet, and literary critic who taught English literature at Oxford University and Cambridge University. After his conversion and return to the Anglican communion at the age of thirty-two, he became a lecturer, lay theologian, and apologist for the Christian faith. Of the more than thirty books he wrote, the best known are *Mere Christianity, The Screwtape Letters,* and *The Chronicles of Narnia.*

16. Francis A. Schaeffer (1912–1984) was an American Presbyterian minister, philosopher, theologian, and founder of the L'Abri (French for "the shelter") community in Switzerland. He was very popular among evangelicals during the late sixties and early seventies for his apologetics. His followers believed he could counter the intellectual challenges of science, philosophy, and modern culture, and answer the questions that troubled them during a revolutionary era.

17. Francis A. Schaeffer, *The God Who Is There* (London: Hodder & Stoughton LTD, 1968).

18. Acts 8:26–40.

was reading, and being without a teacher, I gave up. That was the last contact I ever had with Schaeffer. I never read, or tried to read, anything by C. S. Lewis during that period—not even his classic, *Mere Christianity*. This was probably because nobody around me had a copy of it or was reading it. I also knew I would be unable to read and understand it.

Nonetheless, I never quit searching for what I sensed I desperately needed and wanted, although I had no clue where it was, how to find and gain it, nor even what it was. I was like a blind man asking for directions to an unknown, maybe nonexistent place, from people he assumed could see everything clearly, had been there, and knew where it was. No one in the Christian community, however, seemed to understand what I was asking, much less how to help me—which seemed awfully odd to me. Either they were cruelly toying with me, or wisely leading me to find out for myself. Or worse, they were tragically as blind and unknowing as I was.

Now that I was back, I had no interest in wasting a day of my life, lazily going through the religious cultural motions of the local congregation. I had been there and done that. Surely I had not been sought out in the far country and brought home by God simply to attend services and meetings, read a few verses and a daily devotional in the morning, be a good person and do good deeds during the day, and then say my prayers before falling asleep at night. I wanted to know what this Christian faith was. I wanted to understand it all. Especially now that I was being put in charge of others, I wanted to know what I was doing and talking about. It was for their sake, as well as my own.

All I had to go on were a few crumbs of elementary knowledge, and even less understanding of the Christian faith that remained with me from the past. Somehow I missed the whole loaf of bread. Part of the problem, I am sure, was that I had not paid attention. I was probably daydreaming, or scheming about the next prank I would pull on one of my Sunday School friends, or the new chord I was learning to play on the guitar.

Second, I had been immersed in a culture, but that was all it was: a culture. The hymns and gospel music, the rituals of "walking the aisle" and "getting baptized," the prayer meetings and covered-dish suppers were as common and familiar to me as riding my bicycle and playing baseball. I was at home. However, that was as far and as deep as it went. I never wondered what this community really was. No one did. I never heard anyone explain or analyze it. It simply was. And it was what everybody assumed it was. I spoke the same broken language of the Christians around me, but never knew what we were saying or intending by it. And I began to suspect that they didn't either. It was just the way everybody talked when we were at First Baptist, at home during evening devotional time, or going about our routine business in Southern Christendom.

But now that I was back, these greater things took on the weight of real importance for me for the first time. I wanted to get behind the scenes, underneath the floorboards, and into the closets and attic of the church, to find out what this community and its faith were all about. What could possibly be hidden here, that even these people do not know about? I knew I didn't know. And I would not be satisfied until I did. Simple, superficial religious cultural involvement was no longer adequate or acceptable to me.

I quickly concluded that the local religious community is not the best place to find this fuller, deeper knowledge and understanding. As the old proverb goes, "If you want to know about water, don't ask a fish." Fish, being fish, do not know they are in water, much less what water is.

However, I was a fish, who had grown up in these waters, but who had been thrown out on land, beyond this pond for a while, then caught and returned and thrown back in. I was a fish turned into a fisherman. And so I was keenly aware and curious. I wanted to learn everything I could about H_2O. But there was no one, and no one knew of anyone, who could instruct and guide me, or give me the education I so desperately needed and wanted.

Staying with this water theme, let me tell you about my first experience with snorkeling. My wife and I were vacationing on Kauai, one of the main islands of Hawaii. On a beautiful tropical day, I went swimming in the clear water, while Beth stretched out on a towel on the sandy beach, getting some sun. I saw other people snorkeling, and thought that would be fun. So I rented a mask and fins from a small hut next to the beach. I put them on, as I had seen others doing, and waded out into the water. When I plunged my head under and saw all the brightly-colored fish in the clear water down below, I was overwhelmed by what I saw for the first time in my life. I jumped up and yelled in great excitement to Beth, "You won't believe what's down here! It's a whole other world!"

That is how I have come to view congregations and Christians. We are people who relax on the soft sands and bask in the spiritual light on the shore, or wade a bit into the shallow religious end of the lagoon. But we have never gone in, put our heads under and looked beneath or beyond the surface. Our involvement is basically and superficially cultural, and very limited and diminished at that. The shout of an excited novice snorkeler is met with blank stares. Most people are completely unaware there is anything more—that deeper waters exist—and under the surface are unimaginable mysteries, where few venture to explore, examine, and explain. Christians are satisfied, and not the least bit curious.

The group of one hundred young people I led on Saturday night, for example, did not share my passion. They were content being with their friends, having an emotional experience or two, and feeling spiritual by belonging to something as religious, yet counter-cultural, as the Jesus movement. Nothing more was needed. There was no appetite for serious education. Deeper exploration was not on their radar.

Therefore, I carefully handpicked seven teenagers, and invited them to join me in the quest for the "much more"—whatever that was. We met separately as an even smaller group, and tried to educate ourselves, since we did not know where to turn for help. I read and studied whatever I could find. I then shared with them what I had learned, and we discussed and prayed about it. We became a tight-knit fellowship, formed around, by, and for what we were learning.

That was my first experience of a teaching-learning community. I have used that early practice of small group theological education as a pattern for my ministry in every congregation I have served. It also provides the basic image or model of the church that is prescribed in this book.

Very soon, however, I found out how ill-equipped and poorly-prepared I was as both a student and a teacher. I did not have even the most basic, prerequisite concepts and skills for knowing and understanding the Christian faith. That was a shocking and humbling revelation for me. Had I not been in the church almost every day of my entire growing-up years? Had I not learned the books of the Bible, memorized Bible verses, and heard the major Bible stories? Had I not sat still (mostly still) and listened to not one but two sermons every Sunday from Dr. Daniel, who really was a good preacher? Had I not been Raised Right and Saved?

The first shock wave hit me at my conversion when, for the first time, I began to see and hear. I had drunk the water, but never tasted it. I had breathed its air, without ever smelling a thing. And I had been in its light, without seeing.

How could that have happened?! Had I not been as enmeshed in the thick of the congregation's life and work as any human being could possibly be? Had I not engaged continuously in its culture of worship, education, and fellowship, participating in its Bible reading, singing, prayer, baptism, and Lord's Supper? Yet, strangely, I never really noticed or knew most of it. And worse, I had never known I did not know. I definitely had never considered that any of it might actually be true.

The second shock came when I discovered, with eyes and ears finally opened, that now that I was gasping for deep breaths of air and struggling to exist in these waters, I was suffocating and drowning at the same time. I could not take in, comprehend, make sense of, articulate, or explain what I was seeing and hearing.

I was like the man in Bethsaida, whose eyes had been lathered with Jesus' spit. He could see people, but they looked like walking trees.[19] I could see, but not with comprehension or clarity concerning what I was seeing. I could grasp there was something there; but I could not immediately say what it was. Everything was vivid and vital to me, yet opaque and hidden from me. I was too functionally illiterate, too biblically and theologically ignorant, to make sense of what I was encountering for the first time, yet wanting so much to understand.

I remember my pastor giving me a short paperback that was a Southern Baptist study course book: *An Introduction to the Bible* by L.D. Johnson.[20] I was eager and ready to absorb its contents. But I gave up

---

19. Mark 8:22–26.

20. L. D. Johnson, *An Introduction to the Bible* (Nashville: Convention Press, 1969). Dr. Johnson (1916–1981) was pastor of First Baptist, Greenville, South Carolina, during the 1960s, and then chaplain and professor of religion at Furman University for fourteen years.

after only three or four pages (just as I had with Schaeffer's book). Again, I could not read it. It was a simple, basic book. But I had never read any Christian writing on a level higher or deeper than a Sunday School quarterly or an Open Windows devotional booklet. I lacked the necessary vocabulary, comprehension skills, and pre-understanding. I did not know how to read theologically, think theologically, or talk theologically, and thus I could not decipher theological writing. I had never done it before, although I had been raised in the congregation and its religious training since birth. I did not even know what theology was. I had never heard of it.

It was not that I lacked intelligence. I have since earned three higher education degrees, including a PhD. I admit that I never took a Bible, religion, or philosophy course at Clemson. I majored in psychology, and minored in sociology and history. Regardless, I should have known of and been trained in theology in my home congregation. Christian theological education is not the responsibility of our colleges and universities; and no Christian should have to attend a seminary in order to be educated biblically and theologically. This is the responsibility of local communities of Christians.

Yet, given that our communities have not and still are not providing this education, I lay full blame squarely at their feet. At the same time, I hold every single ordinary Christian accountable for not being interested and curious, not seeking and demanding this education, not jumping in and fully engaging when a smidgeon or taste of it is offered, and thereby complacently choosing to remain illiterate and ignorant. Frankly, I have never understood this attitude and behavior, and will never be able to accept it.

When I look back on my reentry into the Christian life-world, I realize how blessed I was to have been not only eager and enthusiastic, but also illiterate and ignorant, at the same time. I was ripe for theological education.

To use a second metaphor, adding to the one I gave above concerning fish, I was a newborn, starving and grabbing for breast milk. Piling on metaphors, I was fertile soil for the planting of the seeds of fresh knowledge and brand new understanding. Finally, I was the man who had emptied his house of all furniture; but now returning to it, he needed to refurnish and decorate the place.

Second Leaving

During that important first year back, I slowly came to realize that conversion had not been done to me simply to give me a religious experience, so that I could go around giving my personal testimony. It was not simply a rescue effort to make me come to my senses, quit "slopping hogs in the far country," and come back to where I belonged, and to the good life in my Father's house. It was not a ploy to get me to be a better person, enjoying the full and abundant life. Instead, it was a calling. Vocational recruitment. I had been chosen, approached, and claimed for a greater, more transcendent reason.

Possessing the wisdom of a good pastor and mentor, Dr. Daniel pushed me to explore what this meant and required. I was reluctant to consider the possibility that I was being called to clergy ministry, for I had not only a high view of the pastorate, but also a low view of most pastors I knew. I also knew I was unqualified. I was the least likely and the least promising candidate.

Conversion and calling, however, have a way of making one more courageous than he or she truly is, and has any reason or right to be. Slowly over time, I began to see myself in the strange role of clergy, although Saul's armor was way too big and bulky[21] (and, frankly, never has fit me snugly).

I remember Dr. Daniel telling me that if I was halfway serious about pursing any leanings or inclinations I might have toward Christian ministry, I would have to leave and go somewhere to receive a seminary education. The best place he knew of was his alma mater in the Crescent Hill neighborhood where he was raised: The Southern Baptist Theological Seminary in Louisville, Kentucky.

Ferrol Sams expressed it well when he said that back then the "most highly anointed" pastors and preachers came from "a mystic place called Louisville . . . 'Seminary at Louisville' had exactly the same ring as 'Temple in Jerusalem.'"[22] (By the way, Sams was right about Southern in those days.)

So, early one hot, humid, hazy South Carolina morning in August, 1972, I crammed everything I owned into my 1969 Plymouth

21. 1 Samuel 17:38–40.

22. Sams, *The Whisper of the River*, 3.

Barracuda, said goodbye to my mother and father, and drove up the road, as I wiped away the tears and followed the highlighted map to that "mystic place"—the Southern Baptists' version of the Jerusalem Temple.

I played the prodigal son a second time, although in another sense. Where I come from, most people never leave or go very far. They stay. Or, if they leave, they come back as soon as their college days, military stint, or first job is over. Therefore, anyone who moves away and stays away is considered "the black sheep" of the family.

When one of my mill co-workers overheard me talking about my plans to attend the seminary in Louisville, he asked, "Why would you want to do that?" And he meant it. He couldn't imagine why anyone would possibly want to leave. Plus, he had no idea where I was going, or even what a seminary was. He told everyone at the mill, "At the end of this summer, Keith is going to the cemetery."

The seminary was a long way away from my upbringing in the congregation in South Carolina. Although both were under the same denominational roof, they were worlds apart. I have never been able to describe and explain fully my seminary experience to anyone who has never been there. It is truly its own world. It *is* another world.

However, it was a world in which I quickly felt at home, as though it were the world for which I had been born, and where I truly belonged. After a couple of weeks there, I wrote my mother a letter. (Yes, we actually communicated by writing and snail-mailing paper documents in those days.) I told her I had "died and gone to heaven."

I could not believe all this great knowledge—for which I had been blindly, futilely seeking—was located in this one place, and was being opened and offered freely to me—a young man who was completely incapable and unqualified. I experienced it as the next best thing to sitting down at the table at the messianic feast in the Kingdom.

Again, I have never been able to express fully what being there meant to me and did to me: being in classes, listening to the lectures of the brightest Baptist minds (which Baptists are not known for having), researching in a world-class theological library, reading and studying the works of the church's scholars, worshiping and singing three times a week in chapel services, hearing the sermons of visiting pulpit giants, and living among ministers like myself. I had to search for exaggerated, superlative language then, and I still do. I never imagined a place like this existed on earth, much less that I would ever be one of its residents.

My experience in the life-world of the seminary was close to what Rudolf Otto described as an experience of the holy: *Mysterium tremendum et fascinans* (the Mystery that makes one afraid, and yet at the same time, fascinates).[23] I was, after all, in the place where the mysteries of God are thought about and taught. I was in awe and overwhelmed, especially given my illiteracy and ignorance. But, more than anything else, I wanted to be part of it and to take it all in.

I could not learn enough, fast enough. I read every textbook at least twice, and often three times. I memorized each new word. I looked up its definition, and imitated the professor's pronunciation of it. I noticed how these words were related, and then connected and used in sentences. I gathered up and held onto the concepts behind them, slowly beginning to discern how they came together and functioned in the most beautiful, truthful mosaic of Christian faith. Gradually, I learned to think and talk like a mindful, articulate Christian.

I cannot remember whether it was during my first or second year at the seminary, but one day in class the professor mentioned in passing the vision of Findley Edge (who taught at Southern at the time). In his book *The Greening of the Church,* Edge laid out an unheard of, visionary model of "the local congregation as a miniature theological seminary."[24]

All the expressions for sudden illumination have to be marshaled in order to describe what happened to me in that moment: the penny dropped; the light bulb came on; the bell rang; it finally clicked. I was awakened and captured. I knew why I had been called. I understood why I was so enthralled and enthusiastic about biblical-theological

---

23. Rudolf Otto, trans. John W. Harvey, *The Idea of the Holy* (London: Oxford University Press, 1958). Otto (1869–1937) was a German Lutheran theologian and philosopher, who taught at the University of Marburg's Divinity School. He is regarded as one of the most influential scholars of comparative religion in the twentieth century.

24. Findley B. Edge, *The Greening of the Church* (Waco, Texas: Word Books, 1971), 177–189. Dr. Edge (1916–2002) held the Basil Manly, Jr. Chair of Religious Education at The Southern Baptist Theological Seminary, where he taught for more than forty years. Edge authored more than eighty published works.

education. I knew who I was, and what I was to be about the rest of my life.

From that day on to this present day, I have remained highly aware of and sensitive to this concept of "the local congregation as a miniature theological seminary." Whenever I stumble upon it in my reading, my attention is snagged, and my desire ramps up. I stay with the words, imagining what such a local seminary might look like. I want more than ever to be part of it.

Although the company of visionaries is extremely small, Edge was not alone. Here are some examples:

> The congregation must, accordingly, be reconstructed into the pattern of a small theological seminary with the pastor as the professor. Elton Trueblood[25]

> We propose that the congregation is first a neighborhood theological seminary whose primary purpose is to help its members relate the Christian tradition appropriately, intelligently, and morally to the contemporary world situation and vice versa. Clark M. Williamson and Ronald J. Allen[26]

> The ordered learning occurring in congregations should be theological education. ...The educator on the church staff will have to be a theologian-teacher. Edward Farley[27]

This concept of the congregation as a seminary, or place for ordered learning of the Christian faith-tradition, has remained largely

---

25. Elton Trueblood, *The Incendiary Fellowship* (New York: Harper & Row Publishers, 1967), 45. Trueblood (1900–1994) was a founder of the Earlham School of Religion, a Quaker seminary in Richmond, Indiana. Before teaching there, he held faculty and chaplain positions at Haverford College, Guilford College, Harvard University, Stanford University, and Earlham College. He authored more than thirty books.

26. Clark M. Williamson and Ronald J. Allen, *The Teaching Minister* (Louisville: Westminster/John Knox Press, 1991), 106. Both authors are professors at Christian Theological Seminary, Indianapolis, Indiana.

27. Edward Farley, *The Fragility of Knowledge: Theological Education in the Church and the University* (Philadelphia: Fortress Press, 1988), 88, 99. Farley (1929–2014) was Professor of Theology at Vanderbilt Divinity School for nearly thirty years.

conceptual. Although all of these authors offer brief, basic statements of what it means and what it might look like, their descriptions are like scribbles and doodles jotted down quickly on a napkin during an especially creative, energetic brainstorm over lunch. No clearer, fuller description has been provided, and to my knowledge, no local congregation has ever attempted such a major re-conception and reconstruction—much less succeeded.

Still, after four and a half decades of trying, I continue to sow the seed in hopes of a miraculous fall on good soil.[28] I believed then, and I believe today, that theology belongs to the church. Therefore, it belongs in the local appearance of the church, i.e., the congregation. Each assembly of Christians must be an active teaching-learning community in order to be faithful to its calling and raison d'être (reason to be). This requires learning of the highest order, broadest reach, deepest insight, and longest obedience.

This is not Sunday School, and is far more than offering one or two special, optional study courses along the way. Christians in the pews must discipline themselves to become students in the church's classroom, instructed by a minister who is himself or herself both a scholarly student and a competent teaching theologian in the pastoral role.

This, in a nutshell, is what this book is about.

During my seminary years, I was able to practice this concept of a congregation-seminary hybrid. I was called as youth minister at a small, working class congregation, Rolling Fields Baptist Church, in Jeffersonville, Indiana. I devoted much of my ministry to teaching those high school students Bible and theology—just as I had done in my first youth position at my home congregation. I also offered courses for adults, whenever I was not with the youth and was able to squeeze them into the program schedule. Only a handful of adult members ever came. But I remained dedicated to bringing what I learned in the seminary classroom across the Ohio River and delivering it fresh to them. I remained keenly interested in and desirous for theological education on the local level.

These two worlds (seminary and congregation), however, were worlds apart. I was struck by the difference every time I drove from

28. This is an allusion to Jesus' parable of the sower and soils in Mark 4:1–20.

the small apartment where Beth and I lived in Seminary Village (which we affectionately called "the Gospel Ghetto") in Louisville, across the river, and to E 8th St. and Ewing Lane in Jeffersonville. One might think that since both these worlds were Christian, they would be two sides of the same reality, or would at least be connected by some sort of bridge. But that was not the case. To enter one was to leave the other.

During my seventeen growing-up years, and during the one year of my returning and getting started in Christian ministry, I considered the congregation to be home. It truly was where I lived, moved, and had my being. It was where I belonged and found my identity and purpose.

All of that changed when I left Belton. The seminary became my primary life-world, the place where I belonged, had my being, and felt most at home. It took over in telling me who I was and what I was about. Consequently, the congregation became for me "the other world" that I visited and worked in on Sundays and Wednesdays. I stood at a different vantage point, seeing the congregation both outside and inside. I had never viewed it before from both angles at the same time.

And the more I looked at the congregation through bifocal lens, the more I saw how bewildering this place truly was. The people were an odd mix of saint and sinner, spiritual and secular, complacent and complaining, kind and mean, all at the same time. Often I did not recognize their Christianity, and was perplexed by their thinking (or quite frequently, not thinking). They kept coming, but it was for the friendships and religious activities of social-cultural Christianity, and not for the Christian faith itself. I could not figure out why they cared so little about what was in the Bible, the church's history, or the innards of our doctrinal tradition. It was as though that theological world—the world of their own faith heritage—did not exist. And for them, as far as they were concerned, it didn't.

They could not figure me out either. As one dear, sweet, older woman said to me after a sermon I had preached: "Keith, I don't understand a word you say. But I still love you." I was a kind of alien visitor among them for six years, finding congregational life to be strangely foreign, at the same time it was strangely familiar. That mixed, torn sense in congregations has never let up or left me.

Then my cross-cultural situation got even more complicated. As a doctoral student, I was invited to teach Bible and theology at Simmons Bible College, a school for preparing men and women to serve black Baptist congregations.[29] That immersed me in a third world that ethnically and culturally, even religiously, was not my own. Still, I was quickly adopted as "Brother Teacher," and became an accepted member of their chapel services, congregational worship services, and fellowship dinners (although I admit I never ate the chitlins or collard greens).

Most of my students were older, and had no formal education beyond high school—if that. They possessed no intellectual grasp of the Christian faith. What little knowledge they did have was buried under layers of folk religion and sentimental piety, given to them by their culture and its congregations. However, most did have the one thing most needed: a deep sense of calling that provided the strong drive to seek some education.

It was there in the matrix of those three worlds that I learned to teach. I learned how to bring theology home—to the whole church where it belongs—and to introduce Christians to their own faith-tradition, as tough as that undertaking is. The reunion was never easy, always awkward, and sometimes painful. Believers were reluctant and suspicious, and many of them could never get past their fear, in order to have a meaningful relationship. Yet, when and where that happened, as rare as it was, the joy and delight were exceeding.

Those years were some of the most productive and rewarding for my ministry. I taught and worked with Christians in three different settings at the same time, which gave me a unique perspective on theological education. The first thing that stood out was that, other than the various contexts, and other than tests and grades, there was

29. This school was founded in Louisville in 1879 as the Kentucky Normal Theological Institute. Under the direction of Dr. William J. Simmons, an ex-slave who had helped develop Howard University's teacher training programs, the school flourished, became a full university, and expanded its offerings to include liberal arts, college preparatory courses, and medicine, law, business, music, and theology departments. In 1930, the school became Louisville Municipal College, a "colored branch" of the University of Louisville. After severe demise during the Great Depression years, the school narrowed its mission to the education of young men and women for Christian ministry. It was renamed Simmons Bible College to suit better its mission, and to honor the contributions of its earlier president.

no real difference in the education itself. There is not one education for the seminary, another for the Bible College, and still another for the local congregation. The same theological education is possible at all three locations.

Second, Christians can be students. The assumption that both faith and the Spirit conspire to defeat rational thought, thereby rendering the believer beyond education, or incapable of learning, is blatantly false. It is downright idiotic. Anyone who thinks she is too old, has been out of school too long, or no longer possesses the brain cells for it, is underestimating herself. Christians of all ages and varying intellectual ability and skill can over time be trained to be good, capable students of the theological faith-tradition. I have witnessed it happen a few times.

Third, Christians are uneducated as Christians. Generally and typically, they are not knowledgeable of their own religion, much less its theology. Therefore, when they show up at a seminary, Bible college, or small teaching-learning community for serious education, they have to be made into students, which is something most have never been. This usually involves starting over, from scratch, no matter how many years an individual has been in the local congregation. Contrary to the "osmosis theory," human beings do not absorb knowledge and understanding of the Christian theological tradition simply by showing up and hanging around, or by breathing the air and drinking the water. I am a prime example.

Fourth, ordered, in-depth biblical-theological education can take place in the local congregation, as well as in any college, university, or seminary. There is no law or reason why it is restricted and can only take place in the latter. I was determined to follow-through on the vision of Trueblood, Edge, and Farley (none of whom, by the way, spent his career serving in the local congregation). I would bring theology home where it belongs. I would bridge the gap. I would facilitate the ministry of reconciliation.

Second Returning

During the defense of my PhD dissertation at Southern Seminary, Professors Wayne Ward, Eric Rust, and Paul Simmons (taking the place of Henlee Barnette on my doctoral studies committee) asked me about my vocational plans. I remember their looks of disbelief when I told them. They must have thought I was wildly idealistic and "knew not what I was doing." They were right, in that I did not know how to bring theology to congregations and Christians, and had no clue how such an effort would be unwelcomed and rejected.

My professors encouraged me to pursue instead an academic career in a college, university, or seminary. I knew what they were implying: teaching is not a viable ministry in congregations. And again, they were right, in that such a ministry rarely or barely exists. Still, I knew I had been approached and recruited on Concord Road for the teaching ministry in the local congregation. I have never waivered from that conviction, although I never imagined how difficult and even impossible it would be.

I chose the local congregation, because that is the place where the need for ordered learning is greatest. Not only is the local ecclesial community the primary context of the formation of Christian faith-existence, but this community also lacks a teaching ministry. It does not have a program of biblical-theological studies, access to the resources of the historic Christian tradition, teaching theologians in residence, and an educational culture, as do seminaries and many colleges and universities. Therefore, due to my calling, my intrigue with the "church as seminary" model, and my direct experience teaching laypersons, I was not swayed by my professors. Instead, I was compelled to go where the dire need was.

So I returned home a second time. The first was after deliverance from the secular city, and the second was after graduation from the seminary. My first leaving was prodigal. My second was preparatory.

Both times, after a few years of sojourning in a far country, I returned to the place where I had been born and raised. The local congregation was home for me as a Christian pastor-teacher-theologian, although in some ways it had become more like a foreign mission field, since I had dwelled in other lands, and was returning on a mission to bring a message. I was struck by my mixed identity and purpose when I returned.

After interviewing with numerous congregations, hoping to find one that would support both my calling and my family with a steady paycheck, I accepted a minister of education staff position at Friendly

Avenue Baptist Church in Greensboro, North Carolina. What better role for a young minister, returning home as a budding theologian and teacher, bearing gifts of knowledge and understanding of the Christian faith? I wanted to be an educator—in particular, a minister of education.

For me, it would have been selfish not to bring back what I had received. I knew I had been given an opportunity most Christians would never have. I had been led to regions, shown sights, exposed to mysteries, and had treasures opened to me that they could never dream of or imagine. I wanted to come back and tell them about this experience. But more than that, I wanted to bring theology and its rich tradition home to them.

Why keep them in the dark? They, too, are "fellow-heirs, members of the same body, and sharers in the promise in Christ Jesus through the gospel." (Ephesians 3:6) These greater things belong to them. There is no reason why anyone should have to go away to another world (the seminary), where these valuables are kept, in order to have them and to know them. Moreover, how is it possible for a congregation to be responsible and trustworthy in its handling of the gospel, when it does not have this gospel, or does not know and understand it, and does not give it in full depth and breadth to its members, who are fellow-heirs?

My personal commission was to return home with a great gift. Not only had I been given much—much more than I deserved—but consequently, much was required of me. I wanted my brothers and sisters, uncles and aunts, parents and grandparents by faith back home to enjoy and delight in what I had come to enjoy and delight in. More than anything else, I wanted the local congregation to be the church, which it cannot be without theology. I assumed they would be thrilled and eager to receive it.

To say that they were not is an understatement. I announced that I would be teaching seminary-type courses, and no one moved. Not even the crickets made a sound in the room. I recognized the "deer in the headlights" stare I had seen in Belton and Jeffersonville. But I did manage to round up a handful of members, as I had done before and would continue to do for years to come. I began to give them, little by little, the gift I had been given and had brought back home for them.

My job as a minister of education, however, turned out not to be educating, but administrating. That was made clear to me very quickly. I was supposed to keep the Sunday School, Training Union, Wednesday night missions groups (Mission Friends, GAs, and RAs), and various age groups running. We Baptists love our programs, projects, and activities. We have a lot of them, and are always adding to our collection. We never throw anything away, holding onto them as though they are sacrosanct. Also, somebody has to be in charge of all these "treasures" (which was not the same treasure I was offering). That's why I had been brought there. Apparently, the interest shown by the search committee in my vision of the local congregation as a seminary, and to my serving as a teaching theologian-in-residence, had been feigned.

As long as I kept up with my assigned chores, kept the system humming, kept everybody happy, and kept the trickle of new members coming in order to keep the budget growing, no one paid any attention, or cared whether I offered a class on the side. As long as it was during off-hours, on my own time, and did not interfere with the congregation's regular (real) life and work, I was good. I was only the housekeeper.

That's when I discovered, much to my surprise (I had so much to learn about congregations and clergy ministry), that the minister of education position does not require an educator, or even an educated person. Ministers of education are not biblical scholars, and often not biblical students. They are not theologians or teachers. Instead, they are directors of religious and social programming.

Someone, of course, will raise the question, "What about Sunday School, women's small Bible study groups, and missions classes for children?" In my experience, these programs are specially designed for socialization, enculturation, and perhaps a bit of spiritualization, under a very thin veneer of biblical or missional study. There is little that is properly educational about them. Even worse, to the extent that they are educational, they barely scratch the surface, endlessly repeat and reinforce the same limited, shallow body of knowledge, and frequently teach Christians and the congregation the wrong things. These programs cover up illiteracy and ignorance, while actually increasing it. They give the false appearance and assurance that Christians are being educated, but only add to the deficiencies and inadequacies of Christian belief and practice. More harm than good is often done.

I was determined to change all of this. However, my ministry in Greensboro lasted barely eighteen months, due to the pastor. He had been at the helm of this congregation for over thirty years, and was nearing retirement age. The congregation's leaders decided it would be prudent to bring in a new staff of associate ministers, who would be in place and able to provide guidance when the pastor retired. It was clear they were hoping this time would come sooner than later.

However, contrary to everyone's expectations, the pastor decided he did not want to retire, was threatened by his new staff (especially by his new minister of education), and began to take it out on me. When I most needed and wanted a mentor, I found myself fending off an abuser.

Before long, I was in a severe personal crisis of calling that carried me very close to leaving a third time and never coming back. It was more than the common, typical shock of re-entry for seminarians who have been away for a few years (I had been away seven). Unfortunately, I had landed in a congregation where the emotional-spiritual toxicity was high, overriding everything. I almost walked away from the Christian ministry because of it.

Providentially, just at the time I needed it, a friend told me about an opening at University Baptist Church in Charlottesville, Virginia. I mailed my biographical packet, went for an interview, and soon was relocating to serve as their minister of education. That call saved my ministerial life.

I had no clue, though, what was to unfold there. Within four months, the pastor suffered a severe heart attack while on vacation, followed by quadruple bypass surgery. I took on the preaching and pastoral duties, putting my teaching ministry on hold. Everyone, including myself, assumed this would be temporary. I had always said I was not called to be a pastor, but a professor for laypersons. My mother always warned, "Never say never." But I foolishly *never* gave any credence to that advice. I should have.

Over the next few months, I came to realize—much to my surprise—that I had pastoral gifts, and found great meaning and reward in the pastoral ministry. Besides, given what I had discovered about being a minister of education, I realized I would have more freedom and more opportunity in the pastoral position to teach and guide the congregation theologically.

After serving University Baptist Church as minister of education, interim pastor, and then minister of education again, I was officially installed as senior minister in April 1987. My boyhood pastor and mentor, Dr. D. H. Daniel, traveled to Charlottesville to preach the sermon at my installation service. With that, I became what I had sworn I would never become, yet he knew I was destined to become. I was a pastor.

I will always be grateful to the good folks at University Baptist. They gave me a chance. They loved me (most of them did). They let me try and fail. They encouraged and supported me. It was there in the crucible of their congregational life and work, and in the wider context of Mr. Jefferson's University of Virginia, that I learned how to be a pastor and a preacher, a theologian and a teacher.

University Baptist had a strong ministry of worship and music. I immersed myself in it, and took seriously my need to learn and grow as a liturgist. I purposively did not take the wide, heavily-traveled path of looking to and copying the contemporary popular culture, while jettisoning the church's own theological, liturgical tradition. In sharp contrast, I drew on that tradition for its rich language, rituals, prayers, seasons, symbols, hymnody, and homiletics, and guided the congregation accordingly. Week after week, I worked hard to prepare worship services that were reverent and dignified, yet creative and alive. The result was a form of high church, formal worship that most Baptists do not know, but know for certain that if they tried it, they would not like it.

While in Charlottesville, I continued to be faithful to my calling by making teaching a priority. I taught "the pastor's class" on Sunday mornings before worship, along with workshops, seminars, and special classes during the week. I developed my own theological teaching style and honed my skills in the classroom. Only a few members, or a very small percentage of the total active membership, ever came, just as in my three previous congregations. I could never understand that. Why, when given the opportunity, would more Christians not come? This is about them and their faith. This is what they profess to believe and live. Why would they not care to know what it is, understand it more fully, and mature in it?

Something significant and formative happened to me during those almost twenty years at University Baptist Church. I continued my own education. Unlike most seminary graduates, I did not leave my study and learning behind when I left school. I did not allow myself to become so busy and involved in practical ministerial activities that I neglected my continuing theological education. I did not put my books down, nor buy and read only how-to books. I did scholarly research. My library expanded rapidly, requiring more and more shelf space.

My close friend and staff colleague, Len Willingham—whose childhood physician in Georgia was Ferrol Sams, the writer who introduced us to the "Saved, Raised Right" kid, Porter Osborne, Jr.—gave me a framed calligraphy print of a quote attributed to Desiderius Erasmus: "When I get a little money I buy books; and if any is left, I buy food and clothes."[30] My friend knew me well.

During my years at University Baptist, I increased in knowledge and understanding of what little I had come to know and understand. Seminary can only introduce the broad landscape, get one started, provide the tools, and point the way. It is then up to the student to do the rest. As good and solid as a seminary education is, it is by itself insufficient for Christian life and ministry, especially in today's post-Christian, postmodern age. However, this is all most clergy have. And non-clergypersons do not have it at all.

At Simmons Bible College I had to teach broadly—everything from Bible to theology to worship to pastoral care to remedial English. That set in place a good pattern for me, and gave me invaluable experience. Because I was the only teacher-theologian in the congregations I served, I had to teach broadly in all areas of the Christian faith-tradition. The luxury of specialization was never mine. Even if it had been, I would not have wanted it. The interdisciplinary nature of local congregational teaching and learning is much closer to the true nature of the Christian faith.

New Testament theology was the major area of my PhD work at Southern, along with philosophy of religion and ethics. I completed additional study in philosophy at Indiana University. My dissertation

30. Erasmus (1466–1536) was a Dutch Renaissance humanist, Catholic priest, and theologian, who is known for his "synchronized" Greek and Latin version of the New Testament, and arguments against Martin Luther.

was in philosophical and theological hermeneutics.[31] I continued that study, and the Apostle Paul and the philosopher Hans-Georg Gadamer continued to be my teachers, as I worked out my faith in both the classroom and the pulpit with fear and trembling. But I also had to extend and fill in my knowledge of the Old Testament, church history, and Christian mission. The result was a far richer, more comprehensive, coherent body of knowledge than I otherwise would have achieved.

When I preached or taught on a subject, I bought the best books I could find, read them, and drew from them for my sermons and lectures. I taught myself as I went along. It is amazing how much can be learned by this slow method over a long period of time.

The fundamentalists were resurging and seizing complete control of the Southern Baptist Convention during the 1980s. I knew almost nothing about fundamentalism, since I had neither grown up in a fundamentalist congregation nor attended a fundamentalist seminary. Therefore, I read the "Princeton theologians": A.A. Hodge, B.B. Warfield, and J. Gresham Machen. I studied the thought of Carl F.H. Henry, J. Frank Norris, W.A. Criswell, and Paige Patterson, along with their commentators and critics, such as George Marsden and Cecil Sherman.

This eventually led me to study the broader context of modern theological thought in which fundamentalism had first incubated and emerged, gone underground, and then reemerged. I delved into liberalism and postliberalism, evangelicalism, neo-orthodoxy, paleo-orthodoxy, and radical orthodoxy, which, in turn, led to study of the larger social, political, and cultural movements of the modern and postmodern eras.

I had always been quite interested in secularization and secularism, having had some prior, direct, up-close and personal involvement with this life-world. Many of my early papers in the seminary were on Christianity in the secular age. But then, in congregational ministry, my research and lecturing on this subject expanded naturally to modernity (modernism) and postmodernity (postmodernism). I became a careful observer, analyst, and critic of American popular

---

31. Norman Keith Smith, "The Meaning of the Gospel As a Hermeneutical Problem" (PhD dissertation, The Southern Baptist Theological Seminary, 1979). See footnote #9 on page 17.

consumerist culture, and particularly how it is shaping and directing, even consuming, local congregational culture. Everything I studied and learned was related to the church and its local communities.

For those who may be curious about my theological pedigree, I identify Frank Stagg (New Testament), Eric Rust (philosophy of religion), and James Leo Garrett and Frank Tupper (systematic theology) as the seminary professors who most influenced my thinking. During those years I also read everything I could by theologians Paul Tillich (whose three-volume systematic I devoured one summer), Reinhold Niebuhr, Rudolf Bultmann, Emil Brunner, and Wolfhart Pannenberg. Later, I put myself under the tutelage of the great Karl Barth. I then discovered and still sit at the feet of Leslie Newbiggin, Richard John Neuhaus, Robert W. Jenson, and Stanley Hauerwas. Today I am looking to Gerhard Lohfink, N.T. Wright, Christopher J.H. Wright, Kevin Vanhoozer, Edward Farley, Thomas F. Torrance, Anthony Thiselton, and David Bentley Hart for further guidance. Philosophically, for "heavy lifting," I read Martin Heidegger, Hans-Georg Gadamer, Paul Ricoeur, Bernard Lonergan, Michael Polanyi, and Charles Taylor.

Looking back and putting it all together now, I realize that over those years of post-seminary, congregation-based work, I was being gradually molded into the pastor-teacher-theologian I was called to be. I do not believe my knowledge and understanding could have taken on this particular form in the academic setting of a college, university, or seminary. Only in the local congregation have I been able to acquire the kind of theological perspective and insight I value so highly today.

Finally, I must point out that it was the inertia of the congregation that served as the anvil against which the energy of my repeated strikes of education eventually forged both my personal theology and my theological person. The process, however, was long and painful.

After almost two decades in Charlottesville, I moved sixty miles east on I-64 to Richmond, Virginia. That decision was difficult to make, primarily because I was so deeply and intimately rooted at University Baptist. Other congregations had "come calling" over the years, but I had declined their overtures. This time was different. Through months of prayerful, painful searching, and agonizing back-and-forth discernment, I eventually came to the conclusion that my calling was at a turning point, and I was to broaden my experience by serving another congregation.

In May 2000, I became the pastor of Derbyshire Baptist Church, having high hopes of a long, loving relationship that would take me to retirement. I purposefully put myself in the position of a ministry apprentice, believing that I still had much to learn about being a pastor, and definitely everything to learn about being the pastor of this particular congregation and its constituents. I eagerly seized this opportunity to experiment further with biblical-theological education in another setting with another group of Christians. In the active years I had left, I wanted to develop my abilities and become a master pastor-teacher-theologian.

For the next ten years, I worked on crafting a teaching style of preaching. I learned to prepare and deliver "teaching sermons."[32] Also—and this will surprise no one—my favorite ministry was the pastor's class on Sunday mornings. That became a test kitchen for me to prepare and offer tastings of what I was working on regarding biblical-theological education in the local community of faith. The openness and eagerness of the few who came kept me going in my calling, when everyone else and everything around me was moving in other directions.

I preached at the 8:30 service in the chapel; walked up the hallway and into the classroom to lecture to fifteen to twenty students (the most I have ever had); and afterward, left and walked straight into the main sanctuary for the 11:00 service. I was energized by the synergy of education and worship, teaching and preaching, learning and liturgy. I was working with theology at the intersection. I had never had such an opportunity.

In less than three years, this intersection enlarged and became busier and more complex. The John Leland Center for Theological Studies in Arlington, Virginia, was opening a new site in Richmond for their School of Ministry's diploma in theology program. I was offered an adjunct faculty position in systematic theology and philosophy of religion, teaching one course a semester. I had always known I would teach in a seminary in the later years of my career.

---

32. Ronald Allen offers the best instruction on this type of preaching. See his book, *The Teaching Sermon* (Nashville: Abingdon Press, 1995).

I gladly accepted for several reasons: (1) I had learned I am the type of pastor who needs an extracurricular ministry in order to maintain proper perspective and balance in his primary ministry in the congregation; (2) I loved theology and teaching, and never turned down an opportunity to be at the party when the two got together; (3) I had always wanted to teach on the seminary level, and to gain that experience; and (4) as I had discovered during my own seminary years, I was most comfortable and at home at the intersection of academy and congregation, learning and liturgy, teaching and ministry, theology and faith.

For the next fourteen years, I taught across the entire curriculum: Biblical studies, theological studies, and ministry studies. Almost all of my students were laypersons responding to a calling that required a career change later in life. The only difference between them and the laypersons I taught in the local congregation was that they were preparing for clergy ministry. I met some very talented, thoughtful, dedicated Christian servants, and had the rewarding opportunity to be involved as a mentor in their personal lives, as well as their ordinations and ministry challenges.

When I left the pastorate of the Derbyshire congregation, the president and academic dean of Leland invited me to join the seminary staff as Director of the School of Ministry. My primary responsibility was administrative oversight of the multiple sites of the diploma program scattered across the state. I did that work for four years, and gained an education in the inner dynamics, structures, regulations, and politics of an accredited theological school.

Leaving the congregation and becoming a seminary administrator was never in my plan. I had intended to stay the course as full-time pastor and part-time professor. However, the congregational system where I was serving became too culturally ingrown and conflicted over power for me. I could not continue.

Also, it became increasingly clear that the membership never saw the vision, never understood the concept of the local congregation as a theological community, and never would. Just as I had found in four previous settings, there was little real interest in the work of studying, thinking, learning, and growing theologically. Members were happy with their small groups of friends, activities for the kids, and generally the way things were. The more I began to form and express my thoughts on other, greater matters, the more some resisted and even became agitated.

My last-ditch effort at Derbyshire was to try to start a conversation on the church: What is the church? What does it mean to be called and created by God rather than by ourselves? What part in the mission of God have we been assigned, and what is expected of us? How do we avoid the wide path of popular, consumerist cultural success being taken by congregations today, and instead take the rarely traveled path of historical-biblical-theological faithfulness? What if our primary question is not "What works?" but "Are we allowing ourselves to be worked into the body of Christ, the communion of saints, and the fellowship of the Spirit?"

I wrote out multiple pages of theological points for discussion. I took the educational ministers, the entire staff, and the deacons on separate retreats to initiate this discussion. But the more I talked about the church, and called this congregation to understand itself as the church, the community of theological faith, the more the resistance around me set in and locked down. It was turned into a personal attack, which was vicious at times. The bullying and mobbing increased over the last eighteen months of my tenure, finally forcing my resignation.

After preaching my last sermon there on September 5, 2010, I literally drove my car to the edge of the parking lot, got out, removed my shoes, and shook the dust off.[33] With that symbolic act, I left.

Third and Final Leaving

On that day, I knew my departure involved more than merely leaving a particular congregation. I was leaving all congregations. I already had two leavings in my history. I knew what leaving was, and what it entailed. The difference was, this time I was not returning, and would never go back. I left the church, as it is and as we know it. I quit.

I do not say this lightly or loosely. Remember: I was prayed and procreated into the local congregation. I was Raised Right and Saved in the local congregation. I left and returned as a prodigal son of the

33. Read Jesus' instruction in Mark 6:11; Matthew 10:14; and Luke 9:5.

local congregation. I was claimed and converted for service to the local congregation. I went away to seminary to be trained for the ministry of teaching in the local congregation. I faithfully, steadfastly persevered for decades as a staff minister and a pastor, through many difficult circumstances and crises in the local congregation. I know what the local congregation is, inside and out. I have literally been an insider, who could not be more inside. I have also been an outsider, who at one time could not have been more outside. This was home.

The primary way we as Christians experience the church is in and through congregations. Almost all of our knowledge of the church comes through this personal experience, starting at the time we are born into a local congregation, or are later brought into it.

The congregation *is* the church, as far as we are concerned. Just listen to our language: "I grew up in the church"; "I go to church every Sunday"; "What church do you attend?"; "I like the preaching at this church, but the youth ministry is better at the other church."

Church, for us, *is* the local congregation. The two are synonymous. They are one and the same reality in our thinking and experience. There is no difference or distinction. Consequently, there are many "churches," and all of them are "the church." We have no real conception of the church as being in any sense other than or greater than the local congregation.

The Christian theological tradition does have such a conception, and it is central. The church is *communio sanctorum*—the communion of saints. This is an historical, universal, eschatological community of faith. Therefore, the church is not limited to or exhausted by the specific gathering of specific persons in a specific location at a specific time, although the church appears or manifests itself in, through, and as this assembly of persons.

In other words, the church and its local congregations are not identical. But neither are they separable. The church is always other than and greater than any given local congregation, or even all congregations collectively. For this reason, we can say that the local congregation is more or less the church, and the church is more or less present in the local congregation. While inextricably related, the two are to be distinguished.

Ironically, the closer the two are identified, and even equated—as they are by us today—the more they separate and become distanced from one another. By considering itself to be the church, without qualification, the local congregation effectively moves further and further away from the church and its theological faith-tradition, while the church fades further and further into the distant past, abstraction, and irrelevance. To put it another way: if the local congregation *is* the church, then who needs the historical, universal, eschatological church, or communion of saints?

I have always tried to hold the two together in my ministry, without losing their distinction, while consistently maintaining both their relationship and the priority of the church. On the one hand, I was a pastor who loved and served the local congregation. It was home. On the other hand, I was a theologian who loved and served the church. In fact, I loved and served the local congregation only because I loved and served the church first and most of all. I devoted my life to studying and learning about the church, so that I would be able to understand and relate to the particular congregation where I lived and worked, as the church. I have always known not only their bond but also their difference.

Living with both over the years, I have become increasingly alarmed to see this difference ignored, and this bond broken. The congregation has moved further and further from the church. Specifically, how can a local community be the church when it knows and cares so little about the church and its historical-biblical-theological faith-tradition? I have witnessed the chasm growing wider and uglier.

Gradually, and then finally, the divide became too great for me to straddle. I sensed I was like a man standing with one foot on the dock, with the other foot in a boat that was drifting, moving further and further away from the dock. A crisis developed, and a decision had to be made. I finally chose the dock—the solid platform of the church—and stepped out of the congregational boat. No longer was the local congregation home to me, as it had been my entire life. The church became true home, and thus the point of origin and orientation for any association I might or might not have with the local congregation. Theology would not let me do otherwise.

Let me be straightforward: I arrived at the place where I could no longer be part of congregations as they are and as we know them. Through direct, personal experience as a pastor, I had always known congregations are failing to be the church. However, I stubbornly held onto the belief that with enough persuasion through preaching and teaching they would come around and begin taking their identity and purpose as the church seriously. That never happened. I finally could no longer hold out hope that it ever would. And so I left.

I was not burned-out, which is exhaustion and the inability to renew oneself. I suffered that ministerial affliction in 1990, and spent four years recovering. I know what it is. This loss of confidence in and connection with congregations was not that.

I was not overcome with anger over how my ministry was forced to end at Derbyshire. Truth is, I was relieved and grateful when that abusive episode was finally over.

I was not, like Barbara Brown Taylor, making "a new home in the world...well away from all centers of religious command, wherever God shows up."[34] I had not joined the growing ranks of those who have quit organized religion, settling for being merely "spiritual," and now checking the last box "None" in the religious preference section of the latest Gallup poll.

Finally, I did not "lose my faith." If anything, faith was stronger and healthier for me, more vibrant and alive, and more deeply grounded theologically than ever. Instead, I was like the man who believes in love and a marital relationship. But after years and years of dating, he wakes up one day and wonders whether there is any woman who also believes in love and a marital relationship. Is there anyone anywhere who desires to enter into a traditional relationship that participates in the great mystery of Christ and his church?

One day I simply was no longer under any illusion, nor able to work up any more naiveté, trust, or hope. I could no longer be part of, support, and serve what I no longer believed was the church. Congregations as they are—whether traditional, contemporary, emergent, or whatever the latest-greatest flavor or fad might be—and the Christians that make them up, are largely uninterested and not the least bit curious about their own historical-biblical-theological faith-tradition. They refuse to engage in its teaching and learning, even

---

34. Barbara Brown Taylor, *Leaving Church: A Memoir of Faith* (New York: HarperOne, 2006), 166. Taylor (1951–) is an Episcopal priest, Butman Professor of Religion and Philosophy at Piedmont College, Demorest, Georgia, award-winning author, and one of America's most gifted preachers.

when it is offered where they worship and serve. They are not participating in it. They are not embodying it, and thereby have rendered themselves incapable of being the church and serving counter-culturally as God's living witness in today's secular, post-Christian, postmodern world.

Ironically, I still believe in the necessity of congregations for the presence and ministry of the church. It is simply that the church is being betrayed and failed by its congregations.

So I reluctantly and regretfully, with a lot of pain and sorrow, left and walked away, intending never to go back. At the time, and still today, it is a matter of integrity. I am obliged to maintain the integrity of theology, the gospel, and the church, as well as my own as their servant.

It also became a matter of personal protection and preservation. I had to leave the only home I had ever known, the home that had birthed and raised me, the home in which I had birthed and raised my two sons, the home where I had been baptized, married, and ordained, and the home I had dearly loved and sacrificed everything to serve. It had become something else, and was no longer the home of Christian theology. If I stayed I would spend the rest of my life trying in vain to introduce and defend the Christian faith-tradition, and feeling pressured, even to the point of abuse, to give that up and "get with the program." I had survived that environment as long as I could, and refused to do it any longer.

I never feared losing either faith or theology. But I did fear losing the joy of teaching it and writing about it. I feared losing relationship with the historical-universal-eschatological church, which theology taught me to believe in and belong to by faith. For me it was a matter of theological honesty and faithfulness. I had to leave.

Second Conversion

I have always had a strange inner stirring, or restlessness, in matters of religion and faith. That's simply the way I am wired, I suppose. It was always there beneath the surface when I was growing up in Southern Christendom, when I was sojourning in the secular far country, and in every ministry I have had in every congregation I have served. It is an unsettled sense of dissonance or disconnect. It is a gnawing in the gut that something is not exactly right.

About five years before my final leaving, this stirring increased and became prominent and relentless. It was pushing up and pressing on me from my very core. It was as though someone had taken over my house, and was flipping light switches, turning off faucets, shutting down systems, and closing and locking doors inside of me. Things that used to interest me no longer did. Things I had highly valued became worthless. Much of the ministry I once could not get enough of, I now had far too much of. The multicolored congregation was now monochrome. Tasteless. And unappealing.

At the same time, my sense of truth and meaning, right and good, had never been keener. My appetite for things biblical, theological, and particularly ecclesiological, increased and could not be satisfied. Parts of me were being killed off, while others were being brought to existence. Death and life were occurring at the same time within me.

I knew this was not my own doing. I had been through seasons of personal and professional struggle before. But this was different. It was other than and greater than me, which could only be attributed to God. All I knew to do was let whatever this was take its course, and see what happened. I trusted the process, because I trusted God.

However, I never imagined that that process would take me at Derbyshire into "the perfect storm"—an exceptionally rare confluence of circumstances, yielding the worst-case scenario. Like the prophet Jonah in the Old Testament, I rode it out as long as I could, clinging for dear life to the historical-biblical-theological church, as though it were an ark. (I have always liked the traditional symbol of the church as a life-saving boat.)

I was battered unmercifully—more by the crew than by the wind and waves—until, like Jonah, I was thrown overboard and ended up in the depths of the sea monster. Miraculously, I was regurgitated onto dry land, relieved that it was finally over, and thankful that I had come through in one piece.[35]

---

35. Read Jonah, chapter 1. For more involvement with this story, read Eugene H. Peterson, *Under the Predictable Plant: An Exploration in Vocational Holiness* (Grand Rapids: William B. Eerdman's Publishing Company, 1992). Peterson (1932–) is professor emeritus of spiritual theology at Regent College, British Columbia. For 29 years, he served as founding pastor of Christ our King Presbyterian Church in

Safely on the beach, surveying the damage, I realized this had not been just any storm. Congregations these days are the scenes of many conflicts and crises. I have heard plenty of war stories, and have plenty myself to tell. But this one was different. There was far more going on than the usual congregational disturbance, and more than a few prideful, disgruntled members, seeking to take control of things. It had all the markings of divine intervention, judgment, deconstruction, and reconstruction.

By the time I left, I was primed for one of the most significant, self-defining, soul-altering transitions of my life. For one thing, I was not the same person when it was over that I had been before it started. I was different. I was no longer the same minister, pastor, preacher, teacher, theologian, or even person I had been for forty years. Something major had happened and been done to me, shaking me all the way down to the foundations, leaving me radically changed. And I realized that what had been done to me was primarily not the work of those who declared themselves my enemies. Whatever they intended toward me, the Lord God had other, greater intentions.[36]

In the storm's aftermath, I realized I had been through another conversion. This event was bigger than me or the congregation or the present circumstances. This crisis had not been merely professional, but more so, profoundly personal, both theologically and spiritually.

By his gracious initiative, God had claimed and rescued me again, just as God did back in 1971. The first time I was turned around and oriented to Christ. This time, as I like to put it, I was turned around and oriented to Christ's church. Clearly, I had once again been claimed and converted for a reason and purpose. My life took a

---

Bel Air, Maryland. He is the author of more than thirty books, and is probably best known for *The Message: The Bible in Contemporary Language*.

During this period of time, my wife Beth had her own "Jonah dream" (experienced as a terrible nightmare). She found me lying lifeless at the bottom of a swimming pool, but was utterly powerless and helpless. There was nothing she could do to rescue me and bring me back to life. I had drowned.

36. I relied on two verses during this time: (1)"Even though you intended to do harm to me, God intended it for good" (Genesis 50:20); and (2) "We know that the whole creation has been groaning in labor pains until now; and not only the creation, but we ourselves, who have the first fruits of the Spirit, groan inwardly while we wait for adoption, the redemption of our bodies." (Romans 8:22-23)

major turn and was set on a different, unplanned course. It was not by my own seeking or doing.

The second thing I discovered after the storm was that I was now outside the world of the local congregation—and all congregations. Being thrown overboard was the way of being thrown out. I considered that to be an act of serious mercy. This was something I never would have conceived of, much less chosen or done, on my own. Nor could I have done it. I was too tied into pastoral ministry in the congregation. My hands were too tightly gripped on the handle of the plough. Only the move of a more powerful will and purpose could break me away and free me. Only the One who had called me and put my hands there originally could give me permission and begin peeling my fingers back, one by one, calmly yet firmly coaxing, "It's okay. You can let go now. You have plowed this field long enough. It's over."

What I knew for certain was that I was outside what is called "church," all the while being conscious of, more committed to, and closer to the church than ever before. It was a most perplexing, paradoxical place to be. Of course, I knew no one would believe me. "You haven't left," they would say, "That's just the hurt and anger talking. Besides, you are a pastor. Laypersons quit and leave, come and go; but pastors don't."

I also knew no one would understand what I was trying to tell them. "What do you mean you have left the church, or churches, for the sake of the church? That doesn't make any sense. If anything, you are only being idealistic. You are having the dream every minister has of the perfect church. You think you see a mirage, and are believing in a vision of something that does not and never will exist."

Clearly, like Job, I had my own well-meaning friends.[37] One was the accuser: "Learn from this. Where did you go wrong, and what did you do to cause this? Surely you must have done something (or else this wouldn't have happened)."

Another was the optimistic comforter: "Give it time. Get some rest. Bind your wounds. Then, after you have recuperated and healed, you will see things differently, and can return to the mission field (or battle field). You will be better and stronger for it."

37. See Job 4, 8, 11, 15, 18, 20, 22, and 25.

Another was the fatalist: "These things happen. We cannot understand them, and are powerless to do anything about them. Just hang in there, go through it, make the most of it, do the best you can, and then move on."

My friends and family members were worried about me. I could understand. I could see it in their eyes, and hear it in their hesitation and silence, as well as in their faltering words, when I talked about what happened to me, my stormy ending and conversion, and my departure from congregations for the sake of the theological church. They thought I was "mad" in one or more of the senses of this word: intensely angry (furious), unrestrained by reason or good judgment (irrational), given over to delusions of grandeur (narcissistic), tricked by illusions of reality (deceived), or mentally ill (insane).

I appreciated their concern. But I was simply trying to be honest and faithful. I also had to continue on the path to which I have been called, and which I had always been on, restlessly, though now it had taken a strange turn, and there was no prospect of my ever turning back or returning. Home, true home, was elsewhere for me.

A Strange Turning Without Returning

After walking away from congregations and my career among them, I headed out with my older son Matthew to hike a seventy-five mile section of the Appalachian Trail in Virginia. I traded the heavy-laden, wearying burden of a pastor for the much lighter, thirty-five pound load of a backpacker. All of it was quite symbolic.

When I returned, took a shower, got a good night's sleep, and packed clean clothes, Beth and I retreated to Virginia Beach, where we found ourselves hunkered down in a beach house, riding out tropical storm Nicole—again, very symbolic. Those two trips marked a break and a boundary for me. I broke away from the place that had been home for me my entire life, and crossed a line that marked the end and could never be traversed. I would never be going back, and so could only go forward. I truly stopped, let go of and rested from my labor—which is something I had never done since the time I started. I was tired. And I was ready for a new direction and a new future in a new home.

I knew, though, that my recuperating, resting days would be limited. I still had my original calling and vision ahead of me. I had not lost that, nor had it ended. In fact, it was more real and engulfing than ever. It was simply on another course that I did not yet know.

Also, conversion brings a fresh infusion of energy and ambition. It blesses with a second, third, or fourth naiveté, as needed. So, there I was: outside established, typical congregations, though still inside the church and more committed and commissioned than ever to the ministry of theological education among laypersons. Yet I struggled with how that future could be possible. Where will I go to teach? Who's left to teach?

This generated profound, piercing questions in my own mind and heart regarding the church: Where is it? Is the church anywhere? If my experience has taught me anything, it is that our congregations have become something less than and even other than the church. But what else is there, within or beyond these congregations, that could be the church? Is the church present, or even possible, today?

I still believed in the reality of the church, but wondered if there might be many (or any) Christians anywhere who were the church, or were willing to be transformed and become the church. If so, where are they? How do I find them?

Despite evidence to the contrary, I remained confident that the church is real. Compared to what appears to be "real" about our local congregations, the church seems unreal. This is why the church is usually thought of and spoken of more as an idea or ideal, a theory or dream, than as a reality.

However, I continued to trust the gospel and its tradition to tell the truth, knowing that a significant part of this truth is that the church is real, although it reeks of impossibility. We cannot create, construct, or grow the church, despite our best efforts to do so. Possibility comes only by the creating, transforming power of God's Word and Spirit, supremely made known in Jesus Christ. Therefore, the church is not only real and impossible, it is also real and possible—"the impossible possibility."[38] By the grace and power of God, the transcendent church is mysteriously becoming present and actual

38. I am borrowing this term from twentieth century neo-orthodox theologians Karl Barth and Reinhold Niebuhr.

where Christians and congregations allow it to define and determine them.

Still, in my skepticism, I wondered, "Where?" I had not seen it. Or if I had, it was only a rare, quick glimpse of a dim, partial image. I had no clue where I could find the church in more substantial, lasting form. I had left where I had been and would never go back. But where could I go in real time and place among real flesh and blood people to know and be part of the church?

Yes, I had made a strange turn. Very strange indeed.

Within a week following the crisis, a small group of about seventy-five people began meeting for worship and fellowship. They had been at the previous congregation, and had never imagined that they would ever leave. Some of them were charter members. They all were stunned and still in shock. Yet, seeing what their congregation had become, and who their leaders and some of their friends really were, they could not stay, be part of it, and be like them.

Soon they contacted me, asking if I would join them. I declined. I was too exhausted. Too beaten and wounded. But most importantly (I did not tell them this), I had left what is called "the church," and had zero interest in recreating with them something I no longer believed in or could be part of.

After two months of having nothing to do with congregations or Christians, Beth and I decided we might need the company of this group. First, we needed a reality check. Had we only imagined the unimaginable things that had happened to us, and been done to me? Did we interpret them rightly? Did we miss something?

We also required some binding-up and applying of healing salve. We needed some tender personal touch to ease the pain of emotional and spiritual wounds and sore memories, caused by tough impersonal abuse. Some of them had been mistreated, as we had, and would understand. Perhaps they needed us, as well. The embrace of fellow sufferers can heal in ways nothing else can.

So, in the wake of a major storm that hit our area hard (an appropriate symbol), we made our way through downed trees and power lines to join them at a covered-dish supper on a Wednesday night. But Beth and I were clear in our minds that it was only for some comfort food and fellowship. That was all. We did not plan to stay. Just visit.

However, that mid-week gathering turned out to be more than we expected. It was a homecoming, and we immediately felt at home. They invited me to lead worship, preach, and teach. I was uncertain and reluctant, continuing to hold out. I did not actually say "No." But neither could I come up with "Yes." I knew to the bottom of my being that I had been taken out of congregations as they are and as we know them. Why would I go back into another one?

I know it seems contradictory, and perhaps a bit crazy, to those who are reading this, but I reluctantly gave in and agreed to do it. Why? The only answer I can give is, I wondered whether this might be the church. Had all that had happened been nothing more than a painful crisis caused by human beings? Or, had it actually been the birth pangs of a new creation caused by God (especially when none of these people, myself included, ever planned or wanted to leave the womb and take up another life outside)? Could this group possibly be the start of a local manifestation of the church, for which I had long studied and believed in, fought for and suffered? Was this the outworking of the seed I had planted in the soil of the previous congregation? Or more critically, is the church as the church even possible in local form? I had to find out. I could not let this opportunity pass.

Their invitation was made all the more difficult to decline when I learned the name they had carefully chosen for themselves: "New Community." New Community Baptist. New? Is there anything new under the sun? Is the new even possible? Especially with a bunch of Baptists?!

Also—and this was both the shocker and the clincher—they asked me to continue the conversation on the church I had started earlier at the previous congregation. Were they serious? Or were they asking simply to appease me, and possibly tease me into staying with them as their pastor? Can any Christian or group of Christians today talk and think theologically about the church, and also about themselves as the church? Will they give up all that they have ever known, learn a completely new way, and give in and become the church? Could I allow my distrusting self to trust that what I had wanted and worked on more than anything else all these years might have a chance? Right here with these people? My curiosity, I suppose, was simply too great for me to turn down the offer.

So I agreed to be their pastor, although only on a trial basis for six months. In my opinion, all of us were on trial. I would preach and teach on the church. We would continue the conversation. I would call them to be conformed to what we were learning. We would not return to being "just another congregation," as congregations have become and are. Rather, we would seek to become the theological, teaching community that is learning who we are and what we are about as the church.

At the same time, I knew that if this did not happen, or there was no sign that it was going to happen, I would by the end of the six months politely decline their invitation to be their pastor, end our relationship, and continue my search for the local manifestation of the church elsewhere.

Immediately it became apparent that all of this was brand new to all of us. No one had in mind any conception of "new community," but only old forms of community we had all been raised in, complete with all the bells and whistles, sights and sounds, programs and projects, special features and trappings of an established, full-service Christian body in the United States. Naturally, they wanted to construct another typical congregation. It was the only understanding of being Christian and being the church they had. It was all they had ever known. They had never seen, heard about, encountered, or even imagined anything else.

I fully understood. It was all I had grown up with and known, as well. However, I made it very clear that we were not taking that path. Many times I was asked, "Where are we headed? Where do you see this going?" And every time I gave the same response: "I don't know. Why do we have to go anywhere? Why can't we simply be the church? All I can tell you is that we are not going the way we have always gone, and that everybody expects us to go."

I worked hard to explain that, as a faith-community, we would not be constructing ourselves in the same manner or form as others do. In fact, we would not construct ourselves at all, but simply learn who and what we are, as we are being constructed in Christ. We would not compare ourselves to other congregations, nor enter into competition with them. We would not use any of the traditional denominational models, or non-traditional, contemporary, popular cultural blueprints, that are common among congregations today. Instead, we would draw on our own historical-biblical-theological faith-tradition for our definition and formation.

Of course, no one had a clue what I was talking about and had in mind. The concept was foreign to them. They had never heard of anything like this. I was speaking a foreign language about an odd reality from another world. They asked me for an example, but I had none to give them. I knew of no existing community to which I could point and say, "That is what I am talking about. That is what we want to be like." All I could do was tell them what I had read and heard from the Christian theological tradition about the church, and invite them to be confident with me that this was what God was making of and with us.

They must have trusted me, for they set out with me to give this "new community" a hearing and maybe a real chance. I began with a crash course in ecclesiology (doctrine of the church). I preached teaching sermons on the church. This opened up a larger discussion. We worshiped, prayed, ate meals together, looked after one another, and devoted ourselves to this teaching. That was all. But then, what else is there?

We purposefully avoided organizing committees, electing deacons, writing a constitution and bylaws, preparing a budget, setting up membership requirements, working on "outreach" (which often is code for marketing and recruitment), organizing a choir, purchasing a building, and anything else that could easily distract and preoccupy us. Congregations easily develop another, entirely different enterprise that quickly and completely overrides the portions of God's mission for which they were ordained and put in this world. We were clear that we did not want that to happen to us. We wanted to rediscover the purpose for which the church was called and created, and to be about that only.

We were minimalist in a fashion that must have resembled the earliest, post-Pentecost community of Jesus.[39] We were not, however, trying to retrace their steps and recreate a primitive movement. Nor were we looking for a new approach or new model, joining any of the contemporary movements of "simple church," "slow church," or

---

39. I believe the essence of the life and ministry of the local manifestation of the church is defined in Acts 2:42: "They devoted themselves to the apostles' teaching and fellowship, to the breaking of bread and the prayers."

"deep church."[40] We only wanted to concentrate on the historical-biblical-theological tradition of our faith, learn from it, see ourselves in the light of it, and by faith let God create and form us solely by and for the gospel of Christ.

We knew we were attention-deficit, disordered individuals, who had lived our lives in the hyperactive, hyper-stimulating environments of congregational and social cultures—not to mention our sinful humanity and the fact that we come from a long religious heritage of unfaithfulness. If we did not stay laser-focused, we would be easily distracted and taken off-course. Therefore, we intentionally kept it simple and limited to the teaching and learning of the faith-tradition for which we, as believers, are part of the church in the world.

As of this writing, we have been together seven years, and have remained committed to the bare basics of Christian community. Our intentions of continuing are strong. Thankfully, we have been lashed to the mast enough not to give in to the Sirens' song, and crash our vessel on the jagged rocks of their island[41] of "buildings, bodies, and budgets," "plans, programs, and projects," "entrepreneurial ventures, consumer-driven marketing, and transformational leadership," and "hip, hype, and happy." We are staying the course of theological

---

40. Our present Christian landscape is filled with many, various movements, countering the typical forms of congregational life and work. While I resonate with their concerns, and find many of their basic tenets and principles inviting, I am uninterested in emulating them. My motivation is strictly ecclesiological rather than evangelistic or entrepreneurial. Also, for me, there is too much of a programmatic, even slick and gimmicky, feel to a lot of it. Here are some resources for further reading: Thom S. Rainer and Eric Geiger, *The Simple Church: Returning to God's Process for Making Disciples* (Nashville: B&H Publishing Group, 2006); C. Christopher Smith and John Pattison, *Slow Church: Cultivating Community in the Patient Way of Jesus* (Downer's Grove, Illinois: InterVarsity Press, 2014); and Jim Belcher, *Deep Church: A Third Way Beyond Emerging and Traditional* (Downer's Grove, Illinois: InterVarsity Press, 2009).

41. This image comes from the ancient Greek poet Homer's *Odyssey,* composed near the end of the eighth century BCE. The Sirens were beautiful winged maidens whose enchanting voices and songs seduced sailors and lured them to shipwreck on the rocky coasts of their island. The end of their song was death. Therefore, the main character, Odysseus, had his crewmen lash him to the mast of their ship, so that he could hear the Sirens' voices, but not jump overboard to pursue them, nor steer the ship toward them. Eugene Peterson plays off this story in describing pastoral ordination in *The Contemplative Pastor: Returning to the Art of Spiritual Direction* (Grand Rapids: William H. Eerdman's Publishing Company, 1989), 129–139.

teaching and learning, theological life and practice, and theological community formation.

I will be the first to tell you, however, that this approach has not been unanimously supported and followed. Some people came at the beginning to check out the new start, but quickly left to find an established congregation. New Community was too primitive, and would take too long to become a "real church." Besides, as they saw it, we did not seem to be interested in "building and growing the church," and thus were not headed in the right direction of becoming a full-blown, full-service congregation. They wanted programs for their children and youth. So they left.

Others continued longer. But over time, they dropped out, one by one, making their way back to congregations that offered them the things they missed and could not do without. Most of them left by "ghosting," or slowly fading away until they completely disappeared. They were not honest enough with either themselves or us to admit that, while all of this was "nice," the Christian church in its bare, raw theological essence was not enough for them. They needed and wanted more, which invariably turned out to be something other than the church's theological tradition and theological education. If they had to choose between theology and "all the other stuff" offered by all the other congregations, they would choose the latter. Without a word, not even "Goodbye," they made their choice.

Natural attrition, of course, has also taken its toll on our small congregation. Members have moved out of town, divorced, and gone to college. Seven have died. About sixty adults and children remain as active participants in education and worship.

Of those who have stayed the course, I realize some may still not grasp what I am talking about or teaching, or why it matters, even after all this time and effort. Their prior conceptions and practices are that numerous, thick, and set in place. These individuals are perfectly content with their current level of understanding, which is pretty much the same level of understanding they have had since childhood. Why start a whole new, more serious, in-depth round of studying, learning, thinking, and changing now?

I confess that this obstinacy often gets to me, and I become despondent. Maybe the Christian community is only what everybody has always said and known it to be, and what I have always found it to be: (1) therapeutic, not theological; (2) here to meet the felt needs of consumers by offering a wide array of religious goods and services, community services, friendship opportunities, and even recreation; and (3) basically a utilitarian, pragmatic, activist organization for good social, cultural, political, and economic causes.

Who am I kidding? Perhaps I should finally give up the hopeless task to which I have been faithfully devoted all these years, and have gallantly attempted to carry out. Why am I still playing Don Quixote, the man of La Mancha, on horseback, tilting at windmills?[42] It will never happen. Entering the territory of an established congregation, or even a new start made up of people who have been in established congregations their entire lives, and trying to persuade them to assume the theological identity and intentionality of the church, will never work. I know. I have a perfect record of failure to prove it.

Then I receive a phone call or email, or have a conversation, and hear a member of New Community say something theological. Did you hear that? Someone is sounding like a Christian. She is taking her first steps in actually thinking like a Christian. She is joining the conversation of the communion of saints. And she does not realize what she is doing. But she is beginning to view everything, including the mundane matters of her life, theologically. She is doing it within the framework of our Christian faith-tradition, using that tradition's distinctive narrative, language, worldview, and concepts.

This puts me back in touch with the fact that there are those around me who, too, have caught the slightest glimpse of the church, and are fascinated enough to come closer to find out more. I am not alone. Like me, they realize how different this approach is. It is certainly different from anything they have ever experienced, or that their family members and friends can possibly comprehend. It is also sacrificial, demanding the giving up of much of what they have always had. But they are willing to leave behind former things for the sake of those things that promise to be truer and greater. They are

42. Don Quixote is the main character of a classic Spanish novel by Miguel de Cervantes Saavedra, *El ingenioso hidalgo don Quijote de la Mancha,* published in two volumes in 1605 and 1615. Read Edith Grossman's translation, *Don Quixote* (New York: HarperCollins Publishers, Inc., 2003). This novel was adapted as a Broadway musical in 1965, and as a Hollywood film in 1972. The principal song, "The Impossible Dream," became a popular favorite.

willing to go this way. And now that they have, they cannot imagine any other.

I am encouraged by these members, who have attended, paid attention, listened, and allowed themselves to learn. As a result, they have set aside, or at least loosened up, their old lens, filters, and maps, in order to take on the new frameworks and mindsets provided by the church's theological faith-tradition. This tradition has begun to matter to them. They are now moving in the path of becoming its stewards and servants, disciples and teachers, and to being formed as its representative community in the world. They are willing, even eager, to do what is required to be taught and to learn, to know and understand their faith, and thereby be made the church, rather than a typical non-historical-biblical-theological congregation. They do not worry about what they don't have, but rejoice in what they do have as a congregation. It is in this peculiar mood and manner that they come together, worship, study, love, and live in Christ.

I will always be grateful to these believers at New Community for allowing me to be a theologian and teacher among them. They let me "talk theology" to them, even when they do not understand a word I am saying. They ask about my studying and writing. They respect my attempts to "love the Lord with all my mind," and they even join in with me. They allow themselves to be a "living laboratory" for the teaching-learning community that embodies the church.

Being in the company of such budding theological believers at New Community is what gives me hope and keeps me going. The reason is that here, among them, is the most concrete evidence I have thus far that the theological community is actually possible and can be present, despite all appearances and hindrances, even in the context of both secular and spiritual cultures that make it absent and impossible.

I have not returned to the congregation as I have known it, but have made that turn to theology that is real and powerful enough to attract its own audience and form its own community. This is the historical-universal-eschatological church, or theological communion of saints, of which New Community is a faint, partial manifestation.

This is now home for me.

On Not Retiring Theologically

Of course, none of this is easy to explain to family members, friends, and ministerial colleagues. I reject much that passes for Christianity today, and choose no longer to be part of it. I have left local congregations as they are and as we recognize them, although I still believe in and belong to the church as it is made present and known communally. My ministry is now a ministry of stewardship within the household of faith, preserving and transmitting the Christian theological faith-tradition and its gospel. Period. Nothing else.

One way I have tried to explain it is by saying I have retired from certain parts of ministry, and not from others. This seems to satisfy those who ask, since everyone understands retirement. First, I tell them, I have retired from "manure." (Pardon my language; but give me credit for restraining myself, for I can think of at least three or four more graphic, offensive words I could have chosen.) And every pastor knows what I'm talking about!

With congregational ministry comes a lot of garbage, junk, and waste in the form of pointless meetings and tasks; unnecessary busyness; loads and loads of activities that are called "ministry," yet have little to nothing to do with ministry; the accounting of the congregation's faith, ministry, health, and growth by attendance and financial statistics; hidden agendas and ulterior motives; emotional reactions rather than more thoughtful responses; pettiness, whining, bickering, complaining, and sabotaging.

These are the things that have taken over and now consume the attention, energy, and resources of the congregation. These are the things that members, leaders, and staff know something about, value, and want to work on. These are the things that Christians are involved in and talk about, worry about, and vote on. These are the things that have become the pastor's job, which I performed dutifully for an entire career.

But no longer. I now join the Apostle Paul in considering much of my religious heritage and pastoral ministry to be "loss," "rubbish," "excrement," or "dung."[43] One day I decided I had had enough, and I quit. I walked away from all of this unnecessary, meaningless mess

43. See Philippians 3:7-9.

that has come to be "ministry," with the conviction that I would never go there and do that again.

The usual justification for these things is that they come with the territory. I admit that wherever two or three human beings are gathered in the name of Christ, not only will Christ be there, but so will a lot of human garbage, as well. My concern is that we have allowed all these unnecessary, distracting, cheapening pieces of garbage to litter and junk up the place, take over and become not only the territory where we live and work, but also our agenda. They *are* our life and work, when they should not be. From now on, I will take the higher ground:

> My heart has no desire to stay
> Where doubts arise and fears dismay;
> Though some may dwell where these abound,
> My prayer, my aim, is higher ground.
> Lord, lift me up and let me stand
> By faith, on Heaven's tableland,
> A higher plane than I have found;
> Lord, plant my feet on higher ground.[44]

While I have not retired completely from the pastoral ministry, I have lightened the load, and reduced the all-out, all-the-time pace and level of ministry I worked at for decades. I have pushed back and stripped away all that is unnecessary. I have devoted myself to only what is left: the basics, or core functions of the pastor, including presiding over worship services, baptisms, funerals and weddings; preaching and teaching the gospel; overseeing the fellowship and mutual care-giving of the body; and teaching the Christian historical-biblical-theological faith-tradition. What else is there? Or should there be? Seriously.

I do plan for a complete pastoral retirement one day. Unlike many of my ministerial mentors and friends, I will not hang on in a pastorate as long as I possibly can, or until "death do us part." I will not seek or accept an interim pastorate. I will not put my name out to

---

44. This is a verse of a nineteenth century gospel song by Johnson Oatman, Jr. and Charles Hutchinson Gabriel, that I grew up singing in Southern Baptist circles. "Higher Ground," *The Baptist Hymnal* (Nashville: Convention Press, 1991), 484.

do supply preaching when a pastor is on vacation, holiday break, or sick leave. I definitely will not relocate to a senior living community, considering that to be my congregation for chapel services, visitation, and "working the crowd" in the dining hall. While I have enjoyed much of my pastoral career, I am moving and working toward the time when I will make a clean break, and no longer be a pastor.

Of course, there will always be some hard-core, die-hard minister who goes around spreading such platitudes as: "The Bible doesn't say anything about retiring"; "Once a pastor, always a pastor"; and "Old ministers don't retire; they just go out to pastor." (Someone gave me a glass paperweight with these words embroidered on cloth inside.)

I reply: "Watch me." There was a time when I was not a clergyman; and there will be time when I again will not be a clergyman. I have sadly known too many going before me who have been unwilling to let go of this relative, temporary vocation. Or worse, they have no other identity and purpose. I pledged long ago that I would not be one of them.

From the time I left the seminary classroom as a student, I dreamed of returning as a professor. I finally had that opportunity, and loved its challenge for fourteen years. However, I grew tired of reading through ill-written research papers and essays, grading tests, and assigning grades. Preparing and delivering lectures, especially in courses I had taught before, became routine and unchallenging. I found all classroom discussions to be pretty much the same. One day I realized I had been around that block too many times. Therefore, I decided it was time to retire.

In short, I am retiring in stages, dropping off one vocational piece after another. This seems right for me. Eventually, I will retire from the work of the pastor. Yet, even then, when I am retired from all dimensions and roles of my ministerial career, I will never retire from the work of a theologian.

This is the position Stanley Hauerwas lays out in his essay, "How (Not) to Retire Theologically."[45] He does not like the language of retirement, and does not like to think of himself as retired, although on June 30, 2013, he retired from the faculty of the Duke University

45. Stanley Hauerwas, "How (Not) to Retire Theologically," *The Work of Theology* (Grand Rapids: William B. Eerdman's Publishing Company, 2015), 250–265.

Divinity School. He does not regret his decision to stop teaching, but at the same time does not believe that is the equivalent of "retiring." He is a theologian. What could it possibly mean for a theologian to retire? How would one exactly go about retiring from theology? And why would anyone want to? As Hauerwas aptly says, "Theology is a discipline that takes over your life because the subject-matter of theology is life-changing."[46]

I completely agree with him. Theologians do not get to retire. Those of us who are pastors, teachers, and administrators will and should retire from pastoring, teaching, and administering. There will come a time when we will want to, and others will want us to, as well. However, while these forms and seasons of ministry will pass away, the underlying foundation of Christian theology will not. Just as no one can retire from being a human being, or from being a Christian, the person whose existence, identity, character, and calling have been taken over, radically changed, and consumed by theology cannot walk away and let it go. Besides, why would he or she want to?

I have been a pastor, preacher, and teacher in congregations, because I am first a theologian. I have been a seminary professor, staff member, and administrator, because I am first a theologian. I am now writing, because I am a theologian. I am owned by it. It is out of theology that everything in the Christian faith comes and makes sense.

Therefore, the pastor who never reads, studies, or teaches theology, or who can only take a little theology in simple doses every once in a while, puzzles me. Although this is a standard pattern among clergy these days, it is, in my opinion, not the way to be a servant of Christ and his church. The pastor is first and foremost a theologian, and this vocation lasts for a lifetime, which is longer than any job or career.

Besides, after almost a half century of intentional theological study and work, I sense that I have only scratched the surface, and am only now starting to grasp what this discipline is all about. I still feel like a beginning student, excited about being in the water, wading in the shallow end, and working up enough courage to venture into and flounder in the deeper parts.

---

46. Hauerwas, 251.

I am not sure whether what I have done in preaching and teaching was Christian theology at all, much less whether it was good theology done well. I am always rethinking what I have thought and taught. What I am keenly aware of is how little there is behind me that I have learned and come to know and understand, and how much looms ahead of me that I do not yet know. The latter is overwhelming. Yet, it is greatly intriguing, and lures me ahead to continue being its student and its teacher.

At this rate, I will never be able to retire, and death will be grossly premature. There is simply too much theology still demanding my attention and allegiance.

Along with Hauerwas, I will never know enough to retire, and I definitely have a lot more to think about that I am not quite sure I understand.[47] Besides, I believe God continues to claim my life and to give me particular responsibilities and obligations as I grow old and eventually die in Christ.[48]

Finally, I am retiring in stages from being a pastor, professor, and administrator in order to have more time and energy to be a theologian. My career has had to be spent on many non-theological tasks in order to earn a living wage. No institution pays anyone to be a theologian. The congregation employs someone to be its pastor, not its theologian. Even in the divinity school and seminary, the theologian is assigned work on committees and many duties on behalf of the institution in order to justify his or her employment.

The fact that I am now being freed *from* these congregational duties and obligations after all these years only means that I am being freed *for* the specific duties and obligations of theological work. I not only have something to do in my "free time," but I also have something I have to do. For me, this involves doing what I have always done and always loved to do more than anything else: get up, read a theology book, think about it, incorporate it into my understanding, write a sermon or lesson, and find two or three persons who will graciously

47. Hauerwas, 258.

48. This is a dominant theme in a collection of essays by Stanley Hauerwas, Carole Bailey Stoneking, Keith Meador, and David Cloutier, *Growing Old in Christ* (Grand Rapids: William B. Eerdman's Publishing Company, 2003). Another helpful book is by Paul Tournier, *Learn To Grow Old* (New York: Harper & Row, Publishers, 1972).

allow me to teach them what I am learning. I have a need to introduce the unintroduced to the riches of their own theological faith, just as I was once unintroduced, uninitiated, uninformed, and unformed.

Now I have the opportunity through the writing of books to address a wider audience. This is why I cannot retire. There is still too much illiteracy and ignorance in Christ's community, on my part as well as everyone else's.

To put it another way: my work of bringing theology home and reuniting congregations and Christians with their own faith heritage is barely underway. I realize it will never be finished, and on the surface, the work I have done thus far appears to be futile. But I was called, and continue to be called, to this endeavor. Besides, I have invested too much and paid too great a price to turn away now. Finally, what else could I possibly do that would be as meaningful and challenging?

The bottom-line is I cannot stop, and do not want to stop what I am doing to bring theology home. Yes, it is tiring, and I sometimes would like to "retire" from it—or, more accurately, to get a break and some rest from it. But theology haunts and possesses me. My work has been one long attempt to be possessed by and to embody what we believe and say as Christians.[49]

Finally, before I am fully retired by God from my human life and ministry in Christ, I want to continue experimenting with and experiencing what it is like to be part of an intentional theological community, starting with New Community Baptist Church and extending into the formation of other such communities. Surely there are many Christians out there who, like me, long to dwell in the house that theology builds, to learn and live faith here, and to be at home.

---

49. Hauerwas, 265.

2
Meeting

The son cashed out. He demanded the share of his father's property that he would one day inherit. He packed up everything he had and traveled to a far country. Before long, however, he had squandered it all and was flat broke.[1]

During that same time, the far country was suffering from a severe famine. People could not find jobs. It was difficult to put food on the table. So, hungry and in need, this young man went out searching for work. Any work. Finally, a farmer took him on, making him a swine-herder. He looked after somebody else's pigs. He slopped hogs.

I have an idea of what this young man must have experienced, since I grew up on a farm that raised pigs. I watered them and fed them scraps from our table, along with rotten fruits from the orchard. Pigs will eat anything. I chased them down in the woods and herded them back into their pen when they escaped under the cover of darkness. I enjoyed watching them wallow in the oozy mud, and then throwing big rocks into their nasty cesspool for the major splash effects. I saw how they trampled everything underfoot, down into their mucky mire. Like everybody else, I looked at pigs as being good for nothing except breakfast food.

This prodigal son would have had a far more negative view of pigs than the average person. He was Jewish. That meant he could not enjoy pork chops and bacon, which were forbidden by the Torah.[2]

---

1. This story of Jesus, known as "the parable of the prodigal son," is in Luke 15:11–32.

2. Leviticus 11:7; Deuteronomy 14:8.

Moreover, swine were symbols of the unclean, and, therefore, were fit bearers of the demons.[3] Anyone, like this young man, who lived with swine and looked after them would himself be considered unclean. As a Jew, he could not have sunk down into a lower, more degrading, shameful condition than the one he was in. He had hit rock-bottom.

I wrote in chapter 1 that I take this parable of Jesus as my own story theologically and spiritually. As a young man, I left home in Southern Christendom and went to be with people in the far country. They had no regard or respect for the things of my Christian religious inheritance. They did not know its teachings and practices. They did not value its truth, wisdom, or virtues. I learned the meaning of Jesus' strong warning: "Do not throw your pearls before swine, or they will trample them under foot and turn and maul you." (Matthew 7:6)

Eventually, like the prodigal, I came to my senses and realized the terrible condition I was in. You know it's bad when you look at the slop that the pigs are eating, and would gladly eat it, except it is garbage and neither clean nor healthy. So I went back home to be another one of the Father's hired hands.

A year later, I left for a land where I heard they dealt in pearls. The people who lived there were not pig farmers, but pearl merchants. They knew pearls. They loved pearls. They did not trample them down into the mud, but lifted them up for everybody to see and enjoy. They researched pearls. They searched history and the world for fine pearls. And when they found a single pearl of great value, they went and sold everything they had in order to buy it.[4]

By living among them and learning from them, I met and came to know the pearl of great price for the church: theology. But when I brought it back home, theology was met with consternation and disinterest. Congregations and Christians reacted more like swine or swine-herders than pearl merchants. They did not know what this priceless pearl was, or what to do with it. What good were these worthless baubles to them?

Nonetheless, I knew what I had met in that other world. I knew what I had found. I knew what it was worth. And I knew, too, that I

3. Read Mark 5:11–20.

4. Matthew 13:45–46.

had become one of the pearl merchants. I was called to go back to the Father's house and serve it by teaching about the great, priceless pearl of the Christian theological faith-tradition.

How Did You Meet?

Persons in strong relationships—here I am thinking of spouses and good friends—are often asked, "How did you meet?" Everyone loves a good story, and especially a story that involves love. Therefore, I want to tell you how I met theology and came to love the great pearl that has taught and enabled me to know and love the Lord God with my mind.

One might assume, given my upbringing, that I met theology in Southern Christendom at my home congregation of First Baptist Church, Belton, South Carolina. I did, but then I didn't. Theology was there, though in a strangely silent, ghostly, absent way. Therefore, I never actually knew it, noticed it, or paid it any attention. It might as well have not been there. I was in the same frame of religious mind and existence that I have found Christians to be in everywhere I have tried to introduce theology.

Do not assume that my hometown congregation was lacking in faith, or did not love the Lord or the Bible. I was raised in one of the better congregations around. My theological oblivion would have been much worse elsewhere. I am grateful for what I received there.

Still, I had to leave home and go somewhere else, to the seminary, in order to meet theology. The reason is simple: because that was where theology was. Theology did not exist substantially in local congregations—even in those at the buckle of the Bible Belt. Theology was not studied and taught. No one was talking or thinking about theological matters as though they mattered.

In all honesty, though, I must admit that I did not go to the seminary for either theology or theological education. For one thing, at the time, I did not know theology was there. Second, I had no clue what theology was. I simply wanted to be trained and prepared to do the Lord's work back in the local congregation.

Southern writer Ferrol Sams comes as close as anyone to putting his finger on the core of my motivation when he writes that to a child like Porter Obsborne, Jr. (and me), who had been Raised Right: "Seminary at Louisville" had exactly the same ring as "Temple at Jerusalem."[5] It certainly rang true for me. Also, my pastor, whom I wanted to emulate, had been raised in the Crescent Hill neighborhood in the shadows of that great seminary, and had attended it. So where else was I to go?

Southern Seminary was not a community like any I had ever experienced or imagined. First, it was the holiest, most religious place I had ever been. Local congregations can sometimes be holy and religious, especially during spring revival services and prayer retreats. But most of the time, they are about as secular, social, organizational, financial, programmatic, consumerist, and recreational as any other people, while cloaked in more piety, religiousness, and morality.

Second, the seminary was stocked with nothing but highly committed Christians preparing for Christian service. It was where the best—the "crème de la crème," the best of the best of the Lord's servants from hundreds of congregations—were assembled to be a sign or foretaste of what it surely will be like in the Kingdom of God.

Back home I was part of a congregation that had some of these exemplary Christians. They were scattered throughout the fellowship of mostly regular, respectable Christians. There were also quite a few lukewarm, nominal (in name only; or only had their names on the church rolls) Christians, and always a few backsliding (usually "running around" and "drinking too much") Christians.

Not at the seminary. Never before had I been around so many dedicated believers at one time, piled up in one place. I wondered when someone would notice I was there and did not belong.

Third, the seminary was a very academic place, specifically shaped by theology and dedicated to the task of teaching and learning the Christian theological faith-tradition. I had been in an academic place before, i.e., Clemson University (although my sister-in-law Jane and brother-in-law Steve, who are University of South Carolina Gamecocks, would question my description). But I had never experienced academics or higher education at this level of quality and intensity, and certainly not with anything even slightly resembling this particular subject matter. I was a psychology major with a double

---

5. Ferrol Sams, *The Whisper of the River* (New York: Penguin Books, 1986), 3.

minor in sociology and history. I had never taken a course in Bible, philosophy, or world religions. I had no idea whether Clemson even offered such courses. The only background I had was in Sunday School and Training Union, and that was not enough to count as background for what I was expected to master at the seminary.

Unlike the university, the seminary was a one-subject school: theology and its many related disciplines. Since I had never met theology, and had no clue what it was, much less why it mattered, I might as well have been in a foreign land. Ironically, I was far away from home, while at the same time being closer to the true home of the church and faith than I ever had been or ever would be.

Theologian David Kelsey offers an interesting and helpful way to view a seminary. In the larger world of academic institutions, he says, a seminary is "less an ideal city than a crossroads hamlet,"[6] due to its relatively small scale and limited financial resources. But the truly defining factor is where each hamlet is located. Each has grown up at some crossroads.

Traditionally, it has been said that North American seminaries have sprung up and developed "at the crossing of Athens Highway and Jerusalem Road."[7] This is a way of saying that, since the Apostle Paul, the church—along with its theological schools—has existed and been shaped at the intersection of the worlds of Jewish religion and Greek philosophy. The early church father Tertullian expressed it in his famous question: "What has Athens to do with Jerusalem?"[8]

Kelsey, however, believes a more helpful and more historically accurate statement would be that seminary hamlets grow up at the intersection of the "Berlin Turnpike" (German scholarship) and some particular tradition of organized Christianity. Pick one or more: Trent Road (Roman Catholic), Augsburg Road (Lutheran), Geneva Road (Reformed, Presbyterian), Canterbury Road (Anglican), Northampton Road (First Great Awakening), or Azusa Street

---

6. David H. Kelsey, *To Understand God Truly: What's Theological About a Theological School* (Louisville: Westminster/John Knox Press, 1992), 18. Kelsey (1932–) is professor emeritus of theology at Yale Divinity School, where he has taught for fifty years.

7. Kelsey, 30-62.

8.Tertullian (ca. 150–225 CE) was an early church father and Christian apologist. He served as an elder or presbyter in Carthage in North Africa.

(Pentecostal revivalism).[9] I would expand this road map to include the Nicaea-Constantinople Interstate (Orthodox), the Cleveland, Tennessee Route (Church of God), and many more.

Geographically and physically, The Southern Baptist Theological Seminary is located at 2825 Lexington Road, Louisville, Kentucky. When I attended during the 1970s, prior to the fundamentalist takeover, it was located academically where the Nashville Road (the history, beliefs, practices, and organization of the Southern Baptist Convention) met the Berlin Turnpike (the history and traditions of modern higher education).

Southern was considered "the mother seminary" of the Convention's other five seminaries. It stood out, because of (1) the way it traveled to and from what was going on in the larger academic world, especially German biblical and theological scholarship; (2) the way it traveled to and from what was going on in the Southern Baptist Convention, and in its agencies and congregations; and (3) the peculiar point where these two ways and these two worlds intersected, and what happened there and was taught in the classroom at that very busy, energizing intersection.

That is *where* I met theology: where the multiple roads to and from Jerusalem, Athens, Berlin, and Nashville all converged in a unique configuration. After graduating, I left and carried theology on the roads to Greensboro, Charlottesville, and finally Richmond, where local congregations had sprung up. I worked hard to persuade the Christians I met there that Friendly Avenue, West Main Street, Derbyshire Road, and Emerywood Parkway actually do come from and connect back into all these major highways and intersections. We are all part of one large movement, where theology emerged, still emerges, and is to be found. Yet, few believed me, and most stayed home in places that no longer had much, if anything, to do with either Athens or Jerusalem, Berlin or Nashville, or with the theology that came from these worlds.

Now let me tell you *how* I met theology at the Southern crossroads hamlet. As soon as I arrived on the seminary campus and checked into my dorm room, I headed to Norton Hall for orientation,

---

9. Kelsey, 30. Also see Kelsey, *Between Athens and Berlin: The Theological Education Debate* (Eugene, Oregon: Wipf and Stock Publishers, 2011).

psychological and ministerial testing (to weed out those who should not be there), and registration for fall courses. In those days, there was no online registration. There were no computers. The entire process occurred in real time, in-person, on paper, and on a first-come-first-served basis.

The elder brothers and sisters had already been there to choose what they wanted or needed. We newbies got the leftovers. We had to search through the scraps to see if there was anything left we could use to cobble together a schedule of classes. My anxiety level rose higher and higher as I stood in the long line, watching course after course being crossed out on the chalkboard: "Closed."

While waiting, I received sage counsel from an upperclassman, who was there to make a course change. He advised me that, since I was a beginner, I ought to stay away from theology. "Systematic theology is the hardest course offered here," he said. "You need at least a full year before attempting it."

I did not know what theology was. But whatever it was, it did not sound inviting or student-friendly. I quickly made a mental note that, whatever I did, I had to stay away from and avoid theology.

By the time my turn came at the registration table, guess what? The only course still open for the time slot when I needed a course was Systematic Theology I. What was I to do? The upperclassman had wisely warned me not to do it. Yet, what choice did I have? I had to have another course in order to take a full load, and this was the only course left. The title alone sounded ominous: "Systematic Theology I."

In the moment, feeling trapped and doomed, I was weak. I gave in and put my name on the class roster, experiencing all the fear and trembling of signing up to donate a vital organ.

The next nights before classes began were filled with restless sleep. What had I done? What was I in for? What kind of monster was this thing called "theology"? What would it do to me?

The thought crossed my mind of packing up, leaving in the middle of the night, and driving back to South Carolina, where I had been Raised Right and Saved, and there was no theology. Everything there, back home, was safe and non-threatening. Besides, given what I had heard about theology, I would be failing it and packing my bags to go back home soon enough.

On the first day of classes I went to every classroom to begin all my new courses with excitement and enthusiasm—all but Systematic Theology I. When the dreaded hour arrived, I found a desk next to the windows (in case I had to bail out?), and waited for the unknown to strike.

The bell rang, and the professor, Dr. James Leo Garrett, Jr.,[10] arrived, looking the way I had always pictured a seminary professor looking, straight out of central casting. Oddly, he began lecturing out in the hallway, several steps away from crossing the threshold of the room. He came in talking. He kept talking, and did not come up for air or stop until the bell rang and he had crossed the doorway on his way out, still lecturing and fading away in the hallway. He had an encyclopedic mind and a rapid-fire style of lecturing. My skills of comprehension and note-taking were no match. Therefore, I was exhausted by the time class was over.

That first encounter with theology was not at all what I had dreaded. In fact, it turned out far better than I had fearfully expected. Theology was not the enemy I had been told, had imagined, and dreaded. Why had an experienced, educated seminarian warned me to stay away? And why had I listened to him? I could not wait for the next class session. I wanted to hear more about theology. Not only had I met theology and survived, but also, from our first meeting, I was hooked as its student.

For me, it was love at first sight (or first sound). I believe "love" is the right word, for theology is a matter of the heart as well as of the head. Actually, theology, like love, is a matter of both the heart and the head. The 17th century French mathematician, scientist, and philosopher Blaise Pascal famously said, "The heart has its reasons,

---

10. James Leo Garrett, Jr., (1925–) was born in Waco, Texas, where he was raised in Seventh and James Baptist Church. He earned a Bachelor of Arts in English from Baylor University, a Bachelor of Divinity from Southwestern Baptist Theological Seminary, a Masters of Theology from Princeton Theological Seminary, a Doctor of Theology from Southwestern Baptist Theological Seminary, and a Doctor of Philosophy from Harvard University. His long academic teaching career at three Baptist schools extended over thirty years. The two volumes of his *Systematic Theology: Biblical, Historical, and Evangelical* (North Richland Hills, Texas: BIBAL Press; third edition of volume one, 2007; second edition of volume two, 2001) are an encyclopedic masterpiece. In my opinion, he is one of the most educated, brilliant minds Baptists have known, or ever will know.

which reason does not know."[11] I add, "The head has its reasons, which the heart does know. But by both head and heart reasoning together in the whole body, we know the truth. And knowing the truth, we love it."

Theology is knowing and loving the truth, and thereby knowing and loving God in the manner commanded by Jesus: "with all your heart, and with all your soul, and with all your strength, and with all your mind." (Luke 10:27)

What Have I Gotten Myself Into?

No one can possibly know at first sight, first hearing, or first meeting exactly what he has encountered. Sight is limited; hearing is weak; and meeting is superficial. All are liable to misperception. Only after many sightings, hearings, meetings, and exchanges, under many, different circumstances, in and through a long relationship, can one begin to grasp what the other person or entity is, and then come to have a clue about what it truly is he has gotten himself into. This is certainly true with theology.

I met theology initially as a seminary course. That's all I thought it was: one of the multiple courses offered and required by the seminary for completion of the Master of Divinity degree program. Theology is a course of academic study, like English Composition, Chemistry, Introduction to Psychology, Algebra, or American History on the undergraduate level. The only difference is it covers a different subject matter.

I anticipated enrolling in theology's two introductory halves over two semesters, enduring them, checking them off the required list, and moving on to concentrate in New Testament studies with Frank Stagg, psychology of religion with Wayne Oates, and ethics with Henlee Barnette.

However, once I was enthralled as a new believer and lover, I registered for all the theology courses I could take in both the MDiv and PhD programs. What I discovered is that Christian theology is

11. Blaise Pascal, *Pensées,* trans. W. F. Trotter (Mineola, New York: Dover Publication, Inc., 2003), 78.

not a single course, but rather, a broad area of study, consisting of multiple courses grouped together under the traditional heading of "theological studies." At one time, the entire seminary curriculum was referred to as "theological education," and the seminary itself was the "school of theology," or "theology school."

Theology, however, turned out to be far more than a set of scholarly courses offered and taken in an academic environment for a professional education. For instance, it is a language. Theology is the church's language. It is the mother tongue, the first language, or native speech, of those persons who exist by and for faith. Therefore, the goal is not merely to take a few courses and consider oneself educated, but more so, to learn a language, and learn how to talk Christianly, like a Christian.

I was immediately fascinated by the beauty and richness of what Dr. Garrett was saying, and how he was saying it. I had never heard speech like this, spoken like this. But to my ears, he might as well have been speaking a foreign language, or an unknown tongue.

At the same time (and this was truly bizarre), I sensed that his speech was strangely familiar. How could this be? I had never before encountered or experienced such sounds, and especially so many of them piled up together into one long, meaningful discourse. I did not speak the language. I had never heard anyone speak it consistently and fluently, as though he or she were from the far country where this language was vernacular. Yet, somehow I just knew this was my native language, or my mother tongue. Yes, it was long-forgotten, but at the same time, it was part of my heritage and my very being as a Christian.

Of course, I had heard Christian words my entire life. Religious talk and spiritual talk filled the air around me. But they were not the same as theological talk. For one thing, the majority of the theological lexicon was missing from the former. Dr. Garrett used words I had never heard, such as *atonement, incarnation, revelation, and Kingdom of God.* Why had I never heard these words back home?

Words were spoken that were closer to ancient Hebrew and Greek than to modern English. I had no idea how to begin to pronounce them: *Sheol, Yahweh, ekklesia, koinonia, eschatology,* and *logos*. German terms, such as *Heilsgeschichte* and *Sitz im Leben*, were thrown into the mix, making this theological language truly bizarre.

Through all my growing-up years, I had heard bits and pieces of theological language within the much larger blend of folk religion, Baptist piety, American common sense, and popular spirituality. However, I had never heard these fragments assembled, along with the rest of the language that had been forgotten, and spoken so precisely in whole sentences and full paragraphs. They can be joined together to form a whole body of meaningful discourse that a community actually uses to frame its mindset, ground its existence by faith, communicate its most truthful belief and understanding to the world, and, in general, be the church. It was something to hear!

When spoken properly, theology rises above casual conversation, i.e., the way people, including Christians, ordinarily and informally talk to one another every day. It is not sloppy speech or loose talk, but formal and ordered. It abhors vacuous religious clichés, moral platitudes, and spiritual bromides. It cannot fit on a bumper sticker or refrigerator magnet. Theology is thick, rich language. It is put together intentionally and thoughtfully. Its speakers and hearers strive always for greater clarity, comprehensiveness, coherence, consistency, truthfulness, and meaningfulness in what they are saying, as well as greater precision in how they are saying it.

Such speech goes against the way we have been trained to disparage human language: "Words are cheap"; "One picture is worth a thousand words"; and "Don't talk the talk, but walk the walk." Theology restores not only the worth and weight of words, but also the authority of the content these particular words are commissioned to carry and convey. Words matters. Their content matters even more. And the community of faith attempts to speak thoughtfully and articulately, as though its communication matters to God, and may be used to reveal divine truth and meaning to the world.

Obviously, I was unprepared for the theological language I had gotten myself into. Imagine the newborn being thrown into a world of meaningless sounds. That was me. Fortunately, by the interaction of divine grace and human curiosity, I liked what I was hearing. Theology was nonsense; but it was pleasant nonsense. So I began to mimic my teachers and repeat their sounds. I researched the meaning and use of every word I did not know. I practiced out loud the professor's pronunciations. I committed each new word to memory and to my growing vocabulary.

Even more difficult than the words themselves was their collective meaning, or message. I struggled to grasp what the textbook authors were trying to say. At first, reading theology was impossible. I read a couple of paragraphs, and stopped. I found myself going over words without understanding their message or meaning. I went back and reread the same paragraphs—again and again. I read slowly, word-by-word, sentence-by-sentence, as though trudging through chest-deep snow. I stayed with words and phrases I could not comprehend, moving backward and forward in the text, like trying to rock a vehicle out of where it has gotten stuck. Sometimes I had to give up and move on, assuming I needed more background, and that one day I would be capable of reading and understanding the author's writing. Some books had to wait on my shelves for years.

Still, theology was not completely closed to me. With disciplined, persistent effort, I gradually was able to read its writings, acquire its words and constructs, and learn a whole new language. I read every assigned textbook at least twice, and often three or four times. I studied my scribbled class notes over and over. I was determined to learn and understand this language, both spoken and written. I wanted to be like Dr. Garrett and my other professors who knew how to talk (and think) theologically.

I confess that theology was intimidating. Merely being in its presence made me feel inferior and inadequate. Perhaps this is why Christians, like the upperclassman I met at registration, want to stay away, and have as little as possible to do with it. Theology is unfamiliar. We get anxious around what we do not know. We are uncomfortable.

Also, when we are told that theology is our native tongue, and we are supposed to know it, but we don't, we begin to wonder, "Why don't I know this? How did I miss it all these years? What's wrong with me?" We don't like feeling guilty or ashamed; and so we stay away from what is causing it.

Finally, theology strikes us as being very complex and difficult—in fact, too complex and difficult for us to grasp immediately, and probably so complex and difficult we will never be able to grasp it. So, why try? It would take far too much time and effort to be worth it, right? Besides, we have been without theology all these years, and have done pretty well as Christians without it. Why change now?

I believe there is one more reason—perhaps the greatest reason—why we shun theology. It requires us to submit to its grammar and play by its rules. Theology has its own structures, patterns, constructs, concepts, and meanings. It operates as a whole system that must be entered, learned, and lived in and by fully. Most of us would rather pick and choose only a few pieces to blend into the whole religious-spiritual-moral-emotional systems we are busy building for ourselves. Theology, if it is ever to play a part in our lives, can be only a part, and nothing more. It must be immediately relevant and able to fit neatly into our everyday lives, make a difference, and help us to be better, happier persons. Or else, we don't need or want it.

Theology, however, insists on being the life to which you and I must be relevant and fit into, and by which we will be made different and become more faithful, holier persons. We must bend the knee to it, becoming its listeners and learners, putting ourselves under its tutelage. We serve theology, rather than theology serving us.

This goes against the grain of how we have set up our lives and planned to exercise our Christian vocation. We prefer to play by our rules. We believe religion is supposed to be self-expressive, creative, serendipitous, and "from the heart." We do not like to be told what to believe, think, say, or do. However, theology by nature takes the lead, and seeks to have its way over us and with us.

I had to learn this. I had to allow myself to be conformed over time to theology's contour and content. This required me to stay with theology day after day, month after month, and year after year. Such language cannot be acquired and assimilated overnight, or over a few semesters at seminary. Such a life cannot be forged over a period of time less than a lifetime. And such a willful person as I cannot be bent, except by repeated pounding of the hammer on the anvil.

The relationship with theology is not an occasional encounter, an on-again-off-again affair, or an at-arms-length relationship. Theology demands a theological life that is a lifetime of dedicated speaking and hearing, along with continuing reading, studying, and learning. There are no shortcuts.

One more thing: I never had to work so hard and long to decipher a preacher or Sunday School teacher back home, as I did the teachers and scholars of theology. I simply heard the clergyman's or lay teacher's words, immediately picked out something to take with me (if there was anything to take), and moved on. That was that. Quick and easy.

Theological communication was different. It required more time, attention, and effort on my part as its hearer. I could no longer be content to let its words strike my ears and leave a first impression. I could not tune in and out, halfway listening or not listening at all, either daydreaming or dozing off. I had to pay attention and not let my mind wander. I had to concentrate with single focus on what was being said, rather than on what I thought was being said, or what I wanted to hear. Such genuine listening was not a required discipline where I came from. Therefore, it did not come either naturally or easily for me. It was hard work. And I had never associated Christian religion or faith with hard work.

Theological hearing requires thinking. I had never had to "think after" a preacher or teacher. I did very little thinking about what the speaker was saying, much less what he or she was thinking. Thinking was not something I remember anyone ever requiring or encouraging me to do in worship, Sunday School, or youth group. I did not know Christians who did that. Goodness, I didn't even know Christians were allowed to do that sort of thing!

Therefore, theology introduced me to what I call "confessional-critical thinking." This is human thinking that is both confessional and critical. Confession and criticism hold each other accountable.

On the one hand, theology taught me how to respond critically, or reflectively and reasonably, to what I was hearing and reading. I learned to acquire and work with knowledge, to entertain abstract ideas and concepts, to construct mental models and pictures, to discern differences and problems, and to analyze, evaluate, and revise theories.

Theology goes beyond mere informing. It seeks to transform and form the mind of the individual to think critically—which does not mean "negatively," but rather, "carefully, rationally, analytically, and constructively"—about God and about all things in relation to or in light of God.

In other words, I had to give up both shoddy thinking and not thinking at all regarding the Christian church and its theological tradition. I gradually began to examine what I believed, and, more importantly, what the church has believed through the ages and across the nations. I came to think about these things carefully, reasonably, analytically, and constructively.

As I was acquiring the skills of critical theology, I was also learning how to think confessionally, or along the lines of what Christians have known and confessed to be true and meaningful through the centuries. In this way, neither criticism nor confession is allowed to have sole or totalitarian control, for each must meet the demands of the other. We who are believers must be competent in arriving at the affirmation of beliefs that have been through the defining fire of confessional tradition, and also the refining fire of critical reason.

My point is this: Who would have known that by meeting theology I would have gotten myself involved in thinking, and would have had to become a thinker, actually using my mind in matters of faith? I was not this kind of believer before theology. I was not a thoughtful person. I was incapable of thinking theological thoughts. I simply accepted blindly what I was told, or I believed only what would fit quickly and easily into my preconceived belief-system. Therefore, I had to be changed and made by theology's education into the kind of person who can think, talk, and exist theologically in the world.

Another thing about theology that surprised me is that it contains, carries, and conveys cognitive content. This language is actually about something. It says something. Theology is not mere talk for the sake of talking. Neither is it an open, empty box, for us to put into it whatever we choose. It is not raw materials for us to use any way we please. Theology has its own subject matter, as well as its own ways of serving and being loyal to this subject matter.

I do not know why this would have come as such a surprise to me. Physics has its own subject matter. Psychology has its own subject matter. So do horticulture and craft beer brewing. Why not theology, as well?

It never occurred to me that Christianity might be about something more than congregational programs and activities, worship rituals and music, practical piety, good works, and good clean living. I had never considered that there might be real substance behind all this religion —something real that was prompting, sustaining, and guiding this religion. And never once did it cross my mind that the church and all of us who are Christians might be telling the truth, and all of this might actually be true.

Theology does not deal in fantasies or foolish nonsense. It resides in this world, and relates to reality. It never requires "make-believe," or "believing simply to be believing." Theology never takes us to the place where Alice states her inability to believe things that are impossible, and the White Queen responds, "I daresay you haven't had much practice. When I was your age, I always did it for half-an-hour a day. Why, sometimes I've believed as many as six impossible things before breakfast."[12]

Theology talks and thinks about the truth, because it believes there is truth to be talked about and thought about. Theology talks and thinks about things that matter, believing that it matters how we talk and think about them. Therefore, theology is itself to be taken seriously, as serious speech and knowledge regarding reality.

What, then, are these things that matter? What is theology's subject matter? The most concrete answer is "doctrines." Doctrines are statements of what the church has from its beginning and throughout its history come to believe and formulate in its Scriptures, creeds, liturgies, articles of faith, and confessional expressions. Sometimes these beliefs are referred to as "dogma," in order to emphasize their authoritative, normative status.

Theology deals with the decisive, distinctive teachings to which the community of faith is committed. These are the teachings that make this community distinctively, identifiably Christian. Here are the contents of faith's knowledge, understanding, and wisdom that are the fundamentals of what it is to think and talk, believe and behave, Christianly.

Theology, however, is not interested first or foremost in simply conducting a basic sociological or cultural-linguistic study of the beliefs that are associated with the Christian way of life. Its primary aim is not merely to explain doctrines and draw out their practical implications for the church. Nor is the goal to retain and repeat traditional doctrines, believing for the sake of believing them.

In its theological discourse, the church is not simply talking about itself, or about its doctrines and teachings. Rather, it is talking about reality—the same reality that philosophers, historians, and scientists

---

12. Lewis Carroll, *Alice Through the Looking-Glass* (Cambridge, Massachusetts: Candlewick Press, 2005), 104-105.

are talking about. Theology takes its beliefs to be claims of truth. Theology is in a persistent search for the fullness of the truth, i.e., the whole truth and nothing but the truth. The resulting doctrines are always partial and dim expressions of the things to which they point.

Therefore, when the church thinks and talks theologically, it is thinking and talking about what is real, not make-believe—the reality of God and of all things in relation to God. In doing so, theology preserves, clarifies, corrects, develops, teaches, and transmits what the Christian community has come to know and understand about the way things are, and the way they will be. Theology is about what it means to be, or to exist, in such a world. (Note: I have given you here a defining summary of theology.)

This was not an insight that came to me early at the beginning of my relationship with theology, but only toward my later, mature years. By the time I realized what I had gotten myself into, I was already deeply involved in more than an academic course or two, more than a disciplined life of study and learning, more than a professional career, more than a demanding language, more than a form of confessional-critical thinking, and more than a set of doctrinal beliefs. It was too late to stop, or turn around and go back. I had already entered theology's world and taken on its life, or way of life. Theology is a mode of being.

My primary consciousness had become that of being theology's student, or disciple. Later, I discovered that by being its student, I had also become its servant. I had been handed responsibility for caring about theology and taking good care of it. My life's work would be preserving and teaching it. I was called to be a steward of the mysteries of God.

Only after decades of this discipleship and stewardship did it begin to dawn on me how radically I had been acted upon during this long process. During the entire time, I had presumed I had been mastering theology. But the truth was, theology had been mastering me. Rather than theology being drawn into my world to serve me, I was being drawn deeper and deeper into its world to serve it. Instead of theology living where I lived, supporting my life project, I discovered that I lived where it lived, supporting its project.

The Old Testament image of the nation of Israel, and especially its temple, as the "house of the Lord" is meaningful here. The New

Testament appropriates this image for the church. The church is the "spiritual house," "the household of God," "the dwelling place for God," "God's building," and "God's temple." Here is the central locus of God's presence and powerful working in the whole world. This is where God dwells or resides on earth, when most present and powerfully working.

Of course, you and I immediately think of people when we think of the church. This is a human house. But, according to the biblical-theological picture, human beings are not the builders as much as they are the building materials. We do not "build the church," but are ourselves being

- built into a spiritual house, to be a holy priesthood, to offer spiritual sacrifices acceptable to God through Jesus Christ (1 Peter 2:5);
- built upon the foundation of the apostles and prophets, with Christ Jesus himself as the cornerstone. …built together spiritually into a dwelling place for God. (Ephesians 2:20, 22)

Who, then, is the architect and general contractor of this building? Who has conceived and constructed this house? Who sustains and grows this structure? Who owns and oversees this place and its people?

God.

Given its divine origin, order, and purpose, the church is necessarily theological. It is a theological house. Not only is God dwelling and making Himself known and knowable here, but this knowledge of God is also dwelling here. It is being preserved and transmitted here. The self-revelation of God, made known over a long history, and supremely in Jesus Christ, continues to be made known and knowable here.

Thus, we can say that the church is the house built *for* theology, i.e., to be the dwelling place for the knowledge of God. Theology must be housed. And the purpose of this particular house is to house it.

It is equally true that this house has been and continues to be built *by* theology. Theology keeps this peculiar house in place and on task. Theology gives this house its identity and purpose. Theology gives this house its subject matter. Theology orders and guides the lives of those who live here and do the bidding of theology.

The church is the only house in the world that is built by and for theology. All other houses are built by and for other things. For instance, a bank is the house built by and for money. A hospital is the house of healthcare and medical knowledge. A college or university houses academic endeavors, research, and scholarly knowledge in multiple fields or disciplines.

But the church is solely constructed and charged with the unique role and responsibility of housing theology, or the knowledge of God. Therefore, a congregation, or any local manifestation of the church, that is not built by and for theology, and whose household does not exist for the purpose of preserving and serving the knowledge of God, is something else, and not the church.

I have also come to understand that, in a very real sense, theology itself is our dwelling-place. It houses us. We have been summoned to enter and reside in "the house of theology," or "the house that theology has built." Here we are "at home."

This *is* home to those of us who have been lured out of other houses to come and live here, stewarding what this house houses. The matters of this household now matter to us. We now live by and for them, since theology is always converting, constructing, developing, and maturing those who are its residents, or inhabitants, living by faith in the revealed knowledge of God in Christ.

I used to speak about "bringing theology home" in the basic sense of merely reintroducing theology into local settings and individual Christian lives. Not only is that effort difficult to the point of being impossible, it is also a bit misguided. Instead of us "bringing theology home," what is actually happening—if or when it happens—is that theology is still choosing and claiming, gathering and assembling its servants as it has done throughout history and the world. Theology is bringing us back and making of us its house. Theology *is* home.

Only those who let themselves to be drawn in and made theology's own household will find that they are truly "home." Theology is the home of faith and faith's fellowship, to which you and I have to be brought back. Only by our being brought back will theology be brought back, and both will be at home together.

The bringing back of Christians to theology involves more than merely taking a course, reading a book, listening to a sermon or lecture, or learning a language. All of these are excellent, worthwhile, necessary activities that Christians currently are not doing, but they should. In order to return to theology, become theological people, and be the church, believers must take theology courses, immerse themselves in the reading of good theology books, listen to theologically crafted sermons and lectures, and learn the theological language. There is no other way.

However, there is more to this way than basic intellectual and/or academic exercises. Being brought back to theology as home also entails being inducted into theology's community, i.e., the people who live here, for whom theology is home. It involves an educational immersion in this community's long, rich tradition of theological thought, belief and practice, which every resident is expected to respect, obey, study, learn, serve, and take on as his or her own. This ultimately necessitates entering into the life-world of theology, and living there. Only when Christians do this can it be said that they have been brought back home.

Those who return and experience the homecoming enter into a vast communion of theological beings/believers stretching across many generations and people groups. It was at the seminary that I was introduced to this communion, and actually met some of its members in person.

First, there were professors, who had years ago been introduced to theology, just as I was being introduced. They had lived in theology's house all these years as theology's students and servants. They were now at the door, ushering newcomers in, showing them around, teaching them the things by which and for which this house was built, guiding them in how to live here, embodying these things, and exhorting them to take on this community's way of thinking, talking, existing, and witnessing as the church of Christ in the world today.

I was humbled—and awed into silence—to be in the company of such theological scholars, who were at heart theological believers, as Frank Stagg, Eric Rust, Wayne Ward, Dale Moody, Frank Tupper, Henlee Barnette, Wayne Oates, and Glenn Hinson. I wanted to be like them. I wanted to have the love for theology that they had. I wanted to be as studious, reflective, and articulate as they were. I wanted to know and understand at the full, deep level that they knew and understood. I wanted more than anything else to stay with them, and somehow become a member of their community, even if it meant being nothing more than a hired hand. I secretly dreamed of one day being a theologian.

Soon I discovered that through association with these professors, I was being introduced to the greater theological communion itself, of which they were members. It consisted of theological teachers and preachers, believers and behavers, both living and dead, as well as both local and universal.

I remember thinking that surely my experience had to be close to what Simon Peter was privileged to experience on the mountaintop when the transfigured Jesus conversed with the great luminaries of Israel, and outshined them: Moses and Elijah, representing the Law and the prophets.[13]

I was in the company of the Lord's saints, from Paul of Tarsus to Irenaeus of Lyons to Origen of Alexandria to Augustine of Hippo. I read and learned from the theological giants: Aquinas, Luther, and Calvin. I was taken through the crowd to stand near Kierkegaard, Barth, Brunner, Bonhoeffer, Rauschenbusch, the Niebuhrs, Tillich, and Pannenberg. Like Peter, I wanted to stay there and build a large retreat center where all of us could live, and this great moment would never end.

I was like a little child among grownups, eavesdropping on their adult conversation. I dreamed of the day when I would be able to join in. Yet, as much as the thought of that possibility thrilled me, it also frightened me. For who was I—or who would I ever be—that I would dare to presume that I was worthy of even listening, much less having anything to say? Or, that I would be able to say it in such a way that they would recognize and approve of? Or, that I would ever be counted one of them?

What I have learned since is that I was overhearing only a small conversation of a small group, taking place as part of a much larger conversation among a much larger group of faithful witnesses. These were representative thinkers and talkers of the whole *communio sanctorum*, or communion of saints, reflecting and articulating on behalf of the church the full light of God's life and salvation made known in Jesus Christ. Such discourse began long ago, has continued

13. The story of Jesus' transfiguration is told in Mark 9:2–8 (Matthew 17:1–8; Luke 9:28–36).

all these centuries, and will never end, for these theological people cannot stop loving the Lord's truth with all their minds, and declaring the Lord's praise with all their mouths. This is the church.

Before meeting theology, I did not even know that such a community existed. The only Christians I had known were good, committed, ordinary, church-going folks (the majority of them). But they were not theological people. They had little to no knowledge of, much less any relationship with, the theologians of the church. They did not understand or draw from the great theological tradition. It certainly was not home for them. They simply did not live there, or ever go there.

I like Leander Keck's image of mainstream congregations, who are heirs of a great estate, camping out in the front yard because "they neither knew nor cared how to live in the house."[14] Imagine someone coming to these Christians one day to tell them that they are in line to receive a fortune—the pearl of great price. They have had no idea this property is worth anything, much less part of a much larger, richer inheritance. Plus, they are its heirs. Therefore, they can now move back inside the house. They will be ushered in, shown around, and taught how to live in this house as the beneficiaries they are. Their orientation tour is about to begin.

That was my experience. Professors took me from the front yard into the house. They showed me around and inducted me into the larger community of faith, where I would be made a permanent resident. Opened to me were the mysteries, of which I was told I was both an heir and a servant. I was expected to learn how "inheritors of this estate" are supposed to think, talk, believe, value, and live.

These mysteries are the matters by which and for which this house has been built, and this community has been assembled. I refer to them collectively as "tradition." Every house has its own tradition: the bank, the hospital, and the university. All have ways of thinking, talking, believing, valuing, and living that define, distinguish, and direct them. The church is no exception.

Therefore, in meeting theology, being brought back into theology's house, and made at home among the community of theological faith,

---

14. Leander E. Keck, *The Church Confident: Christianity Can Repent But It Must Not Whimper* (Nashville: Abingdon Press, 1993), 16. Keck (1928–) is Winkley Professor of Biblical Theology Emeritus at Yale Divinity School.

I was also introduced to theology's tradition. This house is nothing if not traditional.

Of course, the words "tradition" and "traditional" are spoken and heard negatively today. Who cares about tradition? Who wants to be traditional? One of the objectives of modernity for the past five hundred years has been the dethronement of tradition, and especially Christian religious tradition. The latter is no longer considered to be authoritative or normative for the way modern or postmodern folks think, believe, or behave.

So, where did this authority go? If we have successfully stripped Christian tradition of its former power to determine perception and interpretation of all reality, make decisions about how to live in this world, and require our obedience, what did we do with it? Authority does not simply disappear.

It has been shifted to the individual. Everything now depends on subjective, personal perceptions and interpretations, experiences and inclinations, emotions and feelings, needs and wants, desires and values, self-identifications and self-fulfillments, and decisions made by free choice—all of which are fluid and constantly changing.

However, all legitimate human enterprises—banking, medicine, music, sports—have their own distinctive histories of theory and practice, organization, rules, and standards. If an individual seeks to participate in one of these enterprises, he or she must submit to this enterprise's "tradition." This tradition is authoritative. It is normative. It overrides personal authority, and directs the speech, thought, and actions of the individual.

For instance, in order to play the game of football, the player must enter into the "house" of football and come under the authority of the game itself. Football's tradition, not the player's preferences, determines what football is and how football is to be played.

Granted, this tradition is living and changing. The assumption that "tradition is dead" is dead wrong. Tradition is alive and well where the game is still being played, developed, and matured. The question is, "What is the tradition that is in play here? And within this large, or great, tradition, which smaller traditions are we playing by?"

Likewise, where the Christian religion is in existence and still being practiced, its distinctive "great tradition" is still in play. This tradition is taken as authoritative by and for the individuals and communities that are Christian. It determines what the Christian religion is, and also what is Christian.

Why any Christian or group of Christians would be uninterested in their own tradition, reject it as a burden from the past that must be dropped, or act hostilely toward it, is beyond my comprehension. If Christian faith suddenly and spontaneously appeared in the human heart, or out of thin air, or it were fully a social construction, or invented by each individual who needs to express himself or herself, I would understand. But faith is objective before it is subjective. It derives from reality. It has a history. It has Scriptures, confessions, creeds, articles of faith, doctrines, prayers, and practices. It has established order, process, and content. This tradition is authoritative and normative for the community that belongs to it.

Inexplicably, congregations and Christians all too often do not know or care to know the Christian theological faith-tradition, which is the tradition of the faith that they profess. They effectively deny its importance and authority. At most, they may use it as a salvage yard where they may go to find a few interesting pieces to add to the bricolage[15] of their own religion or spirituality. While they may consider their alienation from tradition to be a sign of relevance, intelligence, or even faith, it is actually a sign of dishonesty and inauthenticity. Christian faith by its very nature is traditional.

I fully agree with Christian historian Jaroslav Pelikan, who has written that "it is traditionalism that gives tradition such a bad name."[16] Traditionalism is the strong upholding of and adhering to the past that resists any and all change. It is the stranglehold of former beliefs and practices, or "the tyranny of the dead." As Pelikan expresses it: "Tradition is the living faith of the dead, traditionalism is the dead faith of the living."[17]

---

15. In art, literature, philosophy, or culture, "bricolage" is something constructed or put together resourcefully out of a diverse range of things that happen to be on hand and available. A religious-spiritual bricolage is an individual's do-it-yourself project of a "new" religion or spirituality, which is a patchwork of materials from multiple religions, spiritualities, psychologies, ideologies, and other sources.

16. Jaroslav Pelikan, *The Vindication of Tradition* (New Haven and London: Yale University Press, 1984), 65. Pelikan (1923–2006) was a preeminent scholar of the history of Christianity, Christian theology, and medieval intellectual thought, who taught at Yale University for over thirty years.

17. Pelikan, 65.

We seek faith that is living and that can make us alive, enabling us to live in this world by faith. This faith has lived in the past. It has brought people alive, and caused them to live in this world by faith. We desire this faith, as well. And, fortunately, our ancestors have left it for us in their writings, sermons, teachings, confessions, hymns, prayers, and poems. Therefore, we are not to neglect or ignore their collective contribution, which is our inheritance. Instead, we are to learn and embody it, so as to know this same faith and the life it engenders.

Edward Farley rightly defines tradition as "the sedimentation" of the experience of people of faith through the ages.[18] Theological tradition is what these people have known, understood, believed, valued, and practiced over centuries in relation to God and to all things as belonging to God. Tradition is what has come out of the long history of human beings, both communally and personally, existing by faith and as students and stewards of the gospel of Jesus Christ. It is what has "settled" out of the currents and undercurrents of the church, and been left behind as faith's "sediment," adding layer upon layer over time,

On the one hand, there are "traditions," which are the customs, beliefs, and practices that characterize a branch of the church (such as Orthodox, Roman Catholic, or Protestant), a denomination, sect, or local congregation. Even so-called "contemporary churches," claiming to be non-denominational and non-traditional, have their own traditions. Christian groups that shun history and cry, "No creed but the Bible," have their own creeds. This cry is one of them. When a congregant complains in protest, "We have never done it that way before," she is referring to tradition in this first sense, i.e., to one of the "traditions" that are local, specific, and limited.

On the other hand, there is "tradition," which is the central expression or manifestation of faith, or what has been left of faith for those who are called to live by faith. This is what has emerged in, through, and out of many traditions as *the* tradition. It consists of those understandings and accompanying behaviors that have come to be primary, essential, and defining for Christian faith-existence. They

18. Edward Farley, *The Fragility of Knowledge: Theological Education in the Church and the University* (Philadelphia: Fortress Press, 1988), 8.

are considered to be identifying and defining, and thus authoritative and normative, for the church.

Some scholars limit tradition to the first five or six hundred years of the church. Tradition is apostolic and patristic faith, enshrined first and most accurately and authoritatively in Scripture, and then in the early church's confessions and creeds.[19] Other scholars focus on classical Protestantism of the sixteenth century, contending that this is *the* tradition. These interpretations and applications are primary and take precedence over those of the past and the present. Finally, still others focus on contemporary constructions. How faith is interpreted and applied today is more important, relevant, and authoritative than all past interpretations and applications.

In contrast, I do not believe our Christian theological tradition is so compartmentalized or polarized. It is not either/or, but both/and. All of the above. I am interested in the central, abiding tradition that spans all historical church periods, and weaves together all Christian religious traditions and all Christian teaching in one long continuity of faith. This may be variously called "the Great Tradition," "orthodoxy," "classical Christianity," "mere Christianity," or "ancient-future faith"—as long as the reference is to the truth and meaning affirmed by the faithful over two millennia.

Think of this tradition as the theological language of people past and present, who are in the same conversation about the same things. You and I don't invent this conversation, as Richard John Neuhaus has noted, but we join it by grace. It is not over, and is still going on today, because there is much that remains to be said. However, only those who actually join this company, learn what has been said and is being said in the conversation, and who conform themselves to its movements, mysteries, and message will be able to say what needs to be said.[20]

---

19. D. H. Williams, *Evangelical and Tradition: The Formative Influence of the Early Church* (Grand Rapids: Baker Academic Books, 2005), 24. Also, see Williams' book, *Retrieving The Tradition and Renewing Evangelicalism: A Primer for Suspicious Protestants* (Grand Rapids: William B. Eerdman's Publishing Company, 1999). Williams is professor of religion in patristics and historical theology at Baylor University.

20. Richard John Neuhaus, "Foreword: An Invitation to the Feast," Thomas C. Oden, *Requiem: A Lament in Three Movements* (Nashville: Abingdon Press, 1995), 12. Neuhaus (1936–2009) was a Roman Catholic priest and founding editor of First Things journal. He was an erudite thinker and prolific writer. His 1984 book, *The*

I am one who has been joined by grace to this community and its age-long theological conversation. I am now both hearer and learner. I am both heir and guardian. What comes out of the past, continuing in the present and projecting toward the future, is the Christian theological tradition, delivering resources of faith for faith in all times and places. We do not have to invent or reinvent all truth, all wisdom, all values, all meanings, or all practices that belong to this particular way of life. Because of tradition, we are assisted with perception of the way things are, insight into what is really going on, wisdom regarding who we are, what we are about, and what we humans are up against, and guidance as to how we can be true to our vocation and reach our destiny in Christ.

I use the term "faith-tradition" to specify the particular theological tradition that belongs to faith. I am also indicating the intimate relationship that exists between faith and its tradition. Faith is faith only to the extent that it comes from, abides in, and expresses itself in this tradition. This tradition comes only from faith, and is relevant and valuable only as it leads to faith. There is no such thing as either traditionless faith or faithless tradition. People of Christian faith are always people of faith's tradition, or faith-tradition.

Before meeting theology at the seminary, I was alienated from my own Christian theological faith-tradition. Returning to Keck's image, I was one of those people, when I was a child and teenager, camping out in the front yard along with many other heirs of this estate, who neither knew nor cared about how to live in the main house. Then I left the front yard and went far away. But by education, as a result of calling and conversion, I was brought back and brought inside. By theology's formative impact, I was made into a student and a steward of the mysteries that matter to this house and to all who live in it. They came to matter to me, as well.

This happened only because I was formally, properly introduced to the tradition by which and for which this house was built. Teachers taught me the tradition that has Christ as its cornerstone, the apostles and fathers as its foundation, and the reformers and other thinking believers throughout history as its builders and building materials.

Naked Public Square, placed him at the center of the debate concerning religion in American public life.

Before I knew it, I was being built into its very structure. I became a "traditional" person, i.e., a person of theology's faith-tradition.

Another way to explain this is to say that I became a resident of "another world," which is the world theology constructs in obedient response to the revelation of the truth and meaning of God in Christ. Persons who exist in this world are not merely active in the world of theology's tradition and education, but they are also active in this world that everybody else lives in. But they live in it theologically, or by faith that is shaped by the Christian theological tradition.

The church bears witness to the truth of God in the midst of the world by not living in the same world as the world does, but rather in a whole, new and different world—the world perceived in relation to God made known in Jesus Christ. Theology, then, does not become part of a person's world, as much as a person becomes part of the world of theology.

This is what it means to be a "contrast society," "citizens of the Kingdom," or "resident aliens." As the church, we are theological people whose home is the strange, new world of the Bible, while also dwelling in the familiar, old world of modern-postmodern, post-Christian society. Because we live, move, and have our being in the former world, we are "in but not of the world" in which most people live, move, and have their being.

Meeting theology meant I became involved in a peculiar "life-world," or "all-embracing context in which people always move, by which they are always surrounded, and which makes its contribution to their formation."[21] Every society and every person lives, moves, and has being within some life-world. But not all life-worlds are either the same world or the same life. The environment or milieu of the church is the Christian theological life-world. This is a life-world in which residents exist by faith. They speak, think, act, relate, live and die within the interpretive framework of the Christian faith-tradition.

Therefore, theology is the life-world, or faith-world, of the people of God. Using the Latin term *habitus,* we can say that theology is a

---

21. Wilfried Härle, *Outline of Christian Doctrine: An Evangelical Dogmatics* (Grand Rapids: William B. Eerdmans Publishing Company, 2015), 143. Härle (1941–) is professor emeritus of systematic theology and ethics at the University of Heidelberg, Germany.

"habit" we get into. From its beginnings, Edward Farley has noted, the Christian community has claimed a revealed knowledge of God, that has the character of wisdom—a wisdom becomes our "habit," or "cognitive disposition and orientation of the soul," and state of existence whose end is salvation.[22]

I emphasize that this "habit" becomes the "habitation" of those persons who exist by faith. It is the dwelling-place where they reside. Hence, I speak of the Christian church as "theology's house," or "the house that theology has built and continues to build."

Only as I continued under the tutelage of theology, over decades, did it later begin to dawn on me what I had gotten myself into years before: a language, a knowledge, a mode of being, a community, tradition, life-world, and enduring state of the soul.

When I finally left the mountaintop and the seminary hamlet at the intersection where the Jerusalem, Athens, Berlin, and Nashville roads converge, I took theology with me. I packed up the books, furniture, wife, kid, cats, and houseplants, and we moved from Kentucky to North Carolina. I drove into the parking lot of the congregation, knocked on the front door, and announced: "I'm back! Guess what I found (or, it found me) while I was away?"

Why Is Theology So Far Away?

The road from the hamlet back home turned out to be longer than I had thought it would be. This was due to more than geographical or cultural distance, but more specifically, to the theological distance of the seminary and local congregation from each other. They are "worlds apart."

Because theology resides in the academic world of the seminary, it is far removed from where clergy and laypersons worship, work, and live as Christians. Bringing theology home, then, entails bridging a wide gulf, which neither side seems to be interested in bridging.

The question that naturally emerges is, "Why is theology so distant from local congregations and ordinary Christians?" Or, "How did the

22. Edward Farley, *Theologia: The Fragmentation and Unity of Theological Education* (Eugene, Oregon: Wipf and Stock Publishers, 2001), 35–36, 39.

body of Christ, the church, get itself in this condition of one hand holding theology, while the other hand is empty? And neither knows what the other is doing?"

The answer requires a brief historical overview. Theology did not suddenly disappear from congregations during the twentieth or twenty-first centuries, as we might assume. This separation occurred during the church's early years, and has developed over centuries to what it is today.[23]

Christian theology was birthed when the church was born—both in the cradle of Judaism. The first responders to what happened on the day of Pentecost in Jerusalem devoted themselves to hearing and learning the apostles' teaching.[24] They became students of Peter and the others.

Naturally, those who had been most closely associated with Jesus as his disciples, or students, during his teaching ministry were responsible for the teaching ministry of this new community. They were now "apostles," meaning "ones who are sent out." They understood themselves to have been authorized by Jesus and empowered by the Spirit to be sent out as Jesus' personal messengers.

Their mission was to proclaim and teach the gospel, or good news, *of* Jesus in two senses: (1) objective genitive: the teachings taught *by* Jesus; and (2) subjective genitive: the teachings *about* Jesus. Both the

---

23. A good, though brief, history of theological education is provided by Justo L. González, *The History of Theological Education* (Nashville: Abingdon Press, 2015). González (1937–) is a Cuban-American Methodist historian and theologian, who is a professor emeritus at Columbia Theological Seminary in Decatur, Georgia. I am greatly dependent here on his work. Also, see Gerald Hiestand and Todd Wilson, *The Pastor Theologian: Resurrecting an Ancient Vision* (Grand Rapids: Zondervan, 2015), 21–52. Hiestand is senior associate pastor of Calvary Memorial Church in Oak Park, Illinois; and Wilson is senior pastor of Calvary Memorial Church in Oak Park, Illinois. Both Hiestand and Wilson are co-founders of the Center for Pastor Theologians. Finally, Owen Strachan provides a brief history of the pastorate in a book he has co-authored with Kevin J. Vanhoozer, *The Pastor As Public Theologian: Reclaiming a Lost Vision* (Grand Rapids: Baker Academic, 2015), 69–93. Strachan is assistant professor of Christian theology and church history at Boyce College and The Southern Baptist Theological Seminary, where he also directs the Carl F. H. Henry Institute for Evangelical Engagement and serves as a Fellow with the Center for Pastor Theologians. Vanhoozer (1957–) is Research Professor of Systematic Theology at Trinity Evangelical Divinity School, Deerfield, Illinois.

24. Acts 2:42.

apostles and those who gathered around them were devoted to the teaching and learning of these teachings.

The geographical expansion of the Jesus-community beyond Jerusalem created many new local gatherings that settled into being ongoing assemblies, communities, or congregations. Wherever these assemblies formed, teaching was central and essential. For a time, the apostles filled this educational role. A major limitation was that they were not always residential or present. Therefore, as the number of congregations increased, and the range of their locations widened, the apostles taught assistants and appointed them to be teachers and overseers of local affairs, including education.

In some congregations—especially those that were more removed from the apostles—one or more members, who were not taught by the apostles, were elected to be teachers. This was based on their knowledge of the apostolic tradition, as well as on their teaching abilities, experiences, and achievements. They were clearly assigned a "measure of faith" and "given the manifestation of the Spirit" that appointed them for the role of teaching.[25]

In sum, theological education in the earliest decades was local and congregation-based. Teaching was central to the life and ministry of the community of faith. Everyone who attended was considered a student of the apostolic theological tradition. Theological education was neither peripheral nor optional, but rather, essential to what it meant to be the church and to be Christian.

Of course, not all members were expected to assume the teaching role. But those who did were expected to take seriously both their teaching ministry and their own studying and learning as students. All—both teachers and students—were mutually responsible for the whole teaching ministry of the congregation. Theological education was considered to be vital to the formation and faithfulness of the community that belonged to Jesus, who was the Master Teacher.

Theological education took place in hours-long worship on Sunday mornings, taking place in two parts: the Service of the Word and the Service of the Table (Communion, Lord's Supper, or Eucharist).[26] The former was essentially educational, modeled after the teaching-

25. See 1 Corinthians 12:4–11, 28–31; Romans 12:3–8; Ephesians 4:11–13.

26. González, 1.

learning worship of the Jewish synagogue. It consisted of readings of the Hebrew Scriptures, the apostolic oral traditions (unwritten or semi-written teachings of the apostles circulating and preserved by word-of-mouth), and written correspondence from teachers, such as Paul. These texts were read out loud, followed by interpretation.

Worship was the only time and place members had to be taught and to learn. There were no separate schools. What believers knew and understood of the Bible, Jesus, and their faith had to be learned in their homes and congregations under the tutelage of homegrown teachers.

Those who directed worship and taught had to be able to read. However, very few members were literate. The majority were women, who were usually uneducated, and also men, who came from lower socio-economic groups and did not have the high-level privilege of an education. Responsibility, then, fell on the one or two exceptions who could read and write.

Reading a biblical text out loud was one important, valuable skill. Interpreting the text theologically as sacred Scripture was another. A member who had received Jewish religious instruction in the Jerusalem Temple, or who had attended a pagan school and learned how to interpret the ancient texts of Greek and Roman poets and philosophers, was highly valued and sought after.

Still, interpreting and teaching a biblical text required specific knowledge and understanding of the history of Israel with God and the work of God supremely in Jesus Christ. The first part of this knowledge was provided only by the Jewish synagogues. It was not provided at all by pagan schools, and could not be acquired through secular studies. Therefore, extremely rare and valuable was a person like Saul/Paul of Tarsus, who was literate in multiple ways: the languages of Hebrew and Greek; the Scriptures of the Jews; the philosophy of the Greeks; the gospel of Christ; and the teachings of the apostles (of which Paul considered himself to be one, having been chosen and commissioned by the Risen Christ himself on the road to Damascus).

As years went by, the challenges to local theological education increased. First, the apostles either died or were martyred. Less and less could anyone claim either a direct or an immediately indirect relationship with one of Jesus' students.

Second, congregations were springing up in cities or regions farther removed geographically and culturally from Jerusalem and Judaism. More converts were Gentiles or pagans, who did not know the religion of Israel, believe in the one God, or follow the moral demands of Israel or the church. Most were completely illiterate, linguistically, religiously, and theologically.

Third, as the first and second generations of believers passed away, third generation Christians were left to be the church. They were not nearly as devoted to teaching and learning the Christian theological tradition as their parents and grandparents. Sustaining commitment and involvement was difficult, making theological education and literacy that much more difficult.

Fourth, major heresies plagued the church, emerging in local congregations. False teachers competed with appointed teachers for students and congregational leadership. They taught docetism (Jesus was not human), antinomianism (Christians are freed by grace from the religious, moral law), Marcionism (rejection of the Hebrew Bible and the Hebrew God), and many other heretical beliefs. That made serving the gospel and maintaining the integrity and continuity of apostolic teaching more difficult, as well as much more crucial.

It became necessary, then, to develop another, more formal, extensive and intensive type of Christian theological education in these communities of faith. It was called the "catechumenate."[27] It was based on the belief that the theological teachings of the church were too important to be imparted to just anyone, or to be thrown around freely or haphazardly, or able to be grasped without careful guidance. Joining the church was to be considered serious business. Becoming a Christian required much more than mere attendance, or simply showing up every once in a while. Faith was more than being born and raised in the fellowship, or volunteering to join up and have one's name on the roll. It certainly was far more than labeling oneself a Christian and claiming to follow Jesus, without having anything to do with Jesus' people, or with Jesus' teachings.

Only persons who demonstrated over time the seriousness of their commitment, by regularly attending services of worship, actively

---

27. The word "catechumenate" comes from "catechesis," meaning "teaching" or "instruction." It refers to both the period of teaching and the curriculum being taught. The teacher is the "catechist," and the student is a "catechumen."

listening to and receiving instruction in the Service of the Word, and living a righteous life, were invited to undergo the rites of initiation: the signing of the cross on the individual's forehead; the laying on of hands; and a pinch of salt, on which a special exorcism had been pronounced, placed in the person's mouth.[28]

The catechumens then entered an extended, formal process of doctrinal, moral, and liturgical instruction, in addition to the Service of the Word, both led by the congregation's pastor. Their lives were closely scrutinized, and they were asked tough exam questions concerning their knowledge and understanding of the church's beliefs and practices. Anyone found to be engaged in unethical practices or to be holding to beliefs from pagan culture or heretical teachers was eliminated.

This educational process lasted at least two, and often three, years, although it could be prolonged indefinitely if the catechumen failed to make the necessary progress in Christian learning and living. The student could also be asked to leave, until he or she showed signs of being ready to reenter and continue.

Among the catechumens who did reach the final stage of the catechumenate, and who successfully completed their initial testing, some were chosen to be baptized. They went through another period of intense preparation, including more rigorous examination of lifestyle and beliefs, and daily exorcisms, while the entire assembly fervently fasted and prayed for them. This period was the origin of our season of Lent.

It culminated in baptism, which was normally administered on Easter morning at sunrise. This ritual consisted of undressing and being anointed with the oil of exorcism, renouncing Satan and all his influences, descending into the water, making a confession of faith (using words close to the Apostles' Creed), being immersed after each of the three divisions of the Creed, dressing and entering the house of worship, receiving the laying on of hands and anointment with the oil of thanksgiving, and joining the congregation for the first time in the Service of the Table, including prayers and the kiss of peace. Initiates were then considered to be members fully grafted into the body of Christ.

---

28. González, 11.

Following catechism, baptism, and first communion, new believers were expected to continue developing in the way of faith that had been set in place, so as to be equipped for:

> the work of ministry, for building up the body of Christ, until all of us come to the unity of the faith and of the knowledge of the Son of God, to maturity, to the measure of the full stature of Christ. We must no longer be children, tossed to and fro and blown about by every wind of doctrine, by people's trickery, by their craftiness in deceitful scheming. But speaking the truth in love, we must grow up in every way into him who is the head, into Christ, from whom the whole body, joined and knit together by every ligament with which it is equipped, as each part is working properly, promotes the body's growth in building itself up in love. (Ephesians 4:12-16)

It was in the congregation that Christians were expected to gain this maturity and to increase in the knowledge and understanding of the mysteries of God revealed in the gospel of Christ and his church. Christian theological education did not end when one had been baptized and joined the church. It was only beginning.

Until the middle of the second century, the local congregation was the sole home and school of theology. In this regard, we might say that clergy and laity were homeschooled. This is not to idealize the education provided by congregations during that early period, nor to set up the ancient catechumenate as a model for all congregations to adopt today. As I have indicated, congregations struggled to do the best they could with the untrained members and leaders they had. Illiteracy and ignorance hindered educational efforts, and the results were often abysmal.

Nonetheless, what should stand out for emulation is the ancient belief and practice of the local community as the locus of biblical and theological education. All believers were called to the stewardship of the Scriptures and the gospel. They were expected to be students, studying and learning what had been entrusted to them, and then to be trustworthy with serving, living, and transmitting it.

Pastors, along with all Christians, were viewed as students. But they had been given an additional, special gift of the Spirit and a special office in the congregation within which to exercise it: the ministry of teaching. Together, laity and clergy formed a teaching-learning community along the lines of the original community of Jesus and his disciples, or apostles. Their life together included the intentional studying and learning of Jesus' teachings, along with the developing body of the church's primary, authoritative, and normative interpretations. The whole church—clergy and non-clergy—were students together, sharing responsibility for the stewardship of the gospel and the ministry of theological education. As González summarizes, "The distinction that we make between theological education for the church as a whole and the training for the pastorate did not exist in the early church."[29]

Consequently, there was no additional or special education for the persons ordained and elected to teach the local congregation. These teachers presided during the Service of the Word, instructed catechetical students, interpreted the Bible, explained the beliefs of Christian faith, and battled heresies without formal biblical or theological training. Worship leaders and teachers had the same Christian education as everyone else—with perhaps the addition of some education in pagan schools. Of course, these leaders were expected to do extra study on their own, or in association with other leaders, in preparation for their educational duties within their respective congregations. But they were not required to know anything more than what the rest of the membership was required to know.[30]

Some of these leaders and teachers were elected to be bishops—variously called "presybters," "elders," "deacons," and "pastors." A bishop served as the chief pastor over several house-churches or congregations in one city or geographical area.[31] Local pastors served these congregations under the bishop's supervision and direction, and often looked to the bishop for mentoring, practical recommendations for pastoral ministry, and biblical-theological education.

Most bishops had been educated in Greek and Roman schools, often in the fields of literature, rhetoric, and philosophy. They were

29. González, 7.

30. González, 14.

31. S. B. Babbage, "Church Officers," in Walter A. Elwell, ed., *Evangelical Dictionary of Theology* (Grand Rapids: Baker Book House, 1984), 244.

relatively learned people, although their education was secular. They received little or no formal instruction in the Bible, and were never formally students of theology. At the time, the church did not have a school for such instruction and training.

Bishops played an important role in filling the gap, by gathering around themselves small groups of pastors for formal instruction in the reading and interpretation of the Bible, the teaching and learning of the doctrinal teachings of faith, and the refutation of heresies. The needs of local congregations for the theological education of its members, and for educated clergy who were qualified and capable to provide it, were great. The bishops provided this education to meet these needs.

A few of these informal bishopric schools developed into major centers of Christian studies. The best known was Justin Martyr's school in Rome, which was patterned after the philosophical schools of his day. Other schools were located in Alexandria and Antioch.

These schools were not specifically dedicated to the training of pastors, or restricted to those who were preparing for ordained ministry. Their purpose was catechetical instruction within a larger purpose of inquiring into, clarifying, expounding, and defending the Christian theological tradition. Thus, many students were laypersons, who wished to know and understand more about the faith they confessed, along with an education in the sciences, mathematics, philosophy, and rhetoric. Pagans, or non-Christians, also attended in order to receive instruction in the secular disciplines, although they were often curious about Christianity, and wanted to add to their growing body of knowledge as a whole.

Of course, many ordained ministers came to these schools for their education, as well. Some later became bishops. However, the vast majority of clergy stayed home, did not attend a bishopric school, and thus remained either informally trained or largely illiterate.

Among the most eminent bishops were some of the greatest thinkers, teachers, and writers of the entire history of the church.[32]

---

32. These influential, intellectual bishops of the early church have come to be known as the "Church Fathers." The time-period in which they lived—from the closing of the New Testament writings (c. 100 CE) to the Council of Chalcedon (451 CE)—is called "the patristic period" (from the Latin word *patres*, meaning "fathers"). Generally, there are three groups of Fathers: (1) eight Apostolic Fathers

They made a serious attempt to express biblical and apostolic truth. They helped sort out the relationship between Christianity and Judaism, and negotiate the church's place in a complex, multicultural, hostile world. The church's faith had to be defended against its enemies, including both heretics (in the church), and hostile emperors and "cultural despisers" (outside the church). Somebody needed to plead for tolerance and protection of this new and different religion. Both false teachings and false charges of atheism, treason, sexual immorality, and even cannibalism had to be refuted. Therefore, the clerical bishops assumed the role of thinking through, shaping, and expressing the beliefs of the new faith centered in Christ, hoping that converts could be gained and disciples could be made.

During the early Middle Ages (c. 400–1000), monasteries became sites for theological scholarship. Monks retreated and formed small communities of study and devotion. While they still practiced the ascetic life, they turned this life into one devoted to the maintaining of the art of writing and reading, the study of the culture and letters of antiquity, the biblical literature and languages, and the translation of the Bible into Latin. These monasteries were "a refuge where ancient knowledge was preserved."[33] Persons who desired this knowledge went to live and study in these small communities.

Several monastic teacher-theologians were committed to the production of original Christian writings, and to the training of clergy in preparation for ministerial tasks. None was more prolific and influential than St. Augustine, Bishop of Hippo. Not only was he a major player in the theological disputes and decisions of his day, but also his teachings and writings were formative for Western theological and philosophical thought in the Middle Ages, and even

---

(including five writings): Clement of Rome, the *Didache,* Ignatius of Antioch, Polycarp of Smyrna, Papias of Hierapolis, the *Epistle of Barnabas,* the *Shepherd of Hermas,* and the *Epistle to Diognetus;* (2) Greek Fathers: Justin Martyr, Clement of Alexandria, Origen of Alexandria, Irenaeus of Lyons, Athanasius of Alexandria, the Cappadoccian Fathers (Basil the Great, Gregory of Nyssa, Peter of Sebaste, Gregory of Nazianzus), John Chrysostom, Maximus the Confessor, and John of Damascus; (3) Latin Fathers: Tertullian, Cyprian of Carthage, Hilary of Poitiers, Ambrose of Milan, Pope Damascus I, Gregory the Great, Augustine of Hippo, Jerome, and Isidore of Seville.

33. González, 24.

continue to shape Christian understanding, teaching, and writing today.[34]

In the high Middle Ages (c. 1001–1300), cathedral schools began to exceed the monastic schools in their numbers and importance. Just as monastic schools had been set up in monasteries, cathedral schools were set up in the cathedrals of Roman Catholicism. The latter were located in mainly urban areas, whereas the former had been in secluded regions, withdrawn from society and the world.

A major reason for cathedral schools was that Europe needed an educated clergy. These schools taught and trained candidates for the priesthood. However, many of the students who attended were not interested in pursuing a career in the church, nor in going into major monastic orders. They wanted the more diverse, advanced education that these schools provided in mathematics, astronomy, geometry, and music, as well as grammar, rhetoric, and logic. The curriculum was secular as well as sacred.

The advanced education of cathedral schools meant that teachers had to be qualified to provide such education. Some clergy were highly educated and qualified to be faculty, especially in the areas of biblical, theological, and ministerial studies. But highly educated, highly qualified non-clerics were also hired. The competition was fierce. So, naturally, those who became teachers were quite proud and ambitious. They took it upon themselves to seek more knowledge, and never to be satisfied with the knowledge they had. Therefore, they became scholars and researchers in their own work, in addition to being teachers in the classroom. Consequently, their students were trained in a more scholarly, research-oriented form of education.

Cathedral schools gradually evolved into what are now known as universities. This development took place during the late eleventh, twelfth, and early thirteenth centuries in Italy (the University of Bologna, 1088), England (Oxford University, 1096; the University of Cambridge, 1209), France (University of Paris, 1160–1250), and Spain (University of Salamanca, 1218).

These institutions existed for the study of the arts, law, medicine, and theology. In fact, from their beginning, universities played a

34. Augustine's two major works are *Confessions,* trans. Henry Chadwick (New York: Oxford University Press, 2009); and *City of God,* trans. Henry Bettenson (New York: Penguin, 2003).

significant role in Christian education. The education of the church, and specifically of its clergy, was largely provided by universities. Candidates for church offices were sent there for specialized, professional ministerial training. The professors were predominantly clergy, and thus, preaching, prayer, and celebration of the Mass were central to the life and work of these schools. Theology was considered to be "the queen of the sciences," or the ultimate subject, serving as the capstone of all other disciplines. The other areas of study, including philosophy, existed primarily to assist, clarify, and defend theology. Many students, who were not preparing to serve as ministers or pastors, came to the universities for theological learning in order to support their own intellectual and spiritual development as believers.

In the United States, several prominent colleges and universities were started in order to train Christian ministers. In 1636, only eight years after settling as the Massachusetts Bay Colony, the Puritans established Harvard College.[35] Other Puritan schools were the Collegiate School in Connecticut (Yale University), founded in 1701; and Dartmouth College, founded in 1769. The Church of England established the College of William and Mary in 1693, King's College (Columbia University) in 1754, and the College of Philadelphia (University of Pennsylvania) in 1755. The Presbyterians founded their own college, the College of New Jersey (Princeton University), in 1746. The first Catholic school of higher education, Georgetown University in Washington, D.C., was established in 1789. Baptists founded the College of Rhode Island (Brown University), 1764; and the first Southern Baptist college was Union University in Jackson, Tennessee, 1823.

---

35. For a history of the American university in relation to the Christian church, see George M. Marsden, *The Soul of the American University: From Protestant Establishment to Established Nonbelief* (New York: Oxford University Press, 1994); James Tunstead Burtchaell, *The Dying of the Light: The Disengagement of Colleges and Universities From Their Christian Churches* (Grand Rapids: William B. Eerdmans Publishing Company, 1998); Warren A. Nord, *Religion and American Education: Rethinking a National Dilemma* (Chapel Hill: The University of North Carolina Press, 1995); Douglas Sloan, *Faith and Knowledge: Mainline Protestantism and American Higher Education* (Louisville: Westminster John Knox Press, 1994); and Philip Gleason, *Contending with Modernity: Catholic Higher Education in the Twentieth Century* (New York: Oxford University Press, 1995).

The high purpose of higher education, as well as secondary education, in America was to nurture and sustain not only the church, but also a Christian civilization.[36] However, during the nineteenth and twentieth centuries, the preeminent, privileged place granted to Christian religion in the university came under increasing scrutiny. The European Enlightenment was reaching American shores and ushering our country into the age of modern science and reason. Professors and administrators began to question what role, if any, religious faith has (or should have) in the modern university.

Today, in the early twenty-first century, the answer is set and clear. The church has lost its established place and role in American higher education. Colleges and universities established under some kind of Christian patronage no longer have a relationship with the church or with their founding denominations. It is questionable whether some of them ever did.[37]

These schools are no longer considered responsible for, nor are they to play any role in, the religious instruction, piety, spiritual well-being, wisdom, or virtue of their students. Faculty are no longer required to be persons of either faith or ordained ministry, as they once were. In fact, such qualifications are more likely to disqualify a candidate for a teaching or research position. Academicians who are Christian believers are culturally pressured to keep quiet about their faith and the intellectual implications of their faith. The presumption is that education is better off without ancient religion and its teaching.[38] Authority has been taken away from Christian tradition, since it is no longer believed that tradition can be truth-bearing or life-relevant. Knowledge, then, is separated from faith, leaving the academy and church estranged.

In many colleges and universities today, a distinction is made between theology and "religious studies." The academy has little to no doubt that theology is not a serious intellectual discipline. It is suspect because it is viewed as involving a pre-commitment of faith to a religious tradition, which makes claims to truth.

---

36. Nord, 63.

37. Burtchaell, xi.

38. George M. Marsden, *The Outrageous Idea of Christian Scholarship* (New York: Oxford University Press, 1977), 4. Marsden (1939–) is Emeritus Professor of History at the University of Notre Dame.

By contrast, the academic field of religious studies sets aside both faith-commitments and the question of truth. Traditional faith is repudiated. Instead, the objective is phenomenal description, or merely describing the *phenomena*, or acts, events, language, rituals, and beliefs of religion. Many religions and spiritualities, including Christianity, are examined, but only as data.

For example, totem poles and their religious significance for the indigenous peoples of the Pacific Northwest coast may be researched. Ancestor worship among Buddhists of Myanmar, or the poetry of the Navajo Indians, may be studied. The scientific methods and tools of modern/postmodern history, linguistics, sociology, anthropology, race, and gender studies are used for this study. But any move beyond this "objective, critical" research is considered to be a move into the territory of theology, and thus is quite improper and suspect.

So what happens to theology, now that the university does not want it? Clearly, theology is unable to defend, justify, and maintain its place in the modern universities, despite the fact that, centuries earlier, it gave birth to these universities. One solution is to tuck theology away in the corner of the university's religious studies department. Another is to create separate housing for the school's founding purpose and subject matter, by relegating theology and its various studies to affiliated, constituent schools, called "divinity schools" (e.g., Harvard Divinity School and Duke Divinity School).

The most common approach is to leave theology to non-university schools called "seminaries." Some of these schools are established and supported by church denominations (e.g., The Southern Baptist Theological Seminary, Louisville, Kentucky, and Union Presbyterian Seminary, Richmond, Virginia), while others are evangelical, multi- or non-denominational (e.g., Asbury Theological Seminary, Wilmore, Kentucky, and Gordon-Conwell Theological Seminary, Hamilton, Massachusetts).

These are the "hamlets" that have emerged, developed, and continue to exist at the few remaining crossroads where the academy and the church still intersect. Their locations, however, vary. Some are located nearer to or directly on the Berlin Turnpike (the academy and higher education). Others are located nearer to or directly on the Nashville Road, Trent Road, or Canterbury Road (the church, a particular denomination, or some spiritual-moral movement of Christian religion).

The coordinates of these schools are not fixed, but are fluid and dynamic. These are living institutions made up of living people in living relations with the living traditions of higher education and religion, culture and church, science and faith. Therefore, theological schools are always shifting toward the academy or the church; or further away from one or the other; or further away from both.

In any case, it would be wrong to assume that the seminary is close to where local congregations or ordinary Christians reside. The seminary is the "far country." Therefore, the individual believer, who stands to have any chance of meeting theology, has to leave his or her home. What do we say? "He (or she) is going to the seminary."

Even if a person takes seminary courses online, he has to look elsewhere, beyond his home congregation, to a school that offers these courses. He must enter a program of study that is not part of the life and work of his congregation, or participated in by any Christian family member or friend he knows. Congregational religious education and seminary theological education are worlds apart, and have been for a very long time.

This estrangement should seem odd and unacceptable to us. Aren't both the seminary and the local community of faith vital parts of the same church—the whole church? The congregation and its members, however, are not near the part of the church where theology is, and where theological education takes place. Likewise, the seminary and its education are not near the part of the church where the vast majority of Christians are, and where everyday, ordinary faith-existence takes place.

Consequently, laypersons are not exposed to or introduced to theology where they live. They will likely never be exposed or introduced. Theology simply is not there except in a residual way, as I will discuss in the next chapter. It is "not from around here." Therefore, if or when theology is brought here, it will always appear to be foreign and forbidding.

How could it be otherwise? The local congregation has lived almost its entire history apart from its own theology and theology's education. Although early on, theology was born and raised in the communities formed by and devoted to the teaching of the apostles, this symbiotic relationship did not last long. While there were good, understandable reasons for theology being handed over to the bishops, then the monks and priests, and finally the professors, the downside is the distancing of theology and its education from the part of the church where almost all Christians live—the local congregation. Therefore, if a Christian wants to meet, come to know, and have a relationship with his or her own theological faith-tradition, this Christian must intentionally leave his or her own local congregation, pay tuition, and become a member of the only community that is still interested in and dedicated to theology and theology's education (i.e., the seminary or divinity school).

Of course, the plan all along has been for a few individuals to be sent to these schools where theology lives, to meet and come to know theology there, and then return home where they will teach theology to their entire communities. Those who are illiterate will become literate in order to come back and help other illiterate persons become literate, as well. Then the whole church will be capable of reading, writing, speaking, and living theologically.

Let's be honest. This plan is not working, and has not for a very long time. First, rarely does anyone from any given congregation undertake a seminary education. Second, rarely does a seminary student receive an adequate theological education, and thereby come to know and understand theology well. Third, rarely does the student, after graduation, return to the local congregation with a calling to teach, and equipped with enough theological wisdom to be capable of teaching others. Fourth, rarely do congregational members open the doors of their house to theological education, even when it is offered by their pastor.

If, on a rare occasion, theology is brought from the seminary back home, the welcome mat is not out.

3
Homecoming

The son who left home and returned was given the royal treatment. "Quickly," his father shouted, overcome with joy, "Bring out a robe —the best one—and put it on him. Put a ring on his finger and sandals on his feet. Get the fatted calf and butcher it. Let us eat and celebrate. My son was dead and is alive again. He was lost and is found!" The entire household began to celebrate—everyone, that is, except the father's first son, the prodigal's older brother.[1]

When I returned home after seven years in the far country of the seminary, there was no extravagant celebration. No party, no band, and no BBQ. Just a small reception in the fellowship hall with store-bought pound cake and Baptist punch.

I did not complain, however, since I did not consider my homecoming to be that big a deal. Unlike the prodigal son, I had not been dead or lost, but only away at school. Besides, new ministers are always welcomed with warm smiles and affirming words, followed by a pleasant, though short-lived "honeymoon."

Nonetheless, I did expect a more open, enthusiastic reception for what I was bringing home with me. I was not returning alone. Surely, I thought to myself, the congregation and its members will recognize

1. This is my rendering of the homecoming in Jesus' parable in Luke 15:11-32. Most reading focuses on the prodigal son's sinful departure (vs. 11-16), ending with his return to and reconciliation with his father (vs. 17-24). Seldom do readers, teachers, and preachers continue with the same level of interest in the refusal of the father's older son to participate in the homecoming celebration (vs. 25-32). I contend that the latter section is especially relevant and instructive for congregations and Christians today.

my companion, theology, and be beside themselves in joy. "We thought you were dead, but you are alive again! You were lost, but now you are found! Let us eat and celebrate!"

But that did not happen. It never happened in any of the congregations where I showed up at the door and introduced theology. Instead, what struck me was the non-response. The non-recognition. The blank look. Nothing.

I would have settled for someone saying in redneck drawl, "Well, look what the cat dragged in!"[2] At least there would have been some acknowledgement of the "vermin" I was bringing into their house. "Now what do we have here? Theology? That's nice."

For those who don't speak or understand the Southern language of "nice," here's the translation: "What are you doing, bringing THAT in here, to us, in our house? I know you found it, or met it while you were away. Students pick up all kinds of things at school. But you need to take it back to where you found it right now. However, if you insist on bringing it in and keeping it, we—being the good Christian folks that we are—will smile and be polite. We won't say anything, while passive-aggressively making sure it never feels welcomed or at home here. We can only hope you will soon lose interest and let go of this little hobby you picked up at the seminary. Keep it to yourself, and don't let it interfere with your real ministry. There are more immediate, more important matters for you to be concerned with in this house. There's work to be done. We have a youth retreat for you to lead this weekend (oh, yeah, we must have forgotten to tell you about it), Sunday School teachers need to be recruited, and the next church newsletter has to be put together and mailed. Welcome back home, servant."

---

2. A domestic cat will often bring indoors a bird or rodent that it has captured or killed outdoors. Once when my family and I were away on vacation, our cat brought a live bird into the house through the cat-flap in the basement door. We returned to find feathers and excrement everywhere. "Look what the cat dragged in" took on real meaning. I think of the good parent who is always on alert for what his or her young child might "drag in" from school or friends: a word of profanity, or a rebellious attitude. Parents of college students worry about who or what their sons and daughters might bring home during a holiday or summer break: an undesirable boyfriend or girlfriend, a foreign ideology or religion, a lifestyle of immoral behavior. Strangely, in my experience, congregations and Christians include theology in this watch-list of foreign, unwelcomed, undesirable "guests."

Can Theology Go Home Again?

Robert Frost and Thomas Wolfe offer differing views of home. Frost wrote in his poem "The Death of the Hired Man" that home is the place where the folks living there have to take you in. Wolfe countered with the title of his novel: *You Can't Go Home Again*.[3]

The local congregation had to take me in. It was home. I was born and raised there—as one of their own. I was one of them. I was a native son. Besides, I was freshly seminary-seasoned and certifiably employable, ready to serve them. Where else could I go, and what else could I do?

Six local congregations took me in along the way. Each was a place where, when I had to go there, they had to take me in. It was home.

However, I discovered that "taking in" does not necessarily mean "embracing, fully accepting, and rejoicing," especially when I came back changed and accompanied. Yes, they had to take me in; but they did not have to like it, or like what I had become. And they did not have to take in my companion called "theology."

Never mind that theology was born in, by, and for the church; that the church has been and still is built by and for theology; and that the local congregation was once theology's home. Today, congregations and Christians have no awareness or remembrance of that. As far as they are concerned, theology is the stranger who must be met with suspicion: "You aren't from around here, are you?" Or, borrowing the language Jesus used about himself, theology is "the prophet who is not accepted in the prophet's hometown."[4]

This has been my experience in every congregation I have served. No exception. I do not believe that by a long streak of bad luck I somehow have always managed to end up in the wrong or the worst congregations. Exactly half of the congregations I served were good, relatively healthy, holy, religious communities. But this should not be taken to mean that they were theologically formed and engaged, or were open and receptive to theological education and to living the Christian theological life. They were not.

3. Robert Frost, "The Death of the Hired Man," *North of Boston* (New York: Henry Holt and Company, 1914), 20. Thomas Wolfe, *You Can't Go Home Again* (New York: HarperPerennial, 1998; originally published in 1940).

4. Luke 4:24.

Also, we assume that somewhere out there in this broad land of ours, there are congregations that are theologically strong and solid. To my knowledge, there are not. Theological eclipse, or absence, is the general condition of Christian communities and individuals in the Western world today. Local congregations simply are not known to be theological places.

During my pastoral career, I accepted this condition, although I was determined to change it. I proceeded under the assumption that most Christian folks are generally committed and earnest people. If given the opportunity—along with enough good, solid theological preaching and teaching on my part, over enough time—they would all eventually wake up from their slumber, come around, and begin paying attention and being interested, wondering what it was their pastor kept talking about. They would begin to desire and seek theological education, and eventually get into the habit of learning and embodying their own theological faith-tradition.

That never happened, except with a very small number of believers. No matter how long, consistently, or well I taught theology and preached theological sermons, only one congregation somewhat cracked open its doors a little, allowed theology to come in and stay, and took some responsibility for it. In the rest, not even the elder brothers and sisters joined in the homecoming—the church staff and deacons, Sunday School teachers and missions leaders, church council and finance committee members, women's Bible study group and men's breakfast fellowship. They never exclaimed about theology, "Kill the fatted calf! Strike up the band. We thought you were dead, but you are alive again! You were lost, but now you are found! Let us eat and celebrate!"

Why not? This situation should baffle and concern us, since we are the church; and the church, by nature, identity, and purpose, is a theological community. Theology is ours. It is our birthright and inheritance. Our very being, or mode of existence, is by and for faith, which is theological. Therefore, in a very real sense, we belong to and derive our lives from theology.

We should be all the more baffled and concerned by the fact that this situation does not baffle and concern us in the least. Why not? Why are our local congregations no longer the place where theology, when it is taken there, will not be taken in? What is it about us and our religious communities that makes it impossible for theology to go home again?

Can We Imagine the Condition of Our House?

Alasdair MacIntyre opens his major book *After Virtue* with a story about a series of environmental disasters occurring around the world. The general public blames the catastrophe on the scientists. Riots break out. Research facilities and laboratories are destroyed. Books are burned. Scientists are arrested, imprisoned, and executed. The teaching of science is forbidden in schools and universities. And an anti-science Know Nothing Party comes into political power.[5]

This tale sounds like something a science fiction writer would write, doesn't it? We have lived so long in a world where science flourishes and dominates the social-cultural worldview and everyday existence that we cannot imagine things being otherwise. Surely such a major catastrophe could never occur in our country. At the first sign of uprising, we would spring into action and take whatever steps would be necessary to stop it and keep science in its rightful place.

But let's stay with MacIntyre's story. Science has been stripped of its authority and power, and people are living unscientifically, if not anti-scientifically. Imagine living in a world where such a disaster has occurred.

As time goes on, a few people become dissatisfied with the current state of things. They remember the earlier glory days of science. They can still recall some of its teachings and accomplishments. They are enlightened enough to know that the anti-science movement is wrong and deadly. And they care enough about the world, its people, and themselves to push back against the status quo and to resist the Know Nothing Party. Eventually, a revolution breaks out, as these rebels attempt to revive science and return it to its former place of prominence.

---

5. Alasdair MacIntyre, *After Virtue: A Study in Moral Theory*, 3rd ed. (Notre Dame, Indiana: University of Notre Dame Press, 2007), 1–5. MacIntyre (1929–) is Emeritus Professor of Philosophy at the University of Notre Dame. His book *After Virtue* is widely recognized as one of the most important contributions to moral philosophy in the twentieth century.

The problem is that they have very little to go on. Remember: the books, equipment, places, and practitioners of science have been destroyed. The teaching of science is forbidden.

Nevertheless, from memory and from what few pieces they had managed to save, or can find, they cobble together a set of teachings and practices. Courses are taught under the revived names of physics, chemistry, and biology. Children once again memorize and recite the surviving portions of the periodical table. They study the theorems of the one or two famous scientists, such as Euclid. Adults continue to use scientific words and expressions. They argue about relativity theory and evolutionary theory, not realizing that they have only a partial knowledge and understanding of what they are talking about. There is great rejoicing and pride that science has been brought back, and their world is again scientific.

However, they are not as successful as they think. Despite their sincere, courageous, and strong efforts, what they have revived and restored is not science. It is a mere resemblance of science—what MacIntyre calls "false simulacra of natural science."[6]

In other words, science *after* the destruction of science is not science as it was *before* the destruction. The two—before and after—are not the same thing. The revived version looks and sounds like science, based on what little people remember, know, and have to go on regarding science. But it is not science—at least not science as science once was and truly is.

First, all these revolutionary-revivalists have to work with are scraps of knowledge, bits and pieces of theory, and a few shreds of practice. Most have not been retrieved. Second, these fragments are scattered and disordered, like random pieces of a jigsaw puzzle scattered out on the floor. Some fit, while most are merely assembled to look as though they fit and can be connected. Third, the "whole," or big picture, of science is missing. The original context, in which the few remaining scientific words, theories, and practices once made sense, has been lost.

---

6. MacIntyre, 2. A "simulacrum" (plural, "simulacra") is an appearance, image, copy, or representation of an original. It may be a good, faithful copy. Or it may be a poor, unfaithful copy; or even a copy that has nothing to do the original at all, while misrepresenting it and substituting itself as real in the place of the original.

Yet, these good, enlightened folks do not realize any of this. They cannot imagine that what they are doing in their world is not science, but merely a truncated, damaged, and disordered form of science. This is because they can no longer imagine what science really is, or was. The old-timers have forgotten, and the youngsters have never known.

This is a very disturbing and depressing story that MacIntyre tells, isn't it? Thankfully, to our great relief, he soon informs us that he has been only telling a fictional story about an imaginary world. No major catastrophe occurred. Science is still science, and still in charge. Everybody can relax, let out a sigh of relief, and sleep well at nights. We are safe.

But then, as soon as MacIntyre has reassured us, he alarms us again. He reveals that he has told us this fictional story in order to set us up for hearing another story, which is a true story, and an even more unbelievable, more alarming story.[7] In our modern Western world, science has not been lost; but morality has. The great disaster of the Enlightenment has occurred, and it has erased our knowledge, understanding, and embodiment of past moral tradition. Now we are in a state of grave disorder.

We have only a few remaining words, phrases, beliefs, values, and practices of morality, but most are still missing. What pieces we do have are scattered and disordered. They do not fit into or comprise a comprehensive, coherent moral system. We have lost the whole. We no longer have the capacity to draw moral resources from a rich moral tradition, to use moral language, to be guided by moral reasoning, and to define and conduct our relations to others in moral terms. Also, we have filled in the gaps with modern inventions and subjectivist, emotivist[8] preferences. Yet, we have no clue that what we have created are merely our own "false simulacra of morality."

Of course, when we hear this, we want to protest. We cannot imagine that our world is without morality, any more than we can

7. MacIntyre, 2.

8. Emotivism is the ethical theory that all value judgments, or moral judgments, are nothing but expressions of feelings, attitudes, preferences, desires, or needs. I believe emotivism is also theological, when a community's or an individual's beliefs are basically expressions of what these persons happen to be valuing, preferring, feeling, desiring, or needing at the time. MacIntyre, 11–12.

imagine it being without science. Besides, aren't we awash in a sea of many and various moralities? Aren't moral values taught in our homes, schools, congregations, and team sports? Aren't most people good, decent moral human beings?

We are oblivious to the radical changes that have occurred to the moral tradition and to ourselves over the past five hundred or more years. Nobody, or almost nobody, realizes that what they are doing is not morality in any proper, full sense of that term. Our condition is invisible to us. We have for too long been too deeply entrenched in it.

Consequently, if the moral tradition were to be rediscovered, we would not recognize it ("doesn't look or sound like morality, or seem moral, to us"). We would strongly resist its return and revival in our house, for, in our view, we already are moral people, who have our own morality. Ironically, on moral grounds, we reject our own moral tradition. Therefore, all we can conclude is that "we are all already in a state so disastrous that there are no large remedies for it."[9]

I am grateful to MacIntyre for "tricking" us into considering the grave disorder of morality in our actual world, by first telling us the story of the loss of science in an imaginary world. Otherwise, we would be unable and unwilling to imagine our loss of morality.

I believe this type of storytelling needs to be taken to the church. Imagine that the historical-biblical-theological tradition of Christian faith has been lost as a result of a series of changes over a long period of time—changes that were perceived as good, necessary, natural, and inevitable. Because a few theological words, beliefs, and practices remain, we Christians assume that our denominations, congregations, agencies, and personal lives are theological. Theology is thought to be alive and well.

However, we have largely, if not entirely, lost our capacity to use theological language, to reason theologically, to view the world and relate to others in theological terms, and to live, move, and have our being theologically. What we possess are "false simulacra of theology," and what we are doing is not theology in any proper, full sense of that term. Yet, we are unable to know this, because we no longer have the whole Christian theological faith-tradition, by which to

9. MacIntyre, 5.

comprehend and compare. We cannot imagine what this tradition might be, or how a theological community might think, talk, and live, and thus, what a disastrous state we truly are in as the church.

Of course, the immediate reaction is disbelief. No one can grasp it, or even imagine it. Such a situation is too bizarre and implausible. If there were a problem, wouldn't we have noticed it? Surely our pastors and leaders would have told us if anything were wrong. But we have not heard a word.

Where is the evidence? Widespread riots have not taken place in the pews. Seminaries have not been burned down, or Sunday Schools closed. Pastors have not been persecuted, or theologians put in jail and executed. Bibles and religious books have not been destroyed, nor the teaching of theology abolished. Everything seems perfectly fine and normal to us.

Therefore, the messenger must be sounding a false alarm, or crying, "Wolf!" We cannot imagine the condition of our house being anything other than theologically sound.

What Is Going On In This House?

Jesus told parables about an estate owner who left his stewards in charge of his household or vineyard while he was away.[10] When he returned home, he found some of his stewards being faithful and prudent. But others were found unfaithful and foolish. They were not being trustworthy with what their master had entrusted to them during his absence.

These stories beg the question: What's going on in our house, the church, and with us as stewards? Given that this house is in the world to house theology, how is theology faring here under our watch? Is theology alive and well? Flourishing? Are you and I being faithful, prudent, trustworthy, and responsible as its servants?

The congregations I have lived and worked among would all answer: "Yes, theology is good here. We are taking good care of it." However, their lack of knowledge, understanding, interest, and

10. Luke 12:42–48; Matthew 24:45–51; Luke 16:1–18; and Luke 20:9–19; Matthew 21:33–46; Mark 12:1–12.

involvement would disclose a different, far more unfaithful situation. They have little to no idea what theology is, much less what it transmits and teaches. They are the least theological people, despite being some of the most wonderful, loving, religiously committed, and good people around. How can theology *not* be flourishing in their houses?

I have always been perplexed by this situation. Why are the minds of congregations and Christians closed to the very reality for which they are called and created? In the house intentionally built of, by, and for theology, why won't its residents at least entertain the idea of taking theology in, being its home again, and being faithful to God regarding it?

I have struggled with this situation for decades. I have struggled for an explanation. The best I have been able to come up with is that this is simply the way it is after theology has been sent away and distanced from the local congregation in schools for centuries. Centuries!

Also, the Western world in which church now exists is post-Christian, as well as modern and postmodern. Our world has worked long and hard not to be a theological world. Consequently, without ordered, ongoing theological education, Christians and their congregations cannot possibly be sustained by the Christian theological faith-tradition. Nor will this tradition be sustained by Christians and congregations.

I used to view the local congregation as an empty place. There was a great void, or vacuum, where theology was supposed to be, but was missing. Picture the bedroom of a son or daughter who is away at college. The room is kept just as it was left, with nothing touched or changed. It is not turned into an exercise gym for Mom, or a home theater for Dad, or passed on to a younger sibling, who needs a bigger room. This room remains as it always has been, except that it is empty, waiting for the day when the college graduate returns home as a "boomerang kid," to live under the same roof with his parents again, until he gets a job and makes enough money to find a place of his own.

This mental picture, I now realize, is wrong when it comes to the local congregation. I have learned through pastoral experience that Jesus provided a far better, more accurate image in his parable about the unclean spirit that left a person. It wandered homelessly in "waterless regions"—dry places, uninhabited deserts, off-grid in the wilderness—for a time, looking for a new resting place. Finding none, this unclean spirit went back to its original house. Not only was nobody home, but the entire place was also empty. It had no furniture or furnishings. It was swept and in order. Inviting. Whoever moved in could do with the place whatever she liked. She could put her personal touches on it, and make it her own.

Therefore, the unclean spirit went back to the desert, rounded up seven other spirits—more unclean and evil than it was—and led them back to take up residence in the empty house. The place was so empty, so inviting, and open to so many creative possibilities.

Jesus concluded his story with these haunting words: "The last state of that person is worse than the first. So will it be also with this evil generation." (Matthew 12:43–45; Luke 11:24–26)

The church, like nature, abhors a vacuum. It will always be full. If emptied, it will be quickly filled again. If genuine theology is stored in a back closet of the church, or sent off to the university or seminary, then something else will soon take its place and give the church its fullness. So I ask: "If not theology, then what are local congregations and their members full of today?"

Let's use the favorite child's finger-play as a guide: "Here's the church; here's the steeple; open the doors; and see all the people." You and I were taught this little rhyme and activity as children, and we have taught it to our children and grandchildren. It states that the church is first a building and then a social group. No wonder, then, that all of us say things like, "I am going to church today"—meaning that I will travel to a physical structure, enter it, and associate inside with human beings.

Note what is missing. There is nothing in our demonstration about religion: worship, Bible study, prayer, *koinonia*, or pastoral care. This is odd. The church is simply a building with a steeple, housing a bunch of people.

If we catch what we are saying, or are questioned, we begin to speak more carefully and completely. We downplay the bricks and mortar part by saying, "The church is not the building, but the people."

Yet, have we moved any closer to a proper definition of the church? When the church is defined simply as people, the implication is that it is just another local assembly, social gathering, friendship group, human institution, community, family ("church family"), or people-helping-people agency. For all anyone knows, this could be a group of train enthusiasts or speed-dating seniors.

Also, does anyone think it odd that the image of the church we give our children lacks God and Jesus? The Scriptures? Theology? Nothing here in our fingers or our words identifies the church as a theological community, or a body of believers embodying the truth made known in the tradition that was formed and continues to be formed around Christ. Therefore, we are left to assume that this building has been built to house people who are not consciously or necessarily here for theology. What, then, brings them "to church"?

Open the door and see all the people, as well all that they are doing. The building is alive with events, programs, and projects. Every day the calendar is packed with activities. There is something for everyone, of every age and every life situation. Consequently, if or when theology is brought home, there simply is no room for it. The room where it once lived, and is supposed to live, has been turned over to many other occupants and other uses. The big flashing "No Vacancy" sign out front has been on for so long, some of the bulbs are burned out. And the sign itself is rusty and barely hanging on its hinges.

In short, no one inside has time for this newcomer, since the entire household is already too busy. Add to this the many, pressing tasks, responsibilities, and demands in members' personal lives every single day, and the odds of welcoming and taking theology in are down near zero. Theology cannot get its foot in the door, much less gain a hearing, despite the fact that it is the reason for these people, their community, and their building.

Why, then, are this building and these people here? The question is its own answer: for the building and the people. The child's fingerplay has it right. Both the building and the people require a lot of attention, time, energy, and money. Meetings upon meetings are held to count the money and the members; maintain, clean, repair, and enlarge the physical plant; manage day-to-day operations; and keep people active and satisfied with the lineup of religious goods and services, social services, therapies, socialization, and secular activities being offered.

Granted, the congregation, as the local manifestation of the body of Christ, is an actual human body. As such, it has numerous human, physical, needs, including shelter. Whether it is a massive cathedral, a quaint chapel, an industrial building, a small store-space in a strip mall, or someone's living room, the community of faith must be sheltered and housed. This requires leased or purchased space, lights and indoor plumbing, heating and air-conditioning, furnishing, cleaning, maintenance and repairs, and eventually renovation. All of this costs money.

Also, the congregation needs someone in the role of pastor. This person may be elected from among the membership and not be paid. However, a community larger than a few dozen members will need someone who can be more firmly in place and "on call," either part-time or full-time. This requires a salary, housing allowance, and health insurance. If the congregation calls a seminary-trained, experienced pastor, then the cost increases. The larger congregation demands more ministers, as well as more buildings.

The result is a lot of fiscal pressure on the congregation to "stay in business" and "keep its doors open." I cannot tell you how many times I have heard these expressions. Only a few rare congregations are endowed, or supported heavily by one or two wealthy patrons. Most are dependent on the relatively small, periodic, voluntary contributions of many members. Therefore, in order to exist, a congregation must maintain the loyalty, enthusiasm, mutual harmony, contentment, and charity of these members, who are its donors. In other words, the staff and lay leaders must keep everybody happy—and giving!

The paramount issue, then, is money. Practically no one will admit it, and, if pressed, will deny it. Yet, this is what committee and monthly business meetings are almost always and exclusively about. This is what leaders think and talk about. This is what they worry about. What they do not worry about is theology.

"Stewardship," then, has become a matter of the budget, not a matter of the gospel. "Church growth" does not mean "equipping the saints for the work of ministry, for building up the body of Christ, until all of us come to the unity of the faith and of the knowledge of the Son of God, to maturity, to the full measure of the stature of Christ." (Ephesians 4:12–13)

While this might be useful as a campaign slogan, the campaign is conducted for recruiting more people (never seniors, but always young people and young families with children and teens), growing the membership rolls, and increasing the annual operating budget.

Money.

I can understand and accept this, to the extent that all institutions are human, and thus mortal, weak, and vulnerable to decline and death. Congregations have a deep, visceral awareness of their fragility, and constantly fear for their future. This is especially keen in our present age when more and more people are religiously "nones," and not looking for or attending local Christian congregations.

Anything can happen: demographic changes in the local neighborhood; a regional or national economic recession; the pastor is caught having an affair; the treasurer embezzles funds; parents don't like the youth minister; somebody says something that offends somebody else; a religious movement—fundamentalism, Pentecostalism, or progressivism—gets a foothold; members idolize a favorite minister and form the congregation around his personality and ministry; the environment becomes toxic due to one or two emotionally disturbed members; or unrest and conflict are caused by three or four bullies attempting a takeover of power.

Finally, natural attrition constantly threatens a congregation. Members are always leaving: "ghosting" and slowly drifting away; becoming dissatisfied about something and going to look for a better fit elsewhere; accepting a new job in another town and moving away; divorcing (one or both spouses divorce the congregation); and becoming ill and/or homebound. And, of course, members are always dying on us. Every pastor knows that every single member sitting before his or her preaching and teaching will one day be gone—and so will the pastor. Every corporate body is vulnerable to so many diseases, illnesses, injuries, and deaths that its membership pool must be continually restocked.

All of this puts tremendous, relentless pressure on the local congregation to provide a wide mix of activities that will attract and retain members. Surveys are common, asking, "What do you need? What would you like?" As the budget allows, the congregation will do everything in its power to give people what they say they want. The agenda is dedicated to programming—maintaining the programs we already have, while adding more—for all ages from cradle to grave, and for a wide range of socio-cultural groups, including singles, seniors, young mothers, and recovering alcoholics.

When considering a new program, the main questions are how well it will be received and supported, and whether it will meet the desires and needs of members and prospective members. Very rarely does theology prompt the idea of such a program as ministry, much less then guide the decision, the formation of the activity, and the practice of the activity. Theology may be brought in after the fact to lend religious credence and political support. However, even this use of theology is becoming less common in congregations today.

Various sub-groups form around these programs. These are social friendship groups and special interest groups. They often become semi-autonomous sub-congregations within the larger congregation, having their own cultures, identities, purposes, and agendas. They also have their own religious and social activities, added to the congregational calendar that is already packed with ball games, movie nights, exercise classes, financial management seminars, child daycare, and small group Bible studies. Members always have something to do, and someone to do it with.

Feeling the need to help somebody less fortunate? We've got a workday coming up for that next weekend. Want to experience the Great Commission firsthand? Sign up for our missions trip to Belize this summer. How do you like your worship? We offer traditional, contemporary, Celtic, jazz, and bluegrass services. Take your pick. Try them all.

In sum, the local congregation has become a marketplace of goods and services, extending far beyond the ones typically thought of as Christian, or even religious. People today are viewed and treated consumeristically, i.e., as customers. They are, after all, "shopping for a church," and asking, "What does your church have to offer me and my family?"

Practically anything will be offered to them, if it is believed that it will cause them to turn aside, come, join the congregation, and stock the programs (and contribute their money) so that more programs can be offered. Congregations that are considered effective and successful, and thus lifted up as examples of "excellence" or "best practices," are those that stay competitive in both religious and secular markets, and keep more and more people coming, interested and involved. These are the congregations that are "working," and that are "growing."

The first question I am almost always asked about my congregation is, "Are you growing?" My usual response about theological and spiritual growth, I'm sure, indicates to the questioner that I must not have heard or understood his question. Or, I am evading it, since I must be ashamed of the fact that we aren't adding new members.

It has always seemed odd to me that every activity, no matter what that activity may be, is called "ministry." Standing in the hallway, talking casually over a cup of coffee, is ministry. Congregations have "golf ministry," "holy yoga ministry," and "Trunk-or-Treat ministry" (on Halloween, children get candy out of car trunks in the parking lot).

All of these activities collectively are viewed as "church." This is what members expect. This is what they are paying for. Therefore, strip away some of these things, or no longer be able to afford them, and watch how many people continue coming to "church" for its "ministry." Offer them theology, its education and life, and they will respond, "What's that?" They will be truly perplexed and dissatisfied, if "that" (theology) is all the congregation offers them.

The chief role of the pastor in this contemporary consumerist congregation is something called "transformational leader." This term basically means that the pastor is expected to produce major change in the life of the congregation and in the lives of its members, helping them to advance to a higher level of morale and motivation that will propel them to a higher level of congregational performance and success, as well as personal fulfillment and satisfaction.

How, then, do we know whether such "transformation" is taking place? By increased performance and success. How, then, are performance and success measured? By increased numerical growth in membership and money, as well as by the energy and satisfaction levels of the members.

The pastor as leader is expected to "run the church" with sound business practices, great people skills, and natural charisma. He or she must function as the storekeeper, who keeps the shelves stocked with the latest-greatest programs, keeps the customers coming, and keeps the shareholders happy. This forces the pastor into "being all things to all people," having the impossible job of CEO, head of marketing, sales, finances, and product development, on top of worship leader, preacher, wedding and funeral officiant, hospital and home visitor, conflict and crisis manager, comforter and counselor, friend, and all-around good person. There is neither time nor energy left over for being a theologian or teacher.

So, we open the door of the building, and ask, "What is going on in this house?" The answer—usually given with great pride—is, "Plenty. Lots of stuff. Practically anything and everything. You name it, we've got it. Come join us and see for yourself."

Yet, what is inconspicuously silent or absent? Christian theology. Theological education is nowhere on the congregation's "must have" or "need to do" list. It is not a common interest, felt need, or big draw. Nor is it on individual believers' or church members' minds. Their own lives are too full and hectic. Like their congregations, they are busy and preoccupied with too many other things to bother with the theological life.

This is not to say that there is absolutely no theology whatsoever in either the congregation's life or the Christian's life. As I have said, fragments of a former tradition can still be found; but these are relatively few in number. Most fragments are missing, along with their original configuration of truth and meaning. The "whole" has been lost. The framework to which all these fragments belong, and from which they receive their proper definition and significance, no longer exists, or is no longer known. Therefore, no complete theological system is available to order these fragments, or to order the lives of human persons, individually or corporately, who possess them.

Human beings cannot exist without some system that gives order and meaning to their lives. If they do not have, know, or understand the Christian theological system, they will find another. Today in our context of radical individualism, they most likely will create one, or make one up. It is fashionable now for folks to design and construct their own religious, spiritual, and moral systems. They combine what few Christian theological fragments they may have with fragments from other sources in order to put together a set of beliefs and values that best suits, supports, and expresses their own religiousness, spiritual sense, or moral preference.

A major contribution of MacIntyre's story is his insight that the world where science has been lost and then later restored, has not actually restored science, but only pieced together and put into operation "false simulacra of natural science." In a similar way, the modern world, having lost morality, is satisfied with "false simulacra of morality."

Likewise, the church without theology does not and cannot remain an empty place for long. It is occupied and taken over by many things. And found among them are "false simulacra of theology"—false, unfaithful copies of Christian faith's theological tradition.

Theological words and doctrinal fragments remain, like fingerprints and other forensic evidence left behind at a crime scene. Some Christians, like CSI technicians, find these fragments and sift through them, trying to decipher them. Most people ignore them. Others, realizing that what they have is fragmentary and inadequate, bring in pieces from all sorts of religions, spiritualities, pieties, moralities, psychologies, and ideologies, in order to fill in the gaps and possibly provide a structure for the entire self-made project.

While Christianity may be the major contributor, there are other fragments from other religious sources, such as Zen Buddhism and New Age neo-paganism. Additional components come from modern and postmodern worldviews, popular culture, popular science, folk wisdom, common sense, current ideology, political correctness, spirituality, piety, morality or immorality, what's trending on social media, and ever-changing personal preferences. Nothing or almost nothing is off-limits, or automatically ineligible for inclusion in one's system.

Quite often these non-Christian and non-theological fragments override the Christian theological ones, and become the dominant, defining, ordering parts of the entire system. Rarely, however, does the individual know or acknowledge this. She is unaware of her sources, and cares little that foreign beliefs and values are being brought into Christianity, and even taking over. She likely will simply call it "my Christian faith."[11]

---

11. For a study of "expressive individualism" in religion, see Robert N. Bellah, et al., *Habits of the Heart: Individualism and Commitment in American Life* (New York: Harper & Row Publishers, 1985). Bellah (1927–2013) was the Elliott Professor of Sociology at the University of California, Berkeley.

Years ago on Easter Sunday morning in Charlottesville, a member of my pastor's class asked me where reincarnation fits in our faith. I answered, "It doesn't." She protested. I went on to explain that we believe in and proclaim resurrection. Reincarnation and resurrection are entirely different interpretations of life and death. They cannot fit into the same belief system. Because God raised Jesus from death, giving him new life, our theological faith-tradition is constructed around resurrection. Reincarnation has no place in our faith.

Her response? "Well, it does in mine." I would not have been so taken back had this individual been a UVA undergraduate. Students are blatant syncretists. But she was a woman in her seventies!

Finally, this "strange brew" gets even stranger (and stronger) with the addition of many and various "isms" of this present secular age: individualism, humanism, relativism, pluralism, hedonism, narcissism, consumerism, Marxism, naturalism, and nihilism—to name a few. The result is a strange bricolage, or kind of creative mix-and-match, do-it-yourself, personalized, all-in-one, patchwork quilt religious-spiritual construction.

Each Christian has his or her distinctive "blend." So does every congregation, and also every small group within it. All consider themselves and their created religions to be "Christian," despite their questionable sources, incompatible parts, confused order, and disparate outcomes that are irreconcilable with either traditional Christian religion or theology. At some point, these systems stop merely falling short as imperfect or impure versions, quit being Christian, and become something else.

Therefore, if or when theology is brought home, the first reaction is non-recognition. Traditional theology does not sound, look, or act like anything we have ever known, or what we think it is supposed to sound, look, and act like. It does not match or fit our creations. It is strange and unknown.

Creators and practitioners of false theological simulacra are usually unaware of what they are doing. They do not know that what they are creating and practicing as religion or faith is actually not Christianity, nor even in the range of what is identifiably, certifiably Christian. If told, they will not believe it. They refuse to hear and entertain such a possibility, especially if they assume confidently that their particular version is "orthodoxy," "evangelical faith," "fundamentalism,"

"Spirit-breathed Pentecostalism," "progressivism," or "what Jesus taught and what he would do today."

Even if persuaded that authentic Christian theology is always other than and greater than all our creations—judging us and calling us to repentance and re-creation—most people will likely stay with what they already have. There is no urgency or reason to change.

First, these systems are ours. They belong to us. They were handed down to us by our grandparents, parents, and favorite Sunday School teachers, youth ministers, and pastors. We may not live by them that closely any longer, but we keep them around, like precious heirlooms, to give us a "Christian" background and our "Christian" identity. We don't need the rest of the biblical-theological tradition in its proper historical framework to give us that. We already have it.

Second, we have invested a lot of effort and energy in making these systems our own, going back to high school and university years. We have spent a lifetime living by them—testing, modifying, and developing them, as needed. They are woven into the fabric of our lives. We have built our houses of marriage, family, career, and congregation, using them. And generally, we like what "we have done with the place."

Third, by comparison to our own creations, traditional theology seems distant. It was and still is a thing of the historical past. It does not come across as modern, scientific, or hip enough today. It is not "where I am, where I live, and what I am going through." While I may borrow from it—if it has something I can use to enhance my own beliefs and values—I am not dependent on this ancient, archaic tradition for either my faith or my life.

Fourth, Christianity is universal and general (for everybody) rather than individualized (for me). I need a religion that is customized to meet my needs and serve the life I live. This is what is so awesome about my version of Christianity. It has *my* name, *my* identity, and *my* beliefs and values written all over it. It is personal, not impersonal. It *is* me.

Fifth, the best thing about our constructions is that they fit us. It is amazing how well "my faith" matches my current worldview, political ideology, psychology, spiritual leanings, moral preferences, cultural involvements, and lifestyle. I do not have to struggle with conflicting understandings, make hard intellectual or ethical decisions, take a stand, change my mind, or go against the grain of the world around me.

Sixth, our own constructions require little or nothing of us. They are self-maintaining. We never have to worship, for instance—unless we want to. We definitely do not have to go to school and take up a life of serious, sustained learning. We never have and never will.

And we're doing just fine! Why disturb or complicate a perfectly good Christian life that is easy, going well, and working? Faith is supposed to be simple and natural, isn't it? As someone once said to me, "All I need to know is Jesus loves me. The rest only gets in the way."

Seventh, a lot is riding on our customized religious cultures and belief systems. This is the way things are, and the way they are supposed to be, as far as we are concerned, because this is the way we have made them and like them. Despite our complaining, the truth is we pretty much have things the way we want them. Therefore, if this status quo is challenged, everything about us senses the pressure, and we push back. We are instinctively protecting the religious-spiritual "houses" we have built, for if they are shaken hard, our entire lives could crumble and come tumbling down.

Any interference—even (especially) if it comes from traditional theology—will be unwelcomed. Christians are sharp to pick up that theology has a mind, language, and existence of its own. Once it enters our houses, it will not leave us alone and on our own. It will remind us that this house is not ours, and was originally built by, with, and for theology. We are merely heirs and stewards of the estate—not its owners.

Yet, who believes this? Or, who can stand to hear it? Theology's intrusion demands a radical paradigm shift. A lot of time, energy, and hard work are required to switch over. Most congregations and Christians are unwilling to put out the effort. Their false simulacra and strange bricolages are sufficient. Everyone is satisfied. To be otherwise would end up costing too much.

Consequently, our congregations are filled with what Ross Douthat calls "bad religion." Our problem, he says, is not that there is too much intolerant secularism and not enough religion in our country—as many on the Christian right believe. Religion is alive and well in America.

But, contrary to what secularists and atheists claim, our problem is not religion itself, and not that we still have too much of it. Rather, it is the presence of too much of the wrong kind of religion, i.e., bad religion. Bad religion is "the slow-motion collapse of traditional faith and the rise of a variety of pseudo-Christianities in its place."[12] It is the invention of "what Christianity means to me." It is the distortion and diminishment of traditional theology, until finally it is abandoned.

This is the same point I am setting forth here. Awash in many "Christianities" that are not the real thing, the real thing gets washed away. Congregations and Christians generally no longer know what the real thing is, nor care to find out. If presented it, they neither recognize nor desire it. They already have all they need. Besides, as far as they know and are concerned, what they have *is* the real thing.

Even the believer whose religious system still contains a significant number of fragments from traditional Christianity rarely knows much about what these fragments are, why they are here, what they mean, and how they function properly in the life of either the church or the individual Christian. This person understands them even less. And thus she is rendered incapable of doing much with them—thinking about them or with them, discussing them intellectually, or embodying them in a lived faith.

These fragments are unable to bear their traditional theological truth and meaning, because the theological tradition itself, or whole system, has been lost, and then replaced by another, pseudo- or non-theological system. It was the former tradition that originally gave these ideas, concepts, constructs, and teachings their significance and use. Therefore, apart from the tradition, they make little sense and are of little use. Or, they are given other meanings, so that they will make sense. They are put to other uses, so that they will be useful. The result is something that seems and sounds like Christian religion or Christian theology, or is being passed off as Christian theology, but is not. It is neither Christianity nor theology.

Douthat pictures the American religious past as a "vast delta" where waters are diverging and reconverging; but they all come from

---

12. Ross Douthat, *Bad Religion: How We Became a Nation of Heretics* (New York: Free Press, 2012), 3-4. Douthat (1979–) is an author, blogger, and op-ed columnist with the New York Times.

and are fed by the same source: traditional Christianity.[13] In my view, we still have lots of religious tributaries, spiritual streams, and moral channels in our society. Many have diverged, but they have not reconverged, and never will. They are no longer connected to either the headwaters or the original, central river of Christianity. They are on their own, while containing and carrying some sediment from their source, which now is merely one of their many sources—and perhaps a minor source at that. We might say that the waters of Christianity have been muddied, diluted, contaminated, dammed, or channeled into other uses and purposes.

A good example is "moralistic therapeutic deism"(MTD). In 2005, Christian Smith, assisted by Melinda Lundquist Denton, studied the religious lives of American teenagers. They discovered that most teenagers (97%) professed some sort of belief in God or some divine reality; and the vast majority self-identified as Christian.[14]

What they did not find, however, was evidence of a recognizably orthodox Christian theological faith. Even young people who have been raised in Christian homes and congregations have not been exposed to and educated in the Christian theological faith-tradition. They do not know what their own tradition teaches, what people who are Christians believe, or how to believe Christianly. They do not understand Christian theology. It makes no sense to them. And they do not care to learn.

Why not? The reason is simple: they already have false theological simulacra and bricolages, and are perfectly happy with them. The neat thing is, these teenagers can be "Christian" and not be Christian at the same time, depending on their life situations, feelings, moods, or needs. Besides, this is what their peers believe and how they live, whether they are Christian, Jewish, Muslim, Buddhist, agnostic, or atheist.

---

13. Douthat, 6.

14. Christian Smith with Melinda Lundquist Denton, *Soul Searching: The Religious and Spiritual Lives of American Teenagers* (New York: Oxford University Press, 2005), 40-41. See Christian Smith with Patricia Snell, *Souls in Transition: The Religious and Spiritual Lives of Emerging Adults* (New York: Oxford University Press, 2009); and Christian Smith with Kari Kristoffersen, Hilary Davidson, and Patricia Snell Herzog, *Lost in Transition: The Dark Side of Emerging Adulthood* (New York: Oxford University Press, Inc., 2011).

According to Smith and Denton, America's youth share a creed that has five main premises:

1. A God exists who created and ordered the world and watches over human life on earth.
2. God wants people to be good, nice, and fair to each other, as taught in the Bible and by most world religions.
3. The central goal in life is to be happy and to feel good about oneself.
4. God does not need to be particularly involved in one's life except when God is needed to resolve a problem.
5. Good people go to heaven when they die.[15]

The first time I read Smith's books, I was struck by the realization that this is what I have found in the congregations I have served: moralistic therapeutic deism. Sadly, many adult Christians see nothing wrong with these beliefs of teenagers, for they believe them, too. (Where do we think our kids got them?) This is their creed, as well. They live by it.

Therefore, these adults, like their children, are now incapable of critically assessing or questioning these five basic premises theologically. They are unable to discern what has been left out (almost all of the Christian tradition), what has been put in (that does not come from or match with the Christian tradition), and what has been "dumbed down" (that weakens, distorts, and destroys parts of the Christian tradition). At best, the entire MTD system is a false simulacrum. At worst, it is a different religion displacing Christianity. In either case, MTD is now so prevalent and commonplace that it could be dubbed "the official American religion."

Local congregations and ordinary Christians are unwilling, and usually unable, to realize this. This is because they do not know there is a Christian theological tradition that is other than and greater than what they presently know and believe. They have never been exposed to this tradition. Or, if they have, they have never been taught it and do not understand it. They certainly are unable to use it to make comparisons and see the differences between Christian faith and false

---

15. Smith, *Soul Searching*, 162–163.

theological simulacra, or bad religion, such as MTD. What is most troubling is that most do not care to see.

However, MTD (sounds like a social disease, doesn't it?—and it is in the body of faith) is only one of many religious tributaries, spiritual streams, and moral channels where we drink, bathe, and swim everyday. Our houses are packed and preoccupied with so many other things that we do not notice how theologically deficient we really are. We do not see it. We have been in this condition too long to notice.

Some church thinkers and leaders have diagnosed our ailment as "amnesia"—spiritual amnesia,[16] or doctrinal amnesia.[17] The theory is that Christians and their congregations are suffering memory problems. They have forgotten theology.

However, my question is, "Doesn't someone have to know something first, in order to forget it? Or fail to remember it later?" The communities and individuals I have met appear to have never known theology. Yet, the idea of Christian amnesia implies that believers today once knew their own theological faith-tradition. They possessed this knowledge and understanding, but have lost it.

This goes back to the Greek philosophers Socrates and Plato. They believed that we human beings acquire our most important forms of moral, spiritual, ethical, existential, metaphysical, and mathematical knowledge from past incarnations, as well as eternity. This knowledge is dormant and latent in each person. In this sense, it is essentially "forgotten," until it is awakened in a moment of "unforgetting"—truly an unforgettable moment. This is the "aha" experience of extra-ordinary insight and clarity, called "anamnesis" (*an-*, un- + *amnesis*, forgetting = unforgetting, or remembering).

Could it be, then, that Christians already possess total, eternal knowledge of everything there is to know, and thus all the theology

---

16. Paul Nixon, *Healing Spiritual Amnesia: Remembering What It Means to be the Church* (Nashville: Abingdon Press, 2004). Nixon is founder of Epicenter Group, a coaching, leadership development, and strategic ministry organization based in Washington, D.C.

17. William J. Abraham, *Waking From Doctrinal Amnesia: The Healing of Doctrine in the United Methodist Church* (Nashville: Abingdon Press, 1995). Abraham (1947–) is the Albert Cook Outler Professor of Wesley Studies at Perkins School of Theology, Southern Methodist University, Dallas, Texas.

they will ever need to know? If so, it is then simply a matter of having this theological knowledge awakened when it is needed. Right now, people are remembering all they need to remember. No more should be expected. If they need to remember more in the future, they will.

However, neither the evidence of my ministry nor my knowledge of theology supports such a theory. Even when theology is brought before congregations, no one stirs. Nothing is awakened. Some only go into deeper slumber. There is no interest or care. There is no resonance, and no recollection. Nothing indicates that they have ever met and known theology.

The philosophical theory of the Greeks assumes that humans are immortal beings who acquire knowledge not only from eternity but also through multiple incarnations and living many lives on earth. While the woman in my pastor's class in Charlottesville would have liked this idea, it does not fit and has no place, as I told her, in the Christian theological understanding of human existence, mortality, death, and resurrection. We do not possess from eternity knowledge of things theological. Such knowledge does not exist in us, merely asleep and forgotten, waiting to be awakened and put to use again. It belongs to God, who alone is eternal and omniscient.

Another diagnosis of our condition is that congregations have become "anemic."[18] The lifeblood of the body of Christ is deficient in the vital material it needs in order to be healthy and holy. Being a theological community, the church requires theology. Without it, or lacking enough of it, the church is weakened and fatigued. It becomes vulnerable to distraction, memory loss, apathy, complacency, idolatry, false teaching, self-distortion, diminishment, and eventually death.

I believe this is the stronger and more appropriate description of the prevailing condition of local congregations and Christians today. Christian theology is the lifeblood that keeps both faith and faith's communities alive and well. Having only a strange mixture of a few leftover bits and pieces of theology, along with fragments of other religions, modern and postmodern ideas and ideologies, popular cultural beliefs and practices, and our subjective, emotivist opinions, feelings, likes and dislikes, we and our religious communities are

---

18. Gerald Hiestand and Todd Wilson, *The Pastor Theologian: Resurrecting An Ancient Vision* (Grand Rapids: Zondervan, 2015), 13–14, 53–64. According to these authors, "*Theology has become ecclesially anemic*, and *the church theologically anemic*." (p. 13)

struggling and suffering, while appearing to prosper and flourish. Without theology in the truest, traditional sense, we are rendered incapable of being the church. We are incapable of sustaining the intellectual and moral life of Christian faith. We cannot know, understand, or embody it. At the same time, we are incapable of being sustained by it.

If or when theology is finally brought home to such a theologically anemic body, it is not recognized as the "body's own lifeblood" that was sent out long ago as a prodigal to the far country. There is no reconciliation and restoring to life. There is no homecoming marked by great celebration: "This tradition of ours was dead and is alive again. It was lost and is found. Now we are found and alive again!"

Theology comes as a stranger, unrecognized and unknown, greeted with suspicion. Yet, if it will join as a contributing member, "get with the program," fit in, support the agenda of the house, attract more members and grow the church's business and budget, it will probably be allowed to stay—as long as it is gets along with the spiritualities, moralities, "isms," emotional undercurrents, and powers now residing in this house.

Some residents may look upon theology as a "crabby, crazy uncle" or "bad guest," who has to be tolerated. After all, it does belong to the family and comes from the distant past. But, even if we have to take it in, this does not mean that we have to allow it to enter the conversation more than occasionally, and never to dominate it. As long as "old theology" pretty much leaves us alone, we will leave it alone, put up with its peculiar words and ways, and do the best we can to get along.

In some congregations, theology will be viewed as a "thief in the night." It will be met with resistance—and even force, if necessary—in order to be rendered irrelevant and harmless. The house must be protected at all costs.

Ironically, without realizing it, the Christian body fights the very reality that comes to give it life, by telling Christians who they are and what they are about. The congregation is fighting the church. It is fighting itself, as well as its source.

So, I ask, "What is going on in this house that keeps theology from coming home again?"

Evidently a lot.

Who's Calling Us Ignorant?

A year or so after I graduated from seminary and was back in the local congregation, I was invited to teach a Saturday workshop on Christian education for Sunday School teachers from the Baptist congregations in the Orange, Virginia, area. I spoke to them about the same matters of biblical-theological education I am writing about here in this book.

My message was strong: "Our members are ignorant, and it is our job to change that. We have to work with great effort to eradicate Biblical illiteracy and theological ignorance in our congregations. And this has to begin with those of us who teach. Even we do not know and understand much about all things biblical, theological, and historical related to the church. Therefore, we have to undertake a life of studying and learning."

My intent was to bring a hard-hitting, yet positive and encouraging charge to these teachers. This prevailing illiteracy, I said, actually gives us the reason for our ministry, as well as the opportunity to fill in the gaps, correct inadequate or false understandings, and develop the skills of reading and studying that Christians lack. We are, like Jesus' disciples, called to "make disciples." Then I devoted the rest of the day to practical ways we can bring historical-biblical-theological education back to our congregations.

After the workshop, the host pastor came over to me to express his appreciation for my coming. But then he said what was really on his mind: "I have a word of advice for you, since you are a young minister just starting out. Take this from a seasoned pro in ministry, who has been around the church a long time. Do not use the word 'ignorant.' People don't like to be called 'ignorant'— even if it is true. If you tell them, you will only make them feel bad. In the case of the majority of Christians I know, they are not exactly ignorant, since they have been in Sunday School, Training Union, missions groups, and Wednesday night study courses their entire lives. They may not know a lot about the Bible and the church, but they know a whole lot more than most people in our society. They simply need to learn more, so they can keep growing in their faith. Besides, as we all know, it's not education or knowledge that matters, but faith. Just tell them their faith can always be richer and stronger by gaining more information about what they believe. Telling them they are ignorant will only discourage them and make things worse."

I received his counsel to the extent of my youth and inexperience. But I knew what I had met at seminary. I also knew that no one had introduced it to me back home when I was growing up, or told me I was ignorant. Now that I was back, I did not see that anything had changed. I was determined to bring the entire Christian theological tradition back to where it belongs and to do everything I could to establish theological education locally in congregations and ordinary Christian lives. It is that important and essential to faith, ministry, and life. This education has to begin with truth-telling—even if it makes us feel bad.

I decided right then and there to keep the words "ignorant" and "ignorance" in my lexicon, and to use them as often as I could. First, these are perfectly good, appropriate words. They indicate that a person or group is not only lacking in knowledge, but also "ignoring" that knowledge. This is precisely what I have found in abundance in our congregations and in the lives of individual Christians. Our house is full of people lacking knowledge and understanding of the Christian theological faith-tradition, avoiding it, and then strongly refusing the education that will remedy their condition of ignorance.

Second, I do not use these words lightly or loosely, but seriously and deliberately. I do not use them to express or to cause ridicule, scorn, humiliation, or contempt. They are not intended as a "put-down," but rather as a protest: "Why are you folks 'putting up' with being 'put down' when it comes to your own theological heritage?"

I set this particular word before Christians as a mirror to help them see themselves more clearly and correctly. I always instruct my audience to remove all negative connotations from my words, taking them to be descriptive rather than derogatory. Let these words simply mean what they mean. We are ignoring theology, which is causing us to be lacking in the very knowledge the church and all Christians require. Who can dispute or deny this?

Third, it is true that this terminology strikes our sensibilities and disturbs us with prophetic force. No one likes to be included among the ignorant. This is not the way we like to think of ourselves. Yet, this is the value of this word and its cognates. They offend us—as they should. They hit us hard with all their shocking, harsh, offensive force, trying to jolt us, and cause us to examine ourselves. Is it I, Lord?

Only then may we possibly be awakened to our personal condition and the state of our house. Perhaps if we realize that we are ignorant of our own historical-biblical-theological faith-tradition, we will stop ignoring it and start listening to it, learning it, and living it. Maybe serious, sustained, and ordered learning will be restored to our lives and to our congregations.

Of course, ignorance, being itself, cannot know itself, and will only continue ignoring itself. Only if or when it is exposed by education to knowledge can it possibly see itself and realize what it is: the opposite of knowledge. Ignorance is the hiding, denying, refusing, distorting, and destroying of knowledge. Only when confronted and called to change and be otherwise can the Christian individual or congregation have any possible chance of becoming more knowledgeable and less ignorant.

This is like the person who says, "When I was growing up in my family, I did not know we were poor—until I met people who weren't." We do not know we are ignorant unless or until we meet people who are not ignoring and lacking theology, but are rich in it. We meet both ourselves and theology in and through them.

After completing my first week in the first grade (my hometown school system did not have preschool or kindergarten at that time), I proudly announced before my entire family at the dinner table that I had learned so much that first week I did not have to go back. I had learned everything there was to know. I could stay home. I knew it all. Going back would only be a waste of everybody's time.

My father was a wise man. He made a bet with me. "Go back to school next week. And if you do not learn anything new—not a single thing—then you don't have to go back. You really have learned it all. You know everything there is to know. You can stay home."

Of course, you know the outcome of this story. I went back, and the teacher taught me something I had never heard or even imagined before. In addition to that lesson, I also learned the lesson that I did not know everything. I was ignorant. But the point is this: I did not and could not know what I did not know until I was exposed to it. Education serves the purpose of telling us what we don't know, in order to open us to what we could know.

Amazingly, in this way, ignorance serves the purpose of promoting education. Without it, there would be no reason for learning and knowing. There would be no motivation or encouragement for the continuation of learning and knowing. In other words, if I am not ignorant, why would I go back the second week?

The good news is that I continued through and completed the first grade, and then stayed on in grade school for eleven more years. I then spent four years in higher education at Clemson University, followed by seven years at Southern Seminary, for a total of twenty-three years of formal education. I did not stop then, but continued on my own, studying and learning, growing in knowledge for another almost four more decades. And today, even after all this time and effort, I still do not know it all. Not even close. So I keep on, continually repelled and compelled by my condition of ignorance.

Frequently I remind my students that I, like them, am a student. I am still reading, studying, and thinking. I am working farther down the educational road beyond them; but we are on the same road. I also say with complete candor, "I remain ignorant of the bulk of the vast Christian theological tradition. What I do not yet know far exceeds what I do know. There is so much more I am ignoring, or am not even aware of. But this pushes me to keep going. Therefore, I urge you to follow me and do the same. Let your ignorance be your guide!"

While I am on this subject, I want to say two more positive things about ignorance. First, it can serve as a vital tool for questioning new data or information that comes to us. "Who or what are you (referring to the strange, new information)? Why should I learn and know you? So what?"

Ignorance prevents us from unquestioningly, mindlessly accepting and immediately taking in every "new knowledge" that comes along. We must be suspicious and somewhat resistant, and at times actually refuse much of what is told or presented to us. A lot of what is being passed-off as "truth" is untrue, false, or even deadly. Therefore, we should ignore it and remain lacking in knowledge of it.

Second, ignorance frees up the resources of attention, time, energy, and effort that are needed for specialized learning and knowledge. If every individual were expected to learn and know everything about everything, then she would not only fail miserably, but she would also be paralyzed. There simply is too much reality for any one person to learn and know. Therefore, she wisely concentrates her education where it is most needed. It is only by not learning, not knowing, and not paying attention to or engaging with all other areas that she is able to focus on this one area, and thereby develop both the knowledge and the skills that are necessary for excelling in it.

For example, if someone is a clarinet player, she effectively ignores what violinists and percussionists must study, learn, know, practice, and develop as skill. She does not study botany or history, unless she is also a professor in either field at the local community college. Ignorance in all other areas allows and even enables her to be who she is and to do what she does in the one or few areas where she cannot afford to be ignorant. Therefore, generally and basically, she is an ignorant person, and must remain so. But this one thing—clarinet playing—she does not ignore and does know, although there still is so much about it that she has yet to learn.

Likewise, the Christian does not have the luxury of ignorance when it comes to what is necessary and essential for Christian faith, and that itself is Christian faith. He can and should remain ignorant of most things, in order to learn and know this one thing.

I am in no way discouraging wider education. Christians need to know a little about many things, because Christian knowledge is of all things in relation to God in Christ. But what I am emphasizing is that, as Christians, you and I are responsible for being continually engaged in theological learning. We are obligated to be full of the knowledge of these matters that truly matter, and that have been entrusted to us. We are expected to be increasing, deepening, and maturing in the understanding that is required by and for faith.

The grave situation is that our local communities of faith—and ourselves included—are mostly lacking in this knowledge and understanding that are required by and for faith. The main subject matter is unknown and is being ignored. Since we are not engaging in the specific education that would go a long way toward correcting and improving our condition, then we are truly ignorant, and need to be called out on it.

Currently, theological ignorance is so widespread and common that it is considered normal. Nobody thinks anything about it. Nobody questions it. Nobody notices it. Nobody can remember a time or a context that was otherwise. Even the notion of it being otherwise does not register. The Christian community on the whole is ignorant of its own ignorance regarding the one thing for which it is called and created to be in this world.

A word that is often preferred to "ignorant" is "illiterate." "Illiteracy" refers to a "reading" inability, or disability. The individual cannot "read" something. She lacks the basic knowledge and skills required for deciphering a written text and making sense of the letters and words on the page. In other words, she cannot read or write.

There are many other types of illiteracy or semi-illiteracy, including health illiteracy, financial illiteracy, technology illiteracy, and cultural illiteracy. Every one of us is illiterate in some way, to some degree, in one or more areas.

I, for example, am illiterate in Spanish (unlike my daughter-in-law, Andrea, who is a professor of Spanish at Shenandoah University in Winchester, Virginia). I cannot read or write Spanish. I cannot understand anyone who is speaking in Spanish; and I certainly cannot respond in the same language. Truth is, I am impaired in all languages except English, although I once studied and was proficient in Latin, German, Hebrew, and Greek.

I am also chemistry illiterate, rugby illiterate, and fashion illiterate. I could go on, but I do not want to make myself feel totally inadequate. One cannot be literate in everything, especially if he desires to be truly, fully literate in one major thing.

Stephen Prothero has called attention to the problem of "religious illiteracy." Paradoxically, he observes, "Americans are both deeply religious and profoundly ignorant about religion."[19] We are a nation of religious illiterates.

Prothero proposes that each of us read the Bible or the Quran—or both. Churches, synagogues, mosques, and temples need to do a better job of addressing our collective ignorance, by following the commandment to "remember" that is emphasized over and over in the Hebrew Bible. Religious leaders can preach more plainly and frequently from their own sacred writings. Congregations must "go back to basics" in the Sunday Schools and religious camps. The

---

19. Stephen Prothero, *Religious Literacy: What Every American Needs to Know—and Doesn't* (New York: HarperSanFrancisco, 2007), 1. Prothero (1960–) is a professor of religion at Boston University.

media, public and private schools, and colleges and universities should take their civic educational responsibility seriously, as well. Together we will be able to increase religious literacy, in order to make the world both more interesting and less dangerous.[20]

I concur with Prothero's assessment and proposal, as far as it goes. I believe all Christians, especially in this present multicultural age, need a basic working knowledge of the world's various religions and spiritualities. Yes, our congregational education should include lessons in Judaism, Islam, the Church of Scientology, the Church of Jesus Christ of Latter Day Saints, Jehovah's Witnesses, and whatever other religions or spiritual movements the members may encounter.

However, this world religions study must be conducted in the context of a much greater, more extensive and intensive, continuing education in the Christian religion. The first need of Christians is to know, understand, and embody their own faith-tradition, and then, as part of that education, learn how to relate to persons, beliefs, and movements that differ from, challenge, and even threaten the church and Christianity.

I am specifically concerned with the Christian community and its own religious illiteracy. It is one thing to be ignorant about other religions (not only Judaism and Islam, but also Buddhism, Hinduism, Taoism, and many more), their political, economic, social, and cultural force, and the major role they are playing in current events and affairs, internationally and nationally. It is another thing to be ignorant about one's own religion—in our case, Christianity. How is it possible for us to remain Christians, or our congregations to be identifiably, distinctively Christian, or the church to be the church rather than something else, unless we are functionally, culturally literate in Christianity?

All of this implies, at root, that congregations and Christians have a "reading" problem, and are suffering from some kind of inability, or disability. Many believers may have been raised in Christian homes, self-identify as Christian, have their names on a church roll, and attend services at least occasionally, if not regularly. But they cannot tell you what they are doing, why, or what it means. They are unable to "read" the signs and symbols, discern the truth and meaning of a

20. Prothero, 17–18.

biblical text or an act of worship, or put it in the larger context of faith. They remain at a child's or beginner's level of participation and understanding.

Because of such illiteracy, these Christians are unable to teach their own religion to their own children. They cannot "give an account for the hope that is in us,"[21] and thereby make known the truth and salvation of God made known in Christ. No one else can come to know what we ourselves do not first know.

Also, how will common misperceptions and misunderstandings of Christianity and its church ever be corrected? How will religious ignorance that is so dangerous for our world today—politically, economically, socially, and culturally—be dealt with and decreased, unless we do our part as teachers of our part of the world's religions? How can the Christian religion survive, unless we ourselves are religiously, Christianly literate?

First, Christians must be literate in the Bible. They must read it in its entirety and be informed of what is in it (and what is not in it). However, the person who does this, and only this, will remain biblically illiterate. Biblical literary involves much more than simply being able to name the four gospels, or know that the last book of the Bible is not "The Book of Revelation<u>s</u>," but "The Book of Revelation." Literacy goes far beyond merely knowing a number of stories, memorizing verses, "getting something out of it," and "saying what it means to me." The literate person is the one who can read the Bible theologically as Scripture. This reader enters the strange new world behind the texts, and allows it authoritatively to bring about transformation, and then increasingly to conform him or her to the gospel of the revelation of God in Christ, which sets faith's mode of existence in the world.

While concurring with Prothero's assessment, I contend that the most serious problem for the church today is deeper than religious illiteracy. It is theological illiteracy. Christians woefully lack the most basic knowledge and understanding of their own theological faith-tradition, within which they can be people of faith. Outwardly, the buildings and the activities of religion continue. But inwardly, the interpretive framework for them is missing.

---

21. See 1 Peter 3:15.

It is one thing to be religious—even very religious, and Christianly so. It is an entirely different thing to know, understand, and embody the theological truth that is the reason for and foundation of the Christian religion, without which this religion itself would be mere window-dressing.

In 1970, James Smart handed the Christian community a provocative book. He asked why the voice of the Scriptures is not spoken and heard more in our preaching and teaching. Why are its message and meaning silent in our minds, and absent from our consciousness as Christians, even among those of us who revere the Bible and are most openly devoted to it? [22]

Can you imagine what he would find in our congregations today, almost a half century later? What might he possibly say to us?

I read Smart's book in seminary, and then took its searching (and scorching) message back with me when I returned home to serve among Christians in congregations. I promoted biblical education, attempting to restore not only the voice, but also the content of the Scriptures in the preaching and teaching of the church, and thereby in the consciousness of Christian people. I did everything I could to fulfill the need Smart had identified.

More specifically, I was gravely concerned for the theological content of the Bible as Scripture. It is neither the literature as such nor the history behind it that we are ultimately after—as vitally important as both are for the entire enterprise of interpretation. We are seeking the Bible's theological teaching.

Also, we must realize that this teaching comes to us today only within a larger tradition of theological teaching. This is the church's "teaching of the teaching," or "interpretation of the interpretation." Neither the Bible nor this larger tradition can be properly understood apart from the other. Yet, how many congregations preach and teach this whole counsel? How many Christians have ever read and studied it, or know anything about it?

---

22. James D. Smart, *The Strange Silence of the Bible in the Church: A Study in Hermeneutics* (Philadelphia: The Westminster Press, 1970), 15–16. Smart (1906–1982) was a Presbyterian pastor, a lecturer in homiletics and Christian education at Knox College, and Jesup Professor of Biblical Interpretation at Union Theological Seminary, New York. He was an influential proponent of a theological approach to Christian education.

It is a strange silence. One may still hear some scattered sounds around that sound like theology, but these are fragmented, garbled, and broken—like a radio not quite tuned to a good station. I often wonder if we aren't like foreign visitors struggling to carry on a conversation with what few words we know, without remembering what conversation we are supposed to be having. But we manage to "get by," as illiterate people do. We are uncomfortable, and far from fluent or proficient, talking this language among ourselves, and especially when we are trying to communicate with the world. So we join other conversations, speaking other languages.

It is strange. Strange indeed. Christians claim involvement in a theological tradition in which they cannot fully or truly be involved, since they have little knowledge, understanding, or experience of it. Their illiteracy renders them incapable of being part of this tradition, and, therefore, of living the Christian theological life. Yet, does anyone besides me think this situation is absolutely bizarre?

What Is It?

The homecoming of Christian theology to the local congregation, and Christians meeting it again, or for the first time, is similar to the Hebrews meeting manna.[23] Somewhere between Elim and Sinai, in the wilderness of Sin, the people complained against their leaders, Moses and Aaron, that they were hungry. The Lord God, they said, had brought them out there in order to starve them to death. It would have been better if he had just left them in Egypt, and killed them there. At least when they were slaves, they had bread to eat. Pharaoh fed them.

One morning when the dew had lifted, there was an odd, flaky substance on the ground. It was white and as fine as early morning frost. When the people saw it, they turned and looked at one another in bewilderment. Then they looked back at the substance and said, "What is it?"

I believe this was one of those incidents that helped them earn their reputation as "children of God." What are the first words that

23. Read Exodus 16.

come out of children's mouths when they come to the table and see what their mother or father has prepared and put on their plates? They do not recognize it. Their immediate reaction is that they don't like it and are not going to like it. "What is it?"

Every morning, six days a week, for forty years, this fine, white, flaky stuff showed up on their doorstep for breakfast. From day one, they called it "manna," and the name stuck. It literally meant, "What is it?" Every day they got up, looked at what had been provided, and said, "Manna." ("What is it?") After being brought out of the land of Egypt, they existed on this strange "bread from heaven,"[24] which was their sustenance all the way to Canaan. But to them, it was always "What is it?" Manna.

I believe theology is the church's manna. Theology is bread for the sustaining of the life of the community following Christ in the wilderness of the world. Yet, most Christians today are not quite sure what it is. They do not recognize it, and definitely do not have a desire, or hankering, for it. Their hunger is being fed and satisfied at other tables. Even when spoon-fed, they act as though it is not on their plates—the proverbial "horse on the dining room table." Their eyes glaze over. They don't see it. No curiosity. No interest.

A few will dutifully "try it," as their parents made them do when they were children. But then they quickly move on to enjoy their religious starches and sweet spiritual desserts. Some occasionally like to sprinkle a little theology over their food to season it, and give their religion a churchy taste. But theology is not a staple, or regularly on the menu of most Christian cuisine.

Try bringing it home to the church where it belongs, and putting it out on the table. See what happens. Theology is the "What is it?" of God's people today.

So What?

The question of "What is it?" quickly becomes "So what?" Non-recognition turns into non-interest, and even defiant non-compliance: "Why should we eat this? We don't have to, and we won't."

24. See Jesus' teaching in John 6:25–59.

In Jesus' parable of the prodigal son, the father's older son is out in the field working. At the end of the day, as he is returning to the house, he hears music and laughter. One of his servants tells him what is going on. His younger brother is home, and their father is hosting a great banquet in his honor to celebrate.

The older son becomes angry and refuses to go in. Even when his father comes out to beg him to come and enjoy the festivities, he refuses. He lays out his case, arguing that the party is being thrown for an unfaithful son, when he has been the faithful son. Yet, has his father ever thrown him a party?!

This story does not have a completely happy ending. Ironically, this "faithful son" is unfaithful. He refuses to obey the father's will. Social custom dictates that he "be there," joining in, eating, drinking, and dancing. After all, he is a member of this family, his father's first-born son, and his brother's brother.

But he is non-compliant. "So what if this loser is back? What do I care? I want nothing to do with him or this situation. Things were better around here when he was gone. As far as I'm concerned, he should have stayed lost and dead."

Most Christian brothers and sisters take the side of this brother when their own flesh-and-blood theological faith-tradition is brought back home. They refuse to join the reunion and reestablish relations. They do not think they are being defiant. There may not be any outward show of animosity or burst of anger, no passive-aggression or outright rejection. To them, it is simply a matter of free choice. And they freely choose not to like what is going on, make room in their lives, or have anything to do with it.

Jesus told another parable about a great banquet.[25] Many were invited, and everyone RSVP'd they wouldn't miss it for the world. However, when the day came and the event was ready, every single invitee declined to attend.

One said, "I have bought a piece of property that I must go and see." (Who buys property sight unseen?) Another said, "I have bought five yoke of oxen, and I am going to try them out in the field" (Can't this wait?). And my favorite: "I just got married, and my wife won't let me out of her sight." (Yeah, right.)

25. Luke 14:15–24.

Now, all the invited-yet-declining guests were polite. No one was rude. Everyone had "good excuses." (A congregational member from West Virginia once told me, "An excuse is a lie wrapped in the skin of a reason.") They simply played the part of the elder brother, refusing to join in.

The owner of the estate, who was throwing the big party, was understandably angry. Matthew's version of this parable[26] describes the man as "enraged." Granted, in this version, some of the invited guests were not socially polite or kind. They "made light" of the event and shrugged it off, as though it were nothing to them. Others became belligerent and violent. They seized the messengers, beat them, and killed some of them.

In other words, they all had better things to do. Even murder was for some invitees better than having to get dressed, walk or drive over, be among the elite at the royal wedding reception, eat a lavish meal, and dance the night away.

Insane, right?

It would be one thing if, in the whole scheme of things, this gathering was one of those occasions that does not really matter. Oh, we might suppose it matters in some way to somebody somewhere, but not to us on this day, or to most people where we live. It's just not that important—at least not right now. Maybe later. We can think of a dozen activities we would rather be doing, along with a lot more we probably ought to be doing. Therefore, it comes down to personal preference, and how each of us freely chooses to spend his or her attention, time, money, and energy.

Frankly, attending the main event of theology's homecoming, and then living in the same house with theology is not high on our list of priorities, and is not our idea of having a good time religiously or spiritually. Theology seems boring. It strikes us as old, outdated, and foreign—for another time and place. It is neither relevant nor applicable to our lives today.

Also, we are grown-ups and no longer small children who have to eat what is put on the table in front of us. Today we go by what we're hungry for, and what sounds or looks good in the moment. Nobody tells us what to eat. We decide what to put on our plates and in our

26. Matthew 22:1–14.

bodies. We design our own religious and spiritual diets. In fact, we make our own food out of what we have foraged from the religious-spiritual marketplace. We have our mealtimes—and our houses—the way we want them, without a lot of help from theology. Who needs it? Why mess things up?

It is not as though theology or theological education is required for being Christian today. Right? Our congregations have never gotten serious about us being serious about our discipleship as members. Name one Christian you know who has taken up the theological life, or the intellectual life. When was the last time anyone asked you about what you were reading, or recommended a solid Christian theological book? Or invited you to a lecture by a visiting theologian?

There is no law, policy, regulation, or contract that obligates the believer to be theologically literate. It is not as though anyone will ever be brought up on charges for failing to be educated, or refusing to comply. There's nothing to which we should comply. Theology is fully optional, as far as everyone is concerned.

Most congregations and Christians, then, have never opted in. And when given the opportunity, they freely choose to opt out. And they see nothing immature, irresponsible, or unfaithful about any of this. They're not doing anything wrong. Being in a constant state of indifference and disengagement is not only acceptable, but it is also expected. It is perfectly okay to "make light" of these matters by having nothing to do with them, because the invited guest to the banquet is devoting all her resources to career, family, and personal pursuits, including a lot of Christian religion—all good things.

In effect, the congregation and individual members, who play the part of the elder brother, are saying, "So what?" And when the owner of the house is enraged, they act surprised: "What??"

Where Is Home?

In the story we tell ourselves, the congregation—or the church in its local manifestation—is home. This is where we were born and raised. This is where we were baptized and married, and saw our children being baptized and married. This is where we buried and grieved our loves ones. This is home, and this is where we are most at home.

One might say we are homebodies. We have never left and have no plans of ever leaving—this side of the grave.

Theology, on the other hand, did leave, and has been away for longer than anyone can remember. It strayed and went away from us—not us from it. Theology, then, is the prodigal. If it would only "come to its senses," change to look and sound contemporary, and come back, hat in hand, to reside in our house as a humble servant, fitting in and supporting our spirituality, mindset, and lifestyle, then we may be able to make a little room for it. We will not necessarily attend the party and rejoice. But we will allow it to hang around and help out as a servant, if—and this is a big "if"—we ever happen to need it.

In recent years, I have slowly come to realize that I have been operating by this view. I saw myself bringing theology back. I opened the door and introduced it to the folks inside, who live in this house. But the homecoming never went as planned, and the reunion never happened. The brothers and sisters ignored theology.

Now I believe it was not theology, but us, who left home long ago. You and I are the prodigals. We are the ones who must come to our senses, change, and come back, hat in hand, as humble servants, fitting into and supporting the house theology has built and in which it dwells.

In other words, we are not the ones who are home, while theology is away, trying to make a comeback. The reverse is true: theology *is* home, and we are far away, seeming to have little to no interest in coming back. We like where we're living now. Theology is no longer home for us. We have moved on.

Therefore, we are resisting much more than the re-introduction of theology into our lives. We are resisting our lives being re-introduced to theology. We don't want to be theology's servants again. We don't want to be theological people. We don't want theology to be our home.

4
Playing

When we read or hear Jesus' parable about the father's celebration dinner for his prodigal son, or his parable about the king's wedding feast for his son, our attention becomes fixed on those who do not participate. Let one child in the school classroom act out and refuse to join in the group's activities, and the entire class—teacher and other students—focuses on this one unruly, noncompliant child.

In these parables, despite the negative people, there are a few who do join in. They do come and participate. They do sit down at the table, eat the lavish meal, and enjoy the laughter and conversation. They may not be the first-born sons and daughters. Their names may not have been on the honored guest list. But, unlike others in the community and in their own household, they do not act out and hold out. They do not have better things to do. Or they did, but all of these very important dates, scheduling conflicts, and obligations go out the window when they have the chance to be part of the biggest event anyone can remember. They would not miss this for the world. They would be foolish to miss it. And so they are here. They are in the banquet hall, thoroughly receiving and enjoying the rich reward.

In the story of my ministry in congregations, a few Christians have broken ranks and come closer to see for themselves what this theology is. They sit down to listen. Even when this prophetic stranger (theology) has clearly "gone to meddling," entering their temple to remake the place, they do not put up much of a fight. They continue to be open and responsive. They continue to learn and to change. As a result, they discover the riches of their own household's faith-tradition, and rejoice: "Theology was dead, and is alive. It was lost and is now found."

Who are these people? What makes them different from everybody else? Why do they respond and join in, when others do not?

I call them "players." When theology is brought home to their congregations, a game begins. Somehow it captures their attention and interest, and involves them. They are lured out of the Christian crowd and its anonymity to join in and play the game. Others are not.

Theology does not faze the latter. Why not? They are heirs of the family inheritance of the mysteries of God in Christ, aren't they? What is it about this peculiar game that attracts and wins over only a few, but then can have such transforming power over them?

Are You Ready to Play?
(Play As the Clue to Theological Explanation)

In his magnum opus, *Truth and Method,* the twentieth century German philosopher Hans-Georg Gadamer wrote a section titled "Play As the Clue to Ontological Explanation."[1] Although he does not venture into the area of theology, I believe his concept of "play" can be helpful to us as we seek a clue to the homecoming that theology sets into motion and requires. It can also aid us in discerning the type of alternative teaching-learning community that theology is calling and creating and sustaining.

Briefly, Gadamer seeks to free the concept of "play" from its subjective meaning that dominates modern thinking about reality and human beings. This is the notion that the "player" wholly determines the "play"—both the game being played and the way it is being played, or being played out, as well as its outcome.

For instance, we say, "Beauty is in the eye of the beholder." The subjective meaning is that I, as seeing subject, determine beauty. There is no beauty until I see it. And it is as I see it.

---

1. Hans-Georg Gadamer, trans. Garrett Barden and John Cumming, *Truth and Method* (New York: The Seabury Press, 1975), 91–119. Gadamer (1900-2002) was a German philosopher at the University of Heidelberg, who was a major figure in the development of twentieth century hermeneutics. "Ontology" is the branch of philosophy concerned with being, becoming, existence, and reality.

Think instead of beauty as the mode of being of a work of art, a natural landscape, or person. It has its own essence, independent of the perception or consciousness of the person who is seeing or not seeing. In this sense, we can say that beauty is already playing. Something is going on. The game is underway. It does not wait for the beholder to get it started, or to determine whether it will be or not, or what it will be.

In fact, the play draws the beholder into its realm, and into a game that precedes and far surpasses her. She begins "to be played." Beauty plays upon her by absorbing her into itself, holding her there in its spell, and fulfilling its purpose in and through her—if she plays, and loses herself in the play.

To put it another way: the game masters its players. It teaches the person it plays how to play, and what it means to play. It changes her, and she becomes what she was not before, and could not on her own have become. She is, as it were, another person. She no longer exists for herself, or by herself. She exists now for the greater game.

Applied theologically, I take Gadamer's understanding to mean that Christian faith is not primarily or essentially a matter of subjective experience, religiosity, or spirituality. It is not a life-project that you and I construct, cause to work, or make produce good results. It is a mode of being that comes only from being caught up in and transformed by the mission of God.

Theology talks about God moving, acting on, and working with the world He has created, including all persons and all things. Think of this as "the play of God." Also, think of theology itself as divine play, or a way of God being playful, playing His church in His world.

God is primary and prior to, other than and greater than, all else. God does not depend on anyone or anything for God's being. The same can be said about theology. It exists independently of us, in the sense that it exists whether we know it or not, whether we believe it or not, and whether we are interested and involved, or not.

Contrary to our common assumption, theology is not the equivalent of "what I believe," or even "what the church believes." Theology has its own essence, greater than those who come in contact with it and work with it. Therefore, what the individual, congregation, or denomination believes and practices will reflect and represent theology, though partially, imperfectly, dimly, and often falsely. Primary emphasis, then, must be on theology itself, rather than on ourselves. Equally mistaken is our presumption that theology is lifeless and useless, unless or until we pick it up and give it life and use. If the truth be known, theology is always going on, with or without us. Without theology, you and I are the ones who are lifeless and useless as Christians and as the church.

However, called in Christ, you and I are being played. We do not play theology, as much as it plays us. Its purpose is to catch us up in its play so that we will lose ourselves in it, give ourselves to it, and thereby be transformed and made its players. In this sense, theology creates its own community. This is a community that is held in theology's spell, drawn into its play, and kept there. Members become capable of being played, and also of playing the game that is theology.

Theology does not leave its subjects as they are, unchanged. The very encounter and ongoing experience with theology alters the human psyche, mind, heart, being, and life. Those who give themselves to it as its students and servants will never master it; but it will master them.

Theology, then, is a sacred and serious game. Therefore, it is only to be played seriously. The Christian congregation or Christians individuals who do not join in, or who treat these matters lightly and loosely, as though they are unimportant and irrelevant, are disrupting, spoiling, and ruining the play. They themselves are not to be taken seriously.

At the same time, there is a sense in which theology does not require the absolute, "dead seriousness" of many activities in this world. The individual who allows himself to be involved in this game, and to be played, finds that he forgets himself. He gets caught up in theology's own movement, and loses track of his own life for the sake of a greater reality and purpose. By losing his life, he gains it.[2] Such life-losing in theology is quite transforming, enlivening, and renewing. And, yes, it is enjoyable. This is why he plays.

Let's be clear that in conceiving of theology as play we are not suggesting that it is a "mere game" that Christians play. Many people commonly assume that the church creates its own game, expecting its members to play along. They also believe that the church's academic

---

2. See Mark 8:34-37.

theologians are merely creating and playing their own mind games. The implication is that Christianity is little more than an exercise human beings have devised for their own amusement and power. It is a trivial pastime, or hobby, some people like to engage in just for fun. Moreover, it is make-believe. It has no reality, meaning, or purpose beyond itself. Basically, it is a total waste of time, unless one happens to like this sort of thing—spending one's free time dabbling in theology—and its brings some reward of pleasure or well-being.

This, however, is not Gadamer's conception of "play." "Play" refers to reality being reality, always self-moving and already showing or presenting itself. Human beings are approached in ways that can neither be anticipated nor controlled. Still, the individual is invited and even lured into the movement and presentation of what is playing, or in play, which is greater than and other than himself. In order to participate, he must "lose himself." He must give up and give in to what is drawing him in. He must play along. And in the process, given the way in which what is playing moves and presents itself, he himself is played. He is made a player. He not only participates in the game, but is also being transformed by it, and conformed to its nature, shape, and movement.

Therefore, we can say that, in a very real, meaningful, and useful way, theologians are the persons who have been caught up in and changed by the self-movement and self-presentation of theology. It has absorbed them into itself, and now holds them in its spell. It takes over their consciousness, their minds and hearts, as well as their human ways of perceiving, knowing, understanding, relating, and living. It gives them its specific task, and makes them its stewards and students. They devote their entire lives to it, and find their entire lives affected and directed by it.

Theology's own sacred seriousness makes them serious in playing; and only this seriousness makes the play of theology wholly play. And as players, they serve the game both by playing it and by preserving its content and conventions. Truth is, they are the ones who are being preserved by being not only informed, but more importantly, transformed and formed by theology.

So, who's playing whom?

My grave concern is that professional theologians are about the only ones left in the game—at least with any regularity, expertise, seriousness, or enjoyment. But they are playing in their own academic worlds, which rarely, if ever, intersect with the places where ordinary Christians live in local settings. Some professionals are even making up their own games, misusing and abusing theology for their own agendas and ideologies, as well as using it for their own professional gain.

Theology, however, plays in and on the whole church, not only in professional circles on professors and pastors. All believers are called into play. Playing this particular game is what makes and keeps them believers. Apart from theology, they are non-players, and thus cannot be theologians, or even Christians. Only those persons who actively participate, or play, believe. Everyone who plays is a believer.

Sadly, local congregations are playing many games today. Theology is not one of them. It certainly is not the main game, especially if theology is understood as truth and meaning playing upon human lives, requiring of them the deliberate, disciplined exercise of serious, sustained learning and living. If theology is still in play in any slight way in a congregation's packed life and work, it is typically in service of the congregation's total religion game.

On the one hand, in most "traditional" congregations, theological words may still be heard sprinkled throughout common everyday religious talk, as well as in Sunday school classrooms and public religious worship services. On the other hand, many "contemporary" congregations are deliberately ridding their services of all theological language, so as not to turn off prospects, or confuse members, who "have no clue what these words mean anyway."

Theology cannot be taken seriously, and certainly cannot be defining or determinative, in settings where Christians see themselves as creating the Christian game, deciding how it will be played, or whether it will be played at all. Theology cannot be played well—if at all—when Christians no longer know what the game is, but think they do. Or, they do not care, for they like the games they have, i.e., the ones they have created for themselves, and that are currently playing under the names of "faith," "church," and "Christianity."

We have it backwards. It is like our eyes that mechanically see everything upside down. The process of refraction through a convex lens causes the image of the object we are seeing to be flipped. Thankfully, though, we have brains. The human brain receives the raw, inverted sensory data, makes it fit with what it already knows, and turns it into a coherent, right-side-up image.

The theological faith-tradition does this for the church and for the Christian. Our natural, normal human way of living and coming at things is inverted. Theology takes this inverted data, makes it fit with what it already knows, and turns it into a coherent right-side-up image. It turns all things, including our selves, upside down and around by "conversion." This is done in order to correct our sight, and help us come at all things rightly in relation to God.

This is the paradigm shift I believe is required for congregations and Christians. We must again begin seeing and coming at things theologically. But this is impossible, unless or until we learn, know, understand, embody and live theologically. And this is impossible, unless or until we are willing to be turned around. We must allow theology to change and teach us. We must imagine that, instead of us playing theology, or playing around like children with theology, or playing our own games with only a few leftover theological pieces, theology is already in play, and is vying to play us, play on us, and play with us.

Finally, this is impossible, unless or until we are ready to lose ourselves and be played. We must be played by this particular game, in this particular way.

Gadamer placed the following poem by Rainer Marie Rilke on in the middle of a single page in the front material of *Truth and Method.* I believe it summarizes well the experience of theology's players.

> Catch only what you've thrown yourself, all is
> mere skill and little gain;
> But when you're suddenly the catcher of a ball
> thrown by an eternal partner
> with accurate and measured swing
> towards you, to your centre, in an arch
> from the great bridgebuilding of God:
> why catching then becomes a power –
> not yours, a world's.[3]

---

3. Gadamer, v. René Maria Rilke (1875–1926) was a Bohemian-Austrian novelist and poet, whose writings are known for their religious, mystical intensity.

So, are you ready to play? Are you ready to join and be part of theology's activity? Are you ready to be played with?

Will Anybody Play?

In Jesus' parable in Luke 15, the elder son seems to be alone in his refusal to play. Who in his or her right mind would miss out on such a joyous event, including great beef brisket?!

On one occasion Jesus went to the home of a leader of the Pharisees for the Sabbath meal. The host had invited other Pharisees and lawyers as his guests, along with Jesus. During the meal, one of the guests said to Jesus, "Blessed is the person who will eat bread in the kingdom of God!" Jesus responded with a parable about someone who gave a great dinner and invited many, but when the day came, they refused to participate in the great feast.[4]

This story was Jesus' way of saying, "Yes, you are right. Blessed is the one who will eat bread in the kingdom of God. However, do you realize how hard it is for people who are already in the house (i.e., Pharisees, chief priests, scribes, and the rest of the inside religious community) to enter and participate? They refuse to join the party, even while having an open invitation, are on the A-list, and are first in line. Yes, truly I tell you, blessed is the one who will eat bread in the Kingdom—if that person will actually do it!"

Jesus ended this parable in Matthew's version with these words: "For many are called, but few are chosen." (Matthew 22:14) The call of God goes out to many; but only a few respond receptively and are chosen.

Using the concept of play, we could say that God throws the ball to many. We cannot say for certain whom, how, when, or why. But sadly, most refuse to catch it. Or, if they do catch it, they drop it. For whatever reasons of preoccupation and disinterest—or there may be no real reason at all—most people do not accept the throw, and do not play. They do not allow themselves to be chosen for the game, despite the fact that they, of all people, have been given the special, most extraordinary blessing of being picked first and called to play.

4. Luke 14:15–24.

The older brother and the religious community are not a few stragglers, naysayers, party-poopers, or exceptions. They are the many, the crowd, the entire house, and the norm. They have substituted their own games, and are now catching only what they are throwing to and among themselves, or what the popular culture is tossing them. They are unmoved by the divine invitation, no matter how compelling. They do not recognize it as the heritage and destiny of their own faith-tradition. They remain uninterested, even after being encountered. Therefore, the question is not whether all are called, but rather, whether a few—or any—might be chosen.

Is there anyone here who will respond and play, and as a result, be played?

Imagine a national mathematical society holding a convention. One particular person in attendance, like others, considers herself to be a mathematician. She conducts research projects in the field of mathematics. She works on advanced mathematical theorems and problems. She tutors children in mathematics. She has registered for this convention, paid her money, taken a flight, and shown up for the opening session.

But then she is baffled and disappointed by her experience at the convention. Attendees do not seem to know much, if anything, about mathematics. A few of the keynote addresses, lectures, and breakout sessions touch on mathematics; but they are all over the place, and are about many other things. Nevertheless, everyone seems to enjoy getting together, and they are having a great time. All of them are saying they will be back next year. She wonders, "Why? For what?"

Imagine you play an instrument: a violin. You have been thinking lately about how wonderful it would be to play classical music in a classical music group. You also would like to learn more about music along the way, while honing your skills as a musician. You want to be in the world of music with musicians like yourself.

One day a friend tells you about a local orchestra that is open to newcomers. So you check it out online, and get directions. You go to the next meeting and walk in carrying your violin case, feeling uneasy and out-of-place.

Everybody seems friendly enough, and genuinely glad you came. Coffee and doughnuts are served. There is a lot of chit-chat. People slowly make their way to the chairs in a circle, which (you think to yourself) is an odd arrangement for an orchestra. You also notice that no one else in the group brought an instrument. You feel very exposed and embarrassed, as though you have worn a costume to a party that is not a costume party.

The meeting gets underway late, because everyone is catching up and talking about their weekends. You are ready to play, but no one seems too eager to get started. The secretary reads the minutes of the last meeting. The treasurer and outreach leader give their reports. Someone provides an update on a member who is in the hospital, and requests prayer.

Finally, the person who is obviously the guest speaker for the night gives a short talk about "being a good musician," which essentially is a good person who does good things for other people, trying to make this world a better place. Someone follows-up with a meditative rendition of "Chopsticks" on the piano. The group sings a couple of choruses, and the meeting is over. Everyone hugs. It really is a warm group of people where you might be able to find some new friends. You leave and go home, carrying your unopened violin case.

One more picture: Imagine that on a crisp Sunday afternoon in October, Vince Lombardi, the football coach of Green Bay Packers legend (my wife Beth, son Daniel, and brother-in-law Phil are die-hard "cheeseheads") walks into an NFL football stadium to watch a game. The first thing he notices is the relatively low attendance. Some sections of the bleachers are thinly populated. Why are fans not flocking in here? What has happened to cause such a loss?

On the next Saturday afternoon, he picks another game—this time in one of the largest university stadiums in the land. The place is packed. The fans are excited, and the place is pulsating.

However, Lombardi notices that the crowd seems more interested in what is happening in the stands among themselves than they are in what is happening on the field. This event is all about tailgating before the game, being with friends, and enjoying a day of recreation and entertainment.

Yet, what really shocks this coach is what is happening on the field (or, what is not happening). He does not recognize what they are doing. What game are they playing? They call it "football," and there are a few elements of football in it. But it is essentially another, very different game.

Rattled and upset by what he is witnessing, this legendary coach finds the announcer's booth, grabs the microphone, and interrupts the game. He addresses everyone who is there, prophetically and passionately, reminding them of the great game of football and of the great players who once played it. He pleads for them to come out of the stands, get off the field, and leave whatever this is. Go into the classroom, and learn what this game is, he pleads, and then return to playing it. He holds a football in his right hand above his head, and says, "This is a football."[5]

"Who is this old dead man?!" the crowd shouts, "And why do we have to listen to him? So what if this isn't football the way he used to play it back in the day, but still thinks it ought to be played. This is how we play it. This is what we want, and everybody is having a good time. Besides, who can argue with the success of our big stadiums, big games, big crowds, big TV advertising, and big salaries?"

Note the common theme running through all three illustrations, as well as Jesus' parables: human beings stubbornly refuse to participate in the game to which they are called. The older son refuses to be the older son in the family and its celebration. Dinner guests invited to a great wedding banquet refuse to be dinner guests. Mathematicians refuse to be mathematicians, actively engaged in the discipline of mathematics. Musicians refuse to be musicians, preferring instead to do just about anything and everything except study, learn, play, and embody music seriously. Football players, coaches, and fans are not about football, but about their own games.

This is what I have found in local congregations. They are neither playing nor being played by the play of Christian theology. Yet strangely, this goes unnoticed. When pointed out, it does not bother them. When theology is brought in, and theological education is attempted, it is refused. And no one seems the least bit worried that this might be causing great harm to the church.

If congregations did not apply the term "Christian" and did not name themselves on the sign in the front lawn as "church," I would not expect theology and theological education to be present. I would not be critical, and I would not complain. If these communities were

---

5. This famous phrase is what Vince Lombardi reportedly said to his players in training camp in 1961. David Mariness, *When Pride Still Mattered: A Life of Vince Lombardi* (New York: Simon & Schuster, Inc., 1999), 274.

established specifically and openly for friendship, socio-psychological therapy, community social services, motivational talks, and business success, I would not try to impose theology—as long as their members were actually friends, therapists and patients, community organizers and social workers, motivational speakers and motivated individuals, and successful businesspersons. However, I would ask them to stop using theological identifiers for themselves, since nothing about who they are and what they are doing is distinctively theological, ecclesial, or Christian.

Jews, Muslims, Hindus, or Sikks do not have to be informed or engaged when it comes to the Christian theological faith-tradition. The reason is that they are not Christians. They do not claim to be Christians. Likewise, atheists, agnostics, neo-pagans, spiritualists, and secularists are exempt. Yet, as soon as a person or a group begins using the language of Christianity—church, God, Christ, Scripture, and faith—they come under the demands of Christian theology. No longer are they excused from theological education and theological knowledge, understanding, wisdom, and embodiment. They have been chosen to play and to be played (or are claiming to have been). Therefore, the absence of such participation is itself an indictment of them and their congregations. What other enterprise can you think of that does not expect all its members to be well-informed and well-formed by that enterprise's tradition?

Again, can you imagine a community of musicians who know little to nothing about music, and do not care to learn? They do not exist musically, and do not relate either to their world or to one another musically. Therefore, what's really going in their collective house and individual houses is something other than, and often contrary to, music. Because of them, the musical community is declining and even disappearing from the world. It cannot survive without true musicians, who are playing and being played.

The real, ultimate tragedy is that music itself is lost. Apart from a community dedicated to music, for whom these matters truly matter, music cannot possibly survive—especially not in the non-musical, anti-musical world in which we live. Music requires a stewarding community made up of musicians, who care about and take care of music, and who seriously teach and explain, study and learn, know and understand, protect and preserve, develop and perfect, embody and live, and transmit it. Otherwise, music fades away and becomes extinct.

Likewise, theology defines and determines everything that is called "church" and that is related to the Christian religion and its faith. Theology is the expression of "the game that is being played, and that is playing us." Therefore, we can only be the community that exists of, by, and for faith, when the theological tradition of this faith is defining and determining us, to the point that it brings us into existence and sustains us, gives us our reason to be, our identity and intentionality, is embodied by us in the way we think, talk, relate, and live, and finally, is the business we are in—the primary work that we are actually doing.

Yes, I do expect all congregations to be theological communities, where all Christians are expected to be theological persons, and where they can be educated as theologians. I strongly contend that the survival of both theology and the Christian community are at stake. Unless we honestly face, admit, and battle our own theological ignorance with urgent concern and dedicated action, the entire enterprise will be lost. And perhaps this has already happened. If so, it is that much more imperative that a few of us become a genuine community of theological faith, devoted to the retrieving, teaching, learning, and preserving of our own theological faith-tradition.

Who Are Theology's Few Players?

In the congregations I have served, I have met a few Christians who became intrigued by the prospect of "catching more than what they had thrown themselves," or that their congregations and fellow believers were tossing around. They began to play another, greater game. And by playing, they began to be played. They caught "the ball thrown by an eternal partner," and, in the process, were caught and changed by this strange, new, very different game.

Who are these few? Why them—these particular persons—rather than others? And, perhaps most confounding: Why *any* at all?

Theology is not a latest-greatest trend. It is not a popular pursuit. It is not a topic brought up in polite conversation. It is not a field of study parents want their children to major in in college. It does not produce the type of books folks have on their nightstands, much less take along to read on the beach. It is not considered essential, or even all that important, for the Christian life. It is not a subject most people know anything about, even in Christian congregations. So, why in the world would anyone have anything to do with it?

Let me ask this question another way: What would cause a plain, ordinary believer to go against the currents of popular culture and its religion, leave the crowd, and cross the line into theology? Over the years, I have had the privilege of knowing some of these contrarians. I was there when it happened. The ball was thrown by God out into the crowd with such accurate and measured swing that it came toward them. Why it was thrown toward them can only be left up to the mysterious grace of divine election.

For whatever reason—almost instinctively (though initiated and empowered by grace)—they responded and caught it. With two or three persons, it happened in real time, suddenly. With most of them, it occurred in slower motion over a longer period of time. But by responding to catch the ball, they all were caught. Before they knew it, they were in the game, as its players, being played.

I have learned that it is impossible to pick these persons out of the face-filled, faceless crowd. It is impossible to detect who they are. I cannot look out into the assembly seated in the pews or chairs when I am preaching, and tell whether any of them are there. There is no sign, no clue, or anything else that gives them away. They are hidden and anonymous until the time of calling and revealing.

They do not even know who they are. Randomly ask individuals whether they are among those chosen to be theology's students and stewards. They will likely look at you, dumbfounded, not knowing what to say, and not really knowing what you are asking. Some might ask you what you mean, and a couple might stutter, "I don't know." They truly don't.

If someone had come up to me prior to the summer of 1971, and told me that I would one day be not only a student of the Christian historical-biblical-theological faith-tradition, but also one of its called stewards and theologians, preaching and teaching it, I would have assumed my questioner was on an LSD trip. For one thing, I could never have imagined myself being that kind of person and living that kind of life. Never. Also, I had absolutely no idea what theology was;

and, frankly, had no desire to know. I wasn't interested. I had no real relationship with either the church or the Christian faith at the time. Why would I take on any responsibility for them?

Then it happened. I became one of the few. I was thrown the ball, and the rest is the history of my life. My great "burdensome joy"[6] has been the vocation of pastor-teacher-theologian, which has allowed me to meet, be with, come to know, and teach persons like myself, who have been claimed and called into the game. I have worshiped, fellowshiped, studied and learned, grieved and struggled, eaten and laughed with these people. I hold in memory the names and faces of every one of them. They are exceptional in my eyes.

However, there really is nothing exceptional about them in and of themselves. They bear no mark of exceptional intelligence, eloquence, or skill. They are good, ordinary folks. Most are introverts, and thus are reserved when it comes to religious expression. They wear their piety quietly. The lean toward mindfulness, and tend to be more serious, reflective, and thoughtful about matters of faith than most Christians—although people around them may not know this about them.

None majored in religion in college, and none is the scholarly type. They are mothers and housewives, computer techs, doctors, retired teachers, government employees, and small business owners. Most of them are not avid readers, and few, if any, have ever had a solid book of Christian studies in their hands. They have never been trained theologically, although they have sat in Sunday School classes, prayer meetings, worship services, and small group studies their entire lives.

Most tell me that from time to time they wondered if there was "more." There had to be, they thought, although it had never been introduced to them. They did not know where or how to look for it. So they settled into the "Christian life" and the "church routine" along with everybody else. They gave their money, helped with the children in the nursery, and served on more committees than they can remember. They did all the things Christian believers are supposed to do. And for the most part, they were content. But then

6. I borrow this term from James Earl Massey's book, *The Burdensome Joy of Preaching* (Nashville: Abingdon Press, 1998). Massey (1930–) is Dean Emeritus of Anderson School of Theology in Anderson, Indiana. He is the author of eighteen books, and a preacher who is known for his great communication skills.

again, occasionally when listening to sermons and lessons, the talk of the church around them, and ordinary Christian conversation among believers who are good and spiritual in every way, they sensed an emptiness. They were hungry for something else and something more. Would they have this appetite, if they weren't missing something real and necessary?

To the casual observer, these persons are just like everybody else. There is no apparent difference, and they apparently do not know they are different. Even after being around them for years, I am still puzzled and fascinated by them. What makes them different? Why are they different? Are they more curious than most people? Do they possess heightened imaginations? Is their mental ability, or spiritual need, greater? Are they wired differently? Just as a few individuals have perfect musical pitch, while others are tone-deaf, do these few simply have greater, keener ability than the general population to detect and deal with things of faith?

I don't think so. I have not noticed any pattern or regularity of personality trait, intellectual skill, spiritual ability, or character quality that would indicate this. There are no discernable markers or identifiers. In all ways, as I continue to say, they seem quite ordinary and normal. Therefore, I have no explanation as to why they pick up on and respond to the invitation, while others do not.

All I can do is go back to the call itself. The power is in the mysterious, miraculous throwing itself. It consists of "a ball thrown by an eternal partner with accurate and measured swing towards you, to your center, in an arch from the great bridgebuilding of God." Such a throw "throws" the recipient into a radically new situation.

Specifically, the divine approach sets into motion the entire event. Without the initiative and intention of God, there would be no perception, no stirring, no awakening, and definitely no response, since there would be nothing to which one might respond. It is the throwing of the ball that graciously gives both the opportunity and the summons to play. It also gives the potential player the interest, desire, and will to play. Catching, in this way, becomes a power.

How, when, or why this happens with some, and not with others, I will never know. But what I do know is that it happens. And when it does, Christians are never Christian the same way again. They are changed *for* the game, and they are changed *by* it.

I view my ministry as a "throwing around of the ball that has been thrown." Picture it. I stand at the pulpit before two or three hundred people, or at the classroom lectern before two or three, and toss the ball. I throw it out. And I do it Sunday after Sunday, or Tuesday night after Tuesday night. What happens next makes all the difference. What do they do with it?

Every theological preacher and teacher, if honest, will tell you how often the ball hits the floor in front of the pulpit or lectern and lies there. No one picks it up, or even notices it is there. It can hit folks in the head or chest, and they will not flinch. Afterward, they file by, saying, "I enjoyed your sermon today."

But then, one day, in an unpredictable, inexplicable moment, it happens. It happens to someone in the crowd. She sees it. What she has never noticed before—although it has been there the entire time—she now notices. She reaches out and catches it. And in doing so, she is caught by it, and begins to play.

I remember sitting alone one afternoon in a rocking chair in our apartment in Seminary Village. I had finished my school work, and was reading more widely in the thoughtful work of Paul Tillich, who had captured my interest. I was reading his *The Courage to Be*,[7] when I came to the very last section. Everything else was preliminary and preparatory, setting me up. I read the words "God above God." It hit me. I was suddenly struck by the full force of the realization breaking through: God—true God—is above all our ideas and concepts of God. God is greater than and other than what we believe, or can even imagine.

I came up out of my rocker, and began walking quickly around the room, exclaiming, "That's it! That's it! I've got it!" The theological truth was that enlightening, overpowering, and moving for me. How

---

7. Paul Tillich, *The Courage To Be* (New Haven: Yale University Press, 1952). The section I am referring to here—"The God Above God and the Courage to Be"—is on pages 186–190. Tillich (1886–1965) was a German American theologian and philosopher, whom many regard as one of the most influential thinkers of the twentieth century. He taught at Union Theological Seminary (New York City), Harvard Divinity School, and the University of Chicago. My wife Beth and I once took a fieldtrip to the park near New Harmony, Indiana, where Tillich's ashes are interred, quotations from his writings are engraved in large stones, and a sculptured bust of him rests on a pedestal in front of a clearing and a pond. It was well worth the effort and quite inspirational to visit.

could I not jump and shout for joy? How could I not respond? The ball had been thrown to me, and I was drawn into the game. Being played was that exhilarating.

The only way I know, then, to disclose the presence of the few in the crowd is to get them to identify themselves. Put theology before them. Toss them a piece of theology, and by their response—what they do or don't do with it—they will let you know if they are theologically called and ready, or not. They may not respond as quickly and demonstratively as I did when finishing Tillich's book. But theology has the power to draw persons out of hiding into the open, to become what they otherwise would not be. Theology captures those whom it wills to be its students and stewards. Catching the ball is both a desire and a capacity given to them by the One who has made the toss, in other to catch them for the game.

In this book's introduction, I used three extended metaphors from Jesus' teaching. First, drag a line and baited hook through the water; and fish will bite and get caught. Second, speak with the words and accent of the Good Shepherd; and his sheep will hear his voice, recognize it, come out, and follow it. Third, lay out pearls on the table. Swine will trample them down into their mire. But one or two persons, recognizing pearls for what they are, and realizing their true worth, will start buying. They will become pearl merchants. And they will devote the rest of their lives to searching for and trading in fine pearls, driven by the allure of the mother lode—the pearl of great price. They will sell everything they have in order to have it.

Let me offer a fourth metaphor from a science demonstration I remember from grade school. The teacher placed tuning forks side-by-side on the table. She picked one up and struck it with a mallet. It sounded. We could hear it ringing. She explained that this tuning fork was vibrating at a certain natural frequency.

The teacher hit this same fork again. But this time, she brought a second tuning fork near it. She did not hit it, and the two did not touch. Yet, because both were tuned to the same natural frequency, and the first one was vibrating, the second one began to vibrate and sound, as well. It was sounding in synch with the first fork.

I was on the edge of my seat.

Then the teacher asked a student to grab the tines of the first tuning fork in order to stop its vibration. Remarkably, we all could still hear its sound. How? It was not the first fork but the second fork that was continuing to ring. Even when the cause that had set it into motion was silenced, it was not. It continued to vibrate and sound.

I was stunned in utter amazement.

This phenomenon is called "resonance." One vibrating system drives another system to vibrate. And the second system responds to the first by reproducing, amplifying, and moving in synch with it, or resonating with it.

Every time I meet someone who responds openly and receptively to theology, I think of this classroom science demonstration. That person is acting the part of the second tuning fork, while I, as the preacher or teacher, am acting the part of the first—although in the whole scheme of Christian calling, I am always only a second tuning fork, like her. Theology is setting her into motion, as it has set me into motion. And now its vibration, operating through me, is setting someone else into motion.

Theology changes us and causes us to take on its sound, words, concepts, understandings, consciousness, and existence. We resound its truth and meaning. We reproduce, amplify, and move in synch with what has struck us. We resonate.

However, like musical instruments, we must first be "tuned" to the frequencies of Christian theology before we can be played to produce the same sounds. Naturally and normally as human beings, we are not tuned this way. We are tuned to many, different, other frequencies. We have been responding to other forces and energies. Therefore, we must be "retuned" by theology in order to become its instruments, capable of resonating with and reproducing its sounds.

These are words from the first stanza of one of my favorite hymns:

> Tune my heart to sing Thy grace;
> Streams of mercy, never ceasing,
> Call for songs of loudest praise:
> Teach me some melodious sonnet,
> Sung by flaming tongues above;
> Praise the mount! I'm fixed upon it,
> Mount of Thy redeeming love.[8]

---

8. Robert Robinson, "Come, Thou Fount of Every Blessing," *The Baptist Hymnal* (Nashville: Convention Press, 1991), 15. Robinson (1735–1790), an English Baptist pastor, scholar, and hymnist, wrote the words of this hymn in 1757. It is usually set

Our desiring prayer is that God will make us instruments that can be taught and tuned by theology to sing and play with the saints their highest, loudest, most melodic songs.

Is the Game Possible?

Sadly, too many Christians are settled and content with their current tuning, which is largely out of tune with the frequencies of their own historical-biblical-theological faith-tradition. Perhaps they are tone-deaf. Maybe they do not care about the original musical score, for they are enjoying making up their own songs, and singing them any way they like. Or, it could be that they are still banging away at the same level of the poor training they received as children, unwilling to invest in higher quality instruction. They do not believe they need to be fashioned into new instruments, or honed and re-tuned for greater playing.

Then, one day, someone comes along who has been caught by the sound, been retuned by it and for it, and is now resonating and ringing it out loudly and clearly. What will the tuning forks sitting in the pews do? Will they sit there unresponsive? Or join in?

Let's take this science demonstration one step further. If two or more tuning forks are mounted on a sound box or board—like the taunt strings of a guitar or piano—and all are struck, they will all begin vibrating. Their collective sound will be much more complex, richer, and louder than the sound each would make apart from the others, and apart from the sound box or board.

I view the church as the "sounding box or board" for the Christian theological faith-tradition. The true church is a hollow body, void of other interests, preoccupations, and activities that would muffle, drown out, or displace theology. This makes it the prime place for the gospel, because here the gospel has plenty of room to bounce around, sound, and resound.

---

to an American folk tune, "Nettleton," which first appeared in John Wyeth's *Respository of Sacred Music, Part Second* (1813, p. 112). I have fond memories of performing my own arrangement of this hymn for Baptist "piano festivals" in the mid-sixties.

The church also provides "empty space" for human beings to hear what they will not hear elsewhere, and otherwise would be unable to hear. The full, deep, magnificent sounds of theology can come through for listening, learning, and living only in congregations that are ordered for this purpose. How can anyone reside here without joining in the playing and hearing of this particular music? Why would anyone want to play or hear anything else?

It is sad and tragic that ordinary Christians are in such low-, false-, post-, non-, or anti-theological places. If or when theology is brought in, it is ignored and not given room, much less full, free reign of the house. Therefore, the chances of laypersons ever meeting their own theological faith-tradition become slim to none. How, then, will the few be revealed and equipped for playing?

If my assessment is correct, the church is in a disastrous state theologically, for which there is no large, immediate solution. There is no antidote, panacea, quick fix, or cure-all. Our own tradition can no longer save us, because we are keeping ourselves far removed from it—the very source that brings alive and empowers both faith and learning. Ironically, we are who in most need are the ones who resist its redemptive resource. We refuse to return for retuning.

Our condition did not happen overnight, or over a short period of time. It will not be changed and corrected overnight, or over a short period of time. There are no signs that anything is changing, or opening and getting ready to be corrected. In fact, everything points to congregations and Christians moving further and further from theology, and thus becoming deeper and deeper, more permanently fixed in their disastrous condition. We are now so estranged from theology in such a state of ignorance and illiteracy that we may never be able to come back, even if we wanted to.

I know this is not the prognosis anyone wants to hear. We are generally optimistic people. We have the good old American "can do" spirit. We hang on tenaciously to the belief that Christians will always in the end do what is right, and end up on their feet on the straight and narrow path.

Our problem, we like to think, is simply that laypersons have never been taught. They have never had the opportunity. They have never had theology explained to them. If given this opportunity, along with a proper introduction and a little encouragement and guidance, most people of Christ will respond positively and jump at the chance to learn and grow in both theological literacy and faith.

My response is two-fold. First, "Have you ever met any of these people?" And second, "Have you ever tried to introduce and teach theology to a group of Christians?" I have. And it has awakened little interest, and even less participation—as I once believed it would. The factors against it taking hold in our congregations and individual lives in this secular age are simply too numerous, pervasive, dominant, and strong. Therefore, I no longer believe it is possible to bring theology back home successfully. It is time we tell the truth. This household is unable and unwilling to house theology again, or to take up residence and be at home in theology's house.

Methodist historian and theologian Justo González reaches a similar conclusion at the end of his overview of the history of theological education. The return of the theological life to its proper place at the heart of the church in local congregations is more than difficult. It is impossible. There are too many interests, inertia, and more important things against it.[9]

I wholeheartedly agree—although it pains me to say so. The entire vision and effort of reconciling the church and theology, and of bringing about theological faith among all Christians, appear doomed.

But then, González adds this final line: "But what is impossible for humans is possible for God."[10] Amen! I again wholeheartedly agree. While we earnestly conclude that the church has gotten itself in a disastrous state from which it cannot deliver itself (and doesn't seem to want to), God is steadfastly faithful and present, already working in hidden ways to educate and redeem Christ's church theologically. Our task, then, is not so much to make this happen, but rather to allow it to happen. We don't resist the theological reformation God is bringing about. We join it.

Consequently, I remain hopeful. I continue to trust that God is still approaching, confronting, claiming, and summoning out of the crowd those whom Christ is selecting to convert and shape to be his students and stewards of the theological faith-tradition and its gospel. My hope is grounded in the truth and wisdom of the Word, along

---

9. González, *The History of Theological Education* (Nashville: Abingdon Press, 2015), 129–130.

10. González, 130.

with the power of the Spirit. I believe theology is the lure, the voice, the mother pearl, the thrown ball, and the melodious sonnet. And I have witnessed its powerful sway enough times—including in my own life—to know that where it is actively at work, some do respond and return home.

I retain the image of "bringing theology home." I continue the ministry effort. Yet, now I see the other side that is more profound: "bringing the church home." Although we view theology as the prodigal, you and I are the real prodigals. We are the ones who separated and wandered off. Theology did not leave us. We left it. Therefore, neither the local congregation nor the individual Christian life is home. Theology is.

Our calling, then, is not so much to bring theology home as it is for theology to bring us home.

Every once in a while, here and there, one or two can be seen making the long journey back. They are responding to an eternal pitch made to them that they had to catch.

5
Schooling

You are still reading. Others bogged down somewhere along the way, or wandered off and were lost. But you are still following this path, and thereby separating and distancing yourself further from the crowd. Soon you will reach the point where you will be unable to go back.

What is most significant about your reading is that you have entered into the territory of theology, and yet have not turned away. You may not realize it, but theology is the reason you have not turned away and gone back into the crowd. You have become aware of something you have never been aware of before. It has made you curious and demanded your attention. Now you are beginning to see that these matters truly matter. And what's more, they have started to matter to you. They are carrying a sense of significance—and even urgency—they did not before. Now you have to know what's next. This is why you are still here, reading and staying with it. How could you leave?

Theology has presented itself to you, as alive with the reality of God as a bush burning in the wilderness.[1] In the manner of Moses, you have broken your routine and stepped aside to see for yourself what this odd thing is. Your responsiveness indicates that the game has captured you. You are being played.

Remember Moses' fear. He hid his face, afraid to face God. This is normal human response to the Holy. No one can gaze on or grasp God, and live. Therefore, who in his or her right mind, or natural

1. Read Exodus 3:1–10.

frame of existence, would not tremble in the presence of the *Mysterium*?[2]

"It is a fearful thing to fall into the hands of the living God." (Hebrews 10:31) Only the fool does not have the urge to save herself by fleeing, and from then on, mark this place as forbidding and to be avoided. Yet, at the same time, only the fool refuses "the one who is speaking," and does not stay and obey the God who is "a consuming fire." (Hebrews 12:25, 29)

Given that theology is about God, I understand why most people want nothing to do with it. The unknown causes a fearful dread, especially when it is the Ultimate Unknown. Theology is about the Ultimate Unknown, and all things in relation to the Ultimate Unknown. Therefore, ordinary mortals are instinctively afraid of theology, and want to stay away from it.

Second, given what little they do know, or think they know about theology, many Christians find it distant and forbidding. It is not for them. It appears to have nothing to do with them, or to give them. They do not see how it relates to their everyday lives, or helps them cope with all their stresses, worries, and problems. Theology belongs to long ago. It is not immediately and directly accessible.

Besides, third, they already have all they need in order to be believers. Early on, their parents and Sunday School teachers gave them Christian religion with a ready-made basic set of beliefs, values, and practices. They have not done much to it or with it over the years, except drop some of its strictest moral clauses, blend in a few novel ideas they have picked up along the way, and dress it up in the more contemporary clothes of popular evangelical language and culture. They have effectively crafted their own religious bricolage, or simulacrum of spirituality, which contains only a few disordered fragments of theology. But they still believe it is fully "Christian."

The best thing is, it is theirs and not somebody else's. They own it, and not even the church can tell them what it is, or what it ought to be. Their religion is new and fresh, and not some old, stale relic from the past. Also, it's working for them. It does what it is supposed to do at the level of faith on which they are living and serving. Genuine,

---

2. See Rudolf Otto, trans. John W. Harvey, *The Idea of the Holy* (London: Oxford University Press, 1958), 8–40.

full-blown, historical, biblical, ethical, ecclesial theology would only complicate and mess things up. It would distract them from what they consider to be really important about being a Christian: believing in God, and having a personal relationship with Jesus, and living a good life. It would be dead weight. So, who needs it?

Finally, theology comes across as demanding. It requires much from those to whom it is given, which is much more that they want to give. Being a sacred trust, it expects the persons to whom it is entrusted to be trustworthy. This entails taking up the theological life, and, from then on, studying and learning, caring for and taking care of, communicating and transmitting, embodying and living theology. Theology's stewards cannot be lazy or neglectful. They cannot be casual or flippant. They must lose their lives for the sake of it.

Most Christians are simply unwilling to do this. The cost is much too high. They do not believe theology is worth it. They don't want to be entrusted with it, and thus responsible for it. It is unworthy of either their trustworthiness or their resources. To them, it is a waste of time and effort.

The only reason I can think of, then, for you, me, or anyone else to stay with theology is that the bush has burned, and a voice has called out. Standing before the *Mysterium,* Abraham, Isaac, Jacob, Moses, Deborah, Samuel, Isaiah, Mary (Jesus' mother), and a long line of saints stretching down through history—now including unlikely participants like you and me—have been able to do nothing but stammer, "Here I am, Lord." This game has caught us up in its play, and now we have to play. We cannot do otherwise.

Now what? It is one thing to be called and to join in. But it is another to be capable and competent as a theologian. Between the two—meeting theology for the first time, and being a theologian—is a wide gulf. One does not automatically or magically become a theologian by hearing a theological word, picking up a theology book, or thinking about God. Nor is the status of theologian merely a step or two away, and easily reached. The distance is great.

The only way to cross this wide gulf is by an educational bridge. A long process of teaching and learning begins with an initial meeting, and then moves toward the other side as its goal. Theology makes those who are responsive to the ball being thrown by God its students and stewards. Gradually, by playing and being played, they learn the game and become more knowledgeable and skillful. They never stop serving as its students and stewards. And, before they know it, they are already being made theology's theologians.

The person refusing this education, who never becomes a student and steward of the Christian theological faith-tradition, will never become a theologian. Frankly, I am amazed at the skill of so many Christians to avoid being students, and thereby escape ever becoming theologians. Why would anyone work so hard to resist theological education, completely ignoring matters of such vital truth and significance? Isn't a non-learning, non-teachable, non-theological Christian believer a self-contradiction?

School Days

School days, school days,
Dear old golden rule days
'Readin' and 'ritin' and 'rithmetic,
Taught to the tune of a hick'ry stick,
You were my queen in calico,
I was your bashful, barefoot beau,
You wrote on my slate, I love you, Joe,
When we were a couple of kids.[3]

This popular 1907 chorus has given generations of Americans an indelible mental picture of "school." School is where kids are sent to be strictly disciplined and taught the basic subjects necessary for them to grow up to become good citizens, good husbands and wives who have their own kids, and all-around decent human beings. Consequently, education has come to be viewed as an enterprise for children.

Grown-ups went through the regimen when they were children. When they grew up and graduated, they put school behind them. Since childhood has passed, it is assumed that the educational period has passed, as well. It must have worked. The goal of learning has

3. Will Cobb and Gus Edwards, *School Days* (New York: Gus Edwards Music Publishing Company, 1907).

been achieved. Adult men and women are out in the "real world." where they are holding down good jobs, so that they can raise their kids to go to college, become good citizens, contribute to society, and be all-around decent human beings.

This close identification of education and childhood is reinforced by Robert Fulghum in a collection of his essays, *All I Really Need to Know I Learned in Kindergarten.*[4] The book's title is taken from its first essay, in which Fulghum summarizes his personal credo. He believes the most important, valuable lessons in life are acquired during early childhood. Everything after that is extra. What one learns in grade school, high school, college, graduate school, on the job, and through adult interactions and involvements is valuable. However, it does not count for nearly as much as what a kindergartener learns and knows: things like holding hands and sticking together, not hitting people, and so on. As Fulghum puts it, wisdom is "in the sandpile at Sunday School."[5]

Implied is the notion that Sunday School is kindergarten, which is primarily for children, and is child's play. Adults no longer need schooling for their religion, since they received it as children, and already know all they really need to know. Now all they have to do is make sure their own children and grandchildren go to Sunday School, so that they, too, will gain the "wisdom" that basically is playing nice and getting along with others.

No mention is made of teaching children important lessons concerning the church, the Bible, faith, or Christ. Being the people of God, proclaiming the gospel, stewarding the Christian historical-biblical-theological faith-tradition, and existing by faith in this world must not rank "up there" with what is taught and can be learned by everybody "down here."

The purpose of Sunday School, accordingly, is to teach children what they need to know about being successful in relationships, wherever they may go and whatever they may do. The important

---

4. Robert Fulghum. *All I Really Need to Know I Learned in Kindergarten: Uncommon Thoughts on Common Things* (New York: Villard Books, 1988). Fulghum (1937–) is an American author and Unitarian-Universalist minister, artist, teacher, and member of a defunct rock and roll band, "Rock Bottom Remainders," that was made up of popular authors who were amateur musicians.

5. Fulghum, 6–8.

lessons are about living meaningfully and happily for the rest of our lives. We are the subjects who matter—not some distinctive, yet distant, historical-biblical-theological subject matter.

Unfortunately, and sadly, many Christians believe this, or want to believe this. Fulghum's "all I really need to know" credo struck a nerve and became a bestseller. It was widely taught in adult Sunday School classes, preached from pulpits, and discussed in Christian book groups. Many Christians did not discern that it did not fit or match the Christian theological faith-tradition.

The idea that both life in general and the Christian life in particular are simple and uncomplicated is inviting. The thought that, as adults, we do not have to stay in school beyond childhood, continue our education, or read, study, think, and work hard anymore, is simply too good *not* to be true. The lessons we were taught about being good boys and girls, obeying our parents (and all adults with authority), "doing unto others as you would have them do unto you," and going to church, are good enough. This is all anyone needs in order to be a Christian and to be saved. Why, then, would anyone study theology?

Given this all-too-common mindset, our congregations have been turned into anything and everything except schools. Sunday School is a pseudo-school. Parents bring their children, because they believe their children need to learn the simple lessons of fair play, getting along, being good, and acting responsibly. Christian youth need to socialize with other Christians their age, so that they can help each other stay away from premarital sex, alcohol, pornography, and other immoral and illegal activities. (What parents don't realize is that these youth groups can be the places where their kids are introduced to these activities.)

Parents who bring their kids may or may not join their own Sunday School classes. If they do, they will likely attend for reasons other than education, such as adult company and conversation, which is very welcomed after having been with their toddlers and teenagers all week.

Never mind that rarely is any teacher in these Sunday School classes a true student of the Christian theological faith-tradition, or fully and skillfully engaged in serious biblical study. Most Christians cannot imagine, much less name, a teacher who actually reads, studies, learns, and then teaches theology. Consequently, no Sunday

School member is ever required, or even encouraged, to be a student, much less a theologian.

The teacher's job is merely to come up with a short "lesson" each week, loosely based on "the quarterly," which is a standardized curriculum put out by a denomination's division of education or an independent Christian publishing house. This lesson is written on a low educational level, is thin and shallow on biblical commentary, while heavy on the comments of its author, and is intended to stimulate more comments from both teacher and students.

The biblical texts for the day are treated as though they are Rorschach inkblots.[6] A verse is held up, and everyone says the first thing that comes to his or her mind. It is common to go around the room, allowing each member to tell the group "what this verse means to me." This exercise reveals more about the emotional, spiritual, and intellectual state of the speaker than it does about the literary and historical structure of the text, or about the text's theological truth or significance.

Before long—if things go as planned—the whole group is off into a lively discussion of whatever it is that they really want to talk about. The aim is for everyone to have a chance to join in, to speak up and express herself, and then leave feeling that she "got something out of it." Adults never question whether they have learned anything, and are leaving with greater knowledge and understanding of the Christian historical-biblical-theological faith-tradition. At least their children come home with arts and crafts pieces to post on the refrigerator.

This same pattern is repeated with "special study courses," children's missions classes, and youth retreats. Very little learning occurs. In fact, these activities keep participants from learning. The illusion that they are "in class" hides from them the truth that their congregation's education program does not educate; and, as a result, they are not being educated.

---

6. Swiss psychiatrist and Freudian psychoanalyst Hermann Rorschach (1884–1922) developed what is known as the "Rorschach test." An individual is shown ten inkblots, one at a time. An inkblot is an ambiguous blot of black ink on a blank page. The individual is asked to tell what she sees. The theory is that she will "project" onto the inkblots unconscious parts of herself, thereby giving the psychologist insight into her personality and emotional functioning.

I have known too many eighty-year-olds who think, talk, and act theologically as they did when they were eight-year-olds. How is it that these delightful, loving, faithful people can spend their entire lives in Sunday School, every single Sunday, yet have so little to show for it? Our congregations are breeding grounds for religious illiteracy and theological ignorance. Yet, no one is alarmed, or ever sounds the alarm. If someone did, most Christians would hit the snooze button, roll over, and go back to sleep.

The message, spoken or unspoken, is clear: Christians, in order to be Christians, do not need formal, ordered, serious, sustained theological education. All of us already know all we need to know for being Christians, and for living meaningful, fulfilling lives. Amazingly, we have had this knowledge a long time, from our earliest training at home and in a home congregation.

Therefore, as adults, we no longer need the church to be a school, or to provide schooling for us. We do not need a teacher, since we do not need to be taught. We do not have to read and study, since there is nothing significant or essential for us to learn, since we have already learned all the significant, essential lessons. We know everything we need to know in order to be religious, spiritual, and moral persons. All else is extra and optional. We already have all the wisdom we can handle, thank you. Any more would only complicate matters and confuse us.

Besides, as adults, we have moved on beyond education, and now our task is to put what we have learned as children into practice. This is the hard part. Going back to school would only distract us and take away from working hard at practicing, living, and growing in our faith. Our school days are long behind us. School is a thing of the past (which is considered a good thing). We have been there, and have already done that. We will not go back. We don't need to.

The problem, however, is that this mindset effectively leaves Christian grown-ups at an elementary level of faith, equivalent to that of a child. Even more troubling is their belief that this is the way they are supposed to be, as "children of the Heavenly Father." They have not advanced beyond a child's level of understanding to know that when Jesus said, "Whoever does not receive the kingdom of God as a little child will never enter it" (Luke 18:17), he was teaching the same lesson he gave Nicodemus: the Kingdom is entered only by "being born of the Spirit, from above,"[7] and thus like a newborn child.

In no way or sense does this mean that adults are never to grow up, but to remain persons who are child-like in their thinking, and childish in their behavior for the rest of their lives. Jesus was simply explaining how each of us begins, when it comes to the in-breaking Kingdom. Just as we were birthed into this world, we have to be birthed into the strange new world of God's Kingdom. Jesus did not expect anyone who starts as a child in either world to remain a child.

Listen to Paul: "When I was a child, I spoke like a child, I thought like a child, I reasoned like a child; when I became an adult, I put an end to childish ways." (1 Corinthians 13:11) Christians are born of the Spirit, and then are animated by the same Spirit to grow up and become grown-up, mature in every way. Although we begin as little children, we must not stay as little children.

Of course, we take much of what we have learned with us and build on it. At the same time, we leave much of it behind, since it is no longer fitting, adequate, or appropriate for us. We continue acquiring greater knowledge and understanding, as we become more and more capable. The mode of existence that is faith is developmental. The learning of it is life-long. Wisdom, then, is not at the beginning in childhood, as Fulghum says, but at the end of this long learning, maturing process, in adulthood. As disciples, or students, of Jesus, there is no time or stage at which our theological education ends, or becomes optional. We are never as mature or wise as we are called to be (or think we are).

However, Christians do stop. They figure they have had enough, or all they need. So they quit. They leave their schooling behind and walk away, never to return. This is when and where they become fixed in place. They stop learning. They are no longer "growing up in every way into him who is the head, into Christ." (Ephesians 4:15)

This is the disastrous state of too many Christians and their congregations. The writer of Hebrews chastises all Christians who allow themselves to "become dull in understanding." His words are as relevant and hard-hitting for adult believers today as they have always been:

---

7. Read John 3:1–8 in conjunction with John 1:12–14.

> For though by this time you ought to be teachers, you need someone to teach you again the basic elements of the oracles of God. You need milk, not solid food; for everyone who lives on milk, being still an infant, is unskilled in the word of righteousness. But solid food is for the mature, for those whose faculties have been trained by practice to distinguish good from evil. Therefore, let us go on toward perfection. (Hebrews 5:11–6:1a)

This is sound admonition for us. People of faith who consider theological education to be optional, and then do not choose this option, are deciding to stay as infants or young children. By refusing the solid, grown-up food of theology's meat and potatoes, they are opting for the child's religious warm milk and spiritual "chicken soup for the soul." These persons stop growing when they stop reading, studying, and being taught. Without more substantial provision, they allow themselves to "become dull in understanding."

After all these years of Sunday School and religious, spiritual, and devotional activities, they should by now be capable and skilled as instructors and mentors of others. However, they are not. They are still in need of basic instruction and mentoring—instruction and mentoring they are refusing. They are not in school, and do not want to be in school. They are not disciples, and have no interest in becoming disciples. They cannot look back and name one thing they have learned in the past five years. They have lived so long without teaching that they no longer are teachable. They are satisfied and comfortable where they are, clinging to what little they learned a long time ago in the church's kindergarten. They are not growing and moving on toward perfection, or maturity. Yet, they believe they have all they need; and it is enough.

The most severe consequence is that a congregation filled with such uneducated, non-learning Christians does not and cannot offer theological education. It is not itself a theologically grounded and growing community. If an individual comes to this place desiring theology, he will quickly discover that theological education has never really been optional here (as he had been led to believe), since there is no such option. This community does not offer, and has no intention of offering, education beyond the most rudimentary religious, moral level for beginners. Anyone who wants more is out of luck. Theology and its education are not taken seriously here. Not one is a serious student or teacher here. No one is a theologian, or is on her way to becoming a theologian, here. There is no life-long course of study here. We are not living the theological life as theological people, because we are uninterested in theological schooling here. "School" has only negative connotations for us. If someone wants theology, let him go and find it somewhere else.

Called to Be Disciples

Jesus summoned twelve to follow him.[8] They were to "walk behind" him, literally going with him wherever he went. This involved more than tagging along, or merely companioning or accompanying him. They were to "walk in the path Jesus walked." That meant they had to learn the path ("the narrow path") Jesus was taking, and how to take it themselves. Jesus was their teacher, both by the way he walked and by the way he talked about it.[9] In sum, he himself was "the way, and the truth, and the life." (John 14:6)

With Jesus in the role of teacher, the twelve were put in the role of disciple. The word "disciple" means "student." The twelve were called by Jesus specifically to be his students. He intended to be their teacher, and to make them his students, teaching them the "secrets," or mysteries, of the Kingdom. Together as teacher and students, they were a teaching-learning community, or school. Their constant, full-time relationship was instructional, and thus was a concrete form of schooling. Their life together was educational, as they lived in the power of the in-breaking Kingdom and learned its lessons.

---

8. Matthew 4:18–22; Mark 1:16–20; Luke 5:1–11.

9. A platitude floats around among Christians: "Don't talk the talk, but walk the walk." I have never used this expression, and never will. My reasons are: (1) I do not diminish either the value or the necessity of talking; it is essential to Christian faith; (2) I refuse to pit talking and walking against each other; both are important and necessary; each requires the other; (3) walking is a form of talking (i.e., articulating or communicating); and talking is a form of walking (i.e., living, moving, and having one's being); and (4) I believe we Christians should be able to "talk and walk at the same time," as Jesus did, and as he taught his disciples to do.

During one of his post-resurrection appearances, Jesus authorized them to "make disciples…teaching them."[10] He ordered his students to go and do to others what he had done to them: to walk the way and talk about it, teaching others what Jesus had first taught them.

Today you and I belong to this same group of those who have been called by Jesus, are being made disciples, and, at the same time, are charged with making disciples. We are in his company for the purpose of being taught and learning. There is no other reason for us to be here. This is a teaching-learning community, or school, where teachers and learners live together in the way, truth, and life that is Christ. At no time can we honestly say, "We have learned everything there is to know, or that we need to know; and, therefore, we no longer have to go to school." This is nothing but a school here. And there are nothing but disciples in this school.

Consequently, you and I must undergo a major shift in our presuppositions and self-images. Our first lesson is to stop thinking that our education is behind us. All we really need to know we did not learn in Sunday School, and no one can or will learn it all there. As beginners, we have no clue how much we don't know, how much there is to know, and how much we can possibly come to know through continuing theological education. Such limited, misguided thinking is clear, overwhelming evidence of our theological ignorance, and of our strong need for theological education. We must not go "back to school" (in the sense of returning to or staying with what we have previously experienced), but rather go forward to another kind of schooling that will continue for the rest of our lives.

Second, we have to start thinking of ourselves in a way we have never thought of ourselves before—as students. Try this term "student" on for size. Wear it and get used to it. Set firmly in your mind that you are a student. And as a student, your first need is to be taught. You need a teacher. Your task is to learn. Why? Because you are called to follow Jesus, in order that you will be made his disciple.

Third, you need a school where you will be among other students like yourself. Students are not born, but have to be made. And they can be made only in a society of teachers and students—a teaching-learning community, or school. Since our congregations are not

10. Matthew 28:19–20.

schools, you will have to search for a group where theology is taken seriously, studied, embodied, and passed on. You then will have to allow yourself to be taken in, taught, and over time be shaped into the disciple that you are called to be.

Where will you find such a school? Where in Chattanooga, Tennessee, Athens, Georgia, or Boone, North Carolina, is "making disciples" occurring? Where can the ordinary believer be faithful to his or her calling to be a student of the Christian theological life?

Called to Be Seminarians

The church has relegated its educational ministry to special schools that are organized for the training of its professional clergy. Theological education is offered primarily, if not exclusively, at these seminaries and divinity schools, and, therefore, not in the wider, whole church—especially not where the church is appearing locally.

Consequently, the Christian who desires to be a student of the Christian theological faith-tradition must pack up, move, and go live at one of these schools where the knowledge is, and where the teacher-theologians and students are. Fortunate are those who live close enough to one of these schools to be able to commute. However, having a family and holding down a day-job means that the student will only be able to take classes part-time one or two weeknights, or on Saturdays—if the seminary supports this type of student with this type of schedule.

Some schools offer online courses. However, it is difficult to achieve and maintain a high level of rigor and quality in such courses. Second, the absence of face-to-face interaction with others in a community hinders and harms the study of theology—more than it does other studies, such as chemistry. Finally, the financial costs and time demands are still too great for the average Christian.

Also, it is well-known and obvious that this education is designed for clergy, is set on a high level of scholarship, and involves all the academic requirements of grading, test-taking, paper-writing, etc. Consequently, those who are not clergypersons, and who have no need or interest in being trained for clergy ministry, stay home with the rest of the church, where theology is neither taught nor learned.

This situation is acceptable to most of us, since we still carry in our heads the long-held belief that only a few exceptional individuals are called "into the ministry." Most believers are not. Therefore, only these rare few have to "go to seminary." The rest of us don't.

The typical person in the pews or folding chairs on Sunday morning has no reason to go, since she has not been called into the ministry. She is only a layperson. She would stand out as the exception at the seminary. Everyone would wonder what she's doing there. She does not belong there. She would feel as though she were committing a crime, breaking and entering into somebody else's house.

Of course, this traditional expectation of seminary education for clergy is fading quickly, as more and more congregations are demanding less and less from their clergy educationally, as well as ministerially. Why would anyone need to go anywhere to be specially educated, when she is serving a congregation that is shaped more by the popular culture than by the historical tradition of Christian biblical-theological faith? Why would a lead pastor, youth pastor, or worship pastor spend his time and money on something that simply is not needed, since neither ministerial nor congregational success depends on it?

I believe both of these assumptions are false. The whole church—the *laos tou Theou,* or laity of God[11]—is called "into the ministry." There is only one calling, and all believers share this same calling, although it is defined and exercised in different ways. Consequently, as I have said, there are nothing but ministers in this house.

What, then, is our common ministry? It is the ministry of Christ. It is the ministry of being made disciples and making disciples. Again, what major human enterprise does not require education? Name one career that does not demand its members to be its students, who are

---

11. This term conveys the truth that all Christians, both clergy and non-clergy persons, are the *laos* or people of God. Despite my ordination, I have always considered myself a layperson, or member of the *laos*. Becoming a clergyperson did not cost me my place in the people of God. The only difference between others and me in the laity is that I have been appointed for overseeing and officiating certain ministries of the church—especially the proclamation and education of the Word, and the equipping of the saints. I am a minister to the ministers. Still, all of us are ministers in these ministries of the church.

being taught and learning its tradition of knowledge and skill. Christian ministry is no exception.

Every believer, called into the ministry, is called to go to school and to be theologically educated. Any minister—professional or non-professional, clergyperson or non-clergyperson—who stays biblically illiterate, theologically ignorant, and thus ministerially ill-equipped and inexperienced, should be the rare exception. Any minister who remains this way, and is the least bit proud of it, ought to be ashamed.

I am fully supportive of seminaries and divinity schools for the church's theological education and the professional training of clergy. I have attended and earned two degrees at one seminary, and also served as faculty and staff member at another. Schools like these are the only house the church has right now for the teaching and learning of the theological faith-tradition. This body of knowledge is stored in their libraries and classrooms. Highly trained, accomplished scholars are on their faculties. These men and women teach, write journal articles and books, and conduct world-class research in the various fields and disciplines of biblical, theological, philosophical, historical, ethical, cultural, liturgical, pastoral, educational, ecclesial, and missional studies. I hold these dedicated stewards in the highest regard, and in no way want to devalue their contribution to the church (although I do have constructive criticisms of some of their scholarship, and also of their lack of connection and communication with the church they are called to serve).

My proposal does not involve in any way the diminishment of the clergy seminary, or the full shift of its tasks to the local congregation. However, I do push for the terms "seminary" and "theological education" to be broadened to include and apply to the local congregation. This in itself is a radical move. It is like adding oil to water, or letting the peas touch the mashed potatoes on the plate. I am proposing that we merge categories we have never thought of merging—and may believe should be kept separate and never merged. Yet, if the whole church, and not merely a small select group of professional scholars and pastors, is to be theological, and thus faithful to its identity and purpose, then theological education must take place locally where Christians live, worship, and serve, as well as at a distance in schools of advanced, specialized training.

Every man and woman who stands before Christ's church as a clergyperson must know, understand, and embody what he or she is called to stand there to represent. Proper schooling and an ongoing life of study and learning are required, and are not optional. Anything less or otherwise is an abomination and disgrace.

I will go one step further. Every non-clergyperson who takes on any role of teacher, elder, deacon, director, or leader in a congregation must know, understand, and embody what he or she is called to live, represent, and serve, which is theological faith. Proper schooling and an ongoing life of study and learning are required, and are not optional. Anything less or otherwise is an abomination and disgrace.

Let's not stop here, but take it all the way. Every Christian—without exception—must know, understand, and embody what he or she is called to live, represent, and serve, which is theological faith. Proper schooling and an ongoing life of study and learning are required, and are not optional. Anything less or otherwise is an abomination and disgrace.

Why? The reason is simple: every believer, every follower of Jesus, is called to be a disciple (student) and a minister. To be one entails the other, and both require a teaching-learning community, or school.

If an individual is not called, then she does not have to enter into discipleship, ministry, and seminary education. She is not required to know, understand, or embody theological faith. She does not have to go to school. She does not have to be a student. She does not have to be a minister. She is under no obligation to be taught or to learn.

A very specific, unique demand is placed on those of us who are called. We are expected to be Jesus' disciples and ministers, and, therefore, to go to school. The particular schooling we need is theological. It is ministerial. This is the education that a seminary offers. Therefore, every Christian is called to be a seminarian. And every seminarian needs and deserves a quality seminary education.

Like every clergyperson, every non-clergyperson should be given the opportunity and means to be theologically trained, and thereby properly educated and equipped in his or her own faith-tradition for the Christian ministry. Every believer shares with the pastor and the professor the same calling to be a theologian, although they all have different levels, places, areas, and methods of theological ministry.

Therefore, every believer needs and deserves the theological education necessary for this theological ministry.

As I have already mentioned, most Christians cannot pack up and relocate. They cannot afford the high financial cost of online or night classes. They cannot carve out the necessary large blocks of time in their busy schedules to fit the schedule of an educational institution. They do not need the usual curriculum in the way it is designed and taught. And, let's be honest, only the hardcore among us relish the thought of going back to test-taking, paper-writing, and grades.

Therefore, why not bring theological education to Christians where they are? Why not establish a small teach-learning community within a congregation, or between several congregations in the same region? Is it possible to reconceive and reform an entire congregation theologically, along the lines of a lay seminary?

We must begin taking theological education seriously for the whole church. We must rediscover and reestablish it as a primary ministry—if not *the* primary ministry—of the congregation. We must make theological education as near to and available to ordinary Christians as possible.

At the same time, in our congregations, we must make worship, fellowship, education, ministry, and missions theological, and also make theology liturgical, social, educational, ministerial, and missional. Our objective is to teach and train the whole body of Christ, and not only a limited segment of it. All believers are ministers. All ministers are seminarians. And all seminarians require a seminary.

Congregation As Seminary

Half a century ago, Elton Trueblood laid out his vision for the renewal of the church. He believed the world needs the church, because it needs the Christian faith as a redemptive force—a force that is operative only through the church.

However, according to Trueblood, the church is failing to function effectively, or to its fullest potential, as God's instrument and means of redemption in the world. Therefore, the church needs to be renewed within. This is the only way it can or will fulfill its missional role without.[12] The only way this will happen is if the church returns to its identity and purpose as a "society of ministers."

Trueblood began with the church being created and placed in this world as "a chosen race, a royal priesthood, a holy nation, God's own people." (1 Peter 2:9) This is the sole reason for its existence. The church is a priestly house in which all believers, both non-clergypersons and clergypersons, are called to participate in the same life and ministry of Christ, though having different functions and tasks.

Of course, Trueblood was speaking within the church's historical-biblical-theological tradition, while realizing that this particular conception of the church is neither commonly known nor practiced in our congregations. It is foreign to most Christians, who have never heard of it. Therefore, Trueblood acknowledged that the renewal of the church, as he envisioned it, would be a great and difficult task. Still, it is a most vital and urgent task. Otherwise, the church will not be the church, participating in the ministry of Christ. And, without the church, the world will not be encountered by the redemptive force of the gospel of God in Christ.

So, we have our work cut out for us. How do we do this? Where do we begin?

Trueblood identified as the practical starting point the recovery of the teaching role of the pastor.[13] The pastor must serve the local congregation by being its teacher. He or she must teach the body persuasively that it is a royal priesthood, or society of ministers. Individual members must be persuaded—against their incredulity and denial—of the truth of the priesthood of all believers. They must be prodded out of their old understandings and behaviors, and trained into new ones. Otherwise, they will not be liberated and equipped for the ministry to which they have been called, and the redemptive force of the gospel will be lost on the world. Committed Christians must be taught.

Consequently, Trueblood called for the congregation to be reconstructed as a small theological seminary, with the pastor as its

---

12. Read Elton Trueblood, *The Company of the Committed* (New York: Harper & Row Publishers, 1961), and *The Incendiary Fellowship* (New York: Harper & Row Publishers, 1967).

13. Trueblood, *The Incendiary Fellowship*, 44–45.

professor.[14] He did not expand or elaborate beyond saying that the pastor should teach theology, and that this is to be done by the use of books, the guidance of individual study, organized discussions, and lectures. The study of theology is as difficult as it is important. But unless we do this hard work, there will be a disastrous falling way and failure.[15]

In the decades following Trueblood's challenging call, his remained the voice of a lone prophet crying in the wilderness.[16] Only a handful of seminary and divinity school professors picked up on what he said, took on his conception of the church, attempted to give it more detail, carried the discussion forward, and considered what a real-life appearance of his vision in a local congregation might look like. The short-list includes Edward Farley, Findley Edge, Clark Williamson, and Ronald Allen.[17]

Even rarer is any real, constructive attempt by a pastor or minister of education to reconceive and reform a congregation accordingly. To my knowledge, none has succeeded. The closest I have come is New Community Baptist Church in Richmond, Virginia, where I presently serve as pastor. Only by intentionally forming this congregation from scratch in 2010 as a teaching-learning community, openly rejecting all other models, and stubbornly resisting pressures to return to being a "real church," have we been able to approximate the image of the congregation as a seminary.

Fifty years later, Trueblood's vision remains almost completely visionary. I still see it as clearly as ever, and find my way by it, as though by the North Star. I persevere in working toward it and holding out hope that in the future a few congregations and Christians will see it as well, give themselves to it, and serve as theology's disciples and ministers, teachers and students, stewards and theologians. However, this ministry is solitary work.

A sketch of what Trueblood's vision might look like in practice was provided by Findley Edge in the final chapter of his book *The Greening of the Church:* "The Local Congregation As a Miniature

---

14. Trueblood, *The Incendiary Fellowship*, 45, 47.

15. Trueblood, *The Incendiary Fellowship*, 45–46.

16. See Isaiah 40:3-11 and John 1:23.

17. Read these theologians' statements about the "congregation as a miniature seminary" on page 32 in chapter 1.

Theological Seminary."[18] The congregation functions as a seminary by offering a core curriculum of courses in five major areas of study: Bible, theology, church history, missions, and ethics. These are the areas, Edge believed, in which everyone called into ministry should have a basic competence. All students are required to take these introductory courses.

Additional specialized courses are offered to equip students for their various ministries. For instance, individuals whose ministry is with youth will take courses in youth ministry. Others serving in the congregation's music ministry will receive training for their special ministry. All members choose and take elective courses beyond the basic, introductory courses.

The pastor and other ministers on staff (if there are any) are the faculty of this local lay seminary.[19] Their function is to educate and train lay ministers for the Christian ministry in general, and also for their respective specialized ministries. The task of clergy is not to "do all the ministry," but rather to equip others for the doing of many ministries in and through the church. Some students may advance to the point of being prepared and capable of serving on the congregation's faculty, teaching others.

No single teacher, according to Edge, can be expected to be competent and qualified to teach in every area of the curriculum. Therefore, many teachers are needed, with each specializing in one area, or subject matter. One member, for example, may be a serious student and teacher of the Old Testament. When an overview of the Old Testament, or a focused study in the prophets or Psalms, is offered, she teaches it. Someone else has responsibility for courses in the New Testament. Others will concentrate their studies in church

---

18. Edge, *The Greening of the Church* (Waco, Texas: Word Books, 1971), 177–189.

19. I use the term "lay seminary" to refer to any teaching-learning community where the *laos tou Theos* (people of God) are engaged in serious, sustained, ordered Christian theological education. From *laos* comes "laity, or lay." The lay seminary, then, is the "people's seminary," where all Christians—both clergypersons and non-clergypersons—can be involved locally where they live and serve. The lay seminary is not for non-clergypersons only ("laypersons"), just as the traditional seminary is not for clergypersons only. However, the traditional seminary is designed for and attended predominately by those who are preparing for clergy ministry, whereas the lay seminary is designed for and attended predominately by those who are preparing for the Christian theological life and (non-clergy) ministry.

history, ethics, or psychology of religion. They will teach courses accordingly.

Finally, Edge's strong recommendation is that the pastor must not attempt to change the whole congregation into a seminary. He should not introduce this type of education widely, or all at once. The better approach is to "open some doors" and let the "new" slowly emerge on a small, limited scale, alongside the "old." Start with a single experimental class. Call together a "searching group." Get a few members involved.

The vast majority of members will continue doing what they are already doing. They will stay with the Sunday School classes and small groups they have been with for a long time. Many will never be interested in a seminary-type education and ministerial training, for they do not see themselves as ministers, and much less as seminarians. They do not perceive the need to be instructed and trained. Besides, theological education sounds too hard, and would require too much of their time and effort, without having any relevance or reward for the Christian lives they are living.

Nonetheless, the pastor can till the soil of a few members, plant the seed, and cultivate the seedling over time, while it grows. The vision is that eventually the entire congregation will be permeated with theological education, and will become capable of producing and bearing its good fruit.

Edge's model rests on several basic assumptions. First, the pastor is qualified to undertake such a project and to teach. I interpret this to mean that the pastor (a) has been properly and fully educated at a seminary or divinity school; (b) continues to be self-disciplined in biblical, theological, historical, ethical, and cultural studies, as well as practical ministerial study, while acquiring specialized expertise in one area; (c) possesses both the calling and gifts of a teacher; (d) loves teaching, being a teacher, the subject matter being taught, and the students he teaches; (e) views each and every one of his students as a minister and seminarian; (f) believes that theological education for non-clergy, ordinary Christian ministers is necessary, not optional; and (g) is courageous enough to resist the congregation's (and his own) job demands and expectations, in order to make time and energy for the undemanded, unexpected task of establishing a local seminary, serving as its lead or sole professor, and being a Christian theologian-in-residence.

The problem is that most pastors do not come close to meeting these basic qualifications. They are uneducated and unequipped as theologians and teachers. They have been trained and mentored for another job. And so they readily give themselves to all the other tasks required and expected of them as congregational clergy.

Therefore, theological education for lay ministers almost never gets initiated—if it is even thought of or considered. If teaching starts, it is difficult to maintain, and likely will fall by the wayside. The major reason is that the pastor lacks the prerequisite formal education and continuing education for it. He does have a strong sense of calling or vision for teaching. His teaching ability, interest, time, and energy are in short supply. I agree with Trueblood and Edge that the pastor is key. But rarely is this key in place; and if it is, rarely does it get turned to start the engine.

A second assumption of Edge's model is that the pastor will be able to specialize in his teaching, and thus leave courses in other areas to other teachers. Who are these other teachers? And from where do they come? Even if the congregation is large enough to have multiple ministers on staff, most are not teachers. Even if they are qualified to teach in the areas of their practical ministries—such as youth ministry, music ministry, or missional ministry—most are not serious biblical or theological students, and thus are unqualified to teach even in their own areas of specialized ministry, since these ministries are by nature biblical and theological.

One or two retired clergypersons may be members of the congregation. But again, it is uncommon to find one who has been and continues to be a serious student and teacher of the Christian theological faith-tradition.

A college with a religious studies program may be located nearby. Faculty members can be invited to come and teach. But this is occasional, not ongoing, and will not meet the teaching need of a lay seminary. Also, many religion professors are not working in the Christian tradition. Even if they are, they may not be working confessionally. Finally, many are uninterested and quite inexperienced in communicating with and instructing ordinary Christians in local congregations.

Finally, Edge imagines students progressing in their seminary education to the point of being able to fill in faculty gaps and meet the specialized teaching needs of the congregation. While this hope can always be held out as both aspiration and inspiration, its accomplishment would take years—even if an exceptionally gifted, fast-learning student happened to come along. It is unrealistic for the typical congregation right now.

All of this leads me to conclude that we have to accept that the pastor will be the lone teacher. He will have to be a student and teacher of the entire theological educational curriculum. While he may specialize in one or two areas, his teaching ministry requires him to be a generalist. He must become basically proficient in all areas of Christian theology.

Personally, I consider this to be blessing rather than a curse; a joy rather than a burden. Where else—certainly not in a seminary or divinity school—would one be allowed to study and teach so widely, and thereby gain both sight of and insight into the overarching grand narrative and big picture of our faith?

Third, it is assumed that the congregation will allow this new educational ministry to exist in the midst of its many other activities and programs. This may not always be the case, or may only happen sporadically. Congregations are protective of their routine schedules and established ministries. They have ways (subtle and not so subtle) of effectively not supporting, undermining, and squeezing out anything that could possibly interfere with or distract from one of their sacred programs.

For this reason, seminary courses have to be offered on other days than Sunday, and at times when no other major activity is being held. This means that students must find a time-slot in their already-jam-packed schedules, that is not already taken up by other personal, family, work, recreational, and congregational obligations. Or, they must create one.

This leads to a fourth assumption Edge makes, best expressed in the popular phrase, "If you build it, they will come."[20] Again, this may not always be the case, or may only happen in a few places. No

20. This is a popular slogan that is a misquotation of a famous line from the 1989 sports film, *Field of Dreams*. An Iowa corn farmer hears a voice telling him, "If you build it, he will come."

one in the congregation may be interested—not a single member—at least not enough to come out another night, or to add another class to the one she is already taking on Thursday mornings with her women's group, that is viewing a video series on biblical principles for a happier life by one of the most dynamic, popular speakers around these days. Serious study requires a lot of serious effort that, frankly, most Christians are unwilling or unable to make. Besides, most believe they already have more than enough religion and enough knowledge for the Christian lives they are living.

Fifth, it is assumed that this local seminary will be sustainable. It may not be. The small student body that begins is likely to shrink over time. The initial curiosity of some students will quickly be satisfied, and they will drop out. Novelty soon wears off. Others will get bored. Still others will find the teaching too difficult. They had expected it to be simple. It's taking too long. They had expected this to be a quick introduction, and then they would be on their way to something else. It's now dawning on them that theology is a lifelong engagement, and they are not sure they are up for it.

Also, it is difficult for Christians to adjust and take on the mindset and manner required of seminarians. They are accustomed to being in Sunday School and taking special, basic "church study courses." For years they have been trained *not* to be students, and *not* to study or read. They have been trained to think simplistically, or not at all. Therefore, when they attend a seminary-type class taught on a seminary level, they approach it the only way they know how—as another activity in the whole store of religious activities their congregation is consumeristically offering; as another elective that is optional (no one has to attend, for this material is not required); and as a little more information that might be of some interest and help for them. Christian theological education turns out not to fit their preconceptions and expectations, and so they quit.

Most have never heard this subject matter before, although they have been Christians in the church their entire lives. It challenges beliefs they have always believed. It requires them to be disciplined, when they prefer to remain undisciplined. They have never taken notes. They have never held real textbooks that they were expected to read. They have never been asked to take anything this seriously before, to go beyond the superficial, to use their minds, to handle their own faith-tradition, and to work this hard at it. The Christian religion has never required them to study, and has left the level of any study they may choose to do up to them. Once they realize they are not in Sunday School, some will slip away and go back to what they have always had and known.

Sixth, it is easy to assume that a miniature theological seminary, because it is called "seminary" and modeled after a seminary, will truly and fully be a seminary, providing a seminary-quality education. The reality, however, is that such an education is difficult to establish in a local congregation, and even more difficult to achieve and sustain, for all the reasons I have discussed. Both teacher and students will be tempted to view what they are doing together as a simulation. "This is what it is *like* to go to seminary. Here are some of the things seminarians study and learn. But you do know, don't you, that this is not the real thing?"

I think of tourists in Colonial Williamsburg, Virginia, who for thirty minutes pretend to go back in time and are militiamen carrying muskets in the War of Independence. They know this is not real, but it is inspiring to pretend. They are like children, who have discovered an old trunk in the attic, and are playing "dress-up," putting on adult clothes and accessories. They know they are not really adults, and these are not their clothes. They are too small for a wardrobe this big. But it is loads of fun!

Likewise, Christians taking seminary courses are likely to assume they are merely pretending they are going to seminary. Everybody knows congregations are not really seminaries, and ordinary believers are not really seminarians. They are not really in the ministry—at least not the "real ministry." Yet, it is quite informative and inspiring to experience what that educational experience might be like, and to get some idea of what the real ministers in real ministry, who have gone to real seminary, are taught and expected to know. Still, we are too small for an education this big. We don't need this knowledge for our simple belief and everyday practice as ordinary Christians. We can never aspire to nor measure up to such theological heights.

The word *miniature* in "miniature theological seminary" does not help to counter this impression. *Miniature* implies that the lay seminary is not really a seminary. At best, it is a highly abridged, dumbed-down version of clergy education, i.e., "theology lite." At worst, it is nothing more than a souped-up set of Sunday School classes under a new name.

In other words, what is offered on the congregational level can never be a full-bodied, industrial-strength education. And the belief is that it should not be. Don't offer theological meat and potatoes, or else Christians, who have always lived on milk, will turn up their noses and push it away.[21] Education has to be "miniaturized." It has to be reduced, downsized, watered-down, thinned, and pureed for lay consumers, until it is nothing more than the same tasteless, nutritionless pablum they have always had.

Of course, this is not at all what Edge had in mind when he used the word *miniature*. He simply meant that we must not duplicate the institution of higher Christian clergy education fully, or "lock, stock, and barrel," at the local level. Most of the organizational and administrative structures, as well as many of the professional, clerical, and scholarly requirements, should be set aside and not replicated. These are unnecessary, and will be hindering—like Saul's armor on the shepherd-boy David.[22]

There are also problems and weaknesses with seminaries and their manner of theological education that do not have to be transferred, and should not be. For instance, since the eighteenth century, the seminary curriculum has been compartmentalized, specialized, and taught "cafeteria style." The student takes Introduction to the Old Testament, and then Introduction to the New Testament; Systematic Theology I and Systematic Theology II; Church History; Christian Ethics; and so on. Each course is a separate unit of study.

The educational experience is not unified. This leaves the student with a trove of disordered fragments of knowledge, without the unifying, meaning-giving whole. The connection of all these bits and pieces with that which makes theology and its education theological has been severed and lost. This also makes seminary education that much more susceptible to clericalization and professionalization, with the emphasis easily shifting from preparing theologically educated ministers to preparing future leaders for running the church's denominations, congregations, and agencies.

21. See Hebrews 5:12–14.

22. 1 Samuel 17:38–40.

I believe the essence of theological education can and should exist apart from its institutional baggage. It can be adapted locally. A version of a theological school, offering a version of a theological education, can be established for non-clergypersons without sacrificing either content or quality. It can be the same type of education, without having to take place at the same highly regulated level of academics. It should, however, retain the same commitment to serious study and reputable scholarship.

Miniature, then, is not a negative term, as it may seem at first. Theological education would do well to be reduced down to its essence, without having to carry the full, extra weight of either the scholar's academics or the clergy's profession, in order to be made available to the whole church, and not limited to scholars or clergy.

If anything, it is the church that has been miniaturized. The church has become something far less than what God has called and created it to be, and thus what it truly is. Now, with theology present and available, the body of Christ will be given the opportunity to return and be enlarged to its full, intended, proper theological size. But in order for this to occur, theology and its education must be "miniaturized" (in the best sense of this term) to engage the church where it exists locally.

My proposal does not mean that theological education should be diminished, trivialized, or made simplistic in any way. It should not be brought down to the level of where most Christians are, made to serve them there, and kept there. Instead, Christians must be brought up to where theology is when it is done well. This will involve a higher level of serious, sustained teaching and learning, although this level will not be that of academic scholarship. We must leave where we are and meet theology where it is. More precisely, we will meet in-between, in the middle, where the church and its faith-tradition are being reunited. Here we adapt to theology, rather than theology adapting to us.

Granted, because this meeting-point is theological and we are not, this reconciliation and education will take place much closer to where our seminaries and divinity schools are, than where our congregations are. We are the ones who have to undergo a major paradigm shift, and change our positioning and perspective, as well as our mindsets, habits, and patterns of behavior.

The objective of lay theological education, then, is not to find something that will appeal to the crowd, or to the greatest number of members and prospects, in order to attract them and keep them coming back. This is not another program or activity, like all other offerings in the congregation's catalog of consumer goods and services. The sole aim is to bring prodigal believers back to theology, where they will meet the Christian faith-tradition (which is their own), and be connected to the sources of faith itself. Simultaneously, theology will be brought home and introduced back into its local setting, closer to its ecclesial roots.

This is not a call for "lay theology," or "ordinary theology," as though non-professional, non-clergy Christians are incapable of "real theology," and thus, they require something else that is their own special activity. Theology is theology. Laypersons and professionals are working with the same wisdom, although they work with it in different areas, at different levels, and with different methods, having different interests and audiences. Their varied theological workings belong to one and the same grand endeavor, because there is only one theology. Imagine the whole church engaged in the same theology at the same time, with each local community and each individual participating according to many, various gifts and graces.

The vast majority of Christians have not received any formal, professional, scholarly, academic theological education. Nor should they—at least not the formal, professional, scholarly, academic kind. However, they should have the opportunity to receive a theological education. If one has the interest, ability, time, and need for the former, she will be greatly blessed by it. But there is no reason or excuse why this blessing should be withheld and not made available to all believers in the manner that they need it. Theological education is inherent and integral to the Christian vocation. It is the heritage, existence, right, and responsibility of every believer. All Christians, then, should have access to theology and its education through a local seminary established and designed for them.

Finally, Edge's recommendation is to proceed slowly. This is wise counsel. Any attempt to convert either the entire congregation, or a major part of it (such as Sunday School) to the seminary model, is guaranteed to fail. In the process, a lot of unnecessary, nonproductive conflict will be generated. Established groups, classes, and members will be threatened. The best way, then, to plant a local seminary is to begin small, operate quietly, and move carefully.

Edge observes that, "a theological seminary can be very helpful in understanding more clearly how the corporate life of the church should be structured and expressed."[23] The strong implication is that, once planted, the lay seminary will set the pattern, and the whole congregation will eventually fall in line, follow, and grow slowly by it in the way it "should be structured and expressed." Ultimately, the entire assembly will become a teaching-learning community. It will come to function theologically as a whole.

Edge's vision, in my opinion, is too optimistic. I have planted a miniature theological seminary in multiple congregations. Every time, the small start remained small and largely isolated from the rest of the congregation. No school had much, if any, effect on its larger body. In fact, most members remained unaware it was even there, despite my regular publicity and promotion. Somehow the presence of a seminary in their midst did not register with them, or they managed to ignore it. It got lost in the larger array of programs and activities. It was that small and insignificant in the whole scheme of things, and thus in the sight of the leaders and members.

Still, I am proud of what I did. It was well worth my time and effort. A few believers did accept the opportunity and challenge to be theologically educated. They became seminarians. They discovered theology and their own faith-tradition. They came to see that they were "in the ministry." And they began to think, talk, and act in an authentically Christian way. One or two became teachers. I was encouraged and motivated by these first fruits of what could be, although the vision continues to be largely visionary and elusive.

The brave soul who foolishly attempts something as outlandish as a miniature theological seminary—perhaps more than once, as I have done—should be prepared for frustration and failure. But we must persevere in the trust and hope that God is bringing about among us and for us what we cannot bring about ourselves.

This is the part I am prone to forget. The church's reformation is already underway. Paths of theological education are being pioneered, and inroads are being made. We are being called and led by the Spirit

23. Edge, 177.

in ways too deep and mysterious for us to detect or track. The church continues to be prodded toward its theological vocation.

In other words, the play of God is playing the church. The game is prior to and greater than us. A ball that we have not thrown ourselves is being pitched. And, every now and then, by grace, the miracle happens, and one or two or three persons break the spell of the crowd and reach up to catch it—amazing themselves. Before they know it, they are the ones who are caught, and are involved in the to-and-fro movement of theological education and ministry. They do not play theology as much as it plays them.

Our task is to remain open to this movement and its pitch. With wonder and imagination, we must stay in a constant state of vulnerability. We must long to join in and be part of it, to stay with it, and see where it goes and what happens. We don't want to miss this!

Seminary As Congregation

During my pastoral career, I have followed the vision of Trueblood and Edge, attempting to implement their model of the congregation as a seminary. My approach has been to teach core courses from the "theological encyclopedia," which is the traditional division of theological knowledge into four basic areas or disciplines: Bible, systematic theology, church history, and practical theology.[24] I then offered elective courses and single lectures, along with workshops, seminars, and teaching sermons. But for reasons I have already discussed, theology, in the fullness of its glory, did not "take."

My ministry, however, was not a complete failure. A few sheep in each flock were theologically fed and nourished more than they would have been otherwise. Intimations of our faith-tradition did break through, sink in, and take hold. Anything is more, and is better than nothing. A handful of believers in various places were able to gain more knowledge and much greater understanding that helped to clarify, fill-in, correct, deepen, and increase their faith. I am satisfied with that.

24. See Farley, *Theologia: The Fragmentation and Unity of Theological Education* (Eugene, Oregon: Wipf and Stock Publishers, 2001), 49–72.

However, by being among Christians in local congregations, and teaching them all these years, I have learned a lot about the miniature theological seminary. I have consequently moved beyond the original model of Trueblood and Edge. For one thing, the conversion of a congregation into a seminary is impossible. I am not saying that it should not be attempted, for the mere attempt does bring theology home, where its game can play locally, and some can be caught up in it as players.

The most we can hope for is that the seed of a seminary will be pushed into the soil, and a small seedling will develop. The typical terrain in our congregations and individual lives, though, is too hardened, rocky, shallow, and covered in thorny brush for a new plant to take firm, deep, lasting hold, and come to full harvest.[25] Even so, I would like to see more pastors attempt to scatter more seed across their fields, and then work to cultivate any tiny, fledging seminaries that may spring up.

I also urge individual congregations to care more about theological education, and to be more welcoming and supportive when the smallest of seminary beginnings are started in their midst. Finally, I invite pastors, who are associated by denomination or ecumenical fellowship, to create a miniature theological seminary in their local region. Together, by their combined talents and resources, they will be able to provide theological education not only to members of their own congregations, but also to many more Christians living nearby.

In recent years, while serving as pastor of New Community Baptist Church, I have been imaging and experimenting with another model of lay theological education. Instead of a congregation becoming a seminary, what if a seminary became a congregation? One concept is no more far-fetched than the other. Our established congregations are typically too established and set in their ways for theology and its education to enter and find a home. Then, why not let theology build its own house, where believers can enter and find a home?

This model is the converse of its predecessor. The relationship between theological seminary and non-theological congregation is simply turned around. The "congregation-to-seminary" model shifts to "seminary-to-congregation." Rather than the congregation, or a

25. See Mark 4:1–9.

very small part of it, becoming a miniature theological seminary, a seminary is established to be a miniature congregation. I call it a "seminary-congregation." This is a congregation that exists for the sole purpose of being a seminary. It is a group of Christian believers who are taking seriously their call to be Jesus' "teaching-learning community." (Isn't this what a congregation is? Or, is supposed to be?)

Here's how it might work: A pastor-teacher-theologian summons and gathers together those he or she can find, who will be taught. Where Christian teacher and students meet for the purpose of meeting theology, there is a seminary.

The first distinguishing mark of this seminary-congregation is that it is freestanding. It does not originate and stay within an established congregation as part of its educational ministry. It exists and operates independently on its own resources. Seminarians come from the active and inactive rolls of congregations in the region, from the ranks of the "unchurched," and even from the "nones," who have considered themselves to be outside all organized religion.

What they will have in common—that brings and holds them together—is a sense of calling into ministry and of personal need for theological education. They are intrigued by the new possibility of participating in a small community that takes the historical-biblical-theological tradition of faith seriously, is devoted to being engaged with it, and is seeking to be conformed to it as its living witness. They want to be with other students. They want to be taught and to learn.

The second mark of this seminary-congregation is that it is "bare bones." It is seminary, and nothing but seminary. There are no programs, activities, or projects, except theological education. The plan is not to add any.

Congregations are notorious for being "all things to all people." Theology is usually not one of these things. It never is the main thing. But here, in this seminary-congregation, it is the only thing.

Consequently, theology and theological education do not have to compete for attention, time, money, or energy. Participants are freed to devote themselves to the theological life, without being pressured, tempted, or distracted by the wide array of religious, spiritual, social, secular, therapeutic, and consumer goods and services typically offered by Christian congregations.

No one here questions the value of theology, or the need for theological education. The subject matter of the church's theological faith-tradition is never extracurricular or optional, since it is the whole curriculum. No justification is required for including classes in the schedule or the budget. There is no schedule. And there is no budget. The really good part is there are no committees or business meetings! All that this group is, and all that it is about, is the ministry of theological education—teaching, studying, learning, embodying, living, loving, serving, representing, proclaiming, preserving and transmitting the theological faith-tradition. What more is there?

No one has any cause or reason to ask why this community is here, or why any person is here. The answer has already been given, and is reinforced by everything this community does. If someone suggests additional activities or "more ministries," or wants to go in another direction, the response is bewilderment. Hasn't this already been settled? This is who we are and why we exist. To change our identity and purpose would effectively dissolve ourselves as a lay seminary, or teaching-learning community, and make us something else.

Other communities have existed without theology for a very long time, and will continue to exist without it for years to come. In stark contrast, this seminary-congregation would not exist for long without theology. It would have no reason to. Therefore, we make no apology and give no defense. There are plenty of Christian groups around that offer just about anything and everything. None offers theological education. This group does, and it majors in it.

The third distinctive mark of the seminary-congregation is that everyone here is a seminarian. There are nothing but seminarians in this house. Why else would anyone come and participate? This is a gathering of those who have been called out of the crowd into the ministry, first to be Jesus' disciples, and then to be the ministers, stewards, teachers, and witnesses of the gospel and its tradition that have formed around Jesus as the Christ.

Everyone who is here has come to be taught and to learn. After all, this is a teaching-learning community. No one is surprised, then, when he or she is expected to take on the rigors of reading, studying, talking, and thinking. This is the only way one's mind, heart, and entire life can be transformed by and then conformed to what is being received. All members give themselves fully to the life of the disciple, or student, in order to become theologians, having the ministry of the Word by the power of the Spirit. They study to receive God's approval, being servants who work hard to divide the word of truth rightly, so as not to have any reason to be ashamed.[26]

This is what members expect, appreciate, and value about their seminary experience. This is why they are here. Each person freely undertakes the theological life in community, and comes under its disciplines. Of course, regular reminders and encouragement are always appreciated. Sometimes a little pushing is required. But, unlike Christian groups in general, this one is not plagued or paralyzed by apathy, sporadic participation, or work avoidance. Members are willing participants.

An important fourth mark is that children and youth are included. They, too, are seminarians. They are welcomed into this teaching-learning community and valued as students. Although they are taught in their classrooms at their age and developmental levels, they study and learn the same subject matter as adults do, preferably at the same time adults are studying and learning it. The entire seminary is involved in the same educational process of making theologians, young and old.

The fifth and final mark is that this lay seminary views itself as a congregation. Out of theology and its education come all the essential functions of the Christian church. Members not only study and learn together, but they also worship, fellowship, pray, and pastorally care for one another and others. They are a seminary that is a local manifestation of the historical, universal, eschatological communion of saints.

How could they not be? Their commitment is to the theological faith-tradition of the church. All they are is what the church is. All they do is what the church does. They live theologically as the true church lives. In and through education, theology grounds and directs the whole life and work of this community.

Worship, for instance, is allowed to emerge naturally, though intentionally, out of what is being learned from the church's long history of theology and worship. Services are no longer planned and conducted according to the tastes and trends of popular culture, past

26. 2 Timothy 2:15 (my paraphrase).

denominational customs, or the therapeutic needs of worshipers, but rather by the deeper well-springs of theological truth and meaning. Liturgical symbols, rituals, music, and speech flow from and reflect, re-present, or enact in dramatic practice the teaching of the gospel of God's revelatory-redemption made known in Jesus Christ. Theology starts, fills, and leads worship. It gives the message. It sets the tone and rhythm. Worship is theological through and through. Worship is theology being embodied and lived. The theological life is our way of worshiping and serving God.

Children from the youngest ages should worship with the whole community, since this experience is an integral part of their education. They need to hear the body talking the same theological language spoken by the church for centuries. They need to be present when the community is thinking, searching, struggling, and coming to new insight and belief. They must witness people being people of faith. And they must not only learn how to join in the singing, praying, listening, and praising, but they must also learn how to serve the congregation as singers, pray-ers, and readers by being trained, and then by helping to direct the congregation's worship.

The same theological influence can be observed in this seminary's fellowship, caregiving, and service. Their relating to and loving one another, ministering to one another, and reaching out to others with life-giving compassion and companionship are embodiment of the faith-tradition they are learning, and also of the theological people they are becoming. Everything about their practical lives comes from and then comes back under the changing, shaping influence of Christian theology. They are learning the way of Christ and his community by actually studying it, trying it, and getting better at it.

The uniqueness of the seminary-congregation is that it takes theology and theological education seriously, and allows everything about itself to be theological. It is established and structured as a teaching-learning community. It operates and functions as a school that is the one place where Christians can come to learn their own theological faith-tradition, and also learn what it means to be the church living this tradition. Rather than offering many, different, unrelated, often irrelevant ministries, this community offers one whole ministry of education, uniting worship, fellowship, caregiving, and service. Everything else is given minimal attention, or is ignored.

Clearly, this is not a typical congregation. For one thing, it rejects the anti-intellectualism and simplistic, childish piety too often found in the general Christian population. It refuses to believe the common negative images and meanings of theology, theological education, ministry, school, seminary, teaching, reading, studying, and learning. On the contrary, this community embraces these terms, images, and meanings. It employs them to understand itself. It patterns itself accordingly. It intentionally becomes a school for disciple-making. Its sole aim is to teach human beings to read, think, talk, feel, see things, and relate to others as Christians. It seeks to be nothing more, less, or other than the church, or the people of God who live in this world theologically and exist by faith. Their defining, driving desire is to be found faithful, and trustworthy of the trust that has been entrusted to them.

Consequently, this congregation does not ignore its own faith-tradition—the one tradition that makes faith possible, provides the resources that nourish faith, and then gives expression to faith. This community is built on and built for this tradition. It is devoted to the teachings of the gospel as interpreted by the apostles and the age-long communion of saints, or the church, following Jesus Christ.

Members do everything they can to avoid and overcome biblical illiteracy and theological ignorance. They are personally ashamed of not knowing, misunderstanding, failing to embody, and being unable to articulate and explain to others the truth and meaning of their faith-tradition. They are ashamed of all Christians and congregations who are not ashamed, but ought to be.

This seminary-congregation knows it is small (very small), but is not embarrassed. When asked repeatedly the leading question that all congregations are asked, "Are you growing?" the answer always is, "Yes. We are growing in the knowledge and wisdom of faith." Members get used to the blank stares and stammering responses.

While always open and outreaching, desiring more members who will become disciples, the focus is not—as it is with other congregations—on membership and budget, or bodies and bucks. The matters of whether anything is happening, and how well (or poorly) things are going, are measured by theological-spiritual increase, not statistical increase. The congregation simply strives to be faithful, regardless of whether it is successful in the eyes of the denomination, the congregation down the road, one's sister-in-law, or the general public.

Being a seminary, this congregation is unafraid and unashamed of education. It does not opt for discipleship that is little more than having a "personal relationship with Jesus," which too often means little more than "feeling something 'real' or 'spiritual' inside."

This community works far beyond routine religious education, and the special, basic doctrinal-practical instruction given to baptism candidates and new Christians. It is not Sunday School as usual.

Also, this community neither denigrates nor disregards the term "Christian education," preferring instead other terms, such as "Christian formation" and "spiritual formation." The latter are often a way of avoiding intentional, ordered education by devoting time and energy to the routine performance of "spiritual disciplines." Supposedly, believers should work out in a "spiritual gym," doing spiritual exercises for spiritual conditioning, just as people go to the gym for physical conditioning. Such piety is the essence of faith.

Common spiritual disciplines are meditation and contemplative prayer, *lectio divina*, labyrinth-walking and prayer-walking, fasting and frugality, random acts of kindness and "paying it forward." The goal is to "be spiritual" (whatever that may mean to the individual) by actions that all too frequently involve little more than the thin practice of religion, the exercise of a private piety, testing the latest spiritual techniques, dabbling in the supernatural or occult, or experiencing one's own self. "Being spiritual" does not necessarily involve "being theological"—or for that matter, "being Christian."

While loving Jesus, being introduced into Christianity, and growing spiritually are noble and necessary endeavors, they are insufficient in and of themselves for living theologically, or existing by faith. Such a life requires the Christian historical-biblical-theological tradition of the church, which, in turn, requires interpretation, explanation, and application. This requires education. For this reason, the seminary-congregation does not shy away from theological education, but rushes to meet it, embrace it, and embody it. Consequently, loving Jesus, being a Christian, and growing spiritually take on new, deeper, richer meaning within a much greater framework.

Largely because education is all this congregation does, it is "real" theological education. It is not the mere semblance or simulation of theological education that gives participants the impression that they are being educated, when they are not. It is not the people of God eating only "the crumbs spilling over from the hearty meal of the clergy."[27] Nor are Christians being kept on infant's milk, spoon-fed spiritual chicken soup, handed sentimental platitudes like Life Saver candy, motivated by current evangelical pep talks, or given a rehash of secular psychotherapy or activist social-political ideology.

In contrast, the seminary-congregation provides education in the truest, most serious sense of this term. Only the best, most essential, substantial subject matter of the Christian theological tradition is put forth. The congregation itself is constructed by and for the teaching of this tradition, and, consequently, the learning and accumulation of traditional knowledge and skill. Real cognitive, linguistic, doctrinal content is in play, given and received. We don't get to make this stuff up. Nor do we get to ignore it, since we are the church.

The seminary-congregation offers only full-bodied material that is never dumbed-down for Christians—especially not for those who are simple-minded and prefer to stay that way. Those who are called and who come here and accept their chair at this table, return regularly as students and developing connoisseurs of this meal. They are taught how to sit at this table, how to enter into its communion and join the conversation, how to partake of the food, and how to taste and enjoy its unique textures and flavors. By participating, they learn how to digest all they are receiving. And they keep mulling it over, until its full gift of the life of the mind, heart, and whole body is gained, and they themselves become theologians, or theological people.

Finally, the previous model of the congregation as a miniature theological seminary (Trueblood and Edge) is the introduction of theology into a non-theological body. The body's immune system, however, is too strong to allow theology to have much influence or effect. The body as a whole will likely not be changed.

My proposed model of a seminary as a miniature congregation is the introduction of a body into theology. You and I come together, unformed as a body, and with no preconceived ideas or plans for making ourselves one. Rather than theology coming into our lives, we are coming into the life of theology. We are newcomers and guests in

27. Farley, 195.

theology's house. We are here only as beginners, ready to learn and serve theology—not for theology to give us more information and inspiration so that we can go and build our own Christian lives.

Rather than trying to make Christian theology work for us, we allow theology to work on us, making us the students, stewards, theologians, and ministers it needs us to be. In this way, theology takes the lead and creates its own body. It claims us and places us in its classroom. It makes us disciples. It teaches us, and makes us teachable. This is because theology requires a community of persons in and through whom it can be present, alive, and salvific in the world.

All the while, our concern is less and less, "What are we doing with theology?" It is more and more, "What is theology doing with us?" We let theology have its way with us, because we are merely its players, who are being played.

Ordered Teaching and Learning

The theological education offered by the lay seminary—whether it is a seminary-congregation or congregation-seminary—is "ordered." It has to be. It cannot be otherwise. How is it possible for anyone to learn anything, if the enterprise is disordered and the subject matter is being dealt with in a disordered manner? In fact, what exactly would "disordered education" be? What would it look like? Isn't this a self-contradiction?

The word "ordered" implies intentionality, arrangement, discipline, and regularity. Ordered education is self-consciously deliberate. It is not left to imagination or intuition, or to the fleeting whims and fancies of either the individual or the congregation. It is purposeful rather than unplanned, thoughtless, slipshod, incidental, aimless, and all over the map. Education is undertaken on purpose, for a particular purpose. It deliberately attempts to transform human beings by engaging them in the deposit of faith's knowledge, understanding, insights, and skills.

Ordered education is arranged. There is a set plan, method, and sequential process of teaching-learning activity. It is also disciplined, meaning that both teachers and students are disciples, or students, first. They undertake the life of a disciple, or student. This life is disciplined. It is shaped and directed by a specific set of disciplines, including reading, studying, learning, and living, both corporately and individually. The entire process is disciplining for those who are involved.

Ordered education is regular. It occurs on a frequent, recurring basis. Those who are engaged are not sporadic, occasional, on-and-off, or sometimes teachers and students. They are engaged all the time. Education is an important, defining part of who they are and what they are about. It holds their interest and consumes their attention, time, energy, and effort. It becomes a matter of routine for them. There is a definite, constant pattern to their lives. And they stay with it, week after week, year after year. Because the regularity is so ingrained and enduring, the individual can be said to have taken up "an ordered way of life," which is the Christian theological life, or faith-existence.

This education also continues for so long that it can be called "lifelong." There is no end to the subject matter, and no limit to what can be learned. No one will ever reach the point where she has come to know and understand it all, finally accomplished her task, reached her goal, is done, and can retire. There will always be simply too much yet to be explored and gained. Therefore, the seminarian never lets up, and never intends to stop. Besides, the theological life is too rewarding and enjoyable. Why would anyone ever want to give it up?

Ordered education requires a teacher, who facilitates the ordering. Every learner requires an instructor, interpreter, mentor, and guide. Otherwise, how will he know where or how to begin? What to read and study? What to make of what he is reading and studying? What it means to worship, fellowship, pray, and care for one another theologically? What's next?

The lay seminary is not merely a learning community; it is also a teaching community. Someone has to assume the teaching office and exercise a teaching ministry on behalf of and in service to this community. Ideally, a theologian will be available, who is competent to serve as both pastor and teacher. The community existing by and for theological education demands it.

Yes, there will actually be a teacher who actually teaches. This approach goes against the current fashionable theory of religious education professors and practitioners that "everything teaches." According to this theory, simply by attending worship services, going on youth mission trips, and hanging around Christians, one absorbs and acquires all he or she really needs to know in order to be a good Christian. This is, in my opinion, the equivalent of "All I really need to know I learned in kindergarten."

Consequently, according to this theory, there is no need for school, since the congregation, merely by being what it is and going about its religious business—along with a wide selection of secular goods and services—is itself a rich environment for learning. Its culture is the curriculum. Therefore, no teacher is required. No one has to teach, since "everything teaches." No one has to read, study, or acquire cognitive content, either.

While there is some portion of truth here, the much larger portion is that the Christian theological faith-tradition—along with its life and education—requires a teacher, if learning is to occur. Theological understanding is not passively caught like the common cold, merely by coming in contact with the church. It does not happen naturally as part of human development over time. It must be intentionally taught and intentionally learned through a process of theological education.

Equally rejected is the notion that "everybody teaches," or that members of a Sunday School class should take turns "being the teacher." The ministry of teaching must be taken far more seriously. The person who teaches must be far more qualified than the average student: (1) is himself or herself a student of the theological faith-tradition, actively engaged in studying, learning, and embodying it; (2) has reached a higher-than-average level of knowledge, understanding, and wisdom; (3) is thoughtful, rational, level-headed, and mature, as well as both critically- and confessionally-minded; (4) possesses the minimum prerequisite calling and skills of a teacher; (5) is gifted in communicating and introducing theology and students to one another effectively; and (6) loves to teach. Only this qualified and capable a person should be in the role of teacher, attempting to teach.

Granted, in some local situations, no one in the group may fit this role fully or well. However, because the group requires teaching, the best student among them may have to be recruited. She should then humbly accept the teaching responsibility with the group, while doing everything she can to become qualified and responsible as a teacher as quickly as possible. The truth is that every teacher, no matter how advanced and experienced, started out as a totally raw, unqualified, inexperienced novice. The essential trait is that the one who teaches loves the subject matter so much that she becomes a devoted, engaged student and a spokesperson for it. She can then learn to teach.

Ordered teaching is not extra or optional, and thus expendable. It is essential. In order for ordered learning to occur, ordered teaching must be occurring. The teacher will teach in an orderly way. This way goes beyond mere modeling (setting a personal example) and involves ordered speech. The person must talk, and must talk theologically—not only about theology, but also, more importantly, in theology's own words, framework, and content. She must be a theologian, who sounds like a theologian. Because this theology is Christian, she must sound like a Christian. There must be Christian speech, and lots of it.

The teacher, then, must be a lover of words. Any person who pits either faith or practice against language, lauding the former while disparaging the latter, is unqualified to teach. She reveals that she is not a teacher, and never will be with that mindset and attitude. Any Christian who does not think before she speaks, or who speaks without attention to the words used, or to using them correctly and appropriately, with greater and greater precision, should not be allowed to stand in front of a class of students who are all ears, listening to and trying to learn the Christian language.

In contrast, the true teacher-theologian orders his mindset and attitude, as well as his speech, carefully, according to the theological faith-tradition. He attempts to communicate the deposit of faith contained and carried by this tradition. The teacher's words will be honed through hours of preparation and presentation every week in the form of theological lectures and sermons. Then he will go back to his study, library, writing table, and laptop to do it all over again, continually striving to think and speak more clearly and convincingly.

Yes—shock of shocks—the lay seminary does require and rely on lecturing (accompanied and supported by other forms of teaching). Contrary to popular opinion, lecturing is not dead. It is not a method that we have, in our great enlightenment, come to see is not a "best practice," and thus must be replaced by the far more effective "open discussion." The latter can be a good, useful, and effective method of engaging students both with the subject matter and one another, in conjunction with the lecture. But, standing alone, it can be a means of distracting students from the subject matter, and engaging them only with one another rather than with theology.

Subject matter having cognitive content must first be presented, introduced, interpreted, analyzed, and explained, before it can be opened for discussion. Otherwise, how does anyone know *what* is open for discussion, or *how* to discuss it? We do not and cannot know what we are *talking about*, unless we have first been *talked to*, or taught. Or, do we arrogantly and wrongly assume that Christian faith has no real, substantive content, or significance, unless or until we give it some?

As Christians, all of us should be suspicious of our haste to share our uninformed and unformed opinions, immediate impressions and reactions, likes and dislikes, and "what it means to me." We must learn to think and to form our thoughts before speaking. And we must not speak in reaction primarily to our own emotions, ideas, or beliefs, but rather in response to the subject matter being taught, that we are just now hearing and best responding to by thinking about it.

Over time, we get better at thinking along the same lines and in the same forms as the thoughts contained in and conveyed by the subject matter. Then we ask a question or make a comment that comes out of our thinking minds regarding this particular subject matter, and not some other. A discussion opens up among the students and teacher. But it is a discussion that is not open in the sense of being about anything in addition to or instead of the subject matter at hand. Students are given plenty of opportunity to try their voices at speaking the Christian theological language, as well as exercising their minds with Christian theological thought.

Lecturing keeps the spotlight where it belongs—away from ourselves as subjects, and on the subject matter. It keeps the group on track and on task. It discloses truth and meaning that otherwise would remain closed. Priority of time and energy is given to the bringing to expression of theology, in order that this group will be maintained and strengthened as the theological community it is, and these students will have the opportunity to hear, learn, and come to live the Christian theological faith-tradition as their own.

Such education involves the acquisition of new knowledge, understanding, and wisdom. Therefore, it does not and cannot take place apart from an intentional, arranged, disciplined, and regular effort at translation and transmission. This is ordered teaching.

Hopefully, ordered teaching will be met with ordered learning. Students will undertake the theological life. This is an ordered way of life, meaning that it is ordered by the order of theology. Theology has its own order. Therefore, its students are those who are discovering, exploring, and learning this order. They are ordering their thought, speech, and mode of being according to the order of theology.

Imagine Christians who are actually reading solid books, studying concepts and doctrines, reflecting on these things, committing them to memory, reorganizing and reforming what they have previously understood, and all the while learning how to exist in, by, and for this entire tradition of faith. This is the ordered way of life of theology, and, therefore, is the ordered way of theological education.

Finally, ordered teaching and ordered learning require an ordered curriculum. Curriculum is broadly defined as the seminary's course of study. It is the path the community takes. It entails the what, when, where, and how of education. The teacher is primarily responsible for thinking about, deciding, directing, and then improving the content, methods, and tools of the teaching-learning process. Since this curriculum is not hidden, unstructured, haphazard, or left to chance, it is described as "ordered."

I will discuss the lay seminary's curriculum more in chapters 6 and 7. Here I only want to make the important point that the seminary is not a group of people who get together because they like getting together and being with one another. It is not a group that assembles to conduct religious services, and to offer as many activities as possible to socialize, entertain, support, and help one another and others; but then, one day, decides it would be nice to offer a few classes to attract those who might be interested in that sort of thing.

Instead, these individuals gather intentionally for one thing, and one thing only, without mixing or diluting it with many other things. They come for the theological life, or way of life ordered by Christian theology. They seek to exist theologically, which is the manner of Jesus' life and ministry. Because this is not the natural, normal mode of existence of human beings, they acknowledge their need to be made disciples who are capable of being taught and transformed. Therefore, they become participants in an ordered teaching-learning community that is following an ordered curriculum based on the order of theology itself.

What is the alternative? A theologically disordered or unordered congregation?

Jesus' School

Bringing Christians back to theology, and thereby bringing theology home to the local congregation, awakens sleeping prejudices and fears about school. First, we have presumed our school days to be far behind us. But theology says these days are still with us, and always will be.

Second, we think of ourselves as grown-ups. We once were children, but now we are beyond all of that. That was kindergarten. Now we are enrolled in "the real school of life." That was elementary stuff. Now, as adults, we are dealing with much greater, more important, complex, difficult, and costly matters.

Then theology shows up, bringing even greater, more important, often more complex and difficult concerns than any you and I have ever faced. These matters are absolutely demanding and costly, often raising life-and-death issues that can make our big adult projects look like child's play. Our immediate reaction is to stick to the usual, everyday grown-up concerns, or flee and return to the simplistic beliefs, values, and behaviors we learned as children in kindergarten and Sunday School. But theology keeps blocking our escape, calling us to grow up and mature, even beyond adulthood.

We resist this schooling. We will do just about anything to avoid having to join Nicodemus in the Kingdom's classroom as students starting all over at the beginning, like newborns. "Lord, we are adults! We are Christians! We have been in church our entire lives!"

Vehemently we insist that we do not need to go back to school. Maybe someone else does, but we don't. We already know all we really need to know. We already have invited Jesus into our hearts and into our lives. We already have been baptized and belong to the church. We already attend a women's prayer circle, in addition to a

Sunday School class that we dearly love. We already serve in the church's soup kitchen and help with youth basketball.

Besides, real men and women of faith don't need education. It only gets in the way, and tempts us to go astray and lose our faith. The Bible is simple, and I simply do what it tells me. I go by the leading of the Spirit. Everyday, in the moment, I just seem to know what to say and what to do. As long as I am being good, feeling good, and doing good, I'm good. God will be pleased, and I will receive my heavenly reward. That's all that matters.

Then Jesus comes along, pointing and saying, "You. Yes, you there. Come, follow me." Those who leave the crowd to walk along with him are given a strange name: "disciple." It means "student."

Your immediate reaction is to be offended. "I am not a student. I haven't been in school for decades, and have no interest, intention, or plan to return. Who needs it? I certainly don't."

Yet, how can you honestly say you follow Jesus, when he calls you "disciple" and obviously wants to be your teacher, yet you refuse to enter into this educational relationship with him, and to be taught?

Think about it. The Master Fisherman came along the shore of the sea of humanity one day. He threw out his wide net in your direction, aimed straight at you. You were being sought, and you got caught. You became entangled in the net, and were dragged up out of the water.

Now he wants to teach you his mode of existence, or how to live his way of life. This is the primary reason you were fished out. The Fisherman's catch is intended to be his teaching-learning community. All in his net are disciples, or students. There is no one present who is not here to be taught and to learn how to live his way of life in the in-breaking, coming Kingdom of God.

Your first lesson, then, is to accept the name "disciple" and start acting like one. Be Jesus' student in Jesus' own teaching-learning community. Be one of his fish in his school of fish.

This picture of a large body of aquatic animals swimming together, is a fuller, richer image of "school" for the lay seminary, or Christian teaching-learning community, than our images from childhood and youth: institution, organization, business, administration, buildings, classrooms, and formal academic studies. While theological education may, and likely will, in some way and to some degree, involve all of these resources and methods, the lay seminary is much more organic and dynamic. Think of Jesus' community as people who are living and having their being as one great body. They are moving together in the same sweeping, to-and-fro motion of faith, in the same sea of tradition as Jesus, the original twelve, all their students, and all their students' students through the centuries to today. We are like a great school of fish.

People continue to be brought together here to be made disciples. By being Jesus' visible, audible, joinable community of disciples, they are effectively sent, and are in the world to make disciples.

Students themselves do not fish for students, or catch them, for that is Jesus' job. But they do receive those who are being sought and caught, and then go to work teaching them. Those who themselves are being taught are the only ones who can teach others. Only disciples can be disciple-makers. Only those who are fish can be apprentices, who are assisting the Master Fisherman in his work.[28]

School, then, is more than what we do or what we have. It is who we are. We are those who are bound together by and around Jesus, as his community of knowing, understanding, experiencing, embodying, preserving, and transmitting his manner of faith-existence. There are nothing but teachable fish here, learning to live, move, and have their being together in relation to the mysteries of God.

We are Jesus' school.

---

28. Jesus also used the extended metaphor of shepherd and sheep. "I am the good shepherd," he said, "I know my own and my own know me." (John 10:14) After his resurrection, he said to Simon Peter, "Feed my lambs. …Tend my sheep. …Feed my sheep." (John 21:15–17) One of the shepherd's sheep became an under-shepherd.

6
Teaching

May I look at your feet? I apologize for getting up close and personal. This is the only way I will know if you have been sent to teach. You are on the go, and your feet are moving all the time. Are they moving in the direction and vicinity of theological education?

Christian faith comes from being taught, and from what is taught. How, then, is anyone to take up this mode of existence, or way of life, unless he believes in the One whose existence this is (Christ)? And how is he to believe, unless he knows and understands? And how is he to know and understand, unless he has been told, or has been taught? And how is he to be taught, unless someone teaches him? And how is he to have a teacher, unless this teacher has been sent—and actually goes and teaches?[1]

Teachers have beautiful feet. This is because these persons have been called and sent. In responding, their feet have moved. They have left their familiar places and usual routines. And, traveling on foot, they have brought a subject matter, or message, to people, who otherwise would be greatly impoverished, if not perish. This subject matter is received as a much-needed, much-welcomed gift. "Help has arrived. We are saved!" Therefore, these people are so overjoyed that they want to kiss the feet of their messenger-teachers, who have brought to them such life-giving good news.

---

1. Both the image of "beautiful feet" and this sequence of questions derive from my reading of Romans 10:13–17 and Isaiah 52:6–10.

The good news of Christian teaching and learning is the gospel of God's revealed redemption in Jesus Christ. This gospel is couched within a larger theological tradition, where it is developed, preserved, and transmitted.

Congregations and their individual members need this theological tradition, or theology, in order to be theological communities. Theology is "good news" to them. It is their source of life and ministry. It is their life. Without it, they will perish as the church.

Of course, congregations will always be with us. They will never disappear completely, despite being theologically weak or false. Many will become other types of community, and may even flourish. Yet, they will not be the church. They will not be the kind of community that exists by and for theological faith in relation to Christ, whose gospel they claim to believe and represent. Lacking the one thing that makes them what they have been called and created to be, they cannot help but become something else. Therefore, bringing theology home to them—and more importantly, bringing them back to theology as their home—will be their salvation. This is good news. Good news indeed!

Yet, who does this? Or, will do it? Who will bring theology home, and bring Christians back home to theology? Who will do this?

Theologians teaching in local settings are unheard of. A little theology may trickle down from the academic mountaintops into the low places. But what people of faith really need is life-giving water from the deep historical-biblical-theological well. Right now, they are trying to quench their thirst from stagnant ponds, shallow puddles, and even dry holes. Who will plunge these depths and bring its water to them?

My Grandpa Smith (named "Grover Cleveland Smith" after our country's 22nd and 24th President) was a carpenter, who milled his own lumber and built his own house. He dug a well for water. I remember going with him when he wanted a drink of water after working in the fields on a hot day. He limped out to where the well was (he had lost three toes on his right foot in a lumber-sawing accident), and pulled back the wooden cover. I leaned over and peered down into the well to where the water was. It was deep and dark. I could barely see the water. It caused me to pull back instinctively, afraid I might fall in. Still, I could not take my eyes off what was down there. It was what I wanted. I wanted to experience it. I was suddenly thirsty. I wanted to taste it.

Grandpa lowered down an old, beaten metal bucket on a heavy chain attached to a pulley. He let it tip over into the water, and then pulled it back up. It was full. Water sloshed out over the top of the bucket. He reached for a dipper, submerged it into the water, and handed it to me. When I drank, it was the coldest, purest, most perfect water I had ever had! Why would anyone drink tap water from a kitchen faucet fed by the modern miracle of indoor plumbing? Especially when they have a well, and can go to it any time they want, to drink perfect water, or real water—water as God has intended it to be.

My question is: "Who is like my grandfather when it comes to our own theological faith-tradition? Have you been sent to go to the well to drink and then to bring back its water for others?" If so, you have beautiful feet. You are a teacher.

The Missing Teaching Ministry

In his book, *A Teachable Spirit,* Richard Osmer makes the case for the recovery of a strong teaching ministry in local congregations today. American religious life has changed, and is continuing to change in major, long-lasting ways. Mainline Protestant congregations are not doing well. They are rapidly losing members, and also losing the influence they once had in influencing and shaping broader culture. Modern individualism, counter-modern (postmodern) anti-authoritarianism, religious pluralism, and civil religion are forces with which the church now has to deal.

Congregations are at a crossroads, according to Osmer. They have two ways to go: (1) seize "the opportunity to make a more authentic Christian witness in American society than was possible when they were ensconced in a position of cultural influence and power"; or (2) "do little more than minister to the personal needs of individuals and families during moments of crisis or life-cycle transition."[2]

---

2. Richard Robert Osmer, *A Teachable Spirit: Recovering the Teaching Office in the Church* (Louisville: Westminster/ John Knox Press, 1990), 5.

The path our congregations will take depends on whether they will rediscover the classical teaching office as formulated by Martin Luther and John Calvin. If congregations work to recover and relearn the biblical-theological heritage of the Christian faith, and then teach it authoritatively, they will become capable of representing the gospel again, and will thereby bring life-giving good news to the world.

If they do not—choosing instead to do little more than attempt to meet personal and social needs—they will continue their descent into failing to teach with authority, and thus failing to be the church.[3]

The most difficult task, Osmer wisely points out, may be simply noticing that something is missing, and then discerning exactly what it is. Both the teaching office and the theological faith-tradition have been missing for so long that even the most committed Christians, along with their congregations and denominations, have no clue that something is missing. They do not recognize what is not present.

Osmer uses the image of a neighborhood where all the trees are cut down for the houses to be built. A person who then moves in and grows up here never misses the massive oak tree, or the beauty of the maple tree in its autumn color. She never knew they were there. They have never been part of her experience. Therefore, they will always be hidden for her.[4]

This is a good analogy for the situation of most Christians. Not having been taught, and not having been a student, the typical Christian does not miss the theological faith-tradition. She does not and cannot miss what she has never had. She has never known the "massive beauty and splendor" of theology. It has never been part of her experience. Therefore, she is oblivious to the fact that theology is missing. She does not even know that it is supposed to be present, or that this is the reason she is a Christian and there is the church.

She simply does not know that, as a Christian, her calling is to be a steward and student of this tradition. She is unaware that such a reality exists, and that it is not only significant and relevant, but also authoritative. No one has ever brought it out of the church's archives to disclose it to her. No one has taught her to understand it and to allow this theological tradition to determine her existence by being

3. Osmer, 5.

4. Osmer, ix.

the interpretive framework she uses to be a human being and to make sense of her life in this world. She has never been told any of this. She has no idea that any of this exists or is real. She has never had a teacher.

Our congregations are not teaching-learning communities. Ask a member or parishioner, "Where can I go to learn the Christian theological faith-tradition?" He will look puzzled and not know how to answer. What are you asking? What is the Christian theological faith-tradition? He will certainly not direct you to his congregation, or to one down the road.

He might tell you, "Go ask my pastor." My concern is that the pastor will most likely be unable to say honestly, "You've come to the right place. We teach that tradition here. Come and join us in theological education."

Who Will Teach Them?

Whenever the discussion moves to the strange silence of the Bible and theology in the church, the missing teaching office, the dire need of laypersons for serious, sustained education, and the possibility of a local seminary, everyone turns to the ordained clergy for solutions. No one expects denominations or congregations to exert any real effort toward reviving an authoritative teaching office and a teaching-learning community.

We can easily imagine individual Christians banding together to start a food drive to feed the hungry, organize and run a children's summer day camp, or take the youth to help with a backyard Vacation Bible School in an Appalachian region in Kentucky. These programs, projects, and events happen all the time. But no one can imagine a single person talking in the hallway, or speaking up at a business meeting, saying, "You know what we need? A seminary. It's a shame we don't know our own theological faith-tradition. So let's come together, find a competent teacher, and get started. We can do this!"

If an ordered teaching ministry is to be recovered, it will depend on a single clergyperson noticing something vital is missing, discerning what it is, and personally caring and becoming concerned enough to do something about it. This is the only way theological education will get started and take place locally.

Unfortunately, the probability of this happening remains very low. Pastors are too busy to be students, much less teachers. Their congregations do not expect them to be teachers; and there is no vocational incentive for them to become theologians. Therefore, they leave their studies behind when they graduate, leave seminary, and hit the local congregational ground running.

Strangely, even their own seminary education did not prepare them to be educators. They were in a teaching-learning environment, and under the instruction of professional educators. But they heard little, if anything, about the church's teaching ministry. They were not told about the severe crisis of theological knowledge in our congregations, or about the desperate need of Christians for theological education. It was never explained to them that their calling was to help meet this need by teaching. They never heard that their vocation is to teach Jesus' community, respecting them as disciples, treating them as such, and making them so.

Most pastors did not grow up under the instruction, example, and mentorship of a teaching pastor. The only teachers they have known are in universities, colleges, and seminaries. None are in local settings. Therefore, when they serve congregations, denominational agencies, or religious organizations where the teaching office is missing, they are unable to conceive of such a ministry—much less rediscover and reestablish it. They are unaware that their job is the reconciliation of the whole church with its own historical-biblical-theological faith-tradition. It does not occur to them that their feet are on the ground locally for the purpose of bringing theological good news. If pastors do not teach, this good news is lost, and the church remains cut off.

Second, education in our seminaries has become professionalized, specialized, and clericalized. Future clergypersons are trained in the knowledge and skills required for the performance of the pastoral tasks that contemporary congregations consider most important: "We need someone who can plan and direct our worship services, deliver a good sermon, visit the sick, counsel those in crisis, conduct funerals and weddings, keep the staff in line, attract new members, and basically run things." Somehow teaching never breaks into the top ten—if it makes the list at all.

Name a single congregation that has a serious, sustained teaching ministry. Name a pastor who is a teacher, or whose primary calling and purpose in ministry is teaching. Do you know any community of believers that requires, or even encourages, its senior and associate pastors to be theologians and teachers of the Christian faith?

Third, not only are clergy not trained to be teachers, but they also are not trained to be students after leaving the seminary classroom. Studying and learning is for a season. After three years or so in the academic community, the student graduates, and, at that moment, effectively resigns as a student. The time of formal education and training has ended. All diligent studying, learning, and preparing must cease, because it's now time to get busy doing "the real work of ministry."

Consequently, this minister, who is quitting her own theological education, has no reason to invite others to begin theirs. She is now just like them. She is no longer a student. She will go on in her Christian vocation, running on what she acquired in seminary, just as laypersons are running on what they acquired in kindergarten and Sunday School. Neither pastor nor parishioner will be expanding, developing, correcting, deepening, or maturing his or her knowledge, understanding, and embodiment of Christian faith. No one will be learning and excitedly coming back with good news. There is nothing good or new to teach.

Fourth, Edward Farley, who was professor of theology at Vanderbilt Divinity School for nearly three decades, told a truth almost no one ever tells, or will admit: "The typical product of three years of seminary study is not a *theologically* educated minister."[5]

Laypersons back home assume that their ministers are very highly educated, and thus are highly trained, skilled theologians and biblical scholars. They are not. While it is true that seminary-educated clergy have received more formal education than their congregants in these matters, their education has been introductory and elementary. The most a seminary can hope to accomplish is to expose its students "cafeteria style" to the broad swath of Christian studies and Christian ministries, imparting a smattering of knowledge and insight, along

5. Edward Farley, *Theologia: The Fragmentation and Unity of Theological Education* (Eugene, Oregon: Wipf and Stock Publishers, 2001), 4.

with a basic set of tools, methods, and skills that they might need. However, there is simply too much to cover in too brief a period of time. Besides, no one can acquire all he needs to know, understand, and be able to do in ministry all at once, or quickly. Therefore, no short-term seminary student can be theologically educated or highly trained. No graduate is a theologian, biblical scholar, or expert in church history, ethics, pastoral counseling, or liturgy. No pastor arrives back at the local congregation fully educated, equipped, seasoned, and mature. He has barely gotten started.

Still, this seminary education is significant, valuable, and necessary. At least he has begun. He knows what it means to begin and what is involved. He knows how to be a beginner. Hopefully, his seminary experience has achieved its main goal of making him a student, and has trained him in the basic competencies of reading, thinking, researching, articulating, and learning. Therefore, he is in position to tell others how to get started and join him. He is not that far ahead of them. From now on, they will travel together, studying and learning the theological faith-tradition.

Fifth, the intent of seminary education is not to give the student total or complete knowledge and skill, but only to equip the student with the most basic knowledge, skills, and tools needed for a career-long, lifelong pursuit of understanding and application. In time—pointed in the right direction and armed with the right equipment—he will become the theologian and scholar the church needs him to be, so that he will be able to teach others, starting and leading them down the same path that he is going. But this uncharted course of post-seminary, life-long education will be largely informal rather than formal, and personal rather than institutional. Local theologians are "autodidacts," or self-taught persons.

All of this sounds heavy, yet encouraging, doesn't it? There is one problem. Almost no pastor goes this way, deliberately and diligently continuing his theological education. Despite noble ideals and good intentions, school days are soon over and in the rearview mirror. Books have to be closed and put away, since the minister must move on to the ministry for which he has been undergoing all this seminary education and training.

The operating assumption is that theological education and practical ministry are sequential, not simultaneous, and definitely not synonymous. The former is past. The latter is present and future. Therefore, sadly, too many ministers repeat—mindlessly, without thinking—the foolish statement they have heard others say: "What I need to know in ministry, I never learned in seminary." In other words, most of what I learned in seminary I don't need or use anymore. All I need to know for the job I now have, I must learn on the job.

Perhaps the greatest obstacle to continuing theological education is the work of Christian ministry itself. The pastor's day-to-day work is not theological work. It is not educational work. In fact, much of it is not work that requires either learning or teaching. Leading, preaching, visiting, bringing in new members, and starting new programs can all be done—and done quite well, according to the current standards of ministerial excellence—without much, if any, theological knowledge, understanding, or wisdom. Most of the life and work of the typical congregation is non-theological (or at least is conducted this way).

Also, the constant demands and pressures of the job make it tough for the pastor to find the time, focus, and energy for continuing his theological studying and learning—even if he wants to do so. The former are more immediate and pressing. They are "in your face," and never let up.

Besides, the congregation never demands that its pastor prepare and deliver theologically-rich, theologically-deep sermons. The pastor is never asked to teach what he is learning. No one ever inquires out of concern, "Are you studying? Are you managing to set aside time every week for your own continuing education in the things that matter most to our being the church? We deserve no less than your theological best."

Pastors are not rewarded with professional mobility, a better, larger congregation, or financial success for being a theologian or teacher. Even if a pastor goes against the norm and works hard on his own to be a teaching theologian, the congregation most likely will not notice what he is doing, or recognize what he is, or even know what to make of it, or do with it. Theology and teaching carry little weight of authority or value back home. Not only are they not required, but they also are irrelevant, if not interfering and counterproductive. Consequently, most pastors are not theologians—in the same way that most theologians are not pastors—and are not teachers.

Finally, leaving the bulk of theological learning to self-initiated continuing education during the post-seminary period is risky. Once the minister is back home in a congregation, denominational office, or agency position, it is difficult for her to stay self-disciplined apart from a disciplining community like the seminary. Without a formal, planned curriculum, it is difficult to know where to begin and what to read next. The minister has never been on her own, and certainly has no experience or expertise in educating herself. More often than not, she will sporadically feel guilty and make a New Year's or Lenten resolution (probably both) to study more. Yet, each time she will soon get bogged down, or distracted, and end up back in the same routine with the same demanding tasks that allow for little to no theological education. The risks and chances of failure only increase greatly as the years go by.

I apologize for painting such a bleak picture, although I believe it is an honest portrayal and accurate assessment of our contemporary non-theological, non-educational congregations, and their clergy and non-clergy members. Our Christian religious communities simply are not theological communities that make, cultivate, support, encourage, or grow theologians, or theological people.

While we must continue to press upon our congregations, denominations, and seminaries the urgent need for theological reformation, my best counsel is "Don't hold your breath." Change is unlikely to come. If it does, it will likely come very slowly over a long period of time. Evidence points to things staying the same, or moving rapidly in the opposite direction.

Therefore, I squint to peer into the Christian crowd, searching for the one, two, or three individuals who might be hidden there, who might twitch or flinch as a sign of resonance in response to the sound of theology, calling them to its service. Who will be a student?

And if there are students, who will teach them? Is there a minister in the crowd, who will twitch or flinch, and respond to the need? I ask, "Is there a teacher in the house?"

Perhaps the most likely way it will happen is that a teaching candidate will come out of the crowd first, ahead of any students. She will come out as a student, having only a little theological study or experience at seminary, but now desiring more. She has likely done little to no teaching, and has never thought of herself as a teacher.

However, the need of others bothers her more than her own. Someone has to teach them, she thinks. And it has to be her.

In other words, how will anyone else take up the theological life, unless she herself does it and teaches it? How will anyone come to believe in the Christ who existence this is, unless she believes, and then brings to others what is believed? And how will others know what to believe, unless she herself already knows it, and then explains it to them, so that they can know and understand, too? And how will they know and understand, unless she teaches them? And how will she teach, unless she has been sent? Unless her feet move, and she steps forward out of the non-theological crowd to walk in the theological faith-tradition, how will two or three or more come out, as well, in response to the same call, and join her and travel along with her?

The feet of the teacher in Jesus' teaching-learning community are beautiful. So are the feet of students moving in the way of theological education set by her.

The Courage to Teach

Teaching takes courage. Leaving the non-theological crowd requires great courage. Taking up the intellectual life of Christian faith is a brave act. Turning toward others and teaching them is daring. And so few attempt it. Without the virtue of courage, the entire theological educational enterprise languishes and fails, or never gets started.

In October 1950, theologian Paul Tillich delivered the Terry Lectures at Yale University. His lecture series was published in a book, *The Courage to Be,* which became a classic work in philosophical theology.

Tillich defined courage as "the ethical act in which man [sic] affirms his own being in spite of those elements of his existence which conflict with his essential self-affirmation."[6] This is a dense way of saying (and this is my humble interpretation) that every person is faced with anxieties and fears that are threatening to one's very being. The world around us engenders concern, doubt, and

6. Paul Tillich, *The Courage To Be* (New Haven: Yale University Press, 1952), 3.

meaninglessness, resulting in the loss of heart and despair. There is much to be dreaded.

However, the person who is grasped by God, and who participates by faith in the power of God who transcends everything, will persevere and prevail. She accepts and does not try to escape either this threatening situation or her own anxiety, struggle, frustration, skepticism, guilt, and downtroddenness. This person continues to be hit—and often hit hard—by these negative elements. Yet, in spite of them, she acts according to the human being God has created her to be. She exists by faith. It is a matter of integrity grounded in identity: "This is who I am, and who I must be."

In this way, the individual knows not only what to dread, but also what to dare. Therefore, she lives daringly, in resistance and rebellious protest against non-being, fate and meaninglessness, sin and evil, the status quo, the tides and trends, and the odds. This, Tillich says, is "the courage to be."

I believe anyone who attempts to teach Christians in their state of religious illiteracy and theological ignorance, in the context of non-theological congregations, without either a teaching office or teaching authority, has to be full of such courage. The teacher teaches "in spite of." No matter what the negatives are, or how many and how strong they may be, she has been called and sent to this place to serve as a pastor-teacher-theologian. This is why she is doing what she is doing, and will always do it. She lives daringly, in resistance and rebellious protest against all the things that are against such a ministry.

My questions are, "Who does this? Who lives this way? Who dares teach? Who starts a lay seminary? And why? No one is asking for it. No one wants it. It is an exercise in futility. So, why attempt it? Or, stay with it and keep attempting it for a lifetime, with little to show for it?"

The answer—drawing on Tillich's understanding— is, "the person with the courage to be." Only the rare human being who is called to this mode of being and this extraordinary ministry, who accepts and affirms God's acceptance and affirmation of him or her, who is lured and then driven by the Christian theological tradition, and who remains deeply connected to the *missio Dei* (mission of God) that is other than and greater than immediate circumstances and people, will attempt such a ministry. Only the individual who is called and being made capable in Christ will teach. Only a courageous man or woman can or will speak, think, act, and be theologically. As Tillich asserts, it is a matter of integrity grounded in identity: This is who I am, and I can be no other.

The odds and obstacles are against the teacher. The subject matter is all-encompassing. The task is daunting. The audience is difficult. The pastor, then, who stands before all three must possess the unusual strength of mind, heart, character, and body that is required. Plagued with personal weaknesses and inadequacies, shortcomings and sins, lack of knowledge, insight, and understanding, along with fears and doubts, the pastor-teacher-theologian depends ultimately on the grace and power that are the Spirit's and not the Self's. Courage is a gift. And it gives assurance, confidence, boldness, resilience, stubborn determination, discipline, patience, perseverance, and even joy, which are indistinguishable from faith, hope, and love. The courage to teach is the courage to be.

How to Become a Teacher

I once asked a member of the congregation I served how he became a corporate attorney. His answer surprised me. He said he simply put his name on a plaque on his office door, along with the formal title. From then on, everyone thought of him as a corporate attorney, and related to him as a corporate attorney. At the same time, he began to think, talk, and act like a corporate attorney.

Granted, his answer was simplistic, but it conveyed a lot of truth. Similarly, a Christian becomes a teacher by calling himself a teacher, telling others he is a teacher, and then doing what a teacher does, which is teaching. Before long, he is thinking, speaking, and acting like a teacher. Other people see him and relate to him as a teacher. His title and name merge into a single identity and function. He *is* a teacher.

My friend did not mention either education or experience, although obviously a corporate attorney (a good one) must have both. Likewise, the person who senses he is called to the ministry of teaching the laity, or people of God, must be theologically educated and experienced. He must always be more educated and experienced than his students. Also, his education must be more serious, subject matter-oriented, ordered, holistic, in-depth, disciplined, and sustained than the religious education routinely offered by congregations in their Sunday School classes and small groups. Finally, the teacher's self-education and teaching ministry must become a way of life, not a sporadic, short-lived burst of interest and energy. A life devoted to studying, learning, and teaching for a lifetime is required.

The first task of the teacher is to be a student. He must call himself a student, tell others he is a student, and then do what a student does, which is to read, research, study, think, and learn. Only the student-teacher can understand what it is like for ordinary believers under his teaching to be students. He himself is one. Therefore, he is one of them, and is like them.

Also, only the teacher who is still studying and learning as a student will have anything new, important, or worthwhile to bring to his own students and tell them. Only a student—like a graduate school teaching assistant—can show other students the path ahead, since he is still on it. Only a sheep under the leading and feeding of the Good Shepherd can himself be helpful in leading and feeding other sheep.

My word of advice and encouragement to the beginning pastoral teacher, then, is to "leave the church"—literally or figuratively—and "go to seminary." If possible, go when you are young, and before you take on the full load of marriage, family, and career obligations. The community where you worship and serve, as much as you are committed to it, will not prepare you properly or adequately to be a teacher.[7] It cannot. It does not offer theological education to its members (and definitely not the kind and level you need). Members are not living the theological life.

---

7. My assumption here is that the local congregational teacher will be a clergyperson, functioning as a pastor-teacher-theologian. However, in some setting or situation, a committed non-clergyperson may see the great need for theological education, and be moved to teach. Since no pastor is available, who can or will teach, she starts teaching, though lacking a clergy seminary education. With fear and trembling, not knowing what she is doing, she will do the best she can to educate herself and then teach others what she discovers. She will always feel inferior and inadequate, as though she is pretending to be something she is not. Yet, she *is* a student, and she *is* a teacher. Surely Jesus will say to her one day, "Well done, good and faithful servant." I wholeheartedly support and encourage this kind of home-birthed, home-grown education.

I firmly believe that those who teach ordinary Christians should be as educated and competent as those who teach Christians preparing for clergy ministry. Far too long, our congregations have suffered in the pit into which they have fallen, due to "the blind leading the blind."[8] Don't be blind. Don't stay in your own blindness. Don't leave other people in theirs. And whatever you do, don't blindly lead them into more of the same blindness that already afflicts them.

Do your research on theological schools. Ask a couple of pastors for their recommendations (to be taken with a dose of discernment). Choose a seminary that is both academically and ecclesially reputable, even if you have to pack up and move in order to attend. You want the good money and time you will be spending to be invested in a good school. You also want the best theological education you can find and afford. Take your time and do your homework.

I remind you, however, that it is unlikely any seminary will direct you to the teaching ministry on the local congregational level. You may not meet a single student who shares (or even understands) your vision of going back home to be a pastor-teacher-theologian, hoping to establish and direct a small seminary for bringing Christians back to theology. Your professors will probably not have much experience in teaching laypersons, other than the occasional guest sermon or lecture. Therefore, you must have the courage to be a seminary student in training for an unusual vocation.

If possible, while you are in the academic world, continue your formal education beyond the basic master's level—usually the Master of Divinity (MDiv) degree). Enroll in a Master of Theology (MTh) or Doctor of Philosophy (PhD) program. If you can find a Doctor of Ministry (DMin) program that will allow you to concentrate on lay education and theological instruction, I encourage you to consider it. However, keep in mind that a degree beyond the MDiv is not required. You simply want a firm foundation on which you will then build a theological life and ministry over a lifetime.

When you graduate and have your degree in hand, look at it and swear to yourself that no matter what, this is not the end. This paper document is merely your license to enter into clergy ministry, where you will continue your theological education. Whatever happens, you

8. See Matthew 15:14.

will not stop, as most of your classmates will. Almost all of them will have good intentions and make the same pledge. The difference is, you will follow through. You will maintain the education that has only gotten started and set in place.

In order to fulfill your calling, you must continue being a student. You have learned a lot and acquired some basic knowledge and skills at the seminary. However, in reality, it is not much, and it definitely is not enough. Only the person who is an ongoing, active, serious student of the Christian theological faith-tradition has the right to be its teacher. And only the student who is advancing in her knowledge and understanding is being responsible in her teaching. Therefore, you cannot take the non-educational route, given that your work is an educational ministry. You are back home to be a pastor-teacher-theologian-in-residence. Your education has had a good, formal beginning, but has only just begun. Now it must be continued, developed, and matured.

A major difference is that you are now on your own. No professor or fellow seminarian will be with you to direct you, prod you, or even ask you how it's going. Your education is entirely up to you. There is no manual or map. You must set the course and navigate it yourself. You must decide what to read and research, how and when to study, and what disciplines must be in place to sustain your continuing education. You must start out and keep going until you begin to figure it out and get into a sound educational path and routine. You will have to be self-motivated and self-directed, which is not a skill most of us naturally have. You must learn it along with everything else you are learning theologically. Think of discipline as an integral part of discipleship and of the theological life itself.

Do not be surprised or disappointed when you do not receive support or encouragement from your congregation, clergy friends, or family members. They have not studied theology, as you have. And they are not now studying theology, as you are. They probably do not comprehend why you are spending so much of your time, thought, and energy on these matters, when what really matters is going to church, saying your prayers, doing your daily devotionals, having Jesus in your life, being a good person, and helping other people. But then they will say things, trying to be supportive, such as, "If that's what you like…go for it. It's just not for me."

This is okay. In fact, be grateful that they are leaving you alone to do what you like and need to do. Indirectly, you are being given permission to pursue without interference your vocation as a student and steward of the Christian faith-tradition. Still, you will be alone. At times, you will really feel alone, as though you are the only person in the world who is studying and teaching theology. In fact, you may likely be the only Christian where you live, who is studying and teaching theology. You are the only one for whom this theological faith-tradition is "the pearl of great price." It will take courage to diverge from the common path of everyone you know around you, and take this solitary one instead. It will take even greater courage to stay on it.

As the pastor or minister of education of a congregation, you will be overloaded with members' conflicting expectations, in addition to the unrelenting demands of the job itself on your time and energy. There will always be a lot of work leftover at the end of every week, for which you will feel guilty. Nonetheless, you will courageously have to resist some of these pressures and flatly refuse some of this work, in order to reserve time and energy for your studies. You will have to be intentional and persistent about it.

Make your education a priority. If you don't, it will get lost in the mix of pastoral duties. Over time, studying and learning will become thin, fade, and finally disappear. Trust me. If you assume that your studies are important, along with a lot of other important things, and somehow everything will come together and work out, and you will be able to do it all, you are mistaken. Your blindness is coming back. You are headed toward the ditch into which almost all ministers are liable to fall.

Make up your mind right now that your studies come first in your ministry, for they *are* your ministry. They *are* the base, structure, and aim of everything else you do as ministry. The work of reading and preparing cannot be one part among many, with all the parts vying for the same limited time and energy. If that is so, then all the other parts will suck up all the time and energy, leaving none for personal education.

What could possibly be more important than, or come before, studying for the purpose of interpreting and understanding the word of truth rightly, and then of instructing others to interpret and understand it rightly, as well? The God of Christ and Christ's church requires no less.

Where did we ever get the idea that theological studying and learning is not "real ministry," but only something the pastor may choose to do in his "free time"—like a hobby or side-work—when he is not doing ministry? Don't we realize that the pastor who devotes his life to the theological faith-tradition *is* doing *the* ministry for which the whole church has been created and incarnated in this world? Why don't we question our unquestioned assumptions about what qualifies for Christian life and ministry? Why are we not alarmed and very concerned about why theology—along with its life and education—doesn't qualify, and is left out?

My strong advice to you, if you are aware of your calling as a pastor to be a teaching theologian, is to continue your education, with or without the permission of the congregation. Do it anyway. Quietly. You will serve in a local context where Christians themselves have never studied or learned much, and may not even value education or knowledge in relation to faith. You will have to judge what to say, or how much to say, about your studies, as a way of setting a good example and encouraging others to do likewise. Don't be surprised if your studying is viewed as a waste of time, or as a distraction from what you are being paid to do, and maybe a sign of laziness on your part. You will have to have the courage to exist stealthily as a student in this type of setting.

As you look ahead to bringing theology home, and bringing laypersons back to theology as their home, you will surely be overwhelmed. The task is daunting. Theology is far removed from the life and work of the local congregation, and has been for such a long time. Laypersons are deeply, firmly entrenched in their old non-theological ways. Only God is up for this reconciliation.

And yet, God has called you and given you a part in God's mission of reconciliation. God has entrusted you with the message of this reconciliation and the resulting new creation of all things through Christ, and sent you to the church to proclaim and teach it. This is your vocation. And as you are carrying it out, God is appealing to both the church and the world—in and through your teaching—to be reconciled. Therefore, you must be a faithful, responsible teacher by being a faithful, responsible student of this theological good news.

You will wonder where to enter and begin your studies. There is no obvious doorway. Where do you take hold? There is no handle. But let me dissuade you from waiting until you have found just the right entry-point and handgrip. What is crucial is that you start studying somewhere. Anywhere is better than nowhere.

In the next chapter, I will propose a possible starting-point, along with a quick-start guide for your education. The important thing is to get started, and then to keep going. You will learn where and how to go as you go along. Trust me.

Gradually build your personal library as you go. Every workman needs the tools of the trade. Purchase books and resources as you need them, and as you have money. Over time, your collection will grow, and you will have on hand all you need to be both a student and a teacher.

In the next chapter, I provide a shortlist of recommended books for the student-teacher's library. The main criterion is always quality, not quantity. Acquire the best books you can find in the various areas of theology. Purchase and read the classic works of the church's most significant, influential theologians, past and present. Come back years later and reread them.

Sooner rather than later, I urge you to leave your personal study space and go public. Step forward and stand before fellow believers in the role of teacher. Begin teaching. This will take courage (great courage). For one thing, you do not yet see yourself as a pastor-teacher-theologian. You are a pastor, preacher, counselor, and CEO, just like all the other clergy you have known. Your congregation likewise views and relates to you in these roles. They do not think of you as a teacher, and certainly not as a theologian (whatever that is). They will never put the title "Pastor-Teacher-Theologian" under your name on the plaque on your office door (and I do not recommend that you do it). However, this is who you are and what you do, as one who has been called and sent for the ministry of teaching the church, within the larger ministry of reconciliation.

You will have to take on this identity, role, and function yourself. No one else will do it for you, nor ever share fully with you your self-understanding. This is why you have to be courageous, acting out of inner conviction grounded in transcendent calling. Say to yourself, "I am called to be a pastor-teacher-theologian. This is who I am. For this ministry, I have been sent here." Then, go and act like one, although you are not quite sure how a pastor-teacher-theologian acts. Teach. And you will gradually become one, revealing to others who you have created to be and are becoming in Christ.

"Pastor-teacher-theologian" is a compound noun. I have added "teacher" to the more familiar compound noun, "pastor-theologian," compounding it even further. I do this, believing the role of teacher is vital to the ministry of the pastor-theologian. It is not enough to be a pastor and a theologian—which, in most cases, simply means that pastor happens to like theology, continues to read a theology book or two along the way, and often draws on theology for material for his or her sermons and congregational newsletter articles. The church needs and deserves much more than this from it ministers. It requires serious, sustained theological study, research, reflection, and embodiment. It requires careful, continuous theological teaching. It demands nothing less than or other than the full ministry of a true pastor-teacher-theologian-in-residence.

Usually, in this compound noun and its self-image, "pastor" takes precedence over "theologian." The individual is first a pastor, and then a theologian. Her primary identity is that of a pastor, not a theologian. Theological function follows pastoral function (if at all). The former serves the latter, and is additional and secondary. The work of theologian reinforces and enhances the work of pastor, while remaining extra and optional. Consequently, the term "theologian" functions as an adjective, modifying the noun "pastor" and pointing to one task among many that are involved in being a pastor.

In my expanded compound noun of "pastor-teaching-theologian," I take seriously the placement of "theologian" last. The accent is on theologian. It is the primary noun. The other two nouns—"pastor" and "teacher"—function as adjectives, modifying "theologian," and describing two important dimensions of what it means to be a theologian of the church.

The pastor-teacher-theologian has a ministry that is significantly different from the ministry of the typical pastor, who is neither a teacher nor a theologian. Theological ministry is much richer, fuller, and deeper. Its foundation and structure are theological first, and then pastoral. The minister is called to be a theologian, who exercises his or her calling by serving as a pastor, whose primary means of serving is teaching. This minister is a theologian-in-residence, who acts as the congregation's teacher. His or her primary task is to educate the faith-community and its members in their own Christian theological tradition, which is the tradition that makes it possible for them to exist in this world theologically and Christianly—as Christ did, in the manner of faith.

Flip through the current catalog of titles and job descriptions, however, and you will not find this one. What Christian minister carries this image and identity, or functions this way? Who today is a pastor-teacher-theologian?

Go back in church history, however, and you will discover that the early bishops, church fathers, desert monks, medieval priests, and also many American pastors—such as Jonathan Edwards[9]—served the church in this way. They were theologians in the role of pastor, ministering primarily through teaching, preaching, and writing.

Following in their steps, you will have to forge your own "ancient-future,"[10] or "old-new," ministerial way through all the many, different job descriptions, demands, and expectations of the modern or post-modern minister. This will take courage on your part to take on an identity and role for yourself that no one requires or even understands. Simply start studying, preaching, teaching, and writing theologically, i.e., within the church's historical-biblical-theological faith-tradition.

Of course, you will not believe you are ready. Frankly, I would worry about you if you did. In many ways you are not ready. But if

---

9. Jonathan Edwards (1703–1758) was an American clergyman, theologian, and philosopher, who served as pastor of the Congregationalist church in Northampton, Massachusetts, and later as president of the College of New Jersey (now Princeton University). He was a Puritan, a "new Calvinist," and a leading figure in the First Great Awakening. See George M. Marsden, *Jonathan Edwards: A Life* (New Haven: Yale University Press, 2003).

10. The term "ancient-future" comes from Robert E. Webber (1933–2007), who taught at Wheaton College and Northern Baptist Theological Seminary. He was founding president of the Robert E. Webber Institute for Worship Studies in Jacksonville, Florida. His long list of published books include "the ancient-future series": *Ancient-Future Faith, Ancient-Future Evangelism, Ancient-Future Time,* and *Ancient-Future Worship.* The term "ancient-future" means "the road to the future runs through the past." The church's challenge is to go back to its own classical Christian theological tradition, and from there, find points of contact with contemporary, postmodern thought and culture.

you wait until you are fully and finally ready, you will be on hold for a very long time, if not for the rest of your life and career. No one is ever ready, fully prepared, or finally competent for the vocation of teaching the Christian theological faith-tradition—no matter how long he or she does it.

Who would dare to teach the church? Still, the church desperately needs teachers today. And it is only by teaching that one truly becomes a teacher. And only by teaching does one truly become a student. So jump into both at the same time. Do it sooner rather than later.

Teach what you have learned and are learning. Simply tell others. Let them in on it. Do not keep this good, rich knowledge and understanding to yourself, but share it with others. Do it while it is fresh, and do it again later when it is more settled and seasoned. Find ways to do this. Keep experimenting with how best to do this. Studying and learning will propel you into teaching, and teaching will propel you back into studying and learning. This becomes your way of life and ministry. It is the life of a theologian, who is a pastor serving the church through teaching.

You should always know more than your students. Stay at least one step ahead of them. In all likelihood, however, you will be working miles ahead, and will constantly have to go back to get them and bring them along. They will be assured that their teacher has scouted the territory ahead, understands more than they do, and knows the way. Otherwise, why would they want to waste their time and energy with someone who is as blind or lost as they are?

Teach out of what you know, not out of what you don't know. One major power of education is that it always, simultaneously, makes us both knowledgeable and ignorant. By exposing us to what can be known, it exposes what we don't know, and didn't even know we didn't know. Recognize the difference, and teach the former—only what you have come to know. Do not venture into areas where you have little to no educational experience, or into matters about which you know little to nothing. Teach only what you have learned to such a degree that you have a good grasp and understanding, and can communicate and explain it well to others.

I do suggest that you occasionally remind your students that, outside of what you know, there is a far greater region of what you don't know. Let them know how ignorant you still are, even after all these many years. This is why you keep studying and learning, seeking and exploring. Like them, you are continuing to be a student, while simultaneously being their teacher. You are not asking them to do something you are not doing. You offer yourself as a model and mentor. You show and tell them how to relate to and be engaged by the Christian theological tradition, by loving, studying, serving, and embodying it, all the while battling and overcoming ignorance.

Don't overdo it, though. There is nothing more demoralizing or pitiful than a teacher who constantly disqualifies himself, saying, "I don't know much about this, and am probably not the person who should be teaching you." If you don't and you aren't, then why are you teaching? Either speak about what you do know and understand, or study harder and be better prepared before attempting to teach.

Now that I have said this, I will quickly add that teaching does play a vital role in helping the student know what she knows. All of us know more than we can tell. Only by attempting to tell it can we truly, fully know and understand it. In fact, the event of learning is not finished and firmly in place until a person can put it into words, articulate and communicate it, and teach someone else.

I have always believed teaching is a selfish act. By both preparing to teach and then teaching, the teacher always learns more than her students, and usually gets more out of it. She benefits the most.

At the same time, teaching is a sacrificial act. It is the teacher who spends the most time with the subject matter, and works the hardest. The teacher gives up valuable resources of time, energy, attention, and thought, while typically no one else around her is sacrificing anything. Yet, she does it willingly and gladly. She seeks to gain for herself. But then she gives to others what she has worked so long and hard to gain. The teacher wants her students to enter into the same selfish act of going after knowledge and understanding of the Christian theological faith-tradition for themselves. She also wants them to become willing to make the same sacrifice required for gaining it.

I encourage you always to teach "over the heads" of your students. We labor under the false assumption that the teacher is supposed to bring the subject matter to the students, "meeting them where they are," down at their level, and adapting it to them, so that it will be made so simply and easy for them that they cannot possibly not learn it.

While there is some truth here—children, for example, cannot be taught at the same level and in the same way as adults—a major objective of education is to lead individuals away from where they are, and not leave them at the same level where they have been. A most significant aim is to train them to submit to being transformed by, conformed to, and formed by a body of wisdom that is other than and greater than themselves, rather than keeping them delusional and ignorant, thinking that the body of wisdom has to be transformed according to what they want it to be, conformed to their needs, and then formed by how they prefer to use it. Perhaps the most important lesson a Christian can learn is that theology does not serve her, but she serves it.

This is why I strongly urge teaching "above" your students. Teach what is beyond all of us. Teach knowledge and understanding that students do not yet have, rather than repeating what they already have, know, and understand. Teach above the shallow, superficial level where Christians currently believe, think, talk, and live. How else will they come to know that there is any other level, much less attempt to reach it—unless you tell them? And you can only tell them, if this is the higher level where you are studying, learning, thinking, and living.

My one qualifier is that you not teach too far over their heads, lest your teaching stop being challenging, and start being incomprehensible. You will lose them. I am not saying that you should never lose them. I think you should. Students need to sense frequently they are "in over their heads," floundering and drowning, or wandering and lost. Much learning can only happen here in this scary, forbidden territory.

Nonetheless, carefully monitor your "victims." As needed, let up, slow down, and come back to them at their level. Give them more explanation. Let them catch up. Allow them to take in and digest what you have revealed to them, informing and forming their words and thoughts. And, when everybody is ready, you can move on again.

Stay at least two steps ahead of them. Continue introducing new material. Move quickly enough that you do not bore them, but not so fast that you run off without them. Learn the proper rhythm of teaching for your particular students. Vary your pace. Stop and explain. Keep it interesting. And definitely keep it moving.

Frequently circle back around to make connections in the material you are teaching, for you are working with the theological tradition as a whole, as well as with its composite parts. Keep the big picture before them, while you explore and discuss each of the smaller themes, motifs, images, concepts, and so on.

In addition to going above and beyond your students, go deeper. They have never been taken into the depths of their own theological faith. They may not even know there are depths. Their Christian swimming has only been on the surface in the shallow end of the pool. They have never ventured out and plunged beneath. And they do not know how. They are afraid to try.

This is where you serve as their encourager and guide. Tell them about the deep end of faith and the theological depths. Help them overcome their trepidation. Give them the orientation they need to be ready and equipped to go there. Then take them there. You "show and tell." You reveal to them all the amazing truth and meaning that are there waiting for them, and take them there, so that they will personally experience it, and never want to come back—except perhaps to tell someone else and lead them there.

Never underestimate or insult the intelligence of your students. Those who prefer that you do are uninterested in learning. They are only seeking to be confirmed in their current beliefs, without having to do any hard mental work, be challenged to change in any way, or submit themselves to the authority of theology's teacher (you), much less theology itself. They should not be allowed to go anywhere near educational construction while it is going on.

Some Christians, in contrast, are very aware, mindful, questioning, discerning, and confessing people. Sadly and shamefully, their congregations have underestimated and insulted their intelligence their entire lives, by only offering to them simplistic, superficial, and sentimental spirituality and morality. They have never been around thoughtful theological discourse. Their pastors have not delivered to them theologically-astute, thought-provoking, faith-forming sermons. They have never been offered the kind of education that serious theological believers require. When classes are offered, these leave much to be desired. They do not constitute a full course of ordered teaching and learning. Therefore, intelligent, thoughtful Christians quietly languish. They assume this is just the way things are. They must be the exception, or the only ones who want more, or something else. Everybody else seems satisfied. They talk about how much they are getting out of it.

Consequently, I encourage you to find and teach these atypical persons. Do not start by attempting to teach everybody, hoping to attract and retain a large attendance. To do this, you would have to teach only subject matter that is interesting to everybody. You would have to teach at a pace and level everybody can manage. You would have to teach what everybody thinks is relevant, because it applies directly to them, fits what they already believe, gives them practical principles and guidelines for their everyday lives, and helps them be religious, spiritual, moral, and happy people. "Everybody" means more of the "same old, same old," in which nobody is theologically educated, and nobody gains a clue about the theological life.

My advice is that you not waste your time and energy on the religious crowd, or on those who are unresponsive and unteachable. Speak to those who hunger for truthful, meaningful words. Think out loud for the benefit of those who are thinking, and, like you, desire to take on the mind of the Christian theological faith-tradition. Make clear the kind of serious, sustained, in-depth education you are offering, and what will be involved and required. Keep your promise by keeping your teaching true to its intended purpose. Maintain the integrity of theology. Call students to conform to theology, rather than theology conform to them. While no one is excluded, most will exclude themselves (as they should). Cast your pearls out before the Christian congregation, and you will discover who will see and value them, and end up becoming pearl merchants. These are the persons for whom you have been sent.

As soon as you gather two or three, start teaching. As important as *what* you teach is, it is vital *that* you teach. The very act of teaching, that has been missing for so long, is desperately needed. Teach without ceasing. Teach what is important, that needs to be taught.

View your small group as a seminary, since this is what it is. Although it is small, it is a school of theological education—which is what a seminary is. You and your students are a teaching-learning community of those who are called to be Jesus' disciples and disciple-makers. Think of yourselves this way, and explore together what it means to be a congregation, or local manifestation of Christ's church. Worship together out of and around what you are studying and learning. Care for one another. Serve. Enjoy the fellowship of the Spirit in which all of you are participating. Be like the first responders at Pentecost, who "devoted themselves to the apostles' teaching and fellowship, to the breaking of bread and the prayers." (Acts 2:42)

This small seminary may exist within the larger congregation you serve as pastor, or it may be independent. In either case, continue to be a pastor-teacher-theologian-in-residence in your larger congregation, as well as in the smaller one. Preach and teach the Christian faith-tradition, centered in the gospel of Christ and its Scriptures, creeds, prayers, and hymns, despite the members' lack of genuine theological interest. Be faithful to your calling, although you will have to work harder to find ways to communicate effectively with this group of Christians than you do with the few who are in the miniature seminary community.

As an employee, you will be expected to perform all the other duties that have come to be expected of pastors today. You will be required to oversee and direct the entire operation. You must take the lead and help the congregation set and achieve its agenda, goals, and strategies. You will function as chief manager and administrator. You will be an ombudsman and referee. You will serve as hallway greeter and counselor. You will officiate at all the congregation's official events, including funerals and weddings, as well as anniversary celebrations and Vacation Bible School picnics. You will visit the sick in hospitals, nursing homes, and private homes. You will be held responsible for maintaining the morale of the congregation (which means keeping everybody happy). Leaders of your congregation will monitor and judge your ministry by the numbers: how many people are coming, attending, joining, and staying (whether "we are growing"), and how much they are giving (or not giving).

All in all, if you are called to be a pastor, you will find some joy and meaning in being "all things to all people"—yes, even these people. However, you will always be painfully aware that your ministry as a theologian and teacher, while it remains vitally real, important, and alive with you, is surreal, unimportant, and dead in the perception of those around you, whom you serve. They do not see it as you do.

Often you will suspect that you have two jobs; and in a real sense, you do. On the one hand, you are a pastor-teacher-theologian-in-residence. On the other hand, you serve as a pastor-leader-all-things-to-all-people. These two roles are not the same.

Yet, you are called to both. Most of your clergy colleagues are not. They have only one job and one identity: pastor-leader-all-things-to-all-people, because this is what "all people" employ and expect them to be and to do. They do not labor under the demands of teacher and theologian.

But you do. Truth is, you consider your first ministry to be that of pastor-teacher-theologian. However, your second ministry (pastor-leader-all-things-to-all-people) is the one that provides you a job and a salary, allowing you to carry out your first ministry. In this way, you are bi-vocational, just as you would be if you worked full-time as a mechanic at a local garage, while pastoring a small congregation on the side. You are working full-time as a pastor at a local congregation, while teaching theology on the side. The former is what you get paid for. You do the latter for free, and in your "free time."

Still, you view theological teaching as your first, true calling, and the primary reason you are where you are, doing what you are doing. Therefore, you are effectively carrying out a stealth ministry while performing another ministry. You are a theologian who is a pastor doing many things, but who, in and through them all, is teaching his or her congregation.

Whether your theological teaching ministry is recognized and valued, or not, I encourage you to continue teaching. Find students and create opportunities for teaching. Discover new material and new ways for teaching. Learn how to teach by teaching.

If you must, read books and articles on the objectives and methods of effective teaching, or on Christian religious education and spiritual formation. You may find something here to help you. Yet, there is one good, sure way to learn how to teach theology to laypersons, and that is by teaching theology to laypersons. Both theology and laypersons will teach you to teach, and make a teacher out of you.

Teach regularly, as often and as much as possible. Teach creatively, by trial and error, success and failure. Teach different persons in different settings. Persevere in season and out of season. This is the only way to become a seasoned teacher, or master teacher.

The counsel of the Apostle Paul to his student-minister Timothy, given in these two texts, is appropriate here:

> In the presence of God and of Christ Jesus, who is to judge the living and the dead, and in view of his appearing and his kingdom, I solemnly urge you: proclaim the message; be persistent whether the time is favorable or unfavorable; convince, rebuke, and encourage, with the utmost patience in teaching. For the time is coming when people will not put up with sound doctrine, but having itching ears, they will accumulate for themselves teachers to suit their own desires, and will turn away from listening to the truth and wander away to myths. As for you, always be sober, endure suffering, do the work of an evangelist, carry out your ministry fully. (2 Timothy 4:1–5)

> If you put these instructions before the brothers and sisters, you will be a good servant of Christ Jesus, nourished on the words of the faith and of sound teaching that you have followed. …Until I arrive, give attention to the public reading of scripture, to exhorting, to teaching. Do not neglect the gift that is in you, which was given to you through prophecy with the laying on of hands by the council of elders. Put these things into practice, devote yourself to them, so that all may see your progress. Pay close attention to yourself and to your teaching; continue in these things, for in doing this you will save both yourself and your hearers. (1 Timothy 4:6, 13–16)

Teaching Sermons and Lectures

The Christian minister has two main ways to teach: proclamation and instruction, or preaching and lecturing. Unfortunately, most ministers assume that preaching and teaching are two completely separate acts. Like oil and water, neither mixes well with the other. The preacher does not teach, and the teacher does not preach.

Another common assumption is that the minister does not teach—if he teaches at all—by lecturing. While this form of teaching may have been popular decades ago, it is not today. Q&A and open discussion are now the standard, acceptable methods. There is no longer any real desire or need for formal instruction.

These common misunderstandings must be rejected, and in their place the minister must view teaching as the primary, pressing function of her ministry. The need of congregations and Christians for theological education, grounded in theological instruction, is simply too great and pressing. The teacher must become keenly aware that wherever she is, and whatever she is doing in ministry, she is a teacher, who has been called and equipped to teach.

As a pastor, her primary occasions for teaching are in the sanctuary and the classroom. She must enter into both with the intention of teaching, and courageously using both proclamation and instruction, without fretting whether she is unduly mixing the two. Preaching and teaching deal with the same theological subject matter. Also, the preacher and teacher are the same person. How can the two forms of ministry not coincide? And why would we not want them to, enriching and strengthening each other?

Another way to say this is, "Teach everywhere you can, every way you can, and every chance you get." Be a theologian who resides in the household of faith, serving as its teacher. Teach in pastoral counseling sessions, as well as in casual conversations. Teach in newsletter articles and blog posts. Teach, teach, teach.

Jesus' students have been too long without a teacher, like sheep without a shepherd. When he was moved, seeing the great crowd in their wayward condition, what did Jesus do? He began to teach them.[11] This was his first response to and remedy for their condition. You do the same with the flock that is before you and around you.

More than sporadic or occasional teaching is necessary for the theological education of Christians, individually and corporately. Ordered teaching, or teaching that is intentional and systematic, must take place. No one in the congregation will demand it, or even mention it. No one will care if the pastor's sermons are teaching sermons. No one will complain if the pastor is not teaching in the classroom, or is not a teacher at all. Therefore, it is entirely up to you, as the pastor, to initiate theological education and to practice ordered teaching.

---

11. Mark 6:34; also Matthew 9:36.

Go into the sanctuary and teach. Go into the classroom and teach. Preach teaching sermons, and deliver formal lectures. This is not to say that other methods of proclamation and instruction should not be used. They should be. But I insist that the minister not neglect these two methods of ordered teaching and learning. In fact, she should rely heavily upon them for teaching theology; and, therefore, should develop great skill in using both effectively.

What is a "teaching sermon"? It is preaching, or proclamation, conceived, constructed, and communicated as an act of teaching. The preacher intentionally decides to preach in a teaching mode. Her intent in preaching is educational. As she proclaims the gospel in and through scriptural exposition, she wants to instruct the congregation in some matter of the vast, complex Christian theological tradition, in such a way as to give hearers the practical knowledge of faith they need to interpret reality and to exist in this world by faith before God.

As Ronald Allen puts it, "The teaching sermon helps the congregation name the world (and the congregation's experience in the world) in the terms of the gospel."[12] By giving hearers-learners the interpretive framework of the Christian theological faith-tradition, the preacher-teacher enables them to interpret the world and live their lives by faith.

The question in the teaching minister's mind as he prepares to preach is not: (1) "What program, age group, special interest, or special emphasis do I need to promote this Sunday?" (2) "What is this congregation going through, or its members facing, that I should address with Scripture and pastoral care?" (3) "What moral virtue will I emphasize and try to instill in them?" (4) "What political action or social ministry should I urge them to pray for or get involved in?" or (5) "What homework assignment do I give them—some principle, value, or task to 'go and do likewise,' putting into practice what they have heard, that will make a difference in their personal lives at home and work this coming week?" Such questions typically direct pastors in their sermon preparation.

---

12. Clark M. Williamson and Ronald J. Allen, *The Teaching Minister* (Louisville: Westminster/John Knox Press, 1991), 85. A solid discussion of the teaching sermon is provided in chapter 5, pages 83–104. Also, read Ronald J. Allen, *The Teaching Sermon* (Nashville: Abingdon Press, 1995).

A major shift is required. The leading question of the teaching minister, guiding his sermon preparation, is, "What do we need to learn as a community this week and in the upcoming weeks?"[13]

The aim of the teaching sermon is the congregation's education. The entire community is dependent on the pulpit for instruction and guidance in what it needs to learn and understand in order to be the church and to live theologically by faith. Because this is knowledge that Christians lack and desperately need, the preacher teaches whenever he enters the pulpit.

The accent of the teaching sermon is on the sermon's content, rather than on either the preacher's delivery of the sermon, or the hearer's immediate emotional reaction to it. Christians are woefully inexperienced and ill-equipped in this kind of listening and learning. Therefore, the preacher must insist—in and through the manner of his preaching—that people listen. They have to be trained to pay attention, focus on what is being said, and then hear what is actually being said, rather than what they assume is being said, or what they want to hear.

The point of orientation must shift from both preacher and hearer to the message. Christians on both sides of the pulpit must respond to the sermon's content of theological truth and meaning—not solely to each other. They must receive this content as vitally important and authoritative. They must do the work of following it, letting it go through their minds, deliver its insight and understanding, do its converting work, and change their very being and mode of existence in the world.

Fundamentally, Christians must be taught to think. They have to learn to think theologically in an identifiably, distinctively Christian way. Their minds must be transformed, and thereby made capable of considering things that are true and excellent, although secret and hidden, not belonging to any wisdom of this age. Ordinary minds have to be opened to being filled with, influenced by, and conformed to the extraordinary knowledge, understanding, and wisdom of God's redemptive revelation. They must come to seek to have the same mind that is in Jesus Christ and in the tradition that has formed around him. They must be trained to love God with their minds as

---

13. Williamson and Allen, *The Teaching Minister*, 85.

well as with their hearts, souls, strengths, and practices related to their neighbors and themselves.

The role of the minister is to be a Christian thinker in the midst of the congregation and its members. He demonstrates and encourages thinking by thinking. He prepares and preaches well-thought-out sermons. His messages provoke thought. The greatest compliment he can receive in response from members at the door after worship is, "You made me think."

The hearer who does not want to think has to work extra hard not to give in and start thinking (or this person has to stay away). The preacher is relentless in transmitting sound cognitive content. She desires for her hearers to participate in the historical church and its theological tradition. She has discovered the truth and meaning that are there; and she wants them to discover it, as well. She battles the ignorance of unfaith, trying to weaken and break its firm hold. She prays that no one will leave as untransformed, uninformed, and unformed as he or she came in. She longs for the whole community she serves to exist, interpret, and live by faith, as the saints have for centuries, and still do.

Of course, the pastor is responsible only for preaching sermons and delivering lectures that teach the historical-biblical-theological tradition of Christian faith. The congregation and its members are responsible for everything else. The teacher attempts to teach them; but whether or not they are taught is up to them.

The preacher preaches persuasively. Yet, his preaching does not have the power to persuade people who refuse to be persuaded. His calling is not to change minds (or hearts, for that matter), but only to bring to mind theological truth and meaning that, by the work of the Spirit, human minds may be changed to the mind that is Christ's—if these minds are not dead set against it.

It amazes me how resistant to learning many Christians have made themselves. The entire worship service is a thoroughgoing theological exercise. How can they possibly attend and sit here every single Sunday for years, and not be taught? The hymns, songs, prayers, and scripture readings are all theological. How can people not hear, or not be affected at all? How can they not take on this theological mind?

The preacher-liturgist who is a teacher-theologian continues her ministry, regardless of her audience's response or non-response. In her most honest moments, she will confess that she does become frustrated and discouraged. Losing heart is an experience with which she is all too familiar. But she continues, and, week after week, feeds her flock with theologically sound, rich teaching sermons.

Theology provides not only the content but also the framework, or structure, of teaching sermons. Theology is a set of interpretations, understandings, insights, concepts, and convictions, framed as a whole by the supreme revelation of God in, through, and as Jesus Christ. The preacher, then, has a kind of map, and his theological preaching follows its path. He is not left to his own desires or devices, wandering aimlessly, looking for the next sermon, wondering what to preach, or running out of something to say. The grand scheme of the whole historical-biblical-theological tradition of faith is preached, with each sermon leading to the next one, and all of them connected and ordered by the same framework.

This is why I have always preached sermon series, finding them to be the best way to teach from the pulpit. Separate sermons comprise a single series, followed by a second series, a third, and so on. All series are correlated, and all work together to communicate the larger whole of the theological faith-tradition.

While the once-a-week, Sunday-after-Sunday schedule may give this kind of preaching-teaching a simple linear appearance, all my sermons actually are intricately, complexly related—like a tapestry or web. Each teaching sermon derives from, represents, relates to, and adds to every other sermon, as well as to their whole.

Teaching can begin at any point, with any sermon, although some starting-points are preferable to others. Teaching is ordered, but it freely moves back and forth, and all over the place, drawing connections, pulling out information and insight, and disclosing the "big picture" in all its integral dimensions, as well as minute pixels.

For instance, last summer I preached a series of sermons on the Lord's Prayer. This was not random, or something I thought my congregation might enjoy hearing. This series naturally followed a series I had completed on "Stewardship of the Mysteries of God." It then led into a subsequent series on Christian ethics, "How Then Shall We Live?" The Lord's Prayer series was the bridge.

My thought and planning were this: Given that we are stewards of the mysteries of God made known and knowable in Christ, how do we live? What do we do? Well, first, we pray. We pray the way Jesus prayed and taught his disciples to pray about these mysteries. Then, second, his prayer leads us into the practice of the life of faith that is grounded in these mysteries.

In this way, all three series were connected in one larger, longer series. I actually view my entire preaching career over four decades as a single series, or as one great sermon told in many pieces, in many ways, from many angles, in many tellings.

A major advantage of preparing this way is that the preacher has a teaching plan. Preaching is an act of ordered teaching. The pastor knows what's next, and does not have to go searching every week for a message or lesson. The congregation is kept moving on a continual path, rather than bogging down or detouring off on various side trips.

Another advantage is that the preacher can concentrate on one limited subject area at a time, and over a significant period of time. His study is neither piece-meal nor helter-skelter. He stays with a single subject or theme for weeks, allowing him to concentrate his study and preparation.

For instance, my sermon series on the Lord's Prayer extended over seven Sundays. I went to my library for good books on the Lord's Prayer that I had collected over the years. I researched the latest historical, literary, and theological material on Matthew 6:7–13 (Luke 11:1-4), and purchased a few more books. I downloaded several online articles. And, using these resources, I studied the Lord's Prayer for two months, as I was preparing and preaching. I wrote down my reflections and insights as they came to me. I kept myself in the role of a student, striving for new knowledge and greater understanding.

I have never liked sermons that only deliver "old" knowledge and "stale" understanding. Why tell people what they have always heard and already know? Out of my study of Jesus' prayer came discoveries that gave fresh, rich organization and content to my sermons.

While preaching-teaching the Lord's Prayer, I drew on many different areas of Christian theology: Kingdom of God, forgiveness, sin and evil—and, of course, prayer. I constantly kept in mind the larger objective of educating the congregation, not merely in the Lord's Prayer, but more so in the entire biblical-theological faith-tradition. I made certain this larger tradition "bled" into each sermon, and that each sermon flowed back into this larger tradition. The interplay between the whole and its parts was vital. I did everything I could to keep both in play at the same time.

When the Lord's Prayer sermon series was completed, I moved into a series in theological ethics, "How Then Shall We Live?" It naturally came next, being suggested by what we were learning about the Kingdom of God, forgiveness, sin and evil, and prayer. Given that we are stewards of the mysteries of God (the six-month series I preached during the winter and spring before the Lord's Prayer series), and students of Jesus' manner of praying (the summer series), it stands to reason that we are learning far more than merely how to believe. We are learning how to be—to be who we are and what we are about in this world in the manner of Christ. What does this life look like? What is required of us? What are our ethical obligations?

Everything in ordered teaching-preaching points to and leads to something else and to everything else. It is like a precious diamond that is multi-faceted. While each sermon laser-focuses on a single facet, the other facets are always appearing and coming into view, reflecting the whole diamond's cut, clarity, color, weight, brilliance, and dispersion of light (its "fire"). Teaching sermons are facets that reflect—though partially and dimly—the full beauty of the Christian historical-biblical-theological faith-tradition.

In addition to teaching sermons on Sundays, I invite members of the congregation to attend a "pastor's class" before worship on Sunday mornings, or to return on a weekday night for further study. Typically, the few who attend are the ones who take their theological education seriously. They want more than what I can provide in a teaching sermon during a worship service. Therefore, they are ready to invest the extra time in classroom learning.

Also, I believe these class sessions are necessary for the making of a lay seminary. Students must invest more time and energy than usual. A single gathering for a single hour a week is not enough. I ask my students to meet for two hours on a weekday night in a dedicated classroom setting. I lecture on material that either extends or complements what I am preaching on Sunday mornings. Both pulpit and lectern are in synch.

These sessions give my students and me the opportunity to interact more directly and closely, as well as more often. I continually ask them questions, and receive theirs. I have an "open door" policy regarding questions: interrupt me anytime to ask me anything; don't wait for the Q&A times that I build into each class session.

I make it clear that while we will certainly learn from one another, our primary goal is to learn from the Christian theological faith-tradition itself. I push them to be continually engaged with the subject matter. Personal reflections, opinions, and initial reactions are important. But they are neither all-important nor of first importance. We are together as students, not of ourselves as subjects, but rather, of a subject matter that truly matters, even more than ourselves.

I strongly encourage the teacher, not the students, to teach. While students may (and hopefully will) learn something from one another, they should not expect too much. Fellow students are not teachers. More importantly, they are not advanced in their knowledge, understanding, and wisdom concerning the subject matter. This is why they are students. And they usually are beginners. The primary source of learning in the classroom, then, is the teacher. Teaching is primarily, if not solely, the responsibility of the teacher.

In order to facilitate the most learning, the teacher must teach by lecturing, not by "leading discussions"—although discussion between teacher and students, and students with one another, is important. I realize my approach seems outdated and runs counter to what is currently trending. However, I do not see that Christians talking to one another is doing anything to combat Christian illiteracy and ignorance. If anything, Christians today are more uninformed and unformed than ever.

Only a full, strong introduction of knowledge—like a blood infusion—can possibly make any difference. The way to do this is by lecturing. Only lecturing can put theology back in front of believers, and give them something not only to talk about, but also to think about, to believe, to learn, and then to live. Finally, only lecturing will restore the primacy of subject matter over the individual subject, and over a group of subjective individuals.

We are here as the church to study and learn our own theological tradition, for which we are responsible as its stewards. The greater weight of authority is on the tradition, while the greater weight of responsibility is on us. Our educational work is more about what the tradition demands of those of us who belong to it, than about what you and I are experiencing or feeling. This is an exercise in "beliefs clarification," but not in the sense of merely clarifying what you and I believe. It is the clarification of what Christians as Christians have traditionally believed and continue to believe. Thus, it is a correction of all that you and I believe that is misguided, incomplete, or false.

Such major work takes place in and through instruction. It involves interpretation, explanation, and transformation. What becomes clear is that you and I are the ones who must have our prior beliefs clarified, or brought out in the open, examined, measured against the Christian biblical-theological faith-tradition, filled-in, developed, deepened, and then corrected and adjusted to that tradition.

Second, the one who knows and understands the most about theology should be the one who teaches the ones who know and understand less. This places tremendous responsibility on the teacher to be the most diligent, advanced student in the class. The only reason the teacher is given the opportunity and privilege of teaching is because he or she has been called, has undertaken the theological life, and is continuing to study and learn as a trustworthy steward in an advanced way. She then has something to teach that others do not have but need. This places her under obligation to teach it, since what she possesses is vital to the church and to the faith of others.

Students both need and deserve to be taught by a teacher, rather than by each other. Why would anyone look to his neighbor—who is just as ignorant as he is (if not more)—for instruction? Those who are blind should not attempt to lead one another, or else they will only be wandering around in darkness. The way out is for someone with both some sight and insight from a long personal engagement with the historical-biblical-theological faith-tradition to step forward and take the lead. This teacher must know the way. Otherwise, why should anyone follow? Or listen?

For too long, laypersons have tolerated non-students serving as their Sunday School, special study course, and small group teachers. They have sat through numerous videos series by popular Christian celebrities, who, while exuberant and inspiring, know relatively little about our tradition, or worse, teach a "different gospel."[14] It is past time that Christians be more discriminating and demanding. We have put up with subpar, superficial, and suspect teaching much too long.

14. See Galatians 1:8 and 2 Corinthians 11:4.

The teacher must not wait for the congregation to begin insisting that its teachers be theologically qualified. Instead, the pastor-teacher-theologian must go ahead and make himself qualified, by taking up the life of a theologian. He devotes himself to the teachings of the church, its Scriptures, and its orthodox confessions and practices. He believes his calling requires reading and studying. He purposefully moves into areas of knowledge that are new for him, driven by an intense desire to explore and learn what he does not yet know or understand. He is curious and fascinated.

I once heard James A. Sanders, an American biblical scholar, speak at a pastor's conference. In the middle of his lecture, he became emotionally moved and had to stop. He explained tearfully, "I am sorry. It's just that I actually believe this stuff."[15]

Yes, the pastor-teacher-theologian actually believes this stuff. He loves the Christian tradition of thought and talk about God. He is compelled by such love to teach the church, whom Christ loves and gives his life. It is this same love that sends this student of Christ back into the community of faith as its teacher. He teaches where theology is unknown. He teaches where the tradition has been lost. He teaches where teaching does not occur, and may not even be wanted. He teaches despite the fact that people are naturally and normally not students. He teaches where education is egalitarian: all are considered equal in knowledge and understanding, with no one having more truth or meaning than anyone else. He teaches where practically any warm body can assume the role of teacher, or no one is really the teacher.

Lecturing breaks all of these misguided beliefs and practices, putting one person up before a group, speaking, instructing and explaining the subject matter that truly matters to the church. There is no other method more efficient or effective for communicating cognitive content—and, yes, our faith does involve cognitive content. Our typical religious education has unfortunately shown little interest in such communication, or in such content.

Of course, it is required of the lecturer that she be well-prepared, articulate, inviting and interesting. The message needs and deserves a

15. Many times I have found myself similarly overcome with emotion, because of the overwhelming truth and meaning of the Christian revelation. How can I not believe? Or not be moved?

good messenger or witness. So do the recipients. There is nothing worse than a boring person going on and on in a humdrum speech, or unengaging monologue. It gives lecturing a bad name.

Good lecturing requires a good lecturer—a teacher who is good at what she does, and is consistently following the "practice, practice, practice!" dictum in order to get better. The good lecturer is devoted to learning more and more of the subject matter, learning the students, learning the best way to communicate and bridge the gap between the two, and pulling all of this together repeatedly in the classroom.

At the same time, students must be trained to listen to and to learn from a lecture. Most do not know how to do this. Usually such training will occur as the educational experience itself takes place and progresses. The very manner in which the teacher teaches through lecturing will communicate, "Listen! Pay attention. Stay with me. Think. This is important." At times, the teacher will have to say these words out loud in order to provoke non-listeners to listen, or listeners to become better listeners, actually hearing the message of the subject matter. Most students will fall in line and begin developing this essential skill, without being aware of it.

The seasoned teacher will learn to build into his lectures brief pauses, or breaks. The lecturer should be lecturing at a rapid enough pace to keep students awake and moving. But periodically, they will need a chance to catch their breath and also catch up with the subject matter. Rest. The teacher must make sure no one has gotten lost or fallen by the wayside. Is everyone still with us?

A break is an opportunity to find out what students are thinking (or not thinking), and where they are being challenged (or not). Invite responses and questions. Ask them questions. Give them time to chew on and digest the new material they are receiving. Ask for their questions. Then return to lecturing. Reserve a few minutes at the end of each session for a brief summary and final discussion. Bring the entire session to a deliberate rather than abrupt close.

My students appreciate the outline of my lecture that I email to them a day or two before each class session. This outline serves as a tool for tracking and staying with me. Some students print out a paper copy for use in class. Others download my file on their laptops, and bring their laptops to class. They take notes by typing them directly into the outline. Then they create document folders and files for my classes, and save them for future reference. Some of my students have over fifteen years worth of theological material at their fingertips on their computers.

I also audio-record all my lectures (and sermons). I make these recordings available "in the cloud" for any student who may want to listen a second time. A few students bring their own recorders or cell phones for this purpose. Anyone who cannot attend a class session can easily catch-up by listening to my lecture online, and will not miss anything or fall behind. This is another way of emphasizing how important our teaching-learning work together truly is.

I encourage teachers to prepare sermon and lecture manuscripts, not relying on a bare outline, a few key words, or one's native skill of extemporaneous speaking. A full manuscript will assist the teacher's pre-class studying, reflecting, and planning. It will also serve to keep the teacher on-track at the pulpit in the sanctuary, or at the lectern in the classroom. Too much freedom leaves one "prone to wander, Lord, I feel it."[16] Without a manuscript, the teacher is more likely to be more influenced by the moment than by the subject matter, or to be too off-the-cuff, flippant, superficial, and disordered.

Afterward, the manuscript serves as a written record, and is one more brick in the building of one's library of learning and teaching. Almost weekly, a student asks me for a copy of my sermon or lecture. She wants to read what she has heard, or he would like to send a copy to a family member or friend. I quickly attach my manuscript file to an email, or send the link to the online account where my audio recordings are stored and are accessible. This is possible only because I have prepared full manuscripts and taped my presentations.

Finally, while I never preach the same sermon or give the same lecture twice, I do return again and again to the same areas where I have preached and taught many times before. I always pull out my old sermon and lecture files for the information and insights I cultivated years before. Why lose all this good material? Then, along with new, fresh material, I craft a new teaching sermon or lecture. I am always trying to say new and different things, along with the same

16. This is a line from the hymn "Come, Thou Fount of Every Blessing." See footnote #8 on page 175.

things in new and better ways. Lectures, as well as sermons, should be progressively richer and deeper, as they come out of a theological life that is continually growing richer and deeper.

Teaching Curriculum

"What will I teach? Where do I start?" These are the first questions of a minister who begins a teaching ministry. He or she is asking for guidance, and is probably hoping to find a pre-packaged study course with a set curriculum, a couple of videos, and a few easy-to-follow instructions—everything the aspiring teacher needs, complete in a single book or box.

Such packages are widely available. I strongly urge you to stay away from them. All of them. First, the theological faith-tradition does not lend itself to being neatly packaged. Its heights, depths, breadths, and lengths cannot be boxed-in.

Second, a significant part of teaching is going through the rigors of one's own study and research, and then wrestling with how best to present what one has learned. No one can or should do this for you.

Third, you do not want the material that someone else has prepared. Rarely is it of high quality or solid content. It is usually unworthy of any attention from thoughtful Christians.

Fourth, most of these programs have been prepared, processed, and packaged for the purpose of being sold on the popular religious market. They are not designed for ordered teaching and learning, or serious theological education, despite claims their sellers may make.

Fifth, do not rely on any program of study that is not your own. While they may be helpful aids, they will make you dependent. You will not be required to make curricular decisions, create lessons, or prepare lectures. It has all been done for you. By not doing your own work, you will never develop fully as a teacher. Name one professor who uses a ready-made kit out of a box.

Whatever the latest-greatest craze may be, or whatever is stirring up congregations and getting Christians excited at the time (and something always is) run from it. Do not pass out copies of the best-selling book that everybody's talking about, and ask your teaching-learning community to read and discuss it. Do not move randomly from one book to another, or one video series to another, or one hot topic to another. This is not serious theological education.

The minister will be tempted to adopt the model of a specialized curriculum that she experienced at the clergy seminary or divinity school. It is the only model of theological education she knows. Teacher and students proceed through a core set of introductory courses in each of the main areas or disciplines: Old Testament, New Testament, systematic theology, church history, ethics, and practical ministry. After these basic courses have been completed, the group then moves to elective courses in these areas, supplemented by "special studies," workshops, and training seminars.

I have already discussed the weaknesses and problems of this approach. The major one is that both teacher and students end up with only a lot of disconnected fragments of information. They come to know a little about a lot of things—which is more than they knew before—but they do not know how to put it all together, fill in the gaps, and see what it all means.

It is like someone handing them one piece of a jigsaw puzzle, and then another, followed by another, and so on. They eventually have a lot of pieces, but not nearly enough to discern the big picture that reveals reality, and shows how these pieces connect and are given their truth and meaning. In others words, raw knowledge may increase, but it is not full knowledge, or advanced knowledge. Understanding lags behind. And wisdom, that is necessary for the embodiment of faith in human existence, remains elusive.

This is why I do not recommend that the teaching-learning community simply undertake a study of "systematic theology," or an orderly, rational, coherent account of the major doctrines of the Christian faith. I am not saying that such a study should never be attempted. In fact, I believe the study of Christian doctrines is essential, and should be included in a broader curriculum. However, despite its systematic structure and approach, this type of study cannot overcome the shortcomings of piecemeal knowledge.

My best recommendation is that the teacher create and develop his or her own curriculum for use in the local seminary. I know this is a large project and a scary prospect, especially in the beginning. You may feel as though you are being asked to perform on a trapeze without a net (and possibly without a trapeze).

However, the resource of the entire historical-biblical-theological faith-tradition is available to you. You have all you will ever need. Your only questions are where to enter, how to take hold, what to deal with first, and how to proceed. The problem is you have too many options, rather than too few, or none.

I propose that you start with a broad, general, overarching view of faith-existence and its theological tradition. Begin with the whole. Give the students a picture of "the lay of the land." Then move to the individual parts, constantly referring them back to the whole, and also relating each part with other parts. Make connections. Show implications. Whatever the immediate focus may be, the angle of vision and point of orientation are always the whole.

Theology sets the course of the educational process. The lay seminary follows this path, tracking along the lines of theology's own basic hermeneutical framework. This leads to an ordered way of learning and living. And this way of life originates in and comes from the order of the theological faith-tradition itself.

Again, using the metaphor of a jigsaw puzzle, do not think of education this way: (1) thousands of pieces are in a box on the table; (2) one-by-one, the teacher takes out a piece for the class to examine and discuss; (3) this piece is laid on the table, outside the box, as the start of a process and a construction project; (4) a second piece is taken out of the box, examined and discussed, and laid on the table next to the first piece; because they don't fit, they are left there separately, until more pieces are added, that may fit; (5) more and more individual pieces are taken out of the box, examined and discussed, and added to the growing collection of pieces; (6) the aim is to get enough of the pieces out on the table, in some form of basic assembly, that will eventually yield some faint idea of what everybody has been searching for and working toward this entire time.

Theological education is all too often approached and conducted this way, as though we are putting together a puzzle, piece-by-piece, until the whole is constructed, and what it is begins to show up. "Let's start with a little New Testament, followed by a little systematic theology, and then a little church history. Oh, we haven't had any Old Testament yet. How about ethics? Anyone interested in ethics?" This is not the best way to study, learn, teach, and embody the Christian theological faith-tradition.

Instead, I propose that students be ushered to the table and introduced to faith-existence and its tradition as a whole. Show it to them first in its largest frame, as it has been assembled by the long line of saints, from the apostles, church fathers and mothers, monks, priests, preachers, philosophers, and theologians. Let your students see what they will be dealing with, and what it looks like.

Then move on to point out individual pieces, or sections of pieces. Explain why they are there, how they connect to and contribute to the whole and also to other pieces, and what they mean. Continually move the students back and forth between the whole and its composite pieces.

So, what is the whole? Where do we begin? In the next chapter, I offer a guide for students. Use it for your teaching, as well as for your own learning. Begin with the broadest overview: (1) this is Christian faith-existence. This is what it means to be a Christian, and to live in this world Christianly; (2) this is the theological tradition that has emerged from faith and for faith; this is what it means to live in this world theologically. Then continue to study this faith and its theology by examining and expositing it more closely, more specifically, and more deeply, always holding it all together and translating it into embodied life, both communally and individually.

Teach out of what you have learned and are learning. Pick up your students, and bring them along the same path you are going. Continue to study ahead of them, preparing the next leg of the journey.

Prepare your own teaching materials out of the same material you are studying. Develop your own teaching style by actually teaching. You know your students. You also know your particular teaching-learning environment, its mood, pace, etc. Only you can determine what to present, along with when and how. But the theological faith-tradition is all there before you.

Remember: theological education for laypersons is so rare that a curriculum for a lay seminary does not exist. Therefore, you will have to construct it. Be creative. This is a major part of your responsibility.

Go and make disciples, teaching them. Not only your feet, but also your entire self, will be beautiful.

7
Learning

The persons whom Jesus called out of the crowd were summoned to be disciples, or students. After his death and resurrection, Jesus authorized them to go and make disciples, or students, by teaching them.[1] The church that resulted was a teaching-learning community. It continued to be Jesus' school.

Today, Christian congregations are no longer schools. They are not places where the theological tradition formed around Jesus is taught. No one would think of going there for theological education. Pastors are not teachers, and members are not students. Most would be offended if a teacher showed up, bringing theology home, expecting them to study and learn it. Their houses are not houses of learning. The Christian life is about many things, but the life of knowing, understanding, stewarding, and embodying the theological mysteries is not one of them.

By reading this book, you have become aware—probably for the first time—of the non-theological state of your own congregation and of your close circle of Christian family members and friends. No one you know and love is a student.

Equally disturbing is the fact that you are not a student. You know and understand a little, but not much more than you did when you were a child or young teen in the church's kindergarten, i.e., Sunday School. Not only are you today still at an immature, irresponsible level when it comes to your own faith-tradition, but also what you believe may be little more than "false theological simulacra." Some of

1. Matthew 28:18–20.

this is not your fault. You have never been taught. I blame denominations and congregations for closing the teaching office.

However, you are not completely off the hook. You bear some responsibility for your own failure. You have done nothing to inquire about your own theological tradition, much less become personally involved in reading, studying, thinking about, talking about, and embodying the wisdom of the Christian theological life. You are doing nothing now to change that. You are on a non-learning path that you have chosen and set in place, and that you will be on for the rest of your life, unless you change your course.

Hopefully, somewhere along the way of reading this book, you have become not only aware of this disastrous state, but even more so, convicted about it. You now have enough sense of calling, along with enough conviction, guilt, and shame, to be driven to go and see for yourself what this theological life is all about. It has your name written all over it—like the call of Moses, Samuel, Isaiah, and each of Jesus' original twelve students.

Yet, now you are in an awkward spot. In order to seek and find the teaching, learning, and living of the theological life, you can no longer look to your own congregation, or to your close circle of Christian family members and friends, as you always have. You certainly cannot depend upon them for your theological education, since they are neither theologically-educated nor theologically-educating. You must look elsewhere. And in this sense, you must "leave" them and "go to seminary."

Fortunately, your leaving will probably not involve an actual departure. Where would you go? The possibility of finding another congregation locally that is a lay seminary, or that takes theological education seriously as one of its major ministries, is extremely low. You might as well stay put.

Still, you will have to depart from the status quo of Christianity as you have known it your entire life. You will have to come out of the non-theological crowd. You will have to separate yourself from the norm, and become "abnormal." You will have to stop trusting your congregation to provide you the knowledge and understanding you need. You will have to take another path in order to follow Jesus as a learner.

Of course, you may be among those who must leave and relocate. Your Christian environment may have become anti-educational, anti-intellectual, and anti-theological. Its worship, fellowship, and service are not conducive to thoughtful, articulate faith. Preachers, teachers, and/or members in your congregation are pushing a hardline left or right position—doctrinally, politically, socially, and morally. It is not an environment that is conducive to learning.

Or, the people around you may be emotionally or spiritually toxic, embroiled in personality-driven drama and power conflicts. You will have to move your membership in order to be in a congregation that—while it may not be overtly supportive of theology and theological education—is at least not opposed and obstructive. Every Christian learner both needs and deserves a religious-cultural community that is, for the most part, safe and sane, healthy and holy.

Currently, you may not be active in any congregation. I encourage you to find a small community where you can fulfill your calling to be taught and to learn. The primary criterion is the quality of this community's theological education. Do not take the pastor's word for it. His or her job is to sell the program and gain members.

Also, another person's idea of theological education may have little to do with either theology or education. Given that you will be investing your valuable attention, energy, time, and money, I advise you to take your time in researching prospective congregations, testing them, and discerning the place most likely to provide sound theological education. Do not settle for anything less than a group of persons who are as serious (if not more serious) about studying and learning the theological faith-tradition as you are. If none is found, you may join a congregation merely for its religious, spiritual, moral, and social formation. But you will have to continue looking for your theological formation elsewhere.

My experience is on the extreme end of leaving. After being a member and minister of five congregations, I left what "the church" had become, and I had experienced. Sadly, the chasm between what the church is denominationally and congregationally, on the one hand, and what the church is theologically, on the other, had became too great. I could no longer hold the two together. Therefore, I went with the latter, which meant walking away from the former. I will never go back. I will not return to a usual or typical congregation, even if it is "traditional" (definitely not "contemporary")—unless it is a teaching-learning community, or seminary-congregation.

The Courage to Learn

It seems strange to me that pursuing a theological education has to be such a radical act of departure for the individual. Yet, this is our situation today. Differentiating oneself from the non-theological crowd is not for the faint-hearted. Taking up the theological life is unheard of, and now is a daring feat. It requires courage. Believing that a layperson is called to be a minister, a seminarian, a theologian, a teacher, and a responsible steward of the mysteries of God in Christ is audaciously bold. Who does this?

Such a life is solitary. No one else you know will be going with you to live it. Although they may wish you well, none will understand why you are going. You will be unable to answer their questions (or perhaps even your own). You don't know where you are going, how you will get there, what will be involved, what will be required, or how you will know when you arrive (if you ever do). All you know is you won't find out unless you go. And you certainly cannot stay where you have been.

But, where do you start? What do you do first? Against all odds, all unknowing, and all inertia, somehow you just start. Only the truly brave attempt something like this.

Why you? Who are you to think that you are being called? That you are destined to be a seminarian, much less a theologian? That the mysteries of God would be entrusted to you? And that you can be trusted with them?

How long has it been since you were in school? Much too long to remember, right? You haven't read a "real book" in years. Your mind is old. The mental cogs are rusted in place. You won't be able to comprehend what a learned teacher is saying. You won't be able to keep up. It will be too hard for you. You will fail.

Much of the courage we need is not for facing theology itself, but for struggling with our own internal doubts and fears. I will not try to talk you out of them, for I believe such hesitations and reservations are realistic. These are a true gauge of where you are and what you are about to do. This is a major undertaking. Who among us is fit for it, or adequately prepared for it? No one. No one has what it takes. Therefore, you find yourself in a situation where calling exceeds capability, and mission slams up against mortality. But the truly faithful end up on the side of doing it anyway, against all good reasons not to. The intimidation is great, but the inspiration is far greater.

You must keep reminding yourself that you are called out of the crowd to be a learner. By this call, you *are* a learner. You do not have to read a certain number of textbooks, attend a year's worth of classes, or pass an exam in order to qualify. You are already a learner. This is your vocation in Christ. You are ready to be taught.

However, this does not mean that you are yet teachable and capable of learning. You are not. But, by being placed in the role of Jesus' disciple, having the identity, purpose, and responsibility of a disciple, you are now in position to be made a disciple. You will be made teachable and capable of learning. In other words, the process of theological education itself will make you who you are, but have never been. Without it, you will never become who you called to be.

It will take great courage for you to allow yourself to be taught, when you show no signs of being ready or qualified, other than a sense of calling and a response of interest. Also, most of us do not want to submit ourselves to being taught. We do not like being submissive to others, or under the authority of tradition. Our natural inclination is avoid learning at all costs, as long as we can.

I have stood before laypersons for years, looking them in the eye, and observing their behavior, as I preached and lectured. The blank stare, with glazed-over eyes, is their best defense. Some have escaped into sleep—like Jesus' disciples in the garden on the Mount of Olives.[2] Still others have refused to look at me, lest they start paying attention and listening. They worked hard *not* to respond, *not* to hear, and *not* to have to think about anything—like Sergeant Shultz in the TV comedy sitcom Hogan's Heroes, who insisted, "I know nothing! I know nothing!"

In this same crowd, however, someone stirs and shows a sign of life. Another person begins to wake up and tune in. Still another is

2. Read Mark 14:32–42.

captured by a word, and starts thinking, wondering about a new concept, or mulling over a key doctrine or insight. I see in their atypical responsiveness the smallest beginnings of the theological life. Education is getting underway with them and for them. The play has started. And it is happening to them, even before they are aware of it.

A few come back the next Sunday, and then the next, responding with the same openness, interest, and engagement. It takes great courage for them to allow this movement to continue, resisting the heavy undertow of non-responsiveness that is always there. They are bold enough—or just plain stubborn and hard-headed enough—to keep listening, hearing, seeing, thinking, and gaining understanding, and coming back for more.

If you desire to be a learner in a non-learning congregation, you will have to be a self-starter, a self-motivator, and a self-learner. The chances of someone else starting with you are slim. Also, no one believes it is his or her responsibility to start you and keep you going. You will have to do it yourself.

Even if you are fortunate enough to have a teacher, he or she will not learn for you. If there is no teacher, you really are on your own. You will have to go the extra mile, and constantly encourage (i.e., put courage in) yourself. Theology is now your life and ministry. No matter what, you must do everything in your power to be its good student and steward.

The Life of Disciplined Learning

Disciples are those who come under discipline. Discipline is the behavior prescribed for those who are disciples. "Undisciplined disciple" is an oxymoron. Moreover, an undisciplined Christian is not a disciple. Most Christians are not disciples, since they have never been disciplined, and resist being disciplined by theology and its education.

Discipline is submission to an order of thinking, believing, talking, relating, and acting. It is accepting that order as authoritative and binding. It is giving oneself to it, coming under its demand and force, and allowing it to order one's entire self and life.

Order is imposed on the individual. This is the discipline. The order disciplines the person in order to train the person in its ways. There are set rules, prescribed tasks and methods, habits of belief and practice, moral dispositions, and codes of conduct. This order takes the lead, directing, correcting, and molding.

The disciple, we might say, is under orders. She obeys and follows. She allows this order to exert its influence, do its work on her, and have its way with her. She suppresses her own desires, what comes naturally to her, and what she would normally do or not do. She is quite restrained and controlled, so much so that she continues this discipline even when she is unmotivated, doesn't feel like it, other tasks demand her time and energy, and everyone around her seems perfectly happy and carefree as Christians without any of these rigors.

This is because her calling and ambition are not theirs. She strives to be made capable and equipped, not merely as a religious person, spiritual person, or good person, but more so as a student, minister, steward, and theologian of the Christian gospel, rightly interpreting and embodying the theological faith-tradition, being faithful and responsible, and thus having no reason to be ashamed. This takes discipline, as well as courage. Such a life, or mode of belief, virtue, and practice, cannot be produced without it.

Theology, then, is the discipline of Christian existence. It is the order that orders the thought and practice of Christian persons, individually and corporately. Coming under this order and learning it is theological education. By teaching and learning, the Christian community and its members become disciples. They are disciplined by the discipline that is theology, so that they will become students, theologians, ministers, and stewards of the mysteries of God, and in particular, the gospel of Christ that is contained in and conveyed by theology.

Of course, we speak of the disciplines of worship, prayer, Bible reading, giving, and serving. These are all theological acts, which are integral to the larger discipline of theology and its mode of faith-existence. Think of them as sub-disciplines. Our intent, then, is not simply to follow the order of a worship service, or to read the Bible in an orderly fashion, or say our prayers daily, simply going through the exercises. Rather, we engage in these practices in order that our selves and our entire existence will be ordered theologically. Theology does its ordering work through worship, prayer, Bible reading, giving, and serving, all of which are part of a greater discipline of theological education.

Finally, by submitting to theology as authoritative, and coming under its ordering as its disciple, the Christian person or Christian community of persons effectively gives theology control over human thought and practice. Theology orders, or commands, a particular knowledge, rather than some other. This knowledge begins to take over, and becomes what the community or the individual knows. Theology's understandings, insights, convictions, and acts become the understandings, insights, convictions, and acts of those who have come under theology's authority and ordering influence. In this way, these persons begin to be controlled by theology, in that they are swayed, directed, and formed by it, and even begin to be responsible for it. Moreover, they begin to control themselves, or discipline themselves, including their time, attention, involvements, and behaviors, according to the control that theology has over them.

In other words, a major part of Christian learning is learning and exercising self-control for the sake of theology. It is largely up to each individual. Anyone who fails to control her time and energies in order to study and learn the Christian theological faith-tradition cannot be theologically educated, and thus cannot exist theologically.

The Making of a Theologian

The aim of theological education is not simply to learn theology, but, more so, to learn theological existence. The discipline of discipleship is for the purpose of learning to exist theologically, and, therefore, is necessary for being a theological person. An individual is made a disciple in order to be made a theologian.

What is a theologian? And, who is a theologian? Most people will probably give the same answer to both questions: "The scholar." The individual who works with the church's doctrines, who researches and teaches in the academic setting of a university or seminary, and who publishes journal articles and books for others in the same field is a theologian. The theologian is a professional, and usually a college or seminary professor.

Granted, this is a simplistic, narrow, exclusive definition. Many church leaders attempt a correction by broadening the term until it includes everyone. Ironically, more often than not, these inclusivists are professional theologians. They are quick to declare, "Everyone is a theologian." Never mind that in their world no one is a theologian who has not earned advanced degrees, published for the academy, and specialized in one of the finer regions of this field of study.

Apparently, though, any person who knows about God, who has had a thought about God, or has spoken about God is a theologian. Believers are included; but so are unbelievers. Everyone! There is no one who is *not* a theologian. Some persons are "anonymous theologians," in that no one knows (they don't even know) that they are theological people, and actually real theologians.[3]

Both definitions, I believe, are distorted and misleading. On the one hand, theology belongs to the whole community of Christ, and not solely to the academic arm of this community. While professional theologians have an important and necessary role to play in studying, interpreting, developing, teaching, preserving, and transmitting the church's theological faith-tradition, it is disastrous for both the church and the church's tradition when theology is left up to the "experts." Not only is this tradition reduced down to an academic science, driven by the questions and concerns of modern-postmodern education, and subject to all the limits and measures of secular scholarship, but it is also cut off from the everyday life and ministry of the rest of the church in the world. Consequently, local congregations and ordinary Christians suffer for lack of theology. At the same time, theology suffers for lack of the whole church. Both languish from amnesia (loss of memory) and anemia (loss of life-blood.)

On the other hand, theology belongs to the whole church, or community of believers, and not to the whole world ("everyone"). Unbelievers have no responsibility for Christian theology. Neither do they automatically become theological, if they happen to say the word "God," entertain a thought about Christ or heaven, or read a verse from the Bible—any more than you and I become athletes when we

---

3. Roger E. Olson, "Everyone Is a Theologian," in Stanley J. Grenz and Roger E. Olson, *Who Needs Theology? An Invitation to the Study of God* (Downers Grove, Illinois: InterVarsity Press, 1996), 12–21.

see someone jogging, run after our kid in the backyard, or sport a pair of Nikes.

Neither is a believer a theologian simply by believing. There is a difference. A theologian is a believer who has "gone the extra mile" (actually, a lot of miles) to take up the Christian mode of existence, while intentionally trying to learn and embody the doctrines, beliefs, virtues, values, and practices of this total way of life. She does this by becoming aware of and paying attention to God, and to everything else as it is defined and determined in relation to God, within the framework of the supreme redemptive-revelation of God in Jesus Christ. She draws on the classical Christian theological faith-tradition for her thoughts and words, practices and actions. She does some hard studying and some hard thinking. She attempts to state as clearly, accurately, and coherently as possible what this faith-existence is, and thus to become capable of existing faithfully, by existing theologically. She is ready to enter into discussion about this faith and its tradition with others. She is a theologian.

Most believers, by this proper definition, are not theologians. Beyond a few residual Christian religious beliefs and practices, they are doing little to nothing to learn, know, understand, embody, think about, or talk about the historical-biblical-theological faith-tradition. They have not taken up the theological life. They are not existing theologically. They have not gone the extra miles.

Yet, all who are in Christ are called to be theologians. Christian faith and the Christian life are by nature theological. There is no way around it, or out of it. Every intelligent believer, then, has an obligation to be theologically transformed, informed, and formed. No one is let off the hook when it comes to knowing and understanding as clearly, coherently, broadly, and deeply as possible the beliefs to which his faith has committed him. Simply because most Christians are neglecting this responsibility does not mean that they do not have to be theologians, and can safely leave all that matters to the specialists, who are the experts. Nor does it mean that we can put a fake badge of "Theologian" on their chests, as though—like children—they are being deputized as "Junior Park Rangers" or "Honorary Firefighters."

An interesting question is, "When does a believer cross the line of merely being a believer, to being a theologian?" Is it as soon as she starts studying the Christian theological faith-tradition as a student? Or, is it later, once she has reached a certain level of knowledge and understanding?

I do not profess to have an exact answer. But I do not believe that education alone, while it is essential, does or can make a student a theologian. Hypothetically, a person could study theology for years, and never become a theologian. Frankly, I suspect some professional theologians have never become theologians. Despite achieving a high level of knowledge and understanding, they have never entered the mode of existence, or way of life, prescribed by this knowledge and understanding. While many ordinary Christians are attempting to live the life without knowledge and understanding, some scholars are attempting to know and understand the life without living it. A theologian is someone who does both, or does one in order to do the other. Theologians are persons who "be" one (a Christian or a theologian) in order to "be" the other (a theologian or a Christian).

Of course, as a beginning learner, you have probably never thought of yourself as a theologian, and would not call yourself a theologian. That would be presumptive on your part. Who are you—the novice that you are—to bear the weighty mantle of "theologian"?

Despite your humility, keep in mind that at the same time you are being made a disciple and being made a minister of the gospel, you are also being made a theologian. This is a three-for-one educational process. You cannot become one without becoming the other two. Theology will teach you and make you what you otherwise would not be—if you are teachable, and if you allow yourself to be made.

Theology builds its own house, and brings people like you into it to make them the students and stewards it needs them to be. It is by entering and taking up permanent residence in this house, doing the work of this house, being a good and faithful servant of theology, its existence, tradition, and education, that you become a theologian. Only theology, requiring your serious submission and participation, can pull off this theologian-making feat.

My suggestion is that you not wait too long before fully accepting the title of "theologian." You will become a theologian before you know you are, or think you are. Therefore, err on the side of being a bit more presumptive than you normally are, or feel comfortable being. The title itself is part of your development. Also, you will need it to keep you faithful to your calling and engaged in your studies. You are a theologian. You are doing what theologians do.

Independent Study

Ideally, every city, town, and rural community would have at least one lay seminary, or local teaching-learning community of faith. Ideally, every Christian would have access to a theological group where he or she can be with other students. A qualified, capable pastor-teacher-theologian would be present to teach this group. And together they would be actively learning and living the Christian theological life.

Unfortunately, the reality is that the individual who is called to be a disciple—in the making as a theologian—will likely not have this opportunity. It does not exist where he lives.

Therefore, he will have to start and proceed on his own as an "autodidact," or a person who teaches himself, and thus is said to be "self-educated." This does not mean that his task is to discover "what he believes" or "why he believes." Theological self-education is not an education in one's self, but rather in theology (which, of course, will shed much light on one's self in relation to God). It simply means that he studies and learns theology without the resources of a school, the instruction of a teacher, or the support of fellow students.

Does the student realize how hard this self-education actually is? How unusual it is for any ordinary Christian to attempt such a work on his own? Or, if he does, how unlikely it is that he will get very far, without a school, without a teacher, and without other students?

But, let's say that you, the reader, are seriously interested in theological education. You know it will have to be independent study. You are determined to take it on. You are aware how hard it will be. And yet, you are willing to do what is required to be a disciple and learn what it means to be a theologian.

Before starting, I encourage you to ask around in your congregation and among your Christian family members and friends. Perhaps one, two, or three others might be interested. You have never heard them say anything about it. To be fair, they haven't heard you say anything, either.

Do you know a pastor who is more studious and thoughtful than most? Would she be interested in joining you, either in a small group or one-on-one? Either as your instructor or as your tutor?

Go fishing. This is how Jesus did it, and how disciples have been made for centuries. Ask around. Bring up the subject. Talk about it. Ask leading questions. Open up the possibility. Invite.

If someone else comes out of the Christian crowd to join you, then you have the makings of a small lay seminary. Where two or three are gathered in the name of Jesus, for the sake of learning and living his way of life, he is there with them.[4]

If no one budges and joins you, then you must go alone. Perhaps another person or two will catch-up later. But you must accept that this is now something you have to do, regardless of whether you do it in partnership or solo.

Take a deep breath of resolve, and start. Resist the thought that you do not know what you are doing. Of course you don't. How could you? But don't let that stop you. Take the initiative. Take the first step. Begin your own theological education. And with that, the making of another Christian seminarian, minister, steward, and theologian begins.

Like most things, self-education is easier said than done. However, I assure you that it can be done, and it will not be as hard as you fear. You have a lot going for you. You can read. You can think. You probably have some elementary knowledge of Christian theology from your upbringing in a congregation and/or a Christian home. Whatever you may lack, you more than make up for it with your sense of calling and your interest, determination, and courage. You can be assured that you will fill in the gaps, broaden your knowledge, and deepen your understanding as you go along.

I have been around persons just like you my entire life. I have heard their insecurities, anxieties, and inadequacies in the face of theology. Everyone thinks he or she is the only one who is having these feelings, without being aware that everyone else does, too. Whatever the activity may be—whether it is kickball on the school playground, philosophy in the college classroom, bringing a new baby home, or walking into a new job—we all hesitate and feel our

---

4. See Matthew 18:20.

inferiority when meeting a task for the first time. It's human nature. And all of us are human. Why would we expect a different set of emotions and experiences in the context of theological education?

Yet, I have also observed these insecure, anxious, inadequate, inferior individuals become comfortable, at ease, and confident around theology. They soon discover that their fears have been exaggerated. Theology is not nearly as daunting as they had thought. Equally shocking, they are not nearly as dumb as they had thought they were!

In fact, most students actually like theology; and some fall in love with it. They all venture into realms in their own Christian faith-tradition that they never knew existed, and most are greatly enriched and matured by this experience.

Like them, you can do this. But you must act out of your positive calling and real need rather than out of your own negative feelings and the lack of support around you. Take the bold initiative to move beyond good intentions, and begin your own theological education.

But where do you begin? What do you do first? Whatever you do, do not conduct a Google search, or consult amazon.com for the "best Christian theology books." Do not browse the religion section at your local Barnes & Nobles store, or the public library, looking for something interesting, and thinking you will know it when you see it. Why are you shooting in the dark for something as important as the starting-point of your own theological education and theological life?

Do not ask your denominational consultants what they have that might help you. Do not listen to a co-worker who tells you that her congregation is sponsoring a study that everyone is raving about. Do not email your daughter's university or seminary professor for his or her suggestions. Do not waste your time asking your pastor, unless you know that your pastor may actually know something about studying and learning theology. Even then, take his or her recommendation with a grain of slightly salty skepticism.

Finally, nobody really knows how laypersons might undertake education for the theological life. How could we? This kind of education has rarely, if ever, been attempted. Yet, this has never stopped anyone from throwing out a random recommendation of a book, article, website, or program in a box. No one honestly admits, "I don't know," or "I'm not sure; but let's work on it together."

Later in this chapter, I will tell you what I have learned from teaching laypersons for over forty-five years. I will give you my best and wisest guidance as to where and how to begin. I will offer a road map that hopefully will be a good guide for you. But first, I want to discuss three major requirements of your theological self-education.

Required Thinking

You will have to think. If you haven't had a real thought in years, or do not like to think, then you do not need to give theological education another thought. What do you think theology and theological education are, if not intellectual thought?

Simply put, theology is thinking about God and about all things in relation to God. Education is learning what to think and how to think. As a student, you will be introduced to thoughts you have never thought. You will be given new ideas, concepts, insights, interpretations, and understandings. Your "old" ideas, concepts, insights, interpretations, and understandings will be exposed and put to the test. Chances are good that many of them will be changed.

The individual who does not want to consider beliefs she has never considered before, who does not want to ponder anything that might cause her any confusion or amazement, and does not want to have any of her presuppositions tampered with and possibly changed, should not be under any delusion that she is interested in or ready for the study of theology.

Theology *is* thinking. It is the church thinking about its own faith, and about all things in the light of this faith. It is the individual or the congregation thinking with the church, as the church. Clearly, then, the person who does not value thinking, refusing to study and learn the church's thinking, while resisting all theological pressure to transform and conform her own thinking, does not care to be part of the church when the church is engaging in mental exercise.

I speak this way—harshly and sarcastically—for I consider non-thinking to be an ugly, despicable trait for any person, and especially for those who call themselves Christians. Thinking is a natural ability and act of every human being. It is a good gift from our Creator. After birth, each of us begins to learn how to think and what to think in order to live in this world. Our thinking develops and matures through the years, as we re-think our thinking, gain new thoughts, deepen or discard old ones, make meaningful connections between them, and live by them. Consciousness, imagination, memory, reason, and discernment are some of the many forms of thinking by which we exist. We humans even have the amazing ability to "think about our thinking," and in this way, to transcend ourselves and be both self-conscious and other-conscious.

Sadly and shamefully, too many believers have somewhere along the way stopped the practice of conscious, active thinking. They now fail to use their minds. They may no longer know how to use their minds, and even stubbornly refuse to do so, not only in their religion but also in all other aspects of their lives. They are mindless. They may even believe their religion or spirituality is antithetical to mindfulness; and this gives them permission, or may even require them, not to think.

Christian preachers and teachers often claim that they are aiming for human hearts or souls, not human heads, when the truth is they are often aiming only for self-expression, or for good impressions and emotional reactions on the part of their hearers. Their communication has little to do with the heart, soul, or head of psychosomatically whole persons. Assuming this to be obedience, these Christians are disobeying the commandment of Jesus: "You shall love the Lord your God with all your heart, and with all your soul, and with all your strength, and *with all your mind* [italics mine]; and your neighbor as yourself." (Luke 10:27)

Without thinking, the individual is vulnerable to taking on the mind of the popular culture, a political ideology, or a false gospel. He does not know that he does not have the mind of Christ. And it is likely that he never will know this, since he never uses his mind, while boasting of it. Theological education is the slow transformation of the human mind, making it less and less conformed to this world, and more and more re-created and made capable of discerning what is true, good, acceptable, and perfect concerning the will of God.[5]

As a student of theology, you will be required to think. You will do a lot of thinking. You will be taught to think. On the one hand, you

5. Read Romans 12:2.

will develop the skill of "critical thinking," or objective, rational analysis and evaluation. You will learn to listen to the thoughts of others; examine them; find their strengths and weaknesses; discern the truth (untruth) and meaning (meaninglessness or nonsense) in them; uncover and assess their information, main concepts, inferences, constructs, insights, assumptions, hidden presuppositions, perspectives, and implications; raise pertinent questions; compare thoughts with other thoughts; and use these for speaking to complex issues and solving major problems. Your own thoughts will mature. Your thinking will sharpen and become clearer, more precise, disciplined, and accurate. You will learn to think, and to think well.

On the other hand, you will also learn what I call "confessional thinking," or thinking about what the church has thought about and confessed for centuries. This is the "the power to comprehend with all the saints what is the breadth and length and height and depth." (Ephesians 3:18) Confessional thinking is the ability to listen to the theological saints, to follow their reasoning and believing, and then to reason and believe "after them," in the sense of affirming and accepting as one's own what they thought in the way they thought it.

Whereas critical thinking relies on distrust and incredulity, confessional thinking relies on trust and credulity. Faith requires both. And, as a student of theology, you will become skilled in both. In other words, you will learn to do something that you currently do not do and do not know how to do: think critically and confessionally in a theological way. You will begin to think like a Christian.[6]

One of the tragedies of intellectual failure is that the person misses out on the joy of thinking. She never has an "Aha!" or "Eureka!" moment. She cannot know what it feels like when disordered fragments of knowledge suddenly come together with such truth and meaning that understanding, insight, or even wisdom results. She

---

6. John R. W. Stott, *Your Mind Matters: The Place of the Mind in the Christian Life* (Downers Grove, Illinois: InterVarsity Press, 1972); John Piper, *Think: The Life of the Mind and the Love of God* (Wheaton, Illinois: Crossway, 2010); Gene Edward Veith, Jr., *Loving God With All Your Mind: Thinking as a Christian in the Postmodern World*, rev. ed. (Wheaton, Illinois: Crossway Books, 2003); Alister McGrath, *The Passionate Intellect: Christian Faith and the Discipleship of the Mind* (Downers Grove, Illinois: InterVarsity, 2010); and John B. Cobb, Jr., *Becoming a Thinking Christian* (Nashville: Abingdon Press, 1993).

never experiences the thrill of stumbling across an unknown idea for the first time. She cannot imagine the pleasure that comes from lying in bed at night, or sitting outside on the patio, pondering the mysteries of our universe, physical and metaphysical, in the light of the redemptive revelation made known in and through Jesus Christ. The God of peace is with those who think about the things that are true, honorable, just, pure, pleasing, commendable, excellent, and worthy of praise.[7]

Thinking is required, but it is one of those requirements that the theological student gladly fulfills. While many are afraid of the dense thicket, preferring to stay on the safe, shallow ground of their childhood religion, a few are much more brave and adventuresome. Like the helpless, but cunning Br'er Rabbit (Brother Rabbit), they plead, "But please don't fling me in de briers!"—prompting the Fox to do exactly that.[8]

Required Talking

I hope you don't mind human talk, and aren't offended by it. As a student of theology, you will be around a lot of it. Theology is nothing but human talk. It is talking about God, or "God-talk." Even thinking about God is talking about God, since such human thought occurs with words.

I hope you are not one of those people who dislike and distrust words. They go around mindlessly saying, "One picture is worth a thousand words," "Talk is cheap," and "Actions, not words, define a person."

What do these people have against words? Why are they devaluing language and the gift of human speech? Don't they know they are using words when they are disparaging words? Don't they realize that God has made them to be linguistic beings?

I once read (yes, words) that the God of the Israelites was the only ancient deity who spoke and thus communicated. All other gods were

7. See Philippians 4:8–9.

8. Joel Chandler Harris, *The Tar-Baby and Other Rhymes of Uncle Remus* (Bedford, Massachusetts: Applewood Books, 1904), 14-15.

silent. Dumb. They did not speak, since they did not exist. Existence exposes and expresses itself by speaking.

Likewise, human beings, made in the image of God, do not fully exist until or unless they speak. God has given us the God-like gift of speech. We are thereby enabled to communicate with and relate to the God who speaks. We are also capable of communicating with and relating to one another. Talking, then, is what it means to be human and to be alive.

Theology is living human talk about God and about all things in relation to God. We talk about nature, society, our bodies, power, money, food, and everything else by using God-words, or words that derive their truth and meaning from the truth and meaning of God revealed in human history, supremely in Jesus Christ.

Theology is the conversation of the church throughout history. It is the articulation of faith. It is believers speaking to one another and to the world about the truth and meaning of God and of all things in relation to God.

The church is the community that talks this talk and talks this way. It speaks this language. This is its native language, or first language. As the body of Christ—a human body—the church thinks in and through words, as do all humans. It communicates in and through words. It lives, moves, and has its being by faith, in and through words. And these words that belong uniquely to faith are summarized in one word: "theology."

Theology, then, is both the church speaking and the church's speech codified, preserved, and transmitted. The Bible is theological speech. Christian creeds, confessions, hymns, prayers, and poems are theological speech. There is no way to get around or away from these words, if the individual or the congregation is Christian, as well as human. But then, why would anyone want to?

As a student, you will be running toward, jumping in, immersing yourself, and swimming in the church's long, deep, swirling ocean of theological speech. This is why I hope you like words, or soon will come to like them. This is all there is—nothing but words. What else could theology possibly be?

What else do we need as believers? When Jesus asked his students if they were offended by his difficult teaching, and if they, like the crowd, were planning to leave, Peter answered, "Lord, to whom can we go? You have the words of eternal life. We have come to believe and know that you are the Son of God." (John 6:60–69)

As a student, you will be directed to these words, and will discover that they are the words of eternal life, full and free, now and forever. This is your language as one who believes that Jesus is the Son of God. Taking part in theological education, you will be introduced to your own mother tongue. You do not know how to speak it, and perhaps can barely comprehend what another person who is speaking theologically is saying. You may know a few words that have been left after the demise and disappearance of this language, but these are disconnected from one another and even from their original framework of meaning. They now carry and convey many, very different meanings. What you have heard and spoken your entire life is, at best, "broken theology" (like broken English or Spanish).

This is because theology is no longer the language of common discourse in our communities of faith. You are not around people who know, understand, and speak it. Even worship services have been stripped of most of the church's traditional theological language, since "nobody understands it anymore anyway."

Therefore, if or when you do hear it, you do not readily grasp it. It sounds strange and foreign to you, like language from another world. You pick up a simple theology book, but cannot make sense of it. While you are fluent in English, the language of spiritual secularism, and "religion-speak," you are not fluent in theology. You do not have a working theological vocabulary. You do not know how to put these words together in coherent sentences, and eventually into an actual conversation. You do not know how to talk theologically, because you do not know how to think theologically—and vice-versa. You cannot live and be alive by theological faith, for you lack the "words of eternal life."

Therefore, you must seek out and find people who do talk, think, and live this way, and hang around with them. They are the ones who are hanging around with the larger *communio sanctorum,* or communion of saints. This is the host of believers who have talked, thought, and lived theologically through the ages and across the nations. Only by being part of such a community, over a long period of time, can you possibly pick up and learn their manner of speaking. Just as you learned English by living in an English-speaking family and society, you will learn theology by living in a theology-speaking community of faith.

Listen to the members of this community as they communicate with one another about the things that matter most to them. Catch their accents and dialects. Borrow their words, idioms, and phrases. Make them your own. It's okay. We are all imitators and plagiarists. Besides, this is not restrictively their language. It is yours, as well.

Practice your new, budding language on anyone who will listen and hopefully converse with you. Attempt to articulate theological beliefs and teachings. Back up and try saying it again in a different way. Keep working on how to say it. Strive to talk like a theologian and sound like a Christian. Do it so persistently that it becomes common discourse as you study, worship, fellowship, and serve. Come to love these words. And in the process, come to love God, your neighbor, yourself, and all things in and through them.

Required Reading

Are you a reader? Are books lying on your nightstand, or beside your easy chair? Are you actively reading any of them? Is reading a daily or regular part of your life? When's the last time you read a serious book?

If you are not a reader, and are hoping to continue getting by with as little reading as possible, then I politely suggest that you are not yet a good candidate for theological education. This education is largely reading. The church's saints have left behind in writing their varied experiences and interpretations of God and of all things in relation to God. Their rich deposit of faith is available to us only in the literary form of commentaries, sermons, treatises, letters, and so on. Access to this tradition, then, is gained by reading. As a student, you will be required to do a lot of reading. Your entire education will take place primarily through reading.

I am not saying that you cannot begin unless you already are an active, strong reader, and have many years of experience with quality Christian literature. Most of my students are not, and do not, when they enter my classroom. Reading is an acquired skill. Reading theology is the specialized skill they are after. And the only way to acquire and develop it is by reading books of theology—reading, reading, and more reading. The theological life is a reading life.

Do not be like a few of my students who have thought they could participate in the classroom part, listening to my lectures and engaging in discussion with other students, without purchasing and reading at home any of the books I required or recommended. They cheated themselves out of a full theological education. Worse, they never joined the greater communion and its conversation. They remained spectators or tourists, and never became theologians.

This is not to imply that reading theology is easy. It is not. Very few Christians have ever read theology. The level and extent of their religious reading is the Sunday School quarterly, daily devotional guide, and popular Christian best-seller (and that may have been years ago). Therefore, when they pick up a good theology book and begin reading, they struggle and do not go far. They back up and start over. They read more slowly, this time paying more attention to the words. But still, they cannot make much sense of them. These words do not immediately grab and hold them. They are quickly bored and easily distracted.

And, in frustration, they blame the author: "Why can't theologians just say what they mean? And say it simply? Why do they have to make it so difficult?"

Remember when you were a child, starting to read? You struggled. Reading did not come naturally or automatically. You had to learn to read. But the important thing was that you wanted to do it. More than anything else, you were committed and driven to doing this amazing act called "reading."

It is no different with theological reading. You begin as a child. You struggle. But, like a child, you must want to read, and want to read so badly, that you are willing to keeping doing it, while failing, until you learn how. (And you don't blame the author!)

Be determined and driven, or else you will likely not make it past the initial stages of not knowing how to read, starting to read, struggling to read, and then giving up. This kind of reading is not quick, simple, or easy. But it is well worth the time and energy. It is its own reward.

First, learn words and construct a working theological vocabulary. Keep a notebook of key terms. Purchase and use a good theological dictionary.[9] When you come across a word you do not know, look it up in your dictionary. Write it down in your notebook, along with a brief sentence summarizing its meaning. While you are at it, learn to pronounce the word properly.[10]

Do the same with the names of theologians, briefly identifying who they are, where they have taught, and the most important contributions they have made.[11] It is important that you become familiar with the leading figures in the historical development of Christian theology, in order to acquire a sense of the greater community of which you are part—a communion of saints that must not remain nameless or faceless.

Start out slowly. Do not rush through the pages you are reading. Theological reading and speed-reading are opposed. When you get bogged down or hung up, or when you are not understanding what you are reading, or you realize you have been going through many paragraphs on automatic pilot without actually reading them or comprehending them, go back and start over. Make rereading a habit.

In my first year at seminary, I reread every textbook multiple times. Why? Because I wanted to learn this language and grasp its truth and meaning. Only by going over and over this theological material did it sink in. I had to sink myself into it and become its student. I gradually

---

9. Here are a few theological dictionaries I recommend, in order: Donald K. McKim, *The Westminster Dictionary of Theological Terms,* 2nd ed. (Louisville: Westminster John Knox Press, 2014); Justo L. González, *Essential Theological Terms* (Louisville: Westminster John Knox Press, 2005); Stanley J. Grenz, David Guretzki, and Cherith Fee Nordling, *Pocket Dictionary of Theological Terms* (Downers Grove, Illinois: InterVarsity Press, 1999); Van A. Harvey, *A Handbook of Theological Terms* (New York: Macmillan Publishing Company, Inc., 1964; reprinted by Touchstone, 1997).

10. Use one of the many pronunciation guides available online, such as dictionary.cambridge.org/us/pronunciation/English. For years, I have also relied on William O. Walker, Jr., gen. ed., *Harper's Bible Pronunciation Guide* (San Francisco: Harper & Row, Publishers, 1989).

11. It is helpful to have two or three dictionaries of Christian theologians in your library. Here are a few recommendations: Justo L. González, *The Westminster Dictionary of Theologians* (Louisville: Westminster John Knox Press, 2006); Patrick W. Carey and Joseph T. Lienhard, ed., *Biographical Dictionary of Christian Theologians* (Peabody, Massachusetts: Hendrickson Publishers, Inc., 2000); Timothy George and David S. Dockery, ed., *Theologians of the Baptist Tradition* (Nashville: Broadman & Holman Publishers, 2001).

learned how to read theology, and in the process, to speak and think theologically, like the theologians I was reading.

Something else happened. I fell in love with both the act of reading and the books I was reading. I did not have that love before. In fact, I never thought of myself as a reader, much less a person who loved to read.

However, I can remember when I was young, and my mother regularly took me, along with my brothers and sisters, to the public library. I loved the smell of the place. I loved being in the shelves, surrounded by giant stacks. I loved seeing so many books at one time. I loved checking out as many books as was allowed, taking them home, trying to decide which one to start with, and then sitting outside on the back steps, or up in a tree, reading. I especially loved reading baseball novels and Sherlock Holmes mysteries. I remember reading a book on the Apostle Paul, written for children.

But somewhere along the way, I lost that love. Even sadder, I did not know I had lost it, and did not miss it. Then I met theology, and the love came back. I have been accompanied by and intimately involved with theological books ever since. Right now, as I write, I look down and see over two dozen surrounding my chair.

But when I first entered theological education, I had to learn how to relate to books all over again. I had to learn what to do with the written text. I also had to learn what the text can do with me.

In other words, I had to learn how to read: first, in the sense of interpreting the text; and then, second, in the sense of allowing the text to interpret, or "read," me. By following the text's logic, thinking its thoughts, discerning and reflecting on its meanings, tracing its teachings, and taking them on as my own, I have learned to allow the text to "have its way with me," and, if truthful and meaningful, to change my mind and my life.

Immerse yourself in the texts of the Christian theological faith-tradition. The church's vast library is open to you. You have access to the primary writings of the Bible, and also to the secondary writings of biblical scholars, past and present. You can read the works of Christianity's greatest minds, from Augustine to Aquinas to Luther to Barth to Newbigin. Read broadly and freely. Do not limit yourself to one or two authors, to one or two topics, or to one or two time periods. This is a conversation that is much longer, broader, and deeper than you can imagine, and you need to overhear and learn as much as possible from all of it.

Not every part of this conversation, however, is equally valuable, meaningful, or even truthful. Therefore, you must develop the skill of discernment, or "selective reading." Not only is it impossible for you to read everything that has ever been written, but also, trust me, you do not want to read, and should not read, just anything. Pick good books. Read the classics. Choose the writings that get to the heart of the Christian faith-tradition, and most adequately and eloquently express its truth and meaning.

You definitely don't want to waste your time, mental energy, or money on lesser books. And today there are a lot of "lesser" books out there, specifically published and marketed for unsuspecting, undiscerning laypersons. Many are little more than spiritual cotton candy or thin religious gruel. Some I would describe as junk theology, or even religious-spiritual pornography.

Here are the basic guidelines I use. First, stay away from Christian writers who are obsessed with a single idea or issue, merely grinding some theological axe.

Second, stay away from writers (and speakers, teachers, and preachers) who are obsessed with relatively obscure parts of Christian theology, always lurking around at the bottom or on the fringes, looking for something strange, avant-garde, or controversial.

Third, avoid books that are full of mere religious jargon, or consist of little more than a series of Bible verses strung like pearls on a string, without offering a single new idea, brilliant insight, or deep thought.

Fourth, do not read books written by pastors, unless you know for certain that these pastors know what they are talking about, and have something to say.[12]

Fifth, do not ask your pastor or a Christian friend for a book recommendation, unless he or she is an active student and reader of Christian theology, and so may have something solid to recommend.

Sixth, do not go to a local bookstore, library, or amazon.com, blindly perusing the shelves to "pick out something that looks good."

---

12. There are a few pastors (active, retired, or deceased) whose books, sermons, blogs, and articles you would do well to read. I include Dietrich Bonhoeffer, George A. Buttrick, and Eugene Peterson in this small, but distinguished group.

Seventh, do not let your reading be blown by the winds of the latest-greatest bestseller that either the popular secular market or the popular spiritual market is lauding. If you hear everyone say, "You have to read this! It is THE Christian book of the year. Every believer should read it," run!

More positively, you will learn the type of books you should be reading. Some books are better than others, even among the best books available. This is why you must generally learn the market of theological writings and be continually discovering and assessing the crème de la crème. Seek to invest your hard-earned money, limited time, and teachable mind only on the best of the best.

This will come with experience. First, you will find the publishers that can be trusted to publish quality theological books. At the top of my list is William B. Eerdman's Publishing Company. I also find Westminster John Knox Press, Abingdon Press, InterVarsity Press, and Baker Academic to be reliable. There are others.

Second, you will learn which theologians to read. An exhaustive list is impossible. But I do not believe any beginning student should have to venture into theological reading without some guidance. Any list is preferable to being left to one's own unskilled senses, to chance, or to heresay.

So, here is my "good theologians shortlist" (names in no particular order): Leslie Newbigin, N. T. Wright, Stanley Hauerwas, Gerhard Lohfink, Richard John Neuhaus, Stanley Grenz, and Kevin Vanhoozer. You are on solid ground with any article or book by one of these writers.

Of course, as soon as I mention these names, I think of others: Alister McGrath, David F. Wells, Thomas C. Oden, Miroslav Volf, and Carl E. Braaten. Conservative evangelical lists might add John R. W. Stott, John M. Frame, and Wayne A. Grudem.

My list grows longer when I include those whom I consider to be the true "heavy-weights": Edward Farley, Robert W. Jenson, Thomas F. Torrance, Anthony Thiselton, Oliver O'Donovan, Colin Gunton, Nicholas Wolsterstorff, John Webster, David Bentley Hart, and Robert L. Wilken.

Don't overlook or neglect the major 20th century theologians, such as Karl Barth, Emil Brunner, Paul Tillich, Rudolf Bultmann, Reinhold Niebuhr, H. Richard Niebuhr, Dietrich Bonhoeffer, Karl

Rahner, Hans Urs von Balthasar, Alexander Schmemann, and John Zizioulas.

Finally, read back into the church's theological history: Jonathan Edwards, Søren Kierkegaard, John Wesley, John Calvin, Martin Luther, Thomas Aquinas, Anselm of Canterbury, Augustine of Hippo, Origen of Alexandria, and Irenaeus of Lyons. There are many, many more. The church is blessed with an innumerable host of thinkers, scholars, and writers. But at least you now have a select list to get you started, and by which you can continue your study for a long time.

What I do not have in mind is the reading of three or four good books, and then you are done. Nor will the reading of a textbook for a short-term course suffice. This is not about "taking a class or two," or "dabbling a little in theological reading every once in a while," or "checking occasionally to see what's out there," or "being on the lookout for something that you could read that might interest you and possibly help your Christian life."

Theological education is serious reading. It is the call to devote yourself to a lifelong career of reading, surrounding yourself with a library of the best books Christians have written and are writing, immersing yourself in their theological discourse, and learning from them their theological wisdom.

This communion of theological saints must become your primary teaching-learning community, supported by any local congregation or seminary in which you may be fortunate enough to be involved. I do not see how either Christian theological education or Christian faith development can take place apart from this greater fellowship of true believers, without "communing" with them through their writings.

Begin reading. Continue reading. As you go, build your personal library, book by book. Chances are you do not live near, or do not have access to, a theological library. Therefore, as part of your self-education, you will have to cobble together a self-made library.

If you are fortunate enough to be in a lay seminary, or small teaching-learning community, purchase and read the textbooks that are assigned. Add them to your library. Search the footnotes, endnotes, and bibliographies in the books for other books the authors are commonly using. Ask your teacher-theologian for his or her best recommendations. Over time, you will begin recognizing the same names of theologians and the same book titles. Purchase them for your library and for future reading.

Be careful. Both buying and reading are habit-forming, and even addictive. Only choose books that are the best of the best, and that you will actually read—unless you have an unlimited bank account and unlimited shelf space in your home or apartment. Believe me when I tell you that books proliferate and take over like kudzu. Desks, floors, walls, and finally entire rooms have been known to disappear. (Ask my wife.)

Include biblical commentaries, dictionaries, and other reference tools in your library.[13] My recommendation is that you not purchase a full set of commentaries, unless the scholarship of the entire set is outstanding, and you have come across a deal too good to pass up. Instead, buy the best one or two commentaries from different sets, as you need them for your studying and/or teaching.

I still believe the 1962 five-volume *The Interpreter's Dictionary of the Bible*[14] is one of the best research tools ever produced. Sets are plentiful from retired or deceased pastors' libraries. So, ask around, or go to the used book section of amazon.com to find a good, clean set —especially the first four volumes (the fifth is a supplementary volume)—at a low price. *The New Interpreter's Dictionary of the Bible*[15] is also available for a greatly reduced price.

I am often asked for the "best translation" of the Bible. While there is no single "best translation," some translations are better than others. All have their weaknesses. But some are weaker than others. Select a strong, solid translation by reputable biblical scholars.

---

13. Here are some recommended resources: Kevin J. Vanhoozer, gen. ed., *Dictionary for Theological Interpretation of the Bible* (Grand Rapids, Michigan: Baker Academic, 2005); Paul J. Achtemeier, gen. ed., *Harper's Bible Dictionary* (San Francisco: Harper & Row, Publishers, 1985); and Bruce M. Metzger, ed. consult., *NRSV Exhaustive Concordance, Complete and Unabridged* (Nashville, Tennessee: Thomas Nelson Publishers, 1991).

14. George Arthur Buttrick, ed., *The Interpreter's Dictionary of the Bible: An Illustrated Encyclopedia,* 4 vols. (Nashville: Abingdon Press, 1962); Keith Crim, Victor Paul Furnish, Lloyd Richard Bailey, Sr., and Emory Stevens Bucke, eds., *The Interpreter's Dictionary of the Bible: An Illustrated Encyclopedia*, supplementary volume (Nashville: Abingdon Press, 1976).

15. Katharine Doob Sakenfeld, ed., *The New Interpreter's Dictionary of the Bible,* 5 vols. (Nashville: Abingdon Press, 2006–2009).

Christians should be discriminating when it comes to the version(s) they use. For your theological study, do not use a paraphrase (such as *The Living Bible),* but a translation. However, do not use a translation simply because your parents or congregation gave it to you, everyone in your prayer group is using it, it "is easy to read," or was on sale. Do your homework. Learn about what goes into translating Hebrew and Greek into English. Select one of the better translations.

I use and highly recommend the New Revised Standard Version of the Bible (NRSV). It is an excellent translation for serious study. Also have on hand for reference and comparison two or three other translations, such as the New International Version (NIV), the Good News Bible (GNB), and, of course, the King James Version (KJV).

By the way, shop online for books, just as you do for clothes and household items. For one thing, you probably will not find these books, or even this type of book, in bookstores. Even Christian bookstores are not known for carrying top-notch theological books.

Second, never pay full retail price for a book, unless you want to order it and support your local bookseller; or you cannot find it anywhere for less, and you must have it. Compare prices online at amazon.com, barnesandnoble.com, and christianbook.com. Do not be afraid of ordering good or very good used books (minor wear, unmarked or slightly marked). I have had good experience with the vendors on Amazon Marketplace. Don't forget tax and shipping.

Read books that are challenging. Why would anyone read a book that is unchallenging? Purposefully select books that are "at your head" or "over your head." Negatively, this means that you should generally avoid books and other literature commonly published for Christians by denominations and popular market publishers. These pamphlets, quarterlies, magazines, and books are written for the mass market and the average reader, who has only a high school education (or less), reads and thinks at a low level, or does not read or think much at all. You can do better. And you should.

Positively, this means that you will be choosing and reading books that will bring you up to their higher reading level. Because they are written by and for thoughtful adults, you will be made a thoughtful adult. Why read a book that does not call and cause you to "love the Lord with your mind"? Why waste your time and money with a book that doesn't teach you any more than you already know and understand? You are a learner. Then read like someone who is trying to learn.

First, read only solid books. Read very little, if anything, that is "light reading," except as a diversion or for entertainment. Second, read weightier books than you otherwise would read. Like a body-builder, continually increase the total weight you are able to deadlift or bench press. I have done some heavy lifting of cognitive content in my time. And I keep doing this exercise in order to stay in shape and to continue increasing in intellectual strength. I am always working on at least one book that is weightier and tougher than I can handle.

Second, think of theological authors as teachers, and their writings as lessons. You do not want a crip course taught by a professor who is a pushover. Instead, you want material that will challenge you, push you, and teach you something. You want to be guided into new territory and put to the test, finally emerging with greater clarity and insight. Only solid, weightier books can do this.

Of course, when you begin, all theology books will likely seem weighty to you. They may all be too heavy for you to lift. Even the least challenging will be over-challenging. This is because you have never done this kind of reading, learning, thinking, or believing before. (I recall my experience as a new convert and seminarian.)

Unfortunately, most theological literature is not written for Christian laypersons. Publishers run a busy market for scholars only. Professional theologians write to and for one another. This is how they gain and maintain academic respect, tenure, and a little income on the side. They are carrying on their own inside conversation, without having the local congregation or average believer in mind.

Certainly, anyone can purchase and read any of these books (if she ever hears and knows about them). These books are not written to or for the whole church. They are not intended for use as textbooks for the teaching ministry of a lay seminary. They require a scholarly mind, as well as much prerequisite knowledge that laypersons do not have, and typically do not need.

What is the alternative? What are non-academic publishers putting out that is geared toward the ordinary believer? The answer is clear: "What will sell." And what sells is "light reading," or the "easy read." Christians have been fed the biblical-theological equivalent of highly processed fast food and sugary sweets for so long that this is all they expect, want, or are capable of consuming and digesting. There is a huge marketplace of cheap religious, devotional, and inspirational literature surrounding and servicing the church.

What, then, is the serious learner to do? The books that are available are too hard or too soft; too complex or too simple. I call this the "Goldilocks dilemma." The middle market, or market in-between, is practically non-existent. In short, theologians generally do not write good, solid, quality books for laypersons. Publishers do not publish and sell this type of book. Therefore, laypersons have very little to choose from, that is both available and accessible to them.

I can think of only a few exceptions. N. T. Wright, for example, is a leading New Testament scholar, who has written major books on Jesus, Paul, and the church.[16] His four volumes in the "Christian Origins and Question of God" series (two additional volumes planned) are highly acclaimed by scholars.

At the same time, Wright is the rare individual who can speak and write to the whole church and its ordinary, non-scholarly saints. He has written a "For Everyone" commentary series on the books of the New Testament. This series is truly "for everyone."[17] So are his books that I call his "simply books" and "surprised books."[18] These are intended for a broader, generally lay audience. I recommend that you read them, along with many of his other books that are accessible to the non-scholarly, yet thoughtful, learner.[19]

---

16. N. T. Wright (1948–) is Research Professor of New Testament and Early Christianity at St. Mary's College, University of St. Andrew's, in Scotland. An Anglican clergyman, he was the Bishop of Durham between 2003 and 2010.

17. N. T. Wright, *New Testament For Everyone,* 18 vols. (Louisville: Westminster John Knox Press, 2011).

18. N. T. Wright, *Simply Christian: Why Christianity Makes Sense* (New York: HarperSanFrancisco, 2006)*; Simply Jesus: A New Vision of Who He Was, What He Did, and Why He Matters* (New York: HarperOne, 2011)*; Simply Good News: Why the Gospel Is News and What Makes It Good* (New York: HarperOne, 2015)*; Surprised by Hope: Rethinking Heaven, the Resurrection, and the Mission of the Church* (New York: HarperOne, 2008)*;* and *Surprised by Scripture: Engaging Contemporary Issues* (New York: HarperOne, 2014).

19. N. T. Wright, *What Saint Paul Really Said: Was Paul of Tarsus the Real Founder of Christianity?* (Grand Rapids: William B. Eerdman's Publishing Company, 1997)*; Paul: In Fresh Perspective* (Minneapolis: Fortress Press, 2005)*; The Last Word: Beyond the Bible Wars to a New Understanding of the Authority of Scripture* (New York:

This book market between the academy and the congregation is sparsely supplied and undeveloped. Occasionally, a theologian will write something that fits here. But laypersons back home never hear about it, and so they never read it. I am thinking of two of Robert Jenson's books as examples: *A Theology in Outline: Can These Bones Live?;* and *Story and Promise.*[20]

When Stanley Hauerwas teams up with William Willimon, the result is a wealth of reading on the Ten Commandments, the Lord's Prayer, the Holy Spirit, preaching, and the church. Begin with *Resident Aliens* and *Where Resident Aliens Live.*[21] Stay with Willimon for a seemingly endless supply of books on theological and pastoral topics. Follow Hauerwas if you are interested in more academic reflections on theology, ministry, ethics, and the church in a secular age. I recommend his essays in *Unleashing the Scripture* and *After Christendom.*[22]

Finally, I invite you to discover and explore the library of books produced by a pastor-theologian, Eugene Peterson. Even when he is addressing the pastor, all Christians will gain wisdom by listening in. My all-time favorite is *Working the Angles.* But I have never read anything Peterson has written that did not inspire me to think,

---

HarperSanFrancisco, 2005)*; Evil and the Justice of God* (Downer's Grove, Illinois: InterVarsity Press, 2006)*; After You Believe: Why Christian Character Matters* (New York: HarperOne, 2010); *How God Became King: The Forgotten Story of the Gospels* (New York: HarperOne, 2012)*;* and *The Day the Revolution Began: Reconsidering the Meaning of Jesus' Crucifixion* (New York: HarperOne, 2016).

20. Robert W. Jenson, *A Theology in Outline: Can These Bones Live?* (New York: Oxford University Press, 2016); *Story and Promise: A Brief Theology of the Gospel of Jesus* (Eugene, Oregon: Wipf and Stock, 2014). Jenson (1930–2017) was an American Lutheran theologian, who taught at Lutheran Theological Seminary in Gettysburg, Pennsylvania, and at St. Olaf College, Northfield, Minnesota, before retiring and taking the position of Senior Scholar for Research at the Center for Theological Inquiry, Princeton, New Jersey. From 2007 to 2010, I had the privilege of learning from him in the Pastor Theologian program of the Center.

21. Stanley Hauerwas and William H. Willimon, *Resident Aliens: A Provocative Christian Assessment of Culture and Ministry for People Who Know That Something is Wrong* (Nashville: Abingdon Press, 1989); and *Where Resident Aliens Live: Exercises for Christian Practice* (Nashville: Abingdon Press, 1996).

22. Stanley Hauerwas, *Unleashing the Scripture: Freeing the Bible from Captivity to America* (Nashville: Abingdon Press, 1993); *After Christendom* (Nashville: Abingdon Press, 1991, 1999). While I am recommending Hauerwas, let me direct you to his *Hannah's Child: A Theologian's Memoir* (Grand Rapids: William B. Eerdman's Publishing Company, 2010).

believe, and live better both as a Christian and as a pastor-teacher-theologian.[23]

There are some books in this middle region, but you will have to go digging for them. I encourage theologians, pastors, and publishers to take a serious interest in this segment of the market. It is wide-open for development. I am now working to do my small part to help construct it and contribute to it. How can pastors and publishers, theologians and teachers, not imagine the open, rich possibilities of writing and publishing books specifically for lay learners, who are students of Christ and stewards of the mysteries of God? These theological saints both need and deserve to be nourished with food that is as tasty, solid, organic, and healthy as what the elite professionals are getting at their tables!

Meanwhile, let me urge you, as a serious reader, to venture into the upper region of theological scholarship. Do not be afraid. You have no legitimate reason to feel that you are unqualified or unworthy, or may be trespassing. You are not. This is your territory as much as it is anyone else's. It belongs to the whole church.

Read scholarly writings that are accessible to the serious student. Become familiar with the theologians who are not so caught up in the rules, interests, and jargon of their own scholarship that they forget how to communicate clearly for a broader readership, and irresponsibly neglect the whole church.

Start with Lesslie Newbigin's *The Gospel in a Pluralist Society*,[24] Gerhard Lohfink's *Does God Need the Church?*,[25] and Christopher J. H.

---

23. Eugene H. Peterson, *Working the Angles: The Shape of Pastoral Integrity* (Grand Rapids: William B. Eerdman's Publishing Company, 1987).

24. Lesslie Newbigin, *The Gospel in a Pluralist Society* (Grand Rapids: William B. Eerdman's Publishing Company, 1989). You may want to access Newbigin through an "introducer and interpreter." I recommend Paul Weston, comp. and ed. *Lesslie Newbigin: Missionary Theologian: A Reader* (Grand Rapids: William B. Eerdman's Publishing Company, 2006). Newbigin (1909-1998) was an Anglican theologian, who served as a missionary in India, a bishop, and ecumenical statesman. He wrote at length and with great insight about the crisis of the gospel and the church in the Western world.

25. Gerhard Lohfink, *Does God Need the Church: Toward a Theology of the People of God* (Collegeville, Minnesota: The Liturgical Press, 1999). Lohfink (1934–) lives and works as a theologian in the Catholic Integrierte Gemeinde (Integrated Community) in Bad Tölz, Germany. Previously, he was professor of New Testament at the University of Tübingen.

Wright's *The Mission of God.*[26] Reading one book by one of the great thinkers and writers will lead to reading another.

Also, select a book of systematic theology that is substantial, yet manageable. I have used Stanley Grenz's *Theology for the Community of God* in my seminary classes.[27] I do not hesitate to recommend it to members of my congregation, and to others who are beginning their theological education.

Peruse my footnotes in this book. I provide you a strong set of books to read. As you read, you will come across references to other books that you will then want to read. Be careful, though. You will likely be tempted to want to read everything!

My point is you will never lack for anything to read. Your difficulty will be having too much that you want to read, and having to decide which book to read next. One day you will wake up and realize how short your life truly is, and that you will run out of good breath before you run out of good books. This is the day when you realize you truly have been hooked as a learner, fished out of the crowd to be a student-follower of Jesus.

A Theological Road Map

You will need a map for your self-education journey. The Christian theological terrain is long and broad. You have never ventured forth in it. How will you know where to begin? Which way to go? Or, how to move and make progress?

Jesus taught his students, "Enter through the narrow gate; for the gate is wide and the road is easy that leads to destruction, and there

---

26. Christopher J. H. Wright, *The Mission of God: Unlocking the Bible's Grand Narrative* (Downer's Grove, Illinois: IVP Academic, 2006). Also, see *The Mission of God's People: A Biblical Theology of the Church's Mission* (Grand Rapids: Zondervan, 2010). Wright (1947–) is an Anglican clergyman and Old Testament scholar. He is currently the International Ministries Director of Langham Partnership International, as well as the principal of All Nations Christian College.

27. Stanley J. Grenz, *Theology for the Community of God* (Grand Rapids: William B. Eerdman's Publishing Company; Vancouver, B.C.: Regent College Publishing, 2000). Grenz (1950–2005) was a Baptist theologian and ethicist, who spent most of his teaching years at Carey Theological College and Regent College in Vancouver, British Columbia, and Northern Baptist Theological Seminary in Lisle, Illinois.

are many who take it. For the gate is narrow and the road is hard that leads to life, and there are few who find it." (Matthew 7:13–14)

Surely Simon Peter must have blurted out, as he always did, what everybody was thinking: "What narrow gate? Where is it? If it is that narrow, how can we possibly enter through it? And if few people find the road on the other side of this gate leading to life, how are we supposed to find it? And if we do find it, and it is as hard a way as you say it is—so hard that almost nobody takes it—how can we be assured there is any chance we will stay on it and follow it all the way to life?"

Here is a good first lesson for you as new theological student: Jesus is the narrow gate, according to his teaching in John 10. He portrayed himself as the good shepherd, who knows his sheep by name and leads them into the fold and out to pasture, keeping them safe from thieves and bandits. His sheep know his voice and follow him. Therefore, whoever enters in and through him, and stays with him, will live. He is their gate to life, or life-gate.

Likewise today, you and I enter and engage the theological life through Jesus. The life he receives from God is the same life we receive and that we live in the world. We go the way he goes.

Obviously, this is not the way that human beings naturally or normally go. Their gate and road, or their shepherd and teacher, is some religious figure, preacher, philosopher, or theorist. They follow that person's lead. Or, they "go with the flow" of the crowd, which is wide-open for anybody and everybody, and is an easy way to go. Or, they simply listen to their own voice, which is the easiest way of all.

But you and I are peculiar, in that we do not go any of these ways. We enter through Jesus and take the road that few find, take, and stay on. Jesus is the one we are listening to and following. He is the one we allow to teach us, and from whom we are learning how to live. We believe that this is the way to truth and life, and the only way that leads to God.[28]

The way of the Christian life and the way of the theological life are synonymous. No person or community of persons can take one way without taking the other. Not taking one means not taking the other. Therefore, those of us who enter through and follow Jesus find

28. See John 14:6.

ourselves on the same road with all Christians past and present who have lived in this world as Jesus did—by theological faith.

However, this road is so untraveled that it is little more than a footpath. In most places, it is barely discernible. Therefore, we need guidance to help us know where this road is, where it leads, and whether we are on this road or some other. Also, how do we navigate it? How do we live in the way of the Christian theological life?

We need a map. Fortunately, faithful people who have gone before us have left behind their travel logs, journal notes, and basic drawings of the way. This long tradition of mapmaking continues today in the work of a few theologians who trace the path the church has taken, the mode of existence called "faith," and its theological life, as well as where we are and the way ahead that we should go. They are practitioners of the dying art and science of what I call "Christian theological cartography."

There are multiple maps. Which one(s) do we use? Whose map? I propose that we do something similar to what I do when I am planning a trip. I consult several online mapping services, such as MapQuest and Google Maps. Also, I still like to have hard paper in my hands, and a broader view before me. So I go to the glove compartment of my car, and pull out the maps I have collected at the welcome centers of several states. With all of this information before me, revealing multiple routes I could take, I decide the best way to go. I chart out my route.

My recommendation is that we do the same in mapping out our theological education. First, we enter through Christ into the territory of the Christian theological faith-tradition that has developed around him, because of him. Second, we consult the multiple mappings of this tradition itself, and follow the way of Christ in the way of the theological saints. Go the way they have gone and are going. Then, as we go along in our studying and learning, and our embodying and existing, we "recalculate" and "reroute," depending on what we encounter along the way. We keep going. And before we know it, we have covered a lot of ground theologically, and are experienced travelers, moving in the way of Christ and his followers.

There is no single travel chart or "best map." No book covers the entire territory, showing where all things are in relationship to each other. This is why we use many, varied sources, allowing these to complement—even conflict with and correct—each other, finally yielding a better map than we otherwise would have.

After doing this for many years in local congregations with laypersons, involving a lot of trial and error, getting lost and finding my way again, I have designed a road map for the theological life and its education. I summarize it this way: "the mission of God as the redemptive drama of the Kingdom of God, for which the communion of saints (the church) is called to be its dwelling-place, existing by faith and engaging the world as stewards of the mysteries of the gospel of Christ."

You and I are not living, moving, and being in this world in the same manner, in the same direction, for the same purpose, or on the same course as everybody else. We are theological pilgrims, following in a long processional behind Jesus and the vast host following him, destined for life in God's Kingdom, or New Creation.

Therefore, let us go this way. Let us study and learn it. Let us preserve and teach it. Let us live it together as a community of faith. We are not left to our own desires or popular opinions. We are not left to wander around haphazardly or aimlessly. We are not left to bog down in immediate circumstances and daily chores. We have a map. Let's follow it.

Our first move is to get the "broad sweep," or overarching view of the entire landscape of the Christian biblical-theological faith-tradition. This is the "big picture." It is the "lay of the land." It is the vision of reality—of the world, humankind, history, and eternity—that is most truthful, meaningful, and trustworthy. By this vision, we not only have the light we need to see our way, but also the way we must go.

Then, as we go, we take in all the sights and sounds, encounters and experiences of this way. We study one part of the theological landscape, and then another, followed by another, and so on. We rely on the travel logs of those who have gone this way before us, who cared enough about the life they were living, following Christ, that they paid attention to it, examined it closely, thought about it, talked about it, and wrote about their understandings of it. We do the same, realizing that others will be coming along behind us, who, like us, will need the theological faith-tradition preserved for and transmitted to them, along with our travel notes. Much depends on our faithfulness.

I believe *missio Dei,* or mission of God, is this whole, or "big picture" of our theological life in this world. Once we know and understand this, we will then be able to know and understand the world itself as the Kingdom of God. This was the essence of the message and ministry of Jesus, who was "sent" as the supreme manifestation, messenger, and means of God's mission. This is also the identity and purpose of the church, as well as the key to the meaning of history and the destiny of the world.

Only in relation to the mission of God and Jesus as the Christ are we able to know and understand the communion of saints, or church. Within this framework, you and I are able to understand that we have been called out of the crowd and united with this communion, which is the dwelling-place of God's mission today. Here we exist by faith as stewards of the mysteries of this mission made known supremely in the gospel of Christ. We engage the world by embodying these mysteries as their faithful witness, being a contrast-society, and thereby offering a more truthful interpretation of all things and an alterative way of living together.

This is what I am referring to as the "big picture," or the basic theological hermeneutical framework of Christian faith and its tradition. Other theologians have spoken of "the Bible's grand narrative" (Christopher J. H. Wright), "the strange new world of the Bible" (Karl Barth), or "the drama of God" (Kevin Vanhoozer.) Theology is our story of reality, history, humanity, and the universe in relation to God and the dramatic mission of God. You and I are the storytellers and actors on the twenty-first century stage of the great theater of the world.[29]

A good, beginning book for studying and learning this broad overview is *The Drama of Scripture* by Craig Bartholomew and Michael Goheen.[30] I recommend that you also read *The Mission of God's People*

---

29. Kevin J. Vanhoozer, *Faith Speaking Understanding: Performing the Drama of Doctrine* (Louisville: Westminster John Knox Press, 2014), 51.

30. Craig G. Bartholomew and Michael W. Goheen, *The Drama of Scripture: Finding Our Place in the Biblical Story*, 2nd ed. (Grand Rapids: Baker Academic, 2014). Bartholomew (1961–) is H. Evan Runner Professor of Philosophy and Professor of Religion and Theology at Redeemer University College in Hamilton, Ontario. Goheen is Director of Theological Education and Scholar-in-residence at Missional Training Center in Phoenix, Arizona, and also Professor of Missiology at Calvin Theological Seminary in Grand Rapids, Michigan.

by Christopher J. H. Wright.[31] The latter book offers questions for guided study. By making this initial broad sweep, you should gain a good understanding of the grand theological landscape.

Your next step is to cover this same area again. But this time, move more slowly, taking more time to explore the terrain. Picture yourself walking along a path through the woods. Later, you walk this same path through these same woods again. On this hike, however, you take a little more time, observing more than you did the first time. You notice things you did not notice the first time. Over future weeks, months, and years, you make multiple trips along this path. You walk it many times. And each time you discover something that is new to you. You learn more and more, as this path becomes your "habit," or way of life.

This is how it is with theology's education and life. Along the way, you will study and learn the many, various parts of the Christian theological faith-tradition, but always in connection with each other and with the whole ("big picture"). Study more specifically and fully the church, Christ, the world as creation, and so on. Always keep your study aligned with and directed by the whole, while moving in all directions to explore each component part.

Once you have the basic path, or track, you will be able to move methodically step-by-step, part-by-part, covering the entire area, going deeper and more thoroughly with each pass. One thing will lead to another. The particular route you take will be your own, while also being in the same territory and along the same basic pathway taken by theological believers throughout history and across the nations.

Keep going. This is not a degree program you will ever complete. This is not a class that requires you to sit through a few lectures and read a textbook, and then you are done. This is not a hobby you can dabble in whenever you happen to have a free moment. This is not a project you can work on, then set aside for a while, until you can get back to it (if you ever do). Instead, this is an ordered course of study that you decisively begin and consistently work on. You must be serious about it, and it must become integral to your routine. You are

31. See footnote #26 on page 305. For additional support and research, read Wright's *The Mission of God: Unlocking the Bible's Grand Narrative*. It is a much fuller work, providing important background and development of themes and concepts.

not taking a theology course. You are undertaking the course of Christian theological faith-existence. Therefore, studying and learning must be ongoing and must be sustained for the rest of your life.

Yes, this is a disciplined way of life that will demand your attention, time, energy, and money. But the amazing thing is, you will never want it to end.

8
Embodying

Christian theology requires a body. In order to be seen, heard, known, understood, studied, learned, taught, and lived, theology must "appear in the flesh." It must be incarnated in concrete, tangible, visible, audible, physical, material, earthly, human form.

Without a body, theology can never be anything more than an abstract idea or theory. It will remain in the ethereal realm of lofty thoughts, idle speculations, imaginative fiction, public opinion, and personal presuppositions. It will be detached and distant from how real people actually exist, live, work, play, and suffer in this world, both individually and communally in marriages, families, societies, congregations, businesses, governments, and nations.

Unfortunately, this is how most persons, including most Christians, view and relate to theology. To them, it is little more than an educational endeavor, mental chess exercise, or spiritual discipline for someone who happens to have the interest, time, and money. Of course, they do not see themselves as this "someone."

The typical Christian thinks, "I am a practical person. Give me specific tasks to do, concrete steps to take, tangible materials to work with, and measurable goals. Unless I can see it with my own eyes, and put my hands on it, the theoretical and spiritual are neither relevant nor real to me."

Without realizing it, this person is expressing what "embodying" means. She likes her religion the way she likes her life: physical, concrete, and practical. However, she fails to realize that theology is always physical, concrete, and practical, as well. It appears in human beings. There is no other way for it to appear. It expresses itself in and by human beings. There is no other way for it to be expressed. Human beings are theological beings when they speak, think, and act theologically. "Embodying theology," then, means that theology shows up physically, concretely, and practically in bodies—in real flesh, like hers.

Yet, by rejecting Christian theology as being too theoretical and impractical, and opting instead for the purely, simply practical, she is effectively pitting practice against theory, rejecting theory, and finally choosing practices that are non-theoretical and ultimately non-theological (since theology is always theory as well as practice).

So, what is she practicing? If not Christian theology, what is she embodying?

This is the type of person who claims to live by and for faith, without ever really asking or being interested in what this faith is. Remember: she is a practical person, who avoids the theoretical and has nothing to do with it. She never examines or questions the intangible, for she stays as far away from the realm of thoughts and ideas as she can. These are unimportant, irrelevant, and non-authoritative to her, because they do not give her something to do, meet her needs, produce anything, or accomplish a goal immediately and directly. Therefore, as far as she is concerned, thoughts and ideas are impractical, despite the fact that she is embodying some thoughts and ideas. She simply is unaware that she is doing this, and is unaware of which thoughts and ideas she is embodying in very physical, concrete, and practical ways.

Consequently, she likely attends a congregation where theology is kept to a minimum, and she will never have to come into serious contact with the Christian historical-biblical-theological faith-tradition. Strangely, in her very embodied life (that she says is Christian) the theology that frames and fills the distinctively Christian life is never embodied. Therefore, she does not belong to and participate in "the body of theology," or "theology's body." Neither she nor her congregation is an embodiment of what the church has always embodied. They are living as the body of something else.

The major misunderstanding here is the separation of human experience into theoretical and practical. While a distinction can be made, there is no separation. All practice is theoretical, and all theory is practical. Theorizing itself is a practice. Practicing itself is a theory, or an act of theorizing. Both are essential to embodiment.

And both occur simultaneously—although we can slow down actual experience, and focus on one in distinction from the other. However, "having a belief, and then putting it into practice," or "acting first, and then later explaining it with a belief" is not the way we actually live. It is also not the way theology works.

Therefore, the question has to be asked of every specific action or practice: What am I embodying here? What am I believing, valuing, and saying in my action?

The separatist never asks such probing questions. As far as she is concerned, she is "practicing her faith," or "walking the walk," rather than "thinking her faith" or "talking the talk." Evidently, for her, thinking and talking are simply not practical enough to be considered real practices.

This is because Christianity, to her, is purely a practical religion, with practice limited only to a few, specific practices. Nothing else counts as practice. Because she has never engaged in the practice of theology, its existence and its education, and knows no one who has, she is unaware that theology is quite practical and is actually practiced. She does not realize that all practices can and should be viewed and lived theologically. At the same time, even religious and moral actions like hers may not embody traditional Christian belief and virtues, and thus not be properly theological or Christian.

This false separation of theory and practice is due largely to the false separation of body and soul, or flesh and spirit. In this view, humans are understood and related to as dichotomies, or bipartite beings. Accordingly, each of us is made up of two parts: a body and a soul (or spirit). There may be three or more parts, if the soul and spirit are considered to be separated entities, and we are further divided into heart, mind, will, and so on.

According to this widespread view of the human being, the body is the outer casing, or shell, while the soul is the inner essence, or being, of the person. The body is material, whereas the soul is immaterial. As material, coming from the earth, the body is mortal. But the soul comes from eternity, and is immaterial. It is immortal. Therefore, while my body is limited, finite, weak, and sinful, the "real me" inside is not. My body has a beginning and an ending, but I am eternal, like the gods. I (the real me) was never really born (except in this earthly, bodily form) and I will never die (not really). Only my body will die and decay, returning to the ground from whence it came: "earth to earth; ashes to ashes; dust to dust." I will never die, but will keep on living forever.

This anthropological dualism, or dichotomous paradigm of the human being, was characteristic of the philosophy of the ancient Greeks, and is commonly held by Christians today. In fact, I cannot recall meeting a single Christian who did not believe it. This is the one belief believed so strongly that almost everyone will get upset if it is questioned, and will speak up to defend it.

However, I believe this model of our humanity is inconsistent with the Scriptures, and is also undermined by recent discoveries and developments in neuroscience. Wellness and illness, life and death, do not merely involve or affect one part of the person (such as the body, or the mind), but rather the whole person. Likewise, relating to the world, and to the people and things around us, involves our selves holistically: heart, mind, and body, without division. There is no physical action or practice that does not involve our thoughts and emotions, just as there is no mental action or practice (thought) that does not involve our emotions and bodies. We humans are psychosomatic wholes. We are not strictly physical beings, as modern materialists believe. There is "more" to us—certainly more than the sum of our parts. But neither are we strictly spiritual beings, either. We don't *have* bodies, but *are* bodies. We are much more unified and complex than either view allows.

The same is true with our apprehending and relating to God, and worshiping and serving God. The whole self is involved the entire time—thoughts, feelings, attitudes, physical actions, and so on. The whole self is the *body* relating to God, not merely part(s) of one's self, such as the heart or soul. The *body* includes but is not limited to "blood and bones." It is a person, or persons. It is humanity, both individually (as in "Any*body* here interested in playing?") and corporately (as in "The *body* of spectators in the stands…").

Theology, then, is hearing, seeing, thinking, talking, experiencing, knowing, understanding, feeling, and acting *bodily* in response to God, and thus to all reality in the same manner. Theology appears or expresses itself *bodily* in and through our *bodies*. The *human body* responds, as the whole person responds. Theology, for those who are theological, is living, moving, and having being. It is being human.

This is what I mean by "embodying." It is allowing theology to have our bodies, and us as a body, using us as its instrument and means of God's revelation and redemption. You and I become the incarnation, or "en-flesh-ment," of theology. We are theology in the flesh. The truth and meaning, wisdom and work, plan and purpose of God are embodied in you and in me. Look at us and listen to us. Hopefully, the world will see and hear here theology's body, the church. And in and through this body, all people will see and hear God.

Of course, we are making an audacious claim for ourselves, for which we should continually ask forgiveness. Who are we to be the embodiment of divine revelation? However, we do not make apology, for this is simply the way revelation and faith work. You and I belong to a whole host of people, who are called out and commissioned to be a "body." We refer to this body as the communion of saints, or the "body of Christ." This is the church. Those who embody the mysteries of God made known and knowable in Christ are the visible, audible, touchable manifestation of these mysteries. These mysteries show up in these persons, through them, and as them. We *are* their body.

Our task, then, is not merely to "put theology into our minds and hearts," or to "put theology into everyday practice." Instead, we must put ourselves—our whole selves—under the authority and influence of theology, allowing ourselves to be transformed, or radically changed, into the human form of thinking, talking, feeling, and acting that theology needs us to be.

Our task is to *be* theology's body. We are called to live holistically as theological people. Without theology, we are nothing more than disordered, disconnected parts, a "bag of bones with a heart," or a mere collection of molecules and atoms, chemicals, electrical processes, and material energies. Without theology, a congregation is just another community or organization, and nothing more than individuals involved in a bunch of different religious, social, and secular activities. Theology is responsible for our wholeness, as well as our distinctive reality.

Christian theology has come from the human bodies of Israel and the church, supremely and definitively incarnated in the human body of Jesus of Nazareth. Theology itself may be called a "body of wisdom and faith" that requires a body for its existence. The latter body must know, understand, preserve, and transmit the former body, on behalf of which it exists. This is the church, which exists today as the theological body of Christ, and thus of what Christ embodied.

Where's the Body?

Perhaps I have watched too many crime investigation shows on TV, but I am convinced that our denominations and congregations are scenes of a major crime. Somebody has silenced, kidnapped, and likely killed the theological body. It is now missing, or remains only in parts, leaving behind some DNA forensic evidence of a past presence. The theological community is little more than "a ghost of its former self." Yet, strangely, nobody is conducting an investigation or a search and rescue operation. Nobody has called 911 to report the body missing.

I am filing here a missing person's report. The theological body no longer exists in the local settings where most Christians live and work. Despite the fact that they are called and created to be a theological community comprised of theological people existing theologically, they are not. The reason is they do not know and understand their own traditional body of wisdom and faith, and, frankly, resist being taught, learning it, and submitting to it. Therefore, they must have become some other body, embodying something else, since they are not the body of theology.

My suspicion, though, is that in this crowd there are two, three, or a few more who are being grafted to the body of Christ, and are allowing their bodies, both individually and collectively, to be made into the dwelling-place of theology, and thus of God. My questions are, "Where are you? Who are you?" My challenge is, "Come out and show yourself. You *are* the body that is missing, for which earnest souls have been searching, and which both the church and the wider world desperately need."

Is Theology Extinct?

Theology is not a mere idea that can continue to live on earth without a body, whether anyone actually incarnates it or not. It is not a belief system that will never die among human societies and individual lives, no matter what. It is not made to be kept in captivity in a museum or in the rare books section of a library, apart from a living, breathing community. Theology requires a living body.

However, congregations and Christians are no longer theology's body, or a theological body. Theology cannot survive disembodied or bodiless. Without human flesh, it fades and vanishes, until it is finally extinct.

None of us likes to think the worst. Surely theology has just wandered off. Give it time. It will be back. Or, theology has simply waned from neglect. If we start giving it a little more attention and cultivating it, it will perk up, come back, and flourish again. Don't worry. There's nothing to be alarmed about here. It will all work out for good. You'll see.

We also protest by pointing to the bits and pieces of theology still lying around, as though this is evidence of anything more than a body that used to be here. We mention the professional scholars. They are theologians. Theology is alive and well with them, right? We point to the denominational seminaries, divinity schools, and universities. Surely there are lots of communities somewhere that still embody theology, right? How, then, can it be extinct?

Tellingly, the person who protests never includes herself or her congregation in this cryptic "community somewhere that embodies theology." This ought to be sufficient evidence that theology *is* extinct for this particular person and her congregation. Just how extinct does theology have to be before it is actually or really, finally and fully extinct?

The International Union for the Conservation of Nature (IUCN), headquartered in Switzerland, maintains a "red list," which is the world's most comprehensive inventory of the global conservation status of biological species and sub-species. This organization assesses the extinction risk of thousands of plants, animals, and birds. Each is assigned to one of the following levels:

1. Extinct (EX) — No known animals remain.
2. Extinct in the wild (EW) — Known only to survive in captivity, or as a naturalized population outside its historic range.
3. Critically endangered (CE) — Extremely high risk of extinction in the wild.
4. Endangered (EN) — High risk of extinction in the wild.
5. Vulnerable (VU) — High risk of endangerment in the wild.
6. Near threatened (NT) — Likely to become endangered in the near future.
7. Least concern (LC) — Lowest risk. No cause for concern at this time.
8. Data deficient (DD) — Not enough data to make a proper assessment of its risk of extinction.
9. Not evaluated (NE) — Has not yet been evaluated against the criteria.[1]

Let's treat theology like a mammal or flower, and assess its extinction risk. Where would it fall on this list? The attitude and behavior of most Christians is "no cause for concern at this moment." Level 7. Either they have not noticed a problem, or have never thought about it, or simply are assuming everything is just fine, since nobody has said anything about it.

I am not so confident or optimistic. I move theology up to at least level 3. It is critically endangered (CE), being at an extremely high risk of extinction "in the wild" (i.e., its natural habitat of local congregations). Given that theology is also "known only to survive in captivity (i.e., in seminaries, divinity schools, and university religious studies departments), or as a naturalized population (i.e., academic scholars and professional theologians) outside its historic range (i.e., the whole church)," I lean strongly toward ranking theology at a higher risk of extinction at level 2.

Either level is much too high, and should be alarming to the church. However, we are in this disastrous state largely because the

1. For more on The IUCN Red List of Threatened Species (Version 2017-2), see: http://www. iucnredlist.org.

church has been morphing for a long time into something else, and diminishing and disappearing as the body of theology. Yet, the church continues to operate at level 9, not evaluating the condition of either itself or theology. The reason is that everyone assumes that theology will always be with us, and thus could never be at serious risk, much less in any real danger. The only other explanation is that theology's survival is not of serious interest or major concern.

Back From the Brink

Marie Wilcox, a great-grandmother in her eighties, is on a mission in the San Joaquin Valley of California. She is learning and teaching the Wukchumni language. She is the last living speaker of the language of her Native American ancestors.

Wilcox grew up hearing, speaking, and understanding the language, thanks to her grandmother, who spoke very little English. After her grandmother died, Wilcox stopped speaking her first language. She soon forgot it. No one else in her tribe remembered or spoke it either.

One day, when her sister began teaching her children the language, Wilcox felt a surge of inspiration. She jumped into action and began teaching herself her mother tongue. When she recalled a word, she wrote it down on an old envelope or piece of paper. She sat up late at night, pecking out letters on a computer keyboard. She worked on her project every day, every chance she got, for seven years. Her daughter joined her as both an assistant and a student.

Now Wilcox has a dictionary, and is working with her grandson to record the Wukchumni language on a tape recorder, making certain that they "say the words right." She wants to leave an archive for future generations. She also plans to continue as long as she can to teach weekly language classes for members of their tribe, who hopefully will preserve and pass it on.

She pauses and becomes pensive: "See, I am uncertain about my language, and who wants to keep it alive. Just a few. No one seems to want to learn. It's sad. …It seems weird that I am the last one.

And, uh, I don't know, it'll just be gone one of these days. Maybe. I don't know. It might go on and on."[2]

What is Marie Wilcox doing? On the surface it may appear that she is simply learning the lost art of speaking and writing an old language, as one might learn to churn butter or forge a wagon wheel. Or, she is doing what a lot of people do when they get old. They nostalgically remember the good old days, work on the family tree, tells stories about the way things used to be, write down wisdom, and leave a legacy for descendants.

Wilcox, however, is doing more than this. She is doing much more than merely hanging onto or trying to recapture the past. When a language becomes extinct, an entire culture is lost. Its history, narratives, songs, rituals, symbols, and sensibilities are gone, along with the body of knowledge and ways of interpreting the world encoded in its language. Without these words, the tribe loses its distinctive identity and intentionality. Although there will always be biological descendants, there will not necessarily always be Wukchumnis. Therefore, by saving their language, Wilcox is saving them as a people, and herself as one of them. Their future depends on their education. Everything depends on what they do or do not do now in terms of their cultural-linguistic tradition.

What is inspiring to me is her presentation of herself (her body) as a "living sacrifice" in the gap. She will be a Wukchumni, whether anyone else will or not. She is determined that the Wukchumni language will not be extinct for her, and will not become extinct when she dies.

Fortunately, she is joined by her sister, daughter, grandson, and a handful of others. Together they are a body that is embodying their own cultural-linguistic tradition by naturally forming and living as a small school, or a local teaching-learning community, engaged in the practice of searching for, retrieving, studying, preserving, and transmitting their heritage. In this way, they are bringing their tradition—and themselves—back from the brink of extinction, and keeping it alive for coming generations. They are its concrete, visible, audible, fleshly, living embodiment.

2. A short documentary, "Marie's Dictionary," has been produced by an award-winning filmmaker, Emmanuel Vaughan-Lee: https://www.globalonenessproject.org/library/films/maries-dictionary.

In the same way, Christian people and their distinctive biblical-theological language cannot exist without each other. Theology requires an ecclesial (church) body within which the theological life can be sustained. Likewise, this body requires theology by which the ecclesial life can be sustained. Neither the theological community nor the theological faith-tradition can be sustained apart from the other. Each keeps the other alive, as well as honest, responsible, and true to what it is and what it is for. Both are necessary for the survival of both.

The Benedict Option

If my assessment of the state of the ecclesial body is true, then theology is endangered and at an extremely high risk of extinction "in the wild." The current denominational and congregational environments are deadening for the theological life. This is because the church is culturally captive, and its faith domesticated, in the post-Christian, postmodern, secular Western world.[3]

There is little chance that either denominations or congregations will wake up, turn around, and exert any real effort to return to the Christian historical-biblical-theological faith-tradition. The religious body seems to lack both consciousness and concern that it now lives, moves, and has its being in a non-theological (often fiercely anti-theological) culture, to which it has dangerously compromised and accommodated itself. This failure is only exacerbated by the fact that the church is oblivious to its own deteriorating condition of theological amnesia and anemia.

For this reason, new, alternative, small communities must be constructed for the purpose of sustaining the theological life. By doing this, they themselves will be sustained by this theological life. These communities will be the human body that Christian theology demands for its survival and flourishing today.

3. A good exploration of the church's captivity and conversion in Western culture has been provided by David J. Kettle, *Western Culture in Gospel Context: Towards the Conversion of the West—Theological Bearings for Mission and Spirituality* (Eugene, Oregon: Cascade Books, 2011).

Given that current, established congregations are unreliable as theology's body, and they show no sign of changing and embodying the Christian theological faith-tradition, Marie Wilcox-type folks will have to take it upon themselves to begin self-teaching, learning the language, and living the life that has been forgotten. Like Wilcox, they will have to come together to form for themselves their own local schools of theological education.

In concluding his classic book, *After Virtue,* Alasdair MacIntyre draws a parallel between our own present age in Europe and North America, and the ancient age in which the Roman Empire declined into the Dark Ages. The loss of civility and the moral life, along with the rule of barbarians, he writes, is not a future or distant possibility, but is already upon us, and has been for some time.[4]

If we have any ground for hope in our situation, it is that the tradition of the virtues (the moral life) was able to survive the horrors of the last dark ages when men and women devoted themselves to the task of strengthening and preserving their own communities, rather than the Empire. They discovered new ways to live and work together, so that the moral life could be sustained.[5] They gathered locally for the sole purpose of maintaining a moral community, and thus keeping themselves moral. They did this by embodying the moral life. And they did this only because they considered the tradition of moral virtues to be so significant, authoritative, normative, and necessary that they devoted their lives to learning, knowing, and understanding the wisdom of this tradition, and then thinking, speaking, and acting accordingly—like moral people. Otherwise, the entire complex of moral community, moral life, and moral tradition is lost in an age when barbarians are in charge and are destroying morality.

MacIntyre's final sentence about not waiting for Godot,[6] but for another, very different St. Benedict is powerful.[7] He is referencing

4. Alasdair MacIntyre, *After Virtue: A Study in Moral Theory,* 3rd ed. (Notre Dame, Indiana: University of Notre Dame Press, 2007), 263.

5. MacIntyre, 263.

6. Godot is the mysterious figure for whom two men are waiting, but who never arrives or shows up, in the play by Samuel Beckett, *Waiting For Godot: A Tragicomedy in Two Acts* (New York: Grove Press, 1954).

7. MacIntyre, 263.

Benedict of Nursia (modern Norcia in Italy), who founded twelve small monastic communities during the period near the turn of the sixth century, when the Roman Empire was collapsing. These were local communities in which the Christian life of seeking and serving God could be sustained, while withstanding the destruction and chaos going on all around them. Benedict's intent was to keep faith alive, so that faith would survive and be available for future generations.

In other words, MacIntyre's call is for someone to step forth who will do in our new dark ages what St. Benedict did in his, which is to construct new forms of local community in which the moral tradition and its life can be sustained. And in this way, they themselves will be sustained as moral people.

In our case, we are in desperate need of new forms of community in which the theological tradition and its theological life can be sustained. Christians must respond to the call to gather in small groups that are consciously and intentionally devoted to knowing and understanding, preserving and transmitting, teaching and learning their own theological faith-tradition. This must be done if the theological life of faith is to survive. It is also necessary for our survival as people of theological faith. The tradition and the community require each other for their continued existence. Otherwise, both are lost. One cannot exist without the other.

We are not waiting, however, for some Godot-like leader in vain. God is already at work among us, raising up teachers and theologians, and rousing men and women of good faith to sense the full weight of the call of God heavily on their lives, enough to make them step forward out of the crowd, and begin doing what no one around them seems willing or interested in doing. These people will gather, and will be open to the gathering of others. Together they will intentionally form themselves into little "schools for the Lord's service," just as St. Benedict did.

The final words of MacIntyre's book hit me with the full force of truth: "Yes!" I am left hanging in illumined suspense, imagining all kinds of possibilities. I keep a copy of this closing paragraph nearby, reading it often for inspiration, encouragement, and hope. My interpretation and application for the church, I am sure, go beyond what MacIntyre had in mind when he wrote these words.

But the principle of a tradition and a community surviving only because each sustains the other remains true and meaningful for us.

Another person who has taken this challenge to heart is Rod Dreher. He has coined a new term, "the Benedict option," for those Christians who recognize the pressing need to gather themselves into communities for the deliberate purpose of living out their faith according to the Great Tradition, and thereby preserving it for future generations.[8] I count myself among these Christians who acknowledge that the world has changed in such drastic ways that Christian theological faith is endangered, and can be maintained only by small communities formed for this purpose.

Dreher then lays out a strategy for limited withdrawal from mainstream culture and the construction of local countercultural communities. These communities seek to rediscover the past, drawing on the authority of the Scriptures and the wisdom of the ancient church. They engage in ancient practices, such as liturgical worship, contemplative prayer, work, asceticism, hospitality, and community life and discipline. This is done in order to recover the Christian virtues found in the Rule of Saint Benedict. They want more than anything else to hold on to their faith in a world that is increasingly hostile.

Dreher believes we Christians are in a time of great danger and grave decision. The choices we make (or don't make) and the actions we take (or don't take) right now will have long-lasting consequences for our children, the church, our nations, and our civilization.[9] We can no longer naively wait, expecting things to turn around and turn out just fine.

I am especially interested in Dreher's discussion of education as central and necessary for Christian survival. St. Benedict called the monastery "a school for the service of the Lord." He believed discipleship was pedagogical, in that both heart and mind must be taught and trained in the ways of faith.

Likewise today, we must establish a schooling system that will recover Christian cultural memory, learn to love the wisdom of the

---

8. Rod Dreher, "Benedict Option FAQ," *The American Conservative,* October 6, 2015. http://www.theamericanconservative.com/dreher/benedict-option-faq/.

9. Rod Dreher, *The Benedict Option: A Strategy For Christians in a Post-Christian Nation (*New York: Sentinel, 2017), 5.

past, preserve it, and pass it on, in order not only to keep ourselves faithful, but also to produce another generation with the same traditional beliefs, understandings, ideals, and values. If we do not educate well, not only will we die as a people of faith, but also, what is left of the Christian faith in our civilization will become extinct and be lost forever.

Dreher, naturally, is concerned about the next generation—our children. He writes an entire chapter on education, discussing how parents must teach their children Scripture and the history of Western civilization. To do this, they will have to take their children out of public schools, put them in classical Christian schools, or homeschool them. Finally, he discusses the Benedict option for young people who are attending a university.[10]

My main concern is adult education. In no way do I disagree with or want to take away from Dreher's emphasis on childhood and young adult education. I trust that my ministry of teaching and writing is complementary and supportive. But I am interested in the grown-ups, who are the parents and teachers of the present and future generations in homeschools, classical schools, Christian schools, and universities (Christian and secular). I am especially interested in and concerned about those who are teaching our kids in local congregations.

Have they themselves been taught? Are they disciples of Christ and serious students of the Christian historical-biblical-theological faith-tradition? Do they know and understand what they are talking about, and what they are teaching their children, or somebody else's children? Are they theologians, who are intentionally and actively embodying theology and existing theologically? Are their practices theologically derived and directed?

Our predicament is that our established congregations, including the Christians who comprise them, are notorious for biblical illiteracy and theological ignorance. How can adults who are mere theological babes themselves, or who may not be theological at all, possibly be expected—despite their good-heartedness and noble intentions—to be competent and responsible in leading others to informed, mature theological faith?

---

10. Dreher, *The Benedict Option,* 144–175.

Dreher wisely notes that we cannot give the world what we ourselves do not have.[11] I add that we cannot give our children what we, as parents and teachers, do not have.

Who's teaching the teachers? Are our instructors themselves being instructed, and learning theology? Otherwise, we are only passing on our ignorance and immature faith, and going through the motions of Christian practices, without truly knowing, understanding, or possibly caring what we are doing, or why.

For this reason, I insist that serious, sustained, ordered teaching and learning be an integral part of the Benedict option and similar efforts. Christians must come together to form new, alternative, small, local bodies of faith. These must be schools, or teaching-learning communities. They must be lay seminaries, where ordinary believers can study and learn together, as well as worship, pray, and serve together. Their worshiping, praying, and serving *are* studying and learning—and vice-versa. Their entire existence together must be both an experience and an education in the Christian theological life.

Our aim cannot be simply to be religious and spiritual, or to be good, moral people. Rather, we are God's people, longing to be made by the Word and Spirit into theological people, like Christ. Our religion, spirituality, morality, and entire lives are grounded in, resourced by, and reflective of a faith that is distinctively theological. Since this faith is expressed in and carried by a theological tradition, we must enter this tradition, learn it, and become part of the body it is always forming to represent its truth and meaning in the world.

Of course, Dreher has his critics. He is looked upon suspiciously by some as an alarmist, a separatist, an apocalyptist, and a trouble-maker. Their general response seems to be, "Don't worry or be afraid. There is nothing wrong here—or, at least nothing that hasn't always been wrong with a church that is human, sinful, and less-than-perfect. Our time is no different, or more dangerous, than any other time."

Therefore, in their opinion, Dreher must be doing only what a Christian blogger and entrepreneur does when he is pushing his

11. Dreher, *The Benedict Option*, 19.

brand. He is merely dealing in "arresting images and memorable monikers," and "mining a memorable phrase," while misreading our cultural circumstances. He exaggerates the spiritual peril. He encourages "some of our debilitating self-deceptions." Therefore, what he offers as the solution is at best unnecessary, and, at worst, harmful to the church. In other words, we don't need what Dreher is offering. We already have the Christian Option.[12]

While Dreher's proposal is not beyond all criticism, I believe that such criticism as this is grossly unfair and unbalanced. Dreher is doing what he can, "banging the pots and pans," to wake up the church and call it to be the church. We need to develop some basic perception of where we are, and what time it is—a perception that we currently do not have. A little more alarm would be wiser and more appropriate, since our larger historical-cultural context itself is more and more alarming. This is not a false alarm or a practice drill. We are in a disastrous situation as the church. And the Benedict Option *is* the Christian Option that we must take.

I am with Dreher, as I am with Stanley Hauerwas, John Howard Yoder, David Kettle, Lesslie Newbigin, Gerhard Lohfink, and many others who have called for the church to be a countercultural community of theological faith in our post-Christian, postmodern Western world. I believe that the dominant, default culture of theological ignorance in our congregations is sufficient evidence that traditional theological faith is endangered. We must hear and heed the call to take dramatic action now and not later. Otherwise, we are ignoring more than our past. We are ignoring both our present and our future. We are putting at grave risk the survival of both the Christian theological tradition and the Christian church.

It is highly likely that my proposal for theological education in the local congregation will be considered just as unnecessary, overly critical, negative, and harmful as Dreher's Benedict Option. It, too, will be criticized by some people into irrelevance, so that it can then be ignored. There are simply too many interests at stake, too much already invested in the programs of our denominations and congregations, and too much inertia.

---

12. For an example of this kind of criticism, see R. R. Reno, "Benedict Option," *First Things,* May 2017. https://www.firstthings.com/article/2017/05/benedict-option.

However, despite resistance, I remain attuned to and confident of the reforming and redirecting of the church that God is already doing, whether the church wants to be reformed and redirected or not. I strain to discern the movement of the Spirit, already making paths for theological education without our awareness. I am waiting and hoping against impossibility for some option—whether Benedictine or not—to emerge from its underground germinating and rooting, appear in "above-ground, out-in-the-open flesh," and give us a body to join. We require a community where faith is incarnated and we are truly who we are and what we are about.

Our situation is growing ever more urgent as the new dark ages of anti-theological nihilism and barbarism press more and more upon us. Our only hope is that somebody, or a few somebodies, will emerge soon, here and there, in many places, coming together and forming intentional, alternative communities of theological existence and education. These persons will be determined to teach themselves and their children and grandchildren their own theological faith-tradition. They will take this tradition as their sacred trust, and strive to be worthy of the trust Christ has in them. They will incorporate into their fellowship and make disciples of any and all persons who will allow themselves to be disciplined. They will be the body that theology needs them to be, as well as the body that needs theology.

Raising the Body

The pressing questions are, "From where will this theological body come?" "How will it come about?" and "Given that this body does not naturally or normally exist in this world, who or what will bring it into existence?"

The only answer I can give is, "A new theological body will have to come from the present non-theological body. But only God can cause this to happen. Only God can take human beings, who are neither theological persons nor a theological people, and make of them a community united by and for theological faith, living the theological life, and being the incarnation of the transcendent, eternal reality that is *Theos,* or God, in this world."

The most likely point of origin is the church. The church appears in many different locations and in many different forms as congregations—wherever Christianity is being expressed and practiced. However, these local assemblies are not known to be theological places. Neither collectively nor individually can they be said to be true, living theological bodies. Theological amnesia and anemia are much too widespread and ingrained. These peculiar diseases of the church have metastasized to the point that the entire religious body is now in such a disastrous state that there is nothing more that can be done.

Meanwhile, denominational and congregational leaders continue working hard to shore up the body with more programs and projects, hoping to infuse it with more members and money. But even if their efforts serve to keep things going and to perk up the fellowship a bit, they will only sustain the body organizationally, socially, culturally, and religiously, and will only be temporary. They cannot and will not revive the body theologically. Checking the breath and pulse of the church body, all that the church physicians can say is, "I'm sorry."

Consequently, if there will ever be a theological body in this world again, it will have to be a new creation. It will have to be raised as a future living body out of the present dead body. The members of it are now "shadows of their former theological self," carrying false theological simulacra, moralistic therapeutic deism, bricolages of religion, spirituality, postmodern secularity, political ideology, and their own free choices, desires, feelings, emotional reactions, and spiritualized experiences. They are not alive with theology, or theological faith. They do not exist theologically. How, then, can they possibly be brought alive and built into the new creation of the new theological body?

None of this can or will occur naturally or automatically. It will not be produced by our own good intentions, team spirit, fervent devotion, careful strategic visioning and planning, coordinated actions, or hard work. It is humanly impossible. Honestly, we would not know where to begin.

I have written extensively about the necessity of our teaching and learning. However, I do not believe that the act of teaching alone can or will make students. I do not believe that an active regimen of studying and learning alone will make us theological people, or a theological community. Only the intervening work of God can do this. Only the Spirit—God as Spirit—can bring the dead to life.

Saying this, I find myself standing next to the prophet Ezekiel, experiencing my own version of his vision.[13] I sense the hand of the One called "LORD," or "Yahweh," bringing me out and setting me down in the middle of a valley. I look out across the vast landscape, and see many and various areas, each covered in bones. This is "Death Valley."

Yahweh asks me a searching question, "Mortal, can these bones live?" First, this name given to me, "Mortal," offends me. I don't like to be reminded that I am not divine, like God, but only a mere human being. I am not immortal. I do not have eternal life. I came from the dust of the earth. It was God who raised me up, like Adam. And I am destined, like Adam and Eve and all mortals, to die and go back, becoming nothing but dust again. One day I will not live—just as these bones lying all around on the ground are no longer living. They are very dry, as they continue to decay and deteriorate into the utter non-existence of being dead. Finally, there is nothing I, or anyone else, can do about these bones. They cannot be helped. They are dead. And I cannot bring them to life. My sorrow is inconsolable.

"Mortal, can these bones live?" I am asked again. All I can say is, "You know, LORD. Only you know." As far as I know, and as far as the powers of this world go, the answer is, "No."

Then Yahweh says to me: "Prophesy. Speak to these bones."

"Prophesy? Speak to them? Why would I do that? Look at them. They're dead. Besides, I have been preaching and speaking into the valley to these dead bones for over forty-five years—and little to nothing! Now you want me to say something to them again? What more can I possibly say? And what good will it do? I am only speaking futilely into thin air and at the ground to a corpse. Lord, I'm tired of doing it. Very tired. I cannot keep doing this, knowing it's never going to faze them, much less make them a living theological body."

---

13. Read Ezekiel 37:1-14. This is my personal retelling of the story.

"Prophesy. Say to these bones, 'Hear the Word of the LORD.' I will cause breath to enter you and you will live.'"

You?? Are you talking about me? Am I, too, among the dying and dead, needing the breath, wind, or Spirit to inflate my lungs and my very being, to raise me up out of theological non-existence, and give me new theological existence?

The wind blows. The Spirit moves. I allow myself to be entered and enlivened. Now, being brought alive, I have to say something. Living beings cannot be silent. So I speak again into death, at the lifeless body. And this time, there is movement. Somebody flinches. I think I see a glint behind the glazed-over eyes. I keep speaking. And the bones keep stirring, ever so slightly at first. Then their response is more active and pronounced. Now they are all moving in the dust, crawling on the ground. They begin to find each other and to come together. They connect and take on flesh.

But there is no breath in them. They are "out-of-breath." There is no theological life entering, filling, animating, and leading them—neither as parts nor as a whole body. They seem to be alive, for they are moving around. But they are nothing more than "the walking dead." They have not yet been in-breathed and revived with theological life.

"Keep speaking, Mortal," I hear Yahweh urging. "Speak to the breath. Turn away from the bones and talk to the wind. Tell it that the Lord God commands it to come and come upon these who are dead, that they may live."

I do this, as commanded. And the same breath that was sent to me is sent to them. The Spirit that brought me alive brings them alive. And they are up on their feet, fully erect—a brand new, living, breathing theological body! Yahweh says to me, "This is the church."

Until now, everyone, myself included, has been looking at this valley and reaching the only honest, realistic conclusion: "There is no hope. Theology is extinct. We are completely cut off. All is lost."

This is true. We must tell the truth. If there is ever going to be an identifiably, distinctively theological body again in the future, it will have come about among the theologically dead by the action of the One who promises, "I am going to open your graves and bring you up from your graves, O my people; …I will put my spirit within you, and you shall live, and I will place you on your own soil; then you shall know that I, the LORD, have spoken and will act." (Ezekiel 37:12b–14)

Our hope for a theological body lies solely in the God who raises the dead. It is God alone who can and will approach us in our dried-up, dusty non-theological state, give us theological life that we do not have in and of ourselves, and place us on the home soil of our own Christian historical-biblical-theological faith-tradition.

Only in this way will we acquire the capacity to hear and see God's mission of speech-acts, supremely revealed in Christ, and to be united, bone and flesh, with one another and with all the saints, as one living theological body. Only then will we be able, individually and communally, to exist by faith.

This is more than mere *resuscitation* or *renewal* (pumping new energy, strategies, programs, and leadership into the church to make it active and vigorous again). What is required goes beyond *reformation* (making changes to update the church, replacing its old, worn-out, irrelevant religious parts with brand new, fresh, up-to-date interpretations and applications).

Given that local congregations and ordinary Christians are theologically dead, they must be more than merely resuscitated, renewed, or reformed religiously, institutionally, or culturally. Such attempts cannot restore them. Only the radical action of *resurrection* will make them a living theological body. And only God can raise the dead.

The church itself came into existence at Pentecost when the same Spirit that mysteriously moved upon Jesus' dead body—breathing the breath or wind of God into him, bodily resurrecting him, opening his grave, and sending him forth alive—came upon Jesus' disciples to do the same to them. They suddenly became a new theological body, or *Theos*-inspired/in-spirited community, up and out in the world. They came forth speaking the *kerygma* (gospel) and enacting the *missio Dei* (mission of God), as part of the same resurrection act of God.

This act is not yet finished. It is still going on today. Wherever the church is found, the Spirit continues to give and sustain theological life. Where there is death, and dry bones litter the valley, the power of resurrection is present and at work. This is our only hope of salvation.

Being the bone and flesh humanity of Jesus Christ, the church is by its very nature a resurrected body. It is a new creation out of chaos. It is new life out of death. And it always will be. God is a resurrecting God, and is still actively, intimately involved with the church. Therefore, you and I have good reason to believe and trust in, to pray and look for, and to position ourselves and participate toward the raising of this body theologically—despite every appearance and every evidence that would indicate otherwise.

God is already doing for us what we are not doing, and cannot do for ourselves. The power of resurrection is at work among us, whether we want to be resurrected or not. The Spirit is not only pushing the church toward theological existence, and along paths of theological education, but is also breathing into us the breath that will animate us to respond, get up and stand, and walk and talk theologically.

Our task is not to make this happen or pull it off. It is absolutely impossible for us. Instead, our task is to allow ourselves to be "called out," and to "come out" of the "dead body," being joined to the new body that the movement of the Spirit is creating. This is the movement of God's resurrection, bringing us back home to the theological life.

Bringing the Body Home

After playing the part of the prodigal, growing weary of it, and then coming to himself, the younger son did not long for home "in thought" or "good intentions," while staying where he was. He did not write or call home, but got up and went to his father. He dragged his weary, unworthy body back home.

When a member of our country's armed forces is killed in service, the first duty of the military, and the first desire of the family, is to bring the body home. It is not enough to "remember" or "celebrate his (or her) life." Nothing seems right until this loved one is back, in some fleshly form, and is re-membered with his or her family in burial.

Likewise, theological education and its theological life are not a kind of "I will be with you in spirit" sentiment. It is a showing up in person, flesh and all. The individual presents his or her whole body in fellowship with the body of saints, in order to be transformed by and then conformed to the body of knowledge and wisdom this body has left behind. Theology is an embodied life.

Therefore, only those who welcome and embrace theology, sacrificially offering their whole selves—head, heart, attention, mood, time, energy, strength, and resources—in service to it, can possibly know the goodness, joy, and pleasure of being part of such a great communion.

I picture a broken, scattered processional of prodigals and battle casualties bringing their bodies back home. At the same time, theology is being brought back. It is as though they are all moving by the Spirit's "homing intuition," in response to the insistent, persistent divine call that they be reconciled.

When they arrive and converge, meeting for the first time, what a homecoming there will be! The band will kick into Chicago's "Does Anybody Really Know What Time It Is" (the song my band always led off with). The fatted calf will come off the grill. And the guests will stay up all night, eating and drinking, dancing, laughing, and catching up. Then, over the next days, weeks, years, and lifetimes, living together, they will truly get to know one another and become the one body of Christ.

Finally. We are home.

Invitation

Maybe it is the Baptist preacher in me. I am inclined to offer an invitation at the end of this book. In the Baptist evangelical world where I have lived and served, "the invitation" follows the sermon, summoning anyone or everyone who has been struck by the message, under the conviction of the Holy Spirit, to "come forward," "walk the aisle," "make a personal decision," "receive Christ," or "make a public profession of faith."

Evangelist Billy Graham set the gold standard of invitations with his famous words: "Every head bowed, every eye closed...I am going to ask you to get up out of your seats, all over this vast arena, and come and stand here...if you are with friends or relatives, they will wait...you get up and come right now." Hundreds came from all directions, as George Beverly Shea led the faithful in quiet, moving singing, "Just as I am, without one plea...."

You have read my book. You have received my message. Now I am going to ask you to make a decision. I assume you have accepted Jesus as the Christ, but may not yet have accepted the disciple-making discipline of theological education that is required for following and serving him.

Will you be a student of the church's tradition, a minister of the gospel, and a steward of the mysteries of God? Will you continue the training that has begun here in your reading? Will you devote yourself in a serious, sustained way to the learning and living of the Christian theological life?

If so, I invite you to make this your solemn commitment. Resolve right now to undertake the tasks and to form the habits that are essential for life-long learning.

I also invite you to take the next step of coming forward to join others in a network of theological education. Although your study and learning will be largely self-directed, there is no reason why you should be completely on your own, or alone.

For this purpose, I have organized Hermeneutic House. This is a ministry of theological interpretation and education. It provides instruction (both onsite and online), publishes books and curriculum resources, offers consultation, and gives encouragement, fellowship, and support to individuals and groups who are engaged in serious, sustained learning. Visit our website, hermeneutichouse.com, for more information.

Feel free to contact me and introduce yourself. Tell me who you are, and what you are doing in your studies. What issues or concerns are you facing? Where are you struggling? I will kindly answer your questions and alleviate any fears or doubts that might be preventing you from moving forward.

If you live in the metro region of Richmond, Virginia, I would like to introduce you to New Community Baptist Church. This is the teaching-learning community I serve as pastor-teacher-theologian. If you belong to another congregation, you can still join us for classes.

Perhaps you have read this book and will now recommend it to others. You plan to buy a few copies to pass along to close friends, co-workers, or family members.

If one of them comes back to you and says, “I think it would be great if we did this together,” please take him or her up on the offer. If the thought crosses your minds, “Let’s start our own lay seminary as discussed in chapter five,” seriously consider it. Why not? I will gladly help you. I can provide a curriculum for your group to use.

Are you a pastor who would like to recover the church’s teaching ministry as a theologian-in-residence? Are you already serving a congregation as its theological teacher? Or, are you a student in a seminary or divinity school, who would like to know more about this special mode of ministry?

Definitely contact me. I would like to know that there are other pastor-teacher-theologians out there, who are working to educate their congregations. We can learn much from one another, as well as be of mutual support. I will openly, honestly share with you out of my experience. A larger fellowship can be quite beneficial to those of us who are local theologians, involved in this unusual ministry.

For those who have read this book, made a personal commitment, and responded to the invitation, I end with this benediction:

> I pray that you may have the power to comprehend with all the saints, what is the breadth and length and height and depth, and to know the love of Christ that surpasses knowledge, so that you may be filled with all the fullness of God.
>
> Now to him who by the power at work within us is able to accomplish abundantly far more than all we can ask or imagine, to him be glory in the church and in Christ Jesus to all generations, forever and ever.
>
> Amen.[1]

---

1. Ephesians 3:18-21.

Acknowledgments

A "great cloud of witnesses" surrounds me as I preach, teach, think, and write. I am keenly aware of these theological saints of the church, who graciously allow me to be in their company as their student. I have sat in the classrooms of a few, but most are living only in the books they have left behind. Their number is innumerable, and their influence is incalculable. I acknowledge my debt to this vast host for preserving and transmitting the tradition that contains the mysteries of God make known in the life and gospel of Jesus Christ.

I also commune with a few of these believers in person at New Community Baptist Church in Richmond, Virginia. My wife Beth and I are covenant members, and I serve as pastor. We gathered in the fall of 2010, and soon dedicated ourselves to being a teaching-learning community. Our ministry is simple: we are stewards of the Christian theological faith-tradition. I know of no other congregation with this identity and purpose, where theology is so defining and directing.

I realize how blessed I am to be among these persons, loved by them, and allowed to be a theologian-in-residence. Where else would I be able to devote my time to the ministry of teaching, or to writing theological sermons, lectures, and books for them and for the whole church? My debt to New Community keeps increasing.

I invited five of the members to work with me in the final editing of this book. They have been my students the longest, and were the group with whom I prepared and test-taught a new biblical studies curriculum in 2014-2015. I am grateful to Jacquelin Aronson, Ed Coleman, Jim McKenney, Joan McKenney, and June Wise for correcting my mistakes and suggesting revisions that have made my work better. They are good examples of the theological student described in this book.

An extra word of appreciation is expressed to Jacquelin Aronson. Two years ago she assumed responsibility for our congregation's educational ministry with children. She and I came up with the idea of teaching them the same biblical-theological material as the adults. Every week she is my student, reading the multiple drafts of the teaching sermon I am preparing, discussing the topics and themes with me, deciding how best to translate this material for the children at their learning levels, and then teaching them. Currently, she is teaching both children and their parents in joint session.

I admire Jacquelin's many gifts and abilities. Her faith is deeply embedded in both mind and heart. She has such interest and enthusiasm about all things theological (which is extremely rare) that I can "talk theology" with her freely and for a long time. She never fails to help me clarify and develop my thoughts, while giving me an opportunity to help her with hers. I am indebted to Jacquelin for our friendship and partnership, out of which has come inspiration for this book. I have also invited her to collaborate with me on a major writing project.

Never during the months of writing have I forgotten those persons who are behind, around, and in front of my writing. New Community is around me now. But behind are the few persons in five previous congregations along the way, who stepped out of the non-theological crowd and came forward to be taught. I can still see their faces, disclosing the wide-eyed amazement that came upon them when they learned something new. I have not forgotten them, but have written with them in mind.

I have also written this book for those persons in front of this book, whom I have not met and taught—yet. Surely there are others like the students of the past and present, who need and would eagerly receive theological education, were it to be introduced and made available to them. I want to offer it. Therefore, I thank these persons in advance for giving me the opportunity.

My parents, Norman and Virginia, have had more influence on my Christian faith than they will ever know. I trust that they have been rewarded with some pride in how I turned out, although no one should ever hold them fully responsible.

I have two grown sons, Matthew and Daniel, who have heard more sermons and lessons from their father than any child should ever have to endure. I like to think they are glad I am finally putting some of this material in published print. Every time one of them, or one of their wives, Andrea and Rachel, has asked me, "How's your book coming along?" I have been encouraged that much more to keep going and to finish. They are really good family. I am especially proud that Daniel designed the cover of this book.

Finally, my debt to my wife, Beth, is beyond description or measure, much less repayment. Forty-six years ago when I brought a few youth together for study and learning—thereby beginning my teaching career—Beth was there among them. Later, when I was working on my doctorate, she took theology courses in college and then earned a seminary degree. A large, significant part of our early marriage was theological conversation. We discussed revelation to eschatology, and everything in-between. Thankfully, these conversations have never stopped, and have grown richer.

God has shown exceeding favor to me by equally yoking me with someone of Beth's ability to think both confessionally and critically, to care about and take care of the Christian faith-tradition, and then embody and live out all that is known and believed. She has without fail trusted my calling and supported my ministry all these years. Therefore, I dedicate this book to her, out of the love and appreciation of a debtor.

Made in the USA
Columbia, SC
01 March 2018